RUSSIAN SCIENCE FICTION LITERATURE AND CINEMA: A Critical Reader

Cultural Syllabus

Series Editor
MARK LIPOVETSKY (University of Colorado, Boulder)

ACADEMIC
STUDIES
PRESS

RUSSIAN SCIENCE FICTION LITERATURE AND CINEMA: A Critical Reader

**Edited and Introduced
by ANINDITA BANERJEE**

Boston
2018

Library of Congress Cataloging-in-Publication Data

Names: Banerjee, Anindita, editor.

Title: Russian science fiction literature and cinema : a critical reader/ edited and introduced by Anindita Banerjee.

Description: Boston : Academic Studies Press, 2018. | Series: Cultural syllabus | Includes bibliographical references and index.

Identifiers: LCCN 2017043784 (print) | LCCN 2017050050 (ebook) | ISBN 9781618117243 (e-book) | ISBN 9781618117229 (hardback) | ISBN 9781618117236 (pbk.)

Subjects: LCSH: Science fiction, Russian—History and criticism. | Science fiction films—Soviet Union—History and criticism.

Classification: LCC PG3098.S5 (ebook) | LCC PG3098.S5 R83 2017 (print) | DDC 891.73/08762—dc23

LC record available at https://lccn.loc.gov/2017043784

ISBN 978-1-61811-722-9 (hardback)
ISBN 978-1-61811-723-6 (paperback)
ISBN 978-1-61811-724-3 (electronic)

Book design by Kryon Publishing Services (P) Ltd.
www.kryonpublishing.com

Cover design by Ivan Grave

Published by Academic Studies Press
28 Montfern Avenue
Brighton, MA 02135, USA
press@academicstudiespress.com
www.academicstudiespress.com

Table of Contents

Introduction

A Possible Strangeness: Reading Russian Science Fiction on the Page and the Screen

"A man is half of what he is, and half of what he wants to be," said Oscar Wilde. If that is the case, then Soviet children of the sixties and seventies were all half cosmonauts. ... The cosmos was everywhere, in school textbooks, on the walls of houses, on the mosaics in the Moscow metro. ... Under the window of every five-story Khrushchev apartment stood miniature models of satellites. On the tear-off wall calendars, one spaceship followed another.

—Victor Pelevin, "Code of the World," 2001[1]

You could say that it all started with Sputnik. Sputnik, meaning "companion" in Russian, was the first artificial satellite to break free of the atmosphere and orbit the earth on October 4, 1957, almost a hundred years after Jules Verne wrote *First Men on the Moon* in 1865 and just one month ahead of the fortieth anniversary of the great utopian experiment of the October Revolution. Sputnik embodied a long-anticipated convergence of science fiction with science fact that reverberated across a planet still recovering from the ravages of

---

1 Victor Pelevin, "Code of the World," trans. Kirill Zikanov, *Frankfurter Allgemeine Zeitung*, February 28, 2001, accessed April 1, 2017, http://www.knigo.com/p/PELEWIN/code_world_engl.htm.

the Second World War, and, in the case of the Soviet Union, from three decades of domestic repression that had recently ended with the death of Josef Stalin in 1953. Though still locked in a Cold War with its geopolitical rival across the Atlantic, the country was entering an era of political, economic, and cultural liberalization at home, with calls for "coexistence" in the international arena under the new leader Nikita Khrushchev—a brief period called the Thaw that was named after a novel by Ilya Ehrenburg, a renowned public intellectual who had himself experimented with writing science fiction after the 1917 revolution.

The ridiculously small sphere orbiting the earth in 1957, twice the size of a soccer ball and weighing only eighty-four kilograms, carried an outsized symbolic weight. It ushered in a whole new way of imagining the self in relation to other worlds far beyond the geographical boundaries and historical travails of our imperfect planet. It embodied a dream cultivated by science fiction writers and technological visionaries that had remained tantalizingly out of humanity's grasp. Most significantly, Sputnik brought everyday life into exhilaratingly close proximity with vast scales of space and time. Part of its appeal was its own accessibility: the satellite could be seen with the naked eye at dawn or dusk from anywhere on the earth's surface, and emitted a chirping signal that could be captured on any short-wave radio. Its launch was the first of many "space firsts" that captivated the world's imagination over the next decade. They included sending the first life form, the legendary dog Laika, on Sputnik II a mere month later; the successful return journey of the canine twins Belka and Strelka in 1960; Yuri Gagarin's first manned mission in 1961; and the flight of Valentina Tereshkova, the first woman in space, in 1963. Until the United States caught up with its own iconic moon landing in 1969, the Soviet Union drew the world into a thrilling participatory spectacle of future-thinking and future-making unfolding in real time.

Each breakthrough was broadcast live on radio and television, providing endless fodder for anticipation and speculation to commentators who adopted a distinctly science fictional tone. Newspapers and burgeoning popular science journals such as *Around the World* (*Vokrug sveta*), *Knowledge is Power* (*Znanie—Sila*), and the *Technology for youth* (*Tekhnika—molodezhi*), newly galvanized by the unfolding drama in outer space, vied for the pleasure of taking every reader along for a ride into the unfathomable.[2] As the contemporary writer and science fiction

---

2 For an overview of science fiction in periodical culture of the early Space Age, see Matthias Schwartz, *Die Erfindung des Kosmos. Zur sowjetischen Science Fiction und populärwissenschaftlichen Publizistik vom Sputnikflug bis zum Ende der Tauwetterzeit* [The discovery of the cosmos: On Soviet science fiction and popular science periodicals from the Sputnik launch to the end of the Thaw] (Frankfurt, 2003).

enthusiast Victor Pelevin so eloquently recalls, the cosmos—as outer space was called in Russian—literally came home through objects and narratives woven into daily commutes and evening playtimes, public art and domestic knickknacks. The infinite universe had become thoroughly intimate, generating its own economy of desire by virtue of its ubiquitous presence in the places and practices of everyday life. Saturating the material, intellectual, and imaginative worlds of both adults and children, the cosmos, like science fiction itself in Fredric Jameson's famous formulation, had reached out and colonized reality.[3]

In the wake of Sputnik, Russia could also make a special historical claim to the condition that Pelevin describes as a foot in the real world and a foot in the cosmos—a mode of being, thinking, and acting that Istvan Csicsery-Ronay has called "the science fictionality of everyday life."[4] Soon after Gagarin's flight, Khrushchev posthumously feted an obscure figure from the early twentieth century on the Red Square. Broadcast with much fanfare on national television and extensively written up in the press, the ceremony transformed Konstantin Tsiolkovsky, a rural teacher of mathematics who first popularized the term "cosmos" in the early 1900s, into the universally beloved grandfather of the Soviet Space Program. Tsiolkovsky stood out among his contemporary visionaries who, like their European and North American counterparts, were obsessed with the prospect of interplanetary communications and space travel. The biologist Alexander Bogdanov, for instance, in his novel *Red Star* (*Krasnaia zvezda*), imagined a Bolshevik utopia on Mars as early as 1908. The filmmaker Iakov Protazanov visualized a Soviet scientist landing on the red planet in *Aelita*, one of the earliest full-length science fiction films, in 1924. Tsiolkovsky's prolific body of science fiction, however, served a further purpose: unlike the purely speculative conjectures of his contemporaries, it communicated the fundamentals of aerospace engineering to its audience. The mathematician wove prescient designs for jet-propulsion engines and gravity-free interiors into fantastical tales of space travel penned between 1895 and the 1920s.

Tsiolkovsky's apotheosis also signaled the triumphant return of science fiction to Soviet life after nearly three decades of being marginalized from mainstream culture.[5] It had been driven underground in the early 1930s

---

3 Fredric Jameson, "Progress versus Utopia; Or, Can We Imagine the Future?" *Science Fiction Studies* 9, no. 27 (1982): 149.

4 Istvan Csicsery-Ronay, *The Seven Beauties of Science Fiction* (Middletown, CT: Wesleyan University Press, 2008), 2.

5 On the media coverage of Tsiolkovsky's public recognition and its impact on the relegitimization of science fiction, see Anindita Banerjee, "Between Sputnik and Gagarin: Space

when socialist realism came to be officially endorsed by the state as the only viable kind of art for a revolutionary society; according to an apocryphal but frequently cited account, Stalin himself had forbidden speculation beyond the realistic horizons of the near future.[6] Under the twin signs of the Space Age and the Thaw, however, enthusiasts of the cosmos began to rediscover and reclaim an earlier golden era of *nauchnaia fantastika* or "scientific fantasy." The Russian term for science fiction, which had first emerged in the 1890s and become increasingly popular in the period leading up to the October Revolution, once again began to appear on the pages of magazines, the cover of books, and in titles and credits on the big screen.[7] In 1962, a journal called *Fantastika* was launched for catering to aficionados of the genre, which reprinted works from the revolutionary era alongside contemporary publications. The same year, a lavish new film returned to Alexander Beliaev's bestselling novel from 1928, *The Amphibian Man* (*Chelovek-amfibii*), for plunging its Space Age audience into another unfathomable, little-explored dimension: the depths of the ocean.[8]

The science fictionality of everyday life that Pelevin associates with his childhood no doubt primed readers and moviegoers for a veritable flood of novels, stories, and films that continue to be venerated as exemplars of the genre to this day. They included *The Andromeda Nebula* (*Tumannost' Andromedy*), Ivan Efremov's saga about intergalactic socialism published almost simultaneously with the Sputnik launch in 1957; the prolific fiction of the brothers Arkady and Boris Strugatsky, whose work through the 1960s and '70s deeply engaged with the mysteries of cutting-edge technological developments yet was palpably critical of their social and political uses; and Andrei Tarkovsky's cinematic masterpieces *Solaris* (1972), lauded as a response to Stanley Kubrick's *2001: A Space Odyssey* (1968), and his later film *Stalker* (1979), set in an ambiguously alien wasteland adapted from the Strugatskys' novel *The Roadside Picnic*. Science fiction, moreover, provided a potent platform for reaching out to the world, not just among the Soviet Union's allies

Flight, Children's Periodicals, and the Circle of Imagination," *Children's Literature in Soviet and Post-Soviet Russia*, ed. Marina Balina and Larissa Rudova (New York: Routledge, 2008), 74–75.

6 Matthias Schwartz, "How *Nauchnaia Fantastika* was Made: The Debates about the Genre of Science Fiction from the NEP to High Stalinism," *Slavic Review* 72, no. 2 (2013): 224–46.

7 Anindita Banerjee, *We Modern People: Science Fiction and the Making of Russian Modernity* (Middletown, CT: Wesleyan University Press, 2013), 1–9.

8 *Chelovek-Amfibii* [The human amphibian], dir. Vladimir Chebotarev, Leningrad, 1962.

in the Eastern Bloc but also farther afield in the West and among the newly decolonized nations of Latin America, Asia, and Africa. Progress Publishers of Moscow released a selection of Tsiolkovsky's essays, notes, and interviews in English in 1970.[9] Tarkovsky's mystifying films won multiple awards at Cannes and elicited much commentary from Kubrick fans worldwide. Throughout the sixties and the seventies, Progress translated contemporary authors as well as selected early-twentieth-century luminaries of science fiction for distribution in many languages and regions.

Sputnik's impact—crossing the boundaries of private life and public culture, domestic enthusiasm and international curiosity, technological spectacle and participatory entertainment, contemporary aspirations and historical visions, and, last but not least, the diverse media of print, film, radio, and television—played an instrumental role in transforming science fiction from Russia into a serious object of study. The opening essay of this reader, arguably the first work on Russian science fiction published in English with an extensive bibliography, was penned in 1971 during the peak of the space fever on both sides of the Cold War. Its author, the Croatian-born literary theorist Darko Suvin, advanced the first theory of the genre in his 1979 book *Metamorphoses of Science Fiction* and became a founding figure of the field of science fiction studies worldwide.[10] With the tantalizing phrase "a possible strangeness," Suvin's contribution sets the stage for understanding why Russian science fiction continued to attract an ever-widening field of scholars and critics over the subsequent decades, even and especially after the Space Age lost its heady fervor and the Soviet Union itself ceased to exist in 1991. The contents and organization of this critical reader reflect the ways in which the Space Age provided both the momentum and the template, much as it had done with the figure of Tsiolkovsky himself, for critics to simultaneously reach backward and forward in time.[11] Their endeavors recover a surprisingly long history of the genre in Russian literature and cinema, in the process revealing a dizzyingly diverse array of formal innovations and thematic preoccupations.

Research on the topic took on a new urgency in the 1980s, when it first became clear that the almost century-long living experiment of creating a

9 Konstain Tsiolkovsky, *The Call of the Cosmos*, trans. V. Danko (Moscow, 1970).

10 Darko Suvin, *Metamorphoses of Science Fiction: On the Poetics and History of a Literary Genre* (New Haven, CT: Yale University Press, 1979).

11 The first historical study of *nauchnaia fantastika* in Russian, published five years after Suvin's seminal essay, was A. N. Britikov's *Russkii-sovetskii nauchno-fantasticheskii roman* [Russian and Soviet science fiction novels] (Moscow, 1976).

utopian alternative to Western industrial capitalism was coming to a close.[12] Under the banner of perestroika and glasnost, several key authors and works that had been suppressed or merely retreated into oblivion were resurrected, reissued, translated, and studied for the first time within and beyond Russia's borders. Bogdanov's *Red Star*, which after its initial success fell into disfavor among Bolsheviks at least in part because of V. I. Lenin's condemnation of its "mystical tendencies," and Protazanov's *Aelita*, which was commercially successful but ideologically suspect in the eyes of the new Soviet commissars, attracted renewed attention from critics and translators. Among other rediscovered early classics were Mikhail Bulgakov's short story *The Fatal Eggs* (*Rokovye iaitsa*) and the novel *Heart of a Dog* (*Sobach'e serdtse*): of these satires about the grand experiment of forging a New Soviet Man in Russia's roaring twenties, the first was published in 1925, while the second appeared in print only in 1987. A similarly uneven publication history lay behind the return to print of the highly experimental early science fiction of Andrei Platonov, a hydrologist and engineer who participated in the Bolshevik project of transforming a largely agrarian country into a technological trailblazer. Evgenii Zamiatin's *We* (*My*), a dystopian novel written in 1921, did not appear in its original language until the late 1980s despite, or perhaps because of, having inspired George Orwell's *1984*. This work is perhaps the most famous example of a sciencefiction text that has been mined endlessly for a key not just to Russia's turbulent relationship with the twentieth century, but to the modern human condition as a whole.

Critical readings of Russian science fiction have continued to grow exponentially since then, and not just within the traditional disciplinary boundaries of literary and cinema studies. The essays collected in this volume confirm what became palpably evident in the Sputnik era: a genre that is perpetually poised, like Pelevin's child-cosmonaut, at the threshold between what is and what could be is not a product of the writer's study or a filmmaker's studio

---

12 Among the foundational studies emerging from this period are Leonid Heller, *De la Science-fiction soviétique: Par delà le dogme* [Soviet science fiction: Some thoughts on ideology] (Lausanne, 1979); John Griffiths, *Three Tomorrows: American, British, and Russian Science Fiction* (London: Macmillan, 1980); and Patrick McGuire, *Red Star: Political Aspects of Soviet Science Fiction* (Ann Arbor, MI: UMI Research Institute, 1985). 1989 and the fall of the Berlin Wall saw another wave of scholarly interest, exemplified by Richard Stites's *Revolutionary Dreams: Utopian Visions and Experimental Life in the Russian Revolution* (Oxford: Oxford University Press, 1989) and Yvonne Howell's *Apocalyptic Realism: The Strugatsky Brothers' Science Fiction* (Middlebury, VT: Russian and East European Studies inthe Aesthetics and Philosophy of Culture, 1994).

alone. From the period when *nauchnaia fantastika* first emerged as a vibrant label at the turn of the twentieth century through its current metamorphoses after the demise of the Soviet Union's governing ideology of scientific materialism, science fiction in Russia has been cocreated and coproduced by an astonishingly large community that included scientists and engineers, philosophers and policymakers, social and political activists, journalists, artists, illustrators, and, above all, consumers, with their frequently flawed material lives and often unfulfilled aspirations. In Russia perhaps more than anywhere else, science fiction served as the battleground for competing attitudes toward not just science and technology but the very idea of their role as the engines of modernity— an endlessly generative and constantly mutating crucible for what Raymond Williams termed "structures of feeling."[13]

In keeping with the disjunctive processes through which science fiction served not so much as a mirror of history or culture as a laboratory of simultaneously thinking, doing, and becoming, the articles in this critical reader expose the genre as inherently transnational, inter-generic, transmedial, and transhistorical. This was as true of what Zamiatin called the art of "displacement, distortion, curvature, [and] nonobjectivity" inspired by the scientific and technological revolutions of Einstein's relativity, aviation, the radio, telegraph, and cinema at the turn of the twentieth century as it was of subsequent radical experiments in transforming bodies, minds, and the physical environment.[14] Following the cautionary dictum of Suvin himself in his later writings about science fiction, the chapters following this introduction refuse to stay within narrow analytical frameworks of purely artistic influences, established literary or cinematic canons, hermetic compartments of historical periods, and monolithic conceptions of ideology flowing unilaterally from

---

13 Raymond Williams, "Structures of Feeling," in *Marxism and Literature* (Oxford: Oxford University Press, 1977), 128–35. Andrew Milner, in his recent book, *Locating Science Fiction*, has similarly defined the genre as a "site of contestation" between incommensurable attitudes, registers, and forms of culture (Liverpool: Liverpool University Press, 2012), 39–40.

14 Yevgeny Zamyatin, "Literature, Revolution, Entropy and Other Matters," in *A Soviet Heretic: Essays by Yevgeny Zamyatin*, trans. Mirra Ginsburg (Chicago: University of Chicago Press, 1970), 112. For intricate histories of science fictional thinking in actual research, development, and policy, see Loren Graham's *The Ghost of the Executed Engineer: Technology and the Fall of the Soviet Union* (Cambridge, MA: Harvard University Press, 1996); and Nikolai Krementsov's *A Martian Stranded on Earth: Alexander Bogdanov, Blood Transfusion, and Proletarian Science* (Chicago: The Univesity of Chicago Press, 2011) and *Revolutionary Experiments: The Quest for Immortality in Bolshevik Science and Fiction* (Oxford: Oxford University Press, 2013).

the state.[15] Instead, they trace the complex "intra- and inter-generic dialogues" identified by Gary Saul Morson through a great diversity of forms and platforms, extending through and flowing between intellectual, ideological, material, and media cultures over the long arc of the twentieth century and beyond.[16] The articles highlight the treasure trove of material that Russian science fiction has provided not only to literary and media studies, but also to intellectual and cultural history and interdisciplinary studies of science and technology.

The four sections of this reader are arranged in a broad chronological order that corresponds with major shifts in Russian history and culture on the one hand and the emergence of science fiction in print and in moving pictures on the other. Such boundaries are hard to enforce, however, and not just because of the uneven history of reception and scholarship as outlined above. Literary and cinematic works of science fiction, perpetually looking beyond the horizons of the here and now, inherently leak through and spill over periods, movements and indeed their own conventions. As a way of accommodating this heterogeneity, this reader strives to balance the perspectives of the telescope and the microscope, interspersing articles that provide rich overviews of particularly instrumental times and themes with those that provide nuanced analyses of authors, directors, and works that are most likely to be encountered in the classroom and revisited for pleasure.

The first section, "From Utopian Traditions to Revolutionary Dreams," begins with Suvin's pioneering essay, followed by Mark Adams's examination of the remarkable life and times of the author of *Red Star*. The next chapter presents an extended inquiry into a question often left implicit in science fiction's fantastical projections of technology, but which in Russia's case became a governing obsession from the eighteenth century all the way to the October Revolution and beyond: how to power the future in both the material and the ideological senses. In the last chapter of this section, Asif Siddiqi similarly traces a thriving prehistory of the popular culture of spaceflight, ranging widely between Tsiolkovsky's visionary writings and amateur clubs of rocket-builders, between mixed-media art exhibitions and early spectacles of photography and cinema.

The next section, "Russia's Roaring Twenties," focuses on the decade immediately following the October Revolution that produced some of the most famous and most controversial science fiction. Following Dominic Esler's

---

15   Darko Suvin, "Narrative Logic, Ideological Domination, and the Range of SF," *Positions and Presuppositions in Science Fiction* (Kent, OH: Kent State University Press, 1988), 64–66.

16   Gary Saul Morson, *The Boundaries of Genre: Dostoevsky's* Diary of a Writer *and the Traditions of Literary Utopia* (Austin, TX: University of Texas Press, 1981), 79.

overview of the incendiary mix of hope, anxiety, and fear that set science fiction apart in this era, three chapters by leading scholars and critics provide in-depth analyses of some of the most abiding early classics of Russian science fiction. Eliot Borenstein looks at language in Zamiatin's *We* as an ideological battleground between collective conformity and the rebellious self. Interpreting Protazanov's *Aelita* as an allegory of Russia's "domestic drama" of economic and social transition, Andrew Horton in the next essay offers a revisionist reading of its techniques and spectatorship. Working at the interface between science fiction and the institutional history of the biomedical sciences, the last chapter of this section by Yvonne Howell locates Bulgakov's monstrous hybrids in the almost equally fantastical culture of Bolshevik eugenics.

The third section of the reader, "From Stalin to Sputnik and Beyond," similarly places the breakthrough science fiction of the Space Age in the cloud chamber of a *longue durée*—a challenge to the view that the utopian aspirations of earlier decades had gone into complete hibernation during the Stalin years. To be sure, there is little science fiction in literary form to show for the period between the early 1930s and the late 1950s. The first two chapters of this section, however, demonstrate that the dream factory of the revolutionary era was kept alive through the wondrous medium of cinema. An excerpt from Michael G. Smith's recent study, *Rockets and Revolution*, illuminates the transnational traffic in multiple media that continued to build upon earlier science fictional projections of spaceflight, culminating in a little-known but remarkable episode of "Stalinist cosmonautics": Vasily Zhuravlev's 1936 film, *Cosmic Voyage*, whose stunning simulations of zero-gravity environments were supervised by none other than Tsiolkovsky. The recently unearthed chronicles of innovative space cinema continues in the next chapter, based on interviews and archival materials obtained from Pavel Klushantsev by Lynn Barker and Robert Skotak. Klushantsev, whose work is only now getting the critical attention it deserves, made documentaries as well as fiction films depicting the cosmos at the dawn of the Space Age; footage from his 1961 film *Planet of the Storms* was sold off to Hollywood, appearing years later in Peter Bogdanovich's 1968 directorial venture, *Voyage to the Planet of Prehistoric Women*.[17] The last two chapters of this section tackle the two greatest icons of science fiction literature and cinema

---

17 On Klushantsev's innovations, see Birgit Beumers, "Special/Spatial Effects in Soviet Cinema," *Russian Aviation, Spaceflight, and Visual Culture*, ed. Vlad Strukov and Helena Goscilo (London: Routledge, 2016), 169–88.

from the Space Age. Csicsery-Ronay's landmark essay investigates the irrepressible paradigms of folklore and fairy tales in the Strugatsky brothers' formidable corpus of work. Andrei Tarkovsky's two forays into science fiction cinema, *Solaris* and *Stalker,* constitute the subject of Christopher Dalton's commentary on the interpenetration between inner and outer space.

The final section of this reader, titled "Futures at the End of Utopia," attempts to map out the nebulous contours of science fiction in the era when writers such as Pelevin look back with both disillusionment and nostalgia at the dreams of futures past. In order to investigate Pelevin's own playful engagement with the present, Elana Gomel turns to postmodernism, which the cultural theorist Mark Lipovetsky has defined as a dominant condition of contemporary life and art.[18] Investigating the kind of fantasy that has replaced the hard science fiction of the sixties and seventies, Vlad Strukov examines Timur Bekmambetov's blockbuster vampire movies, *Night Watch* and *Day Watch,* through the lens of intergenerational disjunction and dysfunction. The critical reader closes with a sweeping view of anti-realist fiction in the 2000s that Aleksandr Chantsev trenchantly calls the "Dystopia Factory."

Even now, a hundred years after the Revolution, sixty years after Sputnik, and more than a quarter century after the demise of the USSR, first encounters with Russian science fiction may come as something of a shock to students, scholars, and fans alike, no matter how well-versed they might be in the massive Anglo-American tradition of literary science fiction or how steeped in its Hollywood-driven cinematic forms. Far from curbing their cognitive wonder, to use another felicitous phrase from Suvin's opening essay, this critical reader hopes to catapult them into further realms of its possible strangeness.

---

18 Mark Lipovetsky, *Russian Postmodernist Fiction: Dialogue with Chaos,* trans. and ed. Eliot Borenstein (London: M. E. Sharpe, 1999).

Part One

From Utopian Traditions to Revolutionary Dreams

The Utopian Tradition of Russian Science Fiction

DARKO SUVIN

Suvin, Darko. "The Utopian Tradition of Russian Science Fiction." *The Modern Language Review* 66, no. 1 (1971): 139–59.

The tradition of science fiction, understood here broadly as meaning all *literature of cognitive wonder*, that is a "possible strangeness" both social and technological, is a time-honored one in Russia. Its strength consists in having blended the rationalist western European strain of utopianism and satire with the native folk longings for abundance and justice. These were embodied, first, in the ubiquitous dream of a land of Cockayne, and in the fabulous voyages (in the case of landlocked Russia, overland ones) toward India, Persia, or China: Marco Polo's Cathay was not more fabulous than the luxurious Kitezh-gorod of folk imagination. Justice to man regardless of the traps and trappings of his social station is the central interest of a second large segment of oral and folk literature. Perhaps it might be enough to mention here only the strong theme of the humble person who is finally exalted. From the wishful and magical fairy stories about Ivanushka the Fool, the youngest or third son who is poorer and apparently more stupid than his brothers but ends up more successful than the norms of class society would allow for, through a fusion with plebeian (especially heretical and sectarian) Christianity, such a theme flowed to the mainstream of modern Russian literature. From Pushkin's and Mussorgsky's mad folk prophet in *Boris Godunov*, through the memorable humble arrogants in Dostoevsky, such as Prince Myshkin in *The Idiot*, all the way to many Tolstoyan and Chekhovian characters, these figures bear utopian values into a world not yet ready for them.

In the middle of the nineteenth century this tradition fused with earlier echoes of imaginary sociopolitical frameworks. The first traces of an exemplary political tale used as vehicle for a fictional blueprint go as far back as Ivan Peresvetov's sixteenth-century *Legend of the Sultan Mahomet*, a plea to Tsar Ivan the Terrible for strong state centralization, which was to be remembered approvingly and appropriately by Stalin. But a real trend in that direction developed in Russian literature following the continent-wide spread of the Rationalist *Staatsroman* in the eighteenth century. From the middle of that century on, utopian writings such as Lvov's and Levshin's extolled ideally harmonious countries of economic abundance and enlightened absolutism. Tredyakovsky adapted Fénelon's *Adventures of Telemachus*; writers like Kheraskov, Dmitriev-Mamonov, and Emin supplied in their works parallels and parables on such an "enlightened absolutist prince" model, usually in a spurious classical setting. In the second half of the century, prince Mikhail Shcherbatov wrote an incomplete *Voyage to the Empire of Ophir* expressing the longings of the higher aristocracy for a privileged life; and More's *Utopia* was translated into Russian in the year of the French Revolution. That event, and the ensuing wars, prompted a speedy suppression of the whole genre for a whole generation. Empress Catherine, who had affected friendship with Voltaire and Diderot while quenching the peasant rebellions, now turned against any "natural right" pleas against serfdom—such as Aleksandr Radishchev's famous *Journey from Petersburg to Moscow* which contained passages of a democratic blueprint for the future—with a mercilessly brutal hand, suppressing the publication and arresting the authorial culprit.

It was only in the 1820s that the official propagandist Thaddeus Bulgarin could publish in his magazine three mildly satirical fantastic-voyage tales. The most substantial of them, his *Untrue Un-Events, or a Voyage to the Centre of the Earth* (1825), is supposedly the manuscript of an anonymous narrator's voyage through three underworld countries—an idea taken from Holberg's *Niels Klim* (also translated into Russian in the eighteenth century, but having ubiquitous myths and folktales as its antecedents), and received for science fiction forty years later by Jules Verne. Bulgarin's narrator falls down a cave in an arctic island into the country of Ignorance, whose grotesque inhabitants live in perpetual darkness, caring only for food, drink, gossip, and gambling. A whirlpool takes him into the dawn-light country of Beastliness, whose ape-like inhabitants are half-blind, and have some superficial and mistaken acquaintance with arts and sciences. Finally, the narrator finds an underground passage to the nethermost country of Enlightedness perpetually lit by the fires of Earth's center, where humans live in the capital city of Utopia and outlying villages. The Enlighted are brought up to be self-disciplined, obedient to lawful authority and to a strict code of life which regulates working, writing, traveling, and even women's fashions. Obviously, though he differentiates his countries by spiritual "enlightenment," Bulgarin's country of Ignorance is a satire on the lower orders of people, mainly on the Russian peasant living under what Tolstoy will, using the same metaphor, aptly call "the power of darkness." The country of Beastliness, in which people are in a way worse than the Ignorantians because they pretend to knowledge they do not possess, is in many ways a jibe at the middle class and the intellectuals just emerging in Tsarist Russia. Finally, the smug patriarchal country of Enlightedness is an autocratic emasculation of More, silent on his basic insights about property and economics, and propagating an idealized stance popular at the Tsarist court from the times of Peter the Great. Although Bulgarin's work is of no aesthetic significance, it nonetheless testifies to a certain interest in the field and to a rather good knowledge of its stock devices, and its obscurantist depicting of social classes as separate races and nations prefigures Wells's triumphant use of this device in *The Time Machine*.

The Russian science-fiction tradition came up to world nineteenth-century standards with prince Vladimir Odoevsky's unfinished *Year 4338*, circulated in manuscript in the 1840s and published only in Soviet times. In this epistolary tale, the Enlightenment tradition—visible in the reliance on new knowledge as well as in the form, taken from Montesquieu's *Persian Letters* with a dash of Mercier's *Year 2440*—is supplemented with Romantic extrapolation by Odoevsky, a disciple of Hoffmann and Pushkin in literature and Schelling in philosophy. Furthermore, although science fiction extrapolation had—in a generally more activistic Europe affected by the French revolution and stubborn utopian hopes—even in lagging Russia already shifted from space to time in Bulgarin's *True Un-Events, or Voyages in the World of the Twenty-ninth Century* (1829), and N. A. Veltman's *Year 3448* (1833), yet Odoevsky's tale was the first significant Russian anticipation. Not that this rich and erudite eccentric, amateur gastronomer, chemist, philosopher, litterateur, etc., went any further than to envisage an enlightened aristocratic empire rewarding both birth and talent. In his view, human nature was rather static, and in social relations there will be only more of the same: a conurbation extends from St. Petersburg to Moscow;

having sold everything else under the sun, Americans are now auctioning off their cities and trying to loot China, this being the only armed conflict left in the world. But Russian officers and peasants returning from the Napoleonic wars had brought a spark of novelty home, and at least once in the intervening years, in the Decembrist revolt of 1825, this spark had threatened to set fire to the antiquated Tsarist structure. For Odoevsky, the new is to be expected from effects of scientific development, about which he is quite sanguine. In his notes to the fragmentary *Year 4338*—often as interesting as the torso itself—he criticizes Mary Shelley's gloomy *The Last Man* for not looking far enough into the future. He envisages, for example, aerostatic communication radically changing the commerce, politics, and morals of the future; expeditions for mineral exploitation of the moon, taking their own atmosphere along and solving the problems of global overpopulation; renewed nomadism; machine authorship of novels and patriotic plays, otherwise (shades of McLuhan) printing and fiction giving way to pure information, "electrical" talking, and public lecturing; scholars who do not publish but lecture daily in a dozen places flying from each to each, and so on.

The novel itself is supposed to have been written with the help of a mesmeric visionary ranging through space, time, and people at will while in a somnambulic state. In this instance, he had tuned into the mind of a young Chinese writing back to a friend in Peking from St. Petersburg of 4338 or 4339, on the eve of a comet's crash onto Earth. Odoevsky obviously never dreamed of a social upheaval of such proportions as to change the hallowed Tsarist name of the city. But again, he interestingly discusses the use of "elastic glass" or "elastic crystal" for clothing, odoriferous gases instead of wines, photocopied newsletters of the important families, teleprinters, air and underground electric traffic, electric lights, heating of northern countries by giant hot air tubes from the Equator, breeding of horses down to the size and use of lapdogs, and so on. The main social game is a "magnetic bath" inducing somnambulism, in which state many people declare their secret actions and sympathies, making hypocrisy impossible; only diplomats are exempt from this game, and therefore have a very low status in the high society. Clearly, the society envisaged is hierarchical and bureaucratic. In one of his notes, Odoevsky—who is sarcastic about middle-class equality—describes a Platonic scientific oligarchy, headed by poet-philosophers. They are flanked by historiographers, linguists, physicists, and other scientists of the second-highest rank. Each historiographer heads in his turn a group of chroniclers, philologists, geographers, archaeologists, each physicist a group of chemists, mineralogists, and other third-rank scientists.

A mineralogist has assigned to him fourth-rank metallurgists, and so on down to the lowest rank of copyists and laboratory assistants. Odoevsky's *Year 4338* can thus be thought of as a liberal-aristocratic answer to Bulgarin, pioneering in scientific extrapolation into the future, but failing to realize that a radically new productivity demands radically new social relations. Since even much of present-day science fiction is still stricken with the same blindness, Odoevsky remains one of the more interesting science fiction writers of the pre-Wellsian age in Europe.

The fact that even such politically timid anticipation could not be printed under Tsarism testifies to the very unfavorable climate of obscurantism science fiction had to contend with in Russia. Thus, the significant fusion of political utopianism and anthropological anticipation, which came about in Nikolay Chernyshevsky's *What Is To Be Done?* (1862), saw the light of the day from the dungeon in which it was written only because of bureaucratic confusion in Tsarist censorship. Even so, it did not get into book form until the 1905 revolution. Nevertheless, its impact was immense, comparable only to Bellamy's in the United States: every high-school girl read handwritten copies under her bench, and for half a century the populists and later the socialists used it in underground education. Much of the veneration was initially due to the legendary figure of the author, the leader of the Russian radical intelligentsia, who was to remain in prison or strict Siberian internment for the rest of his life. A brilliant critic and pre-Marxian materialist who uncompromisingly rejected both Tsarism and the capitalism toward which the regime was groping, Chernyshevsky cautiously smuggled into the novel his ideal of a cooperative and communal libertarian socialism, in which the self-enlightened interest of each would be guaranteed by the free development of all, based on the liberation of labor. But the main reason for the novel's lasting success in stagnant eastern Europe (both Lenin in Russia and Dimitrov in Bulgaria glowingly remembered its decisive influence on their personal commitment to the revolution) was Chernyshevsky's refusal to separate the public and private lives of his heroes. "Freedom now" could have been the slogan of these "new people," and while devoting themselves to the radical cause, they prefigured in their exemplary, free, and sincere personal relationships Russia's utopian future. It can be assumed that Chernyshevsky's novel would—for all the somewhat old-fashioned literary conventions of an admirer of George Sand and Thackeray—strike a responsive chord in today's young people. The liberation of Woman is its main theme, but in the loving happiness Vera Pavlovna pursues there is no break, although there are interesting tensions, between the erotic and the political aspect, just as there is none between the conscious and the subconscious. In fact, the utopian anticipation is formally present in a sequence of four dreams Vera Pavlovna dreams within the novel, a brilliant innovation soon to be picked up and turned against its originators by Dostoyevsky's rebuttal of radicalism in Raskolnikov.

Most clearly utopian in the strict formal sense is the famous "Fourth Dream." A vision in two parts, divided by a self-censored space which stands for the account of the liberating revolution, this dream shows, first, the liberation of female personality through a series of allegorical glimpses leading to the new woman born of revolutionary equality, and second, a future socialist utopia incorporating both Fourier's idea of cooperative producing collectives (*phalanstères*) which would annul the contradictions between town and rural life, and Owen's idea of a new moral world based on equality and made possible by machine productivity. These ideas were widespread in nineteenth-century Europe and America, but Chernyshevsky was, after Cabet, the first to use them in fiction. More importantly, he was the first largely to avoid didactic dryness by making them the supreme emotional interest of his characters. The political dream is also the deepest personal dream of a warm heroine, in a manner which would have been entirely understandable to Dante, Langland, or Marvell, but which had since disappeared from the European cultural mainstream. Chernyshevsky's "Fourth Dream" fused romantic pathos and rational belief in social change. The huge crystal palace in the midst of fertile fields where a happy association of free producers lives and works, each at variegated tasks changing every few hours, symbolizes even architecturally, by its uniting under the same roof a variety of apartments, workplaces, studios, theaters, museums, etc., the balanced harmony of personal and public life. The dream of Vera Pavlovna is thus not unworthy of the great liberating current of "warm" utopias in western Europe, from More and Rabelais to Chernyshevsky's teachers, Rousseau and the utopian socialists, who set up the principle that the emancipation of women is the measure of social liberation. It certainly set the tradition for a whole aspect of Russian science fiction.

A countercurrent to radicalism, equally messianic and anti-bourgeois but with a diametrically opposed point of view, found a most powerful voice in Fyodor Dostoevsky. In his youth a member of an illegal circle which propagated and even tried to experiment with utopian-socialist ideas, Dostoevsky's shattering prison and Siberian experience channelled his utopian concerns into a mystical deification of the Tsarist system. His deepest hatreds were from that time evenly divided between the degradation of man under the impact of capitalist economics and the radical proposals for rational rehumanization; curiously, he had come to think of these opposites as two faces of the same prideful coin. The famous Crystal Palace of the 1851 London World Exhibition became for him the symbol of industrialized inhumanity, dividing brothers into the domineering rich and the gin-sodden, sectarian poor. In his *Notes from the Underground*, written immediately after the publication of *What Is To Be Done?* he sarcastically adduced the irrationality of the individual's free will, the stupidity evidenced by unceasing mass bloodshed, and the general senselessness of world history, against the rationalist builders of new economic relations and of the Crystal Palace. Although unnamed in these repressive circumstances (where even Dostoevsky was censored), there is little doubt that Chernyshevsky's novel was meant. In Raskolnikov, the hero of Dostoevsky's immediately following novel, all radicals recognized a distorted portrait of themselves.

Though he was energetically battering away at the idea of a future Crystal Palace, the ambiguous Dostoevsky remained obsessed with its themes of innocence, brotherly love, and transcending of social antagonisms. True to his religious bent, he placed them in a past and mythical Golden Age, a motif which was to run through his whole work, breaking explicitly out in places like Versilov's speech in *The Adolescent*, the suppressed chapter of *The Possessed*, and finally formalized into a separate work as *The Dream of a Ridiculous Man* (1877). That story is a far cry from the venomous polemics of the 1860s. Although Dostoevsky remained sceptical about the *feasibility* of man's salvation through history—witness the Grand Inquisitor passages in *The Brothers Karamazov*—*The Dream of a Ridiculous Man* is a heartfelt cry for the necessity of such a salvation. It depicts a distraught narrator, who has lost all touch with humanity and who decides to commit suicide. He then dreams that he has died and been transported across space to a perfect twin of our Earth. There, on a Greek island, he finds an unfallen and loving people in a pastoral Golden Age. After a while, however, he corrupts the happy utopians through lies, cruelty, and individualism. A complete civil society soon evolves, with crimes, science, codes of honor and law, warfare, and a full history of slaves and saints, suffering and formal religion. The horrified narrator asks to be crucified but is laughed at, and awakes. He abandons his suicidal intention and devotes the rest of his life to preaching the possibility of happiness and beauty on our planet. For all of Dostoevsky's fulminations against the utopian abolition of suffering, the spell of an earthly happiness has for once managed to assert itself in this neglected gem of his: a tardy, isolated, and wistful but significant concession to the dream of Vera Pavlovna.

Never absent from Russian literature, the anticipatory alternative became especially relevant at times of revolutionary resurgence, which also chipped away at censorship. Such a period were the 1900s, when the utopian flame flared up in many non-science fiction works, for which the future-oriented daydreams of some Chekhovian heroes, such as Vershinin in *Three Sisters*, may be taken as representative. In circumstances which called for active intervention into the here and now, a far-away utopian country, such as the one expounded by the Tolstoyan folk-preacher Luka in Gorky's *Lower Depths*, was already felt as evading the issue. The major science fiction witness to the urgency of intervening was the prominent symbolist poet Valery Bryusov. In his play *Earth* (1904), a youth revolt shatters the glass dome barring humanity from sunshine and open space in a decadent giant city; the revolt is seen in turn as seeking liberation and exposing the city to the risk of annihilation. At the same time as London's more precise *The Iron Heel*, Bryusov thus saw the distant possibilities of a new culture and the immediate prospect of destroying the present one. After the defeat of the 1905 revolution, Bryusov's horizons contracted: the prose version of *Earth* suggests a catastrophic ending, and simultaneously his second story about a future city *The Republic of the Southern Cross* (1907) is frankly dystopian. A huge capitalist metropolis on the very South Pole, capital of the greatest industrial power of the world and again enclosed by an impenetrable dome, falls prey to a deadly epidemic of *mania contradicens*, which makes the sick do the opposite from what they wish to do. Science and society are powerless to prevent its spread, and a resolute bourgeois minority fighting for order is finally overwhelmed by the brutalized inhabitants. The story is a curious prefiguration of Camus's *The Plague*, possibly because both descend from Raskolnikov's dream of a worldwide epidemic at the end of *Crime and Punishment*, but more significantly because they both allegorize the great social convulsions of our century. But Bryusov was readier to pay any price for the destruction of the "ugly and shameful" capitalist system. Though his apocalyptic verse envisaged wolves baying on the banks of the Seine, and happy children burning books in the London Parliament, he apostrophized "the coming Huns" (see also his story *The Last Martyrs*):

> But you, who will destroy me,
> I meet with an anthem of welcome!

Together with his great fellow-symbolist Alexander Blok, who had also envisaged the coming of new "Scythians," Bryusov became thus one of the few prominent non-Marxist writers who took an active part in post-revolutionary cultural life of Soviet Russia.

All of these examples testify to a continued interest in and a significant tradition of Russian science fiction. One could add to them a number of secondary attempts such as Pavel Sakulin's *Russian Icaria* (1912), Alexander Kuprin's popular stories *A Toast* and *The Liquid Sun* (1913), and some technological anticipations written with popularizing aims by engineers and scientists—such as V. Chikolev's *Electrical Tale: It Never Happened, but It Is Not Imaginary* (1895), A. Rodnykh's *Rolling Road* (1902), Professor Bakhmetev's *The Billionaire's Legacy* (1904), and N. Komarov's *Coldtown* (1917)—and culminating in the work of Tsiolkovsky. Komarov's anticipation of a refrigerating technique on a scale to counteract a rise of atmospheric temperature already led into a technocratic sketch of the next two centuries' history. Concentrating on the sociopolitical aspects of such a history, A. Bogdanov-Malinovsky, a prominent though ideologically unorthodox Bolshevik leader, became the most interesting science fiction writer of the prerevolutionary years alongside Bryusov and Tsiolkovsky. His novels about an exemplary Martian society, *The Red Star* (1908) and *Engineer Menni* (1913), especially the former, set the tradition for left-wing Russian science fiction by fusing earthly political struggles with the interplanetary tale, either directly or by juxtaposition within the same work as prefigurations, extrapolations, or alternative paths. Bogdanov's superior Martian technology (including a foretaste of nuclear energy, automation, antimatter, and interplanetary vessels with ionic propulsion), and social organization successfully brought up to date the European "Martian story" (Lasswitz in Germany) in a manner unsurpassed between Wells and the American 1940s. The free, science-orientated social system will be taken up fifty years later by Yefremov, the revolutionary protagonist's illumination and love affair on another planet by Alexey Tolstoy, and both these elements by much of Soviet science fiction in the 1920s and 1960s. Even Bogdanov's activist characters, and in places lyrical style, were to prove trendsetting. Yet for all its vitality, the prerevolutionary science fiction tradition was very tenuous, written at great cost by exceptional, heroic, and isolated figures. The weight of industrial and scientific backwardness combined with the obtuse oppression of Tsarism was too great to allow a flowering of the genre. In the twenty years before 1917, only about twenty-five such books were published. Nonetheless, together with copious translations and imitations of Jules Verne (by, for example, Volokhov-Pervushin, Semenov, Uminsky), they prepared the ground for the flowering. This came with a vengeance in the 1920s, in the first flush of a .

revolutionary regime committed to industrialization and modern science as a means for achieving utopian mastery over man's destiny.

In Russia, this was one of those epochs when new heavens touch the old earth, when the future actively overpowers the present, and the sluggish and disjointed flow of time is suddenly channeled into a wild waterfall, generating a rainbow on the near horizon and capable of dispensing light and warmth from scores of dynamos. Wells visited the Soviet state in the midst of the Volga famine and found Lenin confidently tracing plans of a fully electrified self-governing Russia. Quite rightly, he recognized in the author of *State and Revolution* a utopian dreamer: but Wells the "utopographer" had forgotten that certain utopias are realizable. In the literature of the 1920s this atmosphere evoked a flurry of anticipations and planetary novels. The tireless Bryusov, long an enthusiast of interplanetary travel, dreamed with Pasternak and the Futurists of a scientific poetry, and wrote of billions of worlds ready to hear the call of an earth spiraling in its "planetary revolution" (*Distances*, 1922). Two of his plays discussed the possibilities and pitfalls of interplanetary relations. The tragedy *Dictator* (1921), probably modeled on Wells's *The Sleeper Wakes*, portrays a militarist who wants earth to conquer the universe but is overthrown by the partisans of peaceful labor. *The World of Seven Generations* (1923) takes place on a symbolical comet and has mankind triumphing peacefully, because of its ethical values. Taking off from such a widespread identification of the social revolution with man's leap into the universe, a whole school of Russian versifiers called themselves the "Cosmists," and extolled a somewhat vague "planetary awareness." Much too little is also known about the sociologically doubtless very representative Chernyshevsky- or Bogdanov-type visions of a perfect classless future such as V. Itin's warm *Land of Gonguri* (1922), Ya. Okunev's *Future World* (1923), and several other works of that kind up to V. Nikolsky's *In a Thousand Years* (1927, featuring intelligent plant life and the first nuclear explosion in 1945), E. Zelikovich's *Coming World* (1930), and Ya. Larri's *Land of the Happy* (1931). A number of noted prose writers wrote at the outset of their careers at least one largely or marginally science fiction work, often in a near-future setting and with strong elements of a political adventure or crime story, such as some stories of Nikolai Aseyev, Ilya Ehrenburg's novel *Trust D.E.* (1923), Valentin Katayev's *Ehrendorf Island* (1924), Marietta Shaginian's "Jim Dollar" trilogy beginning with *Mess-Mend* (1924–26), Boris Lavrenev's *The Fall of the Ytl Republic* (1925), and Vsevolod Ivanov and Victor Shklovsky's *Yperite* (1926).

Another and similar type was "the catastrophe novel," which dealt with the social consequences of a new scientific invention (often a kind of "death ray," and brought about by a solitary scientist of the Frankenstein-Nemo type) ending invariably with a catastrophic downfall of the capitalist system and victory of world revolution. One can mention, for example, the self-explanatory titles of Valentin Katayev's novel *The Lord of Iron* (1925) or of two works from 1927— A. Palei's *Gulf Stream*, where a socialist Old World is contrasted with a taylorized and alienated United States, and A. Shishko's *The Microbes' Appetite* operating with robots and chemical warfare. This type of story started out from the Vernean "scientific novel" and broadened it into sociopolitical anticipations of a near future. Its global dimensions latched on to Wells's middle-period romances such as *The War in the Air, The World Set Free,* and especially *When the Sleeper Wakes,* but their primary impulse came from general Soviet anticipation of a world revolutionary upheaval in the first ten years after the October Revolution. The undoubted culmination of this type was Alexey Tolstoy's *Hyperboloid of Engineer Garin* (translated into English as *The Garin Death-Ray,* and touched upon later in this article), whose first version was published in 1925–26. Tolstoy's numerous revisions of this political anticipation in the next dozen years would almost suffice to provide a micro-history of shifting attitudes in and around Soviet science fiction in that period. Finally, the tormented and ironic aspects of a Zamiatin-like skepticism were continued by S. Bobrov's *Revolt of the Misanthropes* (1922), Lev Lunts's expressionistic drama *The City of Truth* (1923), some stories of Venyamin Kaverin, and especially by Mikhail Bulgakov (*The Fatal Eggs,* 1924; *The Heart of a Dog,* 1925), who soon crossed into pure fantasy.

Perhaps the most representative of this 1920s mainstream were some works—even though, or just because, they were only partly or marginally science fiction—of Vladimir Mayakovsky, its most popular poet. In poems such as *About It, 150,000,000,* and *The Fifth International,* in short propagandist pieces such as *Before and Now,* in film scenarios, and most clearly in his three post-revolutionary plays, the mainspring of Mayakovsky's creation was the tension between anticipatory utopianism and recalcitrant reality. A Futurist and admirer of Wells and London, Mayakovsky wrote his witty masterpiece *Mystery Buffo* to celebrate the first anniversary of the October revolution, envisaging it as a second cleansing Flood in which the working classes, inspired by a poetic vision from the future, get successively rid of their masters, of devils, angels, and economic chaos, and finally achieve a terrestrial paradise of reconciliation with things around them. The revolution is thus both political and cosmic; it is an irreversible and eschatological, irreverent and mysterious, earthy and tender return to direct sensuous relationships of men with a no longer alien universe. No wonder that Mayakovsky's two later plays became satirical protests against the threatening separation of the classless heavens from the earth. The future heavens of the sunlit commune remain the constant horizon of Mayakovsky's imaginative experiments, and it is by its values that the grotesque tendencies of petty-bourgeois restoration in *The Bedbug* (1928) or of bureaucratic degeneration in *The Bath* (1929) are savaged. Indeed, in the second part of both plays, the future—though too vaguely imagined for scenic purposes—erupts into the play. In *The Bedbug*, it absorbs and quarantines the petty "bedbugus normalis" in its bestiary. In *The Bath*, the newly proclaimed Soviet Five-Year-Plan slogan of "Time forward!" materializes into the invention of a time machine which communicates with and leaps into the future, sweeping along the productive and the downtrodden characters but spewing out the bureaucrats. The victory over time was for Mayakovsky a matter of central political, cosmic, and personal importance: he firmly believed in a possible immortality for men, and greeted the time-contraction of Einstein's theory of relativity with such hopes. His suicide in 1930 cut him off in the middle of a fierce fight against the bureaucrats whom he envisaged as holding time back, and who had engineered the failure of Meyerhold's first-rate production of *The Bath*.

The seemingly diverging concerns of Evgenii Zamiatin when looked at more closely turn out also to deal with the relationships of the new, future heavens and the old, present earth. The difference is that Zamiatin did not believe in any eschatological end of history. An ex-Bolshevik and rebel against Tsarism, a scientist-specialist in shipbuilding who introduced into his novel *We* (1920?) the atmosphere of the shipyards, and of illegal movement, Zamiatin too despised western capitalism as life crushing. Some of the features of a satirical novel against bourgeois respectability and clerical philistinism which he wrote while in England during the First War, such as the coupons for sex and a Taylorite "table of compulsory salvation" through minutely regulated daily occupations, recur in *We*. Even after leaving the USSR, his major project in the 1930s was a historical novel on Attila and the fall of decadent Rome, a situation that he, with Bryusov and Blok, considered analogous to the East-West conflict of our times. Most significantly, for Zamiatin too the Revolution is the undoubted sun-like principle of life and movement, while he bestowed the name of Entropy on the principle of dogmatic evil and death. An anti-entropic science, society and, of course, literature is needed, he affirmed, "as a means for struggling against hardening of arteries, rigidity, moss and peace ... a utopian literature, absurd as Babeuf in 1797: it will be proved right after 150 years." It is evident that

Zamiatin believed he was a utopian, that, paradoxically, he thought of himself as more revolutionary than the latter-day Bolsheviks, since "the truths of today are the errors of tomorrow: there is no final number" (*On Literature, Revolution and Entropy*). It is thus disingenuous to present him as a primarily anti-Soviet author—even though the increasingly dogmatic and bureaucratic high priests of Soviet letters thought so, never allowed his novel to be printed in the USSR, and induced him to leave his country in 1931. Extrapolating the repressive potentials of every strong state and technocratic setup, including the socialist ones, Zamiatin describes a United or Unique State twelve centuries hence having for its leader "the Benefactor" (a prototype for Orwell's Big Brother and the situation in *1984*), where art has become a public utilitarian service, and science a faultless guide for linear, undeviating happiness. Zamiatin's sarcasm against abstract utopian prescriptions (say, of the feebler Wells) takes on Dostoevskian overtones: the threat of the Crystal Palace echoes in the totally rationalized city. The only irrational element left are people, like the split (Marx would have said alienated) narrator, the mathematician and rocketship builder D-503, and the temptress from the underground movement who for a moment makes of him a deviant. But man has, as Dostoevsky's Grand Inquisitor explained to Christ, a built-in instinct for slavery, the rebellion fails, and all the citizen "Numbers" are subjected to brain surgery removing the possibility of harmful imagination.

Zamiatin's novel, however, is not consistent or of even merit. Of a bold general concept, it hesitates midway between Chernyshevsky and Dostoevsky, undecided what to think of science and reason. After the physician and philosopher Bogdanov, and the mathematician Tsiolkovsky, Zamiatin was the first practicing scientist and engineer among significant Russian science fiction writers. The scientific method provided the paradigm for his thinking, and he could not seriously blame it for the deformations of life. In that case, how come that a certain type of rationalism claiming to be scientific, can be harmful in certain social usages? This question, which came up in science fiction with Butler's *Erewhon* and the best works of Wells, Zamiatin was unable to answer except in mythical, Dostoevskian terms: there is "only one conceivable victory —to be crucified. ... Christ, when factually the victor, becomes the Grand Inquisitor" (in his essay "Scythians?"). Any achievement of a lofty ideal inevitably makes it founder in philistinism. To the extent that *We* equates leninist communism with institutionalized Christianity, and models its fable on an inevitable Fall from Eden ending in an ironical Crucifixion, it has a strong anti-utopian streak. Zamiatin's evocative style shifted the focus to systematic image-building at the expense of the plot, thus making a virtue out of his inability to explicate the chosen situation and to reconcile its poles of rationalism and irrationalism, science and art (including the art of love). However, this obscures the problem of whether *any* utopia—even a dynamic, non-Morean one—must of inherent necessity become repressive and dehumanizing. Zamiatin's social ideology conflicts thus with his own favorite experimental approach: any significant exploration of this theme and situation would have to be conducted in terms of the least alienating utopia imaginable—one in which there is no misuse of natural sciences by a dogmatic science of man.

Yet when all this is said, the basic values of *We* imply a stubborn revolutionary vision of a classless new moral world free from all social alienations, a vision common to Anarchism and libertarian Marxism. Zamiatin thus confronts an anti-utopian, absolutistic, military-type control—extrapolated both from the bourgeois and early socialist state practices—with a utopian-socialist norm. As he wrote in the essay "Tomorrow": "We do not turn to those who reject the present in the name of a return to the past, nor to those hopelessly stupefied by the present, but to those who can see the far-off tomorrow—and in the name of tomorrow, in the name of man we judge the present." This point of view differs from Mayakovsky's in *The Bath* principally by its ascetic concentration on the deformities, without the explicit counterbalance of a vague future. Indeed, it is rather significant how for Mayakovsky, too, the utopian anticipation draws further off in time: in poetry, from the twenty-first century of *The Fifth International* (1922) to the thirtieth century of *The Flying Proletarian* (1925); in dramaturgy, from the twenty-five years of the scenario *Forget the Hearth* (1927) to the hundred years of *The Bath* (1929). Simultaneously with the poetry of Mayakovsky, whom he called "a magnificent beacon," Zamiatin brought to Russian science fiction the realization that the new utopian world cannot be a static changeless paradise of a new religion, albeit a religion of steel, mathematics, and interplanetary flights. Refusing all canonization, the materialist utopia must subject itself to a constant scrutiny by the light of its own principles. These are for Zamiatin centered in an ever-developing human personality, and expressed in the irreducible, life-giving, and subversive erotic passion. For all its resolute one-sidedness, the uses of Zamiatin's bitter and paradoxical warning in a dialectical utopianism seem to be obvious.

The language itself of the novel is a very interesting expressionist medium vouching for at least some cognitive veracity. It is manipulated for speed and economy which Zamiatin himself defined as:

> a high voltage of every word. In one second there has to be condensed
> what before fitted into a whole minute; the syntax becomes elliptical

and airy, the complex pyramids of the paragraph are scattered into stone blocks of independent sentences. … The picture is sharply focussed, synthetic, it has one basic trait only, which could be noticed from a moving car. Provincialisms, neologisms, science, mathematics, engineering have invaded a vocabulary canonized by usage.

Zamyatin is a heretic; in places vague and possibly confused, he probably fails to attain first-rank artistic structure because of the one-sided assumptions which guide his composition—but he is certainly not counterrevolutionary. On the contrary, in his own way he tried to work for a future different from that of the United State. His protagonist is defeated, but the novel as a whole remains concerned for the integrity of man's knowledge (science) and practice (love and art). Even the symbol of "$\sqrt{-1}$" (personalized as the retribalized, "hippie" Mephis in the Green World) is an antithesis to and appeal against a limited rationalism (the United State) which does not simply reject the thesis—as Dostoyevsky's Underground Man did—but includes it in a higher dialectical synthesis prefigured in D-503's oscillation between love and the Integral. Yet unlike Wells, the guilt and possible solution is here placed squarely on man and not on mythical outsiders. Like the formal model of D-503's personalized notes, the laboratory conspectus, the structure of We remains open to new cognitions, restless, anti-entropic, and never finally complete. By systematically and sensitively subjecting the deformities it describes to experimental examination and the extrapolating magnification of science fiction, Zamiatin's method makes it possible to identify and cope with them. In his own vocabulary, the protagonist's defeat is of the day but not necessarily of the epoch. The defeat in the novel We is not the defeat of the novel itself, but an attempt to provoke the reader to thought and action. It is a document of an exasperated clash between the "cold" and the "warm" utopia: a judgment on Campanella as given by Rabelais.

Parallel to predominantly social-science fiction, the 1920s saw also the first wave of Russian science fiction which organically blended sociological with natural-science fiction primarily oriented toward interplanetary adventures. The great pioneer of both Russian astronautics and Soviet science fiction was Konstantin Tsiolkovsky, a mathematics teacher who had begun his speculations on mankind's cosmic destiny in the depths of a Tsarist provincial town by the 1890s. He wrote for propagandist purposes two science fiction booklets illustrating a possible happy weightless life on asteroids, the moon, and on rocket colonies in space (*On the Moon*, 1887; *Daydreams of Earth and*

Heavens, 1894). The Soviet regime enthusiastically took up his unheeded ideas; Tsiolkovsky wrote his best science fiction story *Outside Earth* in 1918, and proceeded to develop his scientific plans with public means, becoming the venerated teacher of the future Sputnik and Vostok constructors as well as of the science fiction fans and writers such as Beliaev. Mention was made earlier of the general enthusiasm for a revolutionary "storming of the heavens" in the 1920s, as expressed by Bryusov, Mayakovsky, and the "Cosmists," and skeptically reflected even in Zamiatin's *We* as well as in his story *The Most Important Thing* (1924). Astronautic study circles, public lectures, and expositions got under way at that time; in the midst of the Civil War the tireless Lenin, having read Lowell on Mars and debated the Martian novels with Bogdanov, went in 1920 to listen to a public lecture on the project of a cosmic ship, and talking with Wells concluded that "if mankind ever comes to other planets all our philosophical, moral and social assumptions will have to be reexamined." In 1925 Moscow University organized a debate on "The Flight to Other Worlds," and in 1925–26 the first specialized adventure periodicals carrying largely or exclusively science fiction appeared, such as *War of the Worlds, Universal Detective, Knowledge is Power,* and *World of Adventure.* In the New Economic Policy heyday of private publishing, the Soviet book market was flooded by immense quantities of translated European and American popular science fiction, such as E. R. Burroughs's Martian cycle. Not counting the perennially popular Verne and Wells, research has traced more than a hundred translated titles (novels and stories) between 1923 and 1930 (as compared with 200 original Soviet novels and stories between 1920 and 1930). In such an atmosphere, the genre was given the accolade of literary quality and respectability by the well-known writer Alexey Tolstoy, who in his novels *Aelita* and *The Garin Death-Ray* blended the adventure of interplanetary flight and conflicts, and the global struggle for a new scientific invention, with a utopian pathos steeped in revolutionary social perspectives in a way calculated to please almost all segments of the reading public. This blend was to remain the basic Soviet science fiction tradition.

In *Aelita* (1922), written while Tolstoy was still an émigré preparing to return to the Soviet Union, this blend is endearingly enriched with a lyrical component, the love of Los, the inventor of the rocketship, for the Martian princess Aelita. Los, the creative intellectual, with his vacillations and individualist concerns, is contrasted to but also allied with Gusev, a shrewd man of the people and fearless fighter who leads the revolt of Martian workers (the Martians are descendants of the Atlantans) against the decadent dictatorship of the Engineers' Council. If the standard adventure and romance were taken over from Wells and the current western popular science fiction (Benoit's *Atlantis* and Burroughs's *A Princess of the Moon* probably—both were translated in the USSR), the politics are diametrically opposed to Lasswitz's, Wells's, and Bogdanov's idea of a Martian benevolent technocracy. Yet if the workers' uprising led by a Red Army man was a clear parable for the times, such as could have been shared by all Soviet science fiction from Mayakovsky to Zamiatin, the dejected and somewhat hasty return which has Los listening at the end to the desperate wireless calls of his beloved is as clearly of a Wellsian gloom (*The First Men on the Moon*). But this ambiguity, which sometimes strains the plot mechanics, makes also for a counterpointing richness, an encompassing of differing attitudes and levels which envisages the price as well as the necessity of an activist happiness. Since the novel's plastic characterization, rich and differentiated language, and consistent verisimilitude (once one accepts the underlying premise), lifted it to the level of the literary mainstream much as Wells had done in Britain, it became the first universally accepted masterpiece of Soviet science fiction. In particular, it lifted its extraterrestrial utopianism out of simple imitations of Verne, Wells, and Burroughs (such as those by Mukhanov, Arelsky, Grave, Yazvitsky, Goncharov) to a height not to be reached again until Yefremov.

Tolstoy's second science fiction novel, *The Garin Death-Ray* (four versions from 1926 to 1937), is a retreat to the "catastrophe" novel: Vernean adventures and Chestertonian detections and conspiracies centre around an amoral scientist who beats the capitalist industry kings at their own game but comes to grief when faced with popular revolt. It moves fast if jerkily; as Tolstoy was a trained engineer, its science is believable (atomic disintegration of a trans-uranium element is posited as well as something resembling lasers), and it remains a prototype of the anti-imperialist and anti-Fascist concern in Soviet science fiction. In its skein, this has always been a vigorous strand, whether as direct political satire (as in Ehrenburg or Lavrenev, or in later works such as Turov's *Island of Gorilloids*, Zuyev-Ordinets's *Panurge's Herd*, or A. Shishko's *The End of Common Sense*), as the more dubious Soviet-invention-and-foreign-spy thrillers frequent from that time on (for example, atomic energy in A. Glebov's play *Gold and Brains* (1929), or as the pamphleteering story popular among the best present-day writers like Lagin, Savchenko, Toman, Dneprov, Varshavsky, etc. In the 1920s themselves, numerous novels clustered around the *Garin Death-Ray* combination of scientific thriller and politically virtuous anticipation (besides those already mentioned, A. Yaroslavsky *The Argonauts of Space*, V. Orlovsky *The Horror Machine* and *The Revolt of Atoms*, N. Karpov *Death*

Rays, S. Grigorev *The Fall of Britain*, F. Bogdanov *Twice Born*, T. Keller and V. Hirschhorn *Universal Rays*, etc.).

Soviet science fiction of the 1920s had thus established a tradition ranging sociologically from facile sub-literature to some of the most interesting works of "highbrow" fiction produced in that golden age. It had embraced further and nearer anticipation, global and interplanetary tales; adventure, politics, utopianism, and technology; ethics and romance; novels, stories, poems, plays, essays, and films (eight silent science fiction films, surely the first in the world, were made up to 1926, beginning with Jack London's *Iron Heel* in 1919 for which the scenario was written by no less a dignitary than the comissar for education, Lunacharsky, and continuing with a rather bad *Aelita* in 1924). It had sketched in most of the themes and *topoi* of modern science fiction—galactic warfare being conspicuously rare—including anti-utopianism, automation, and social consequences of "value-free" natural science. Its common denominator was a sometimes naïve but genuinely enthusiastic, thoroughgoing, and humanist critique of old capitalist Europe and America.

About 1927, Soviet concentration on national industrial expansion at the expense of global revolutionary romanticism, with future sociological horizons narrowing into a planned quantitative growth and thus decreasing in imaginative novelty, began strongly to favour linear technological and natural-science extrapolation. Within a general European movement toward a "realist objectivity" (*Neue Sachlichkeit*), Soviet literary horizons grew less "cosmic" and grandiose: the science fiction estrangement shifted into the field of amazing adventures or inventions. Instead of a world revolution and far-ranging anticipations, detailed but flat descriptions of the technologically changed near future or of science fiction adventures in an abstract, often foreign-sounding (a convention still strong today), or planetary setting came to the fore. This constituted a return to the nineteenth-century traditions of Verne and Wells. Prerevolutionary Vernean writings had not remained without echoes, such as the geologist and geographer V. Obruchev's two novels about prehistoric environments *Plutonia* (1924, a hollow-earth setting) and *Sannikov-Land* (1926, North Pole oasis). As for the never-ceasing Russian fascination with Wells it could simply turn to his short-range extrapolations such as *The Island of Dr. Moreau* or *The Invisible Man*. In this tradition, the most interesting and still widely read, even though basically a juvenile writer was Aleksandr Beliaev, who followed upon his successful first novel *Professor Dowell's Head* (1925) with many stories and about twenty novels (for example, *The Amphibian Man*) which mingled breathtaking Vernean adventures of a romantically alienated hero in a basically fairytale vein with an unusually lively interest in new biological and astronautic themes (brain surgery; atomic fission; several novels in the 1930s domesticating Tsiolkovsky's notions). Yet the black-and-white opposition of his threatened hero to an imaginary capitalist environment was also a form of escapism into black Ruritania, soon mingled with detective and spy-thriller elements.

In fact, the promise of the revolutionary years, which made it appear probable that the Russian school (or indeed schools) would dominate our times in science fiction, and in cinema, painting, theater, was not fulfilled: the historical sense, the dimension of imaginative experimentation—both anti-utopian and utopian—was forcibly expunged from it. The sectarian RAPP (Proletarian Writers' Association) critics opened in 1929–30 a strong campaign against science fiction as a "harmful genre" and succeeded in putting an almost total stop to its publication. From an average of about twenty-five titles per year in the mid-1920s (forty-seven in the peak year 1927), the publication plummeted to four books in 1931, and one each in 1933 and 1934. Only in 1935, properly sterilized, science fiction was partly rehabilitated as a marginal, juvenile, and popularizing genre. Anticipating the future became an uncomfortable pursuit when "Stalin was the only one supposed to 'foresee' the future" (as the Soviet science fiction critic Brandis expresses it), and cosmonautics were mentioned in the same breath with bourgeois cosmopolitism. As a result, in the twenty-five years beginning with Mayakovsky's death and Zamiatin's departure and up to the appearance of Yefremov's *Andromeda*, no significant work of anticipation appeared in Soviet science fiction though the appearance of anticipation by oblique incorporation into the work of major writers such as Yuriy Olesha or Leonid Leonov (one layer of his three-level novel *The Journey Toward the Ocean*, with its picture of future world wars and interplanetary flight, verges on an independent vision worthy of *The Iron Heel*) is a testimony of its latent vitality. But the constitution of science fiction moods and elements into a significant genre in its own right was cut short by the prevailing Stalinist attitude towards science fiction called the "theory of limits," or with more sophistry, the "theory of nearer aims." The Soviet science fiction critic Ryurikov sums up the situation: "Its acolytes ... began trussing up the wings of imagination. They said that literary anticipation had to solve only technological problems of the nearest future, and that it should not attempt to go beyond such limits; only thus will it remain based on socialist realism." Thus, science fiction was reduced to extolling technology, its ethics to pragmatic rules, and its "writers did not even hint at the problems of man's spiritual development on the path to communism." Of all such novels about bigger and better oil-drills, radars, or solar energy uses, the least boring were those depicting Arctic exploration and transformation (Lissovoy, Grebnyov, Adamov, Kazantsev), since this was luckily both in the Vernean tradition and the region of many exploits of the Soviet 1930s. But just as the few remaining anticipation novels were exclusively juvenile, so all of these mixtures of technological adventure and patriotic—sometimes even military—pride (for example, Adamov's *Secret of Two Oceans*) fade more or less into sub-literature. Yu. Dolgushin's novel *The Generator of Miracles*, approaching some bionic ideas, was probably the most interesting among them; serialized in 1940, it was published in book form only in 1959.

Such stagnation within utilitarian horizons and stereotyped situations and characters (the heroic expedition or project-leader, the corrupted intellectual doubter, the foreign spy or saboteur) earned Soviet science fiction from mid-1930s to mid-1950s the reputation of a second-rate crossbreed, neither really artistic nor scientific. A first reaction to this was a growth of detective and adventure elements in the 1950s (Nemtsov, Kazantsev). This was perhaps helpful in momentarily dispelling the reigning monotony, but a meteor alarm instead of a sabotage does not much raise the cognitive or imaginative level of science fiction. (The technological-adventure science fiction—nalogous to that of the 1930s in the United State —based on a morality triangle of a starry-eyed beginner set between a wise elder leader and a careerist and egotistic antagonist is probably still flourishing in the foothills of Soviet science fiction.)

The second great age of Soviet science fiction, after the heterogeneous 1920s, accordingly came about with a specific regeneration of its utopian imaginativeness in the latter half of the 1950s, and it has now lasted more than a decade. The reasons which made it possible are obvious. The Twentieth Congress of the Soviet Communist party in 1956 destroyed the indisputability of Stalinist myths about society and literature. They were further shaken by the sensational achievements of Soviet natural sciences, symbolized by the first Sputnik. The new science fiction wave, rich in tradition and individual talent, eager to deal with an increasing range of subjects, from sociological to cosmological and anthropological, from astronautic through cybernetic to anticipatory-utopian, found a wide audience among the young and the intelligentsia. We have no sure statistics on this reading public, but I think at least the juvenile section might well be larger than its American counterpart. It was perhaps unsophisticated, but impatient of the old cliches and thirsting after knowledge and imagination. Its tastes carried the day in the great "Yefremov debate."

Indeed in the whole history of Russian and Soviet science fiction, only Chernyshevsky's, and probably Mayakovsky's, work had taken by storm young people, especially the younger scientists, and earned the genre such general esteem as did Yefremov's novel *Andromeda*. Subsequent developments in Soviet science fiction can be understood only as growing out of its having, against violent ideological opposition, consummated in 1957–58 the victory of the new wave, which was really the victory of the pristine Soviet Russian tradition, in abeyance since the Leninist 1920s. The writers and critics of the "cold stream" rebuked the novel's heroes as being "too far from our times" and thus unintelligible to the reader, especially to the juvenile reader. In short, they were saying that Yefremov's scope was too daring. "The demand: 'Thus far, and no farther' smells of blind dogmatism," a Soviet critic (Sytin) concluded of such pressure, which had for fifteen years hindered the publication and development of Yefremov's science fiction (his first such story, *The Hellenic Secret* from 1942, dealing with "gene memory," was thought of as mystical and published only in 1966). However, the opinion of "warm stream" critics, and of the thousands of readers who wrote to the author, newspapers, and periodicals, that this was a liberating turning-point in Soviet science fiction, finally prevailed. The novel has since been reprinted twenty-four times, running to millions of snapped-up copies, and translated into twenty-three languages.

Yefremov's work achieved such historical significance because, in its own way, it creatively revived the classical utopian and socialist vision, whose resilience so flabbergasted Wells in his meeting with Lenin. This vision (Marx's, Chernyshevsky's, Morris's, or even the mellower Wells's, just back from Soviet Russia, in *Men Like Gods*) looks forward to a unified, affluent, humanist, classless, and stateless world. Thus, *Andromeda* is situated in the 408th year of the Era of the Great Ring, when mankind has established informational contact with inhabitants of distant constellations who pass on such information to each other through a "ring" of inhabited systems. The earth itself is administered—by analogy with the associative centers of the human brain—by an Astronautic Council and an Economic Council which tallies all plans with existing possibilities; their specialized research Academies correspond to man's sensory centers. Within this framework of the body politic, Yefremov is primarily interested in the development of a disalienated man and new ethical relationships. For all the theatrical loftiness of his characters, whose emotions are rarely less sublime than full satisfaction and confidence (only an occasional melodramatic villain feels fear or hate), they can learn through painful mistakes and failures, as distinct from the superman cliches of "socialist realism" or much American science fiction after Gernsback.

The re-exhumation of socialist utopianism brought back into Soviet fiction whole reaches of the science fiction tradition—the philosophical story and romantic *étude*, classic sociological and modern cosmological utopianism. Yet in Yefremov's novel the strong narrative sweep full of adventurous actions, from a fistfight to an encounter with electrical predators and a robot-spaceship from the Andromeda nebula, is imbued with the joy and romance of cognition. This certainly embraces an understanding of, and intervening into, the outside world of modern cosmology and evolutionist biology. But Yefremov's strong anthropocentrical bent places the highest value on *creativity*, a simultaneous adventure of deed, thought, and feeling resulting in physical and ethical (body and mind being indissolubly connected in this materialist writer) *beauty*. The lofty utopianism of his anthropology is evident even in the symbolic title: the Andromeda nebula recalls the chained Greek beauty rescued from a monster (class egotism and violence, personified in the novel as a bull, and often bearing some hallmarks of Stalinism) by a flying hero endowed with superior science. Astronautics thus do not evolve into a new uncritical cult, but are claimed as a humanist discipline—one of the most significant cross-connections between physical sciences, social sciences, ethics, and art which Yefremov establishes as the norm for his new people. Even the novel structure, oscillating between cosmic and terrestrial chapters, serves to emphasize this connection. Furthermore, this future is not an arrested, pseudo-perfect end of history—the bane of optimistic utopianism from Plato and More to Bellamy. Freed from economic and power worries, man must still redeem time, which is unequal on earth and in space, through a humanist dialectics of personal creativity and societal teamwork mediated, in a clear harking back to the ideals of the 1920s, by artistic and scientific beauty of functionality (for example, Dar listening to the cosmic symphony, or the Tibetan experiment). Creativity is always countered by entropy, and self-realization paid for in effort and even suffering. As a matter of fact, several very interesting approaches to a Marxist "optimistic tragedy" can be found in the book (for instance, in the Mven Mass "happy Fall" motif). Finally, the accent on beauty and responsible freedom places Chernyshevskian female heroines in the center of the novel, interacting with the heroes and contributing to the emotional motivation of new utopian ethics—in complete contrast to American science fiction (with which Yefremov is obviously in a well-informed polemical dialogue).

How difficult it is for a science fiction writer to portray basically different, even if philosophically already sketched human relations, can be seen from some places where the novel's dialogue, motivation, and tone flag, so that it falls back on pathos and preaching which slow down its rhythm. Yefremov's characters tend to be statuesque and monolithic in a kind of neoclassicist way, and his incidents often exploit the quantitatively grandiose: Mven blows up a satellite and half a mountain, Veda loses the greatest ever anthropological find, and to think of the manly Erg blushing or the pure Nisa stepping into, say, offensive jellyfish offal on the iron-star planet is practically blasphemous. Most of this can be explained by the transitional nature of the work, trying to achieve several aims at once: it was the first to open the floodgates closed for twenty-five years, and it overflowed into clogged channels. One feels in it the presence of a reader unused to fast orientation in new perspectives and, as Yefremov himself wrote, "still attracted to the externals, decorations, and theatrical effects of the genre." It cannot be denied that some aspects of Yefremov's ethics and aesthetics, such as the erotic and the intimate interpersonal relations generally seem, though understandable enough in the context of the social mores of an elder-generation Soviet Russian scientist, curiously old-fashioned for a sweeping science fiction glance. His limitations are most clearly manifested in the later long story *Cor Serpentis*, where Terrans meeting a lonely fluorine-based mankind solve its problem by promising to transmute fluorine into oxygen. This story, an explicit counterblast to Leinster's *First Contact* with its bellicose and acquisitive presuppositions, might be a legitimate pacifist-socialist allegory for changing American capitalist meritocrats into Russian socialist ones, yet such a "genocentric" view (if I may coin a term in between egocentric and anthropocentric) precludes a full development of imaginative science fiction vistas, whose point is unity in variety. But even the further discussion of such vistas in Soviet science fiction (for example, by the brothers Strugatsky, Dneprov, Varshavsky, etc.) was made possible by Yefremov's pioneering effort. And on the whole, the success of *Andromeda*'s polyphonic scope, not limited in its large number of protagonists to the consciousness of the central hero, cannot be seriously contested. It is perhaps (with Lem's *Magellan Nebula* in Poland) the first utopia in world literature which shows new characters creating and being created by a new society, that is *the personal working out of a utopia*. Yefremov's basic device of unfolding the narration as if the anticipated future were already a normative present unites the classic "looking backward" of utopian anticipations with the modern Einsteinian conception of different coordinate systems with autonomous norms: twentieth-century science and the age-old dreams of a just and happy society meet in his novel. This made it the nodal point of the Russian and the socialist tradition this essay has been concerned to establish; and that is why it was able to usher in the new era of Soviet science fiction.

Subsequent developments and differentiations can be fully appreciated only from this perspective. Of course, Soviet science fiction embraces, even in the first decade of its modern phase, and at the beginning of a full mastery of themes and approaches, a widening spread of significant works, from astronautic to cybernetic, from the novel about a new invention to technological fable, from psychological study to satire and pamphlet. It has assembled fifty habitual (though not full-time) writers, an insatiable reading public, an expectation of literary clarity and careful craftsmanship, and it has avoided confusing its medium with those of fantasy, gangster novels, horror thrillers, and cloak-and-dagger adventures. But perhaps most important for understanding it is the fact of its leading writers having opted for a *hope* which grows out of the central position of functionally clear human figures. They have, in other words, developed the basic philosophical and literary tradition of socialism—the utopia, equated here with the open horizons of extrapolated humanizing potentialities.

A Select Bibliography On Russian Science Fiction From The Beginnings To 1959[1]

(The standard histories of Russian literature, thought, and theater are not included; nor is primary literature, although some articles by the science fiction writers discussed are obviously pertinent.)

A. EIGHTEENTH CENTURY

N. D. Chechulin, "Russky sotsial'nyy roman XVIII veka" [The Russian social novel of the eighteenth century], *Zhurnal Ministerstva Narodnogo Prosveshcheniya* [Journal of the ministry of public education] 327 (January 1900).

---

1 It is a pleasant duty to record here the helpful exchange of opinions and indications, especially for the study of the oldest Russian science fiction, which I have received from Professor M. J. Holquist of Yale University and from a lecture at his seminar in Russian utopian thinking, as well as the kind services of Yale University Library, Indiana University Library, and the New York Public Library. Work on this essay was helped by a research grant of the University of Massachusetts at Amherst. The responsibility for this bibliography, and for the article preceding it, remains, of course, entirely my own.

K. V. Chistov, *Russkie narodnye sotsial'no-utopicheskie legendy XVII–XIX vekov* [Russian folk legends of social utopia, 17th–19th centuries] (Moscow, 1967).

A. A. Kizevetter, "Russkaya utopiya XVIII st." [Russian eighteenth-century utopias] in his *Istoricheskie ocherki* [Historical outlines] (Moscow, 1912).

M. N. Longinov and N. P. Durov, "Fedor Ivanovich Dmitriev-Mamonov," *Russkaya starina* [Russian antiquity] no. I (1870): 544–59.

Marc Raeff, "State and Nobility in the Ideology of M. N. Shcherbatov," *American Slavic and East European Review* 19 (1960): 363–79.

V. V. Sipovsky, "Filosofskie nastroeniya i idei v russkom romane XVIII veka," *Zh.M.N.P.* (May 1905): 359.

B. NINETEENTH CENTURY

P. N. Sakulin, *Russkaya literatura i sotsializm* [Russian literature and socialism], vol. 1 (Moscow, 1924).

Nicholas P. Vaslev, "Bulgarin and the Development of the Russian Utopian Genre," *Slavic and East European Journal* 12 (1968): 35–43.

N. Brodsky and N. Sidorov, *Kommentariy k romanu N. G. Chernyshevskogo "Chto delat'?"* [Commentary on N. G. Chernyshevsky's novel *What Is to be Done*] (Moscow, 1933).

Joseph Frank, "N. G. Chernyshevsky. A Russian Utopia," *Southern Review*, N.S.3 (1967): 66–84.

A. V. Lunacharsky, *Stat'i o Chernyshevskom* [Essays on Chernyshevsky] (Moscow, 1958).

M. P. Nikolaev, *N. G. Chernyshevsky—Seminariy* N. G. Chernyshevsky: Seminars] (Leningrad, 1959).

N. T. Pinaev, *Kommentariy k romanu N. G. Chernyshevskogo "Chto delat'?"* (Moscow, 1963).

E. I. Pokusaev, *N. G. Chernyshevsky* (Moscow, 1960).

F. Randall, *N. G. Chernyshevskii* (New York, 1967).

Yu. M. Steklov, *Chernyshevsky—ego zhizn' i deyatel'nost'* [Chernyshevsky: His life and work] (Moscow, 1928).

N. F. Bel'chikov, "Chernyshevsky i Dostoevsky" [Chernyshevsky and Dostoevsky], *Pechat' i revolyutsiya* [The press and the revolution] 5 (1928): 35–53.

———. *Dostoevsky v protsesse petrashevtsev* [Dostoevsky in the Petrashevsky circle case] (Leningrad, 1936).

G. I. Chulkov, "Dostoevsky i utopichesky sotsializm" [Dostoevsky and utopian socialism] *Katorga i ssylka* [Conviction and exile] nos. 2 and 3 (1929): 9–36, 134–51.

A. S. Dolinin, "Dostoevsky sredi Petrashevtsev" [Dostoevsky among the Petrashevskys] *Zvenya* [The link] no. 6 (1936).

Joseph Frank, "Nihilism and *Notes from the Underground*," *Sewanee Review* 69 (1961): 1–33.

L. Grossman, *Seminariy po Dostoevskomu* [The Dostoevsky seminars] (Moscow, 1923).

M. S. Gus, *Idei i obrazy F. M. Dostoevskogo* [Ideas and images of F. M. Dostoevsky] (Moscow, 1962).

G. Lukács, *Der russische Realismus in der Weltliteratur* [Russian realism in world literature] (Berlin, 1949).

E. Pokrovskaya, "Dostoevsky i Petrashevtsy" [Dostoevsky and the Petrashevsky Circle], in *Dostoevsky—stat'i i materialy* [Dostoevsky: Essays and sources], vol. i, ed. A. Dolinin, 2 vols. (Petrograd, 1922–25).

Ernest J. Simmons, *Dostoevsky: The Making of a Novelist* (New York, 1962).

V. Tunimanov, "Satira i utopiya ('Bobok,' 'Son smeshnogo cheloveka')" [Satire and utopia ("Bobok," "The Dream of the Ridiculous Man")] *Russkaya literatura* 9, no. 4 (1966).

C. 1900–1930

K. Gerasimov, "'Shturm neba' v poezii Valeriya Bryusova" ["Storming the sky" in Valery Bryusov's poetry] in *Bryusovskie chteniya 1963 goda* [Bryusov readings 1963], ed. K. Ayvazyan (Erevan, 1964).

N. I. Chardzhiev, "Novoe o Mayakovskom" [New materials on Mayakovsky] in *Literaturnoe nasledstvo* [Literary heritage], ed. V. Vinogradov et al. (Moscow, 1958), vol. 65.

A. Fevral'sky, *Mayakovsky—dramaturg* [Mayakovsky the playwright] (Moscow, 1940).

R. V. Ivanov-Razumnik, "Misteriya ili buffo?" [Mystery or bouffe?] in his *Tvorchestvo i kritika* [Art and criticism] (Petrograd, 1922).

N. N. Maslin, *Mayakovsky—ocherki tvorchestva* [Mayakovsky: Sketches of creative works] (Moscow, 1956).

B. L. Mlilyavsky, *Satirik i vremya* [The satirist and his times] (Moscow, 1963).

V. O. Pertsov, *Mayakovsky*, 3 vols. (Moscow, 1956–65), vols. II and III.

Angelo Maria Ripellino, *Majakovskij e il teatro russo d'avanguardia* [Mayakovsky and Russian avant-garde theater] (Torino, 1959).

B. I. Rostotsky, *Mayakovsky i teatr* [Mayakovsky and the theater] (Moscow, 1952).

Viktor Shklovsky, *O Mayakovskom* [On Mayakovsky] (Moscow, 1940).

Laurence Leo Stahlberger, *The Symbolic System of Majakovskij* (The Hague, 1964).

Ya. Braun, "Vzyskuyushchiy cheloveka" [The seeker of humanity], *Sibirskie ogni* [Siberian lights] nos. 5–6 (1923): 225–40.

Edward J. Brown, "Zamiatin and English Literature," in *American Contributions to the Fifth International Congress of Slavists*, 2 vols. (The Hague, 1964), II:21–40.

Christopher Collins, "Zamiatin, Wells, and the Utopian Literary Tradition," *Slavonic and East European Review* 44 (1966), 351–60.

———. "Zamiatin's We as Myth," *Slavic and East European Journal* 10 (1966): 125–33.

Isaac Deutscher, *Heretics and Renegades* (London, 1965), 35–50.

Aleksandar Flaker, *Heretici i sanjari* [Heretics and rebels] (Zagreb, 1958).

Richard A. Gregg, "Two Adams and Eve in the Crystal Palace," *Slavic Review* 24 (1965), 680–87.

Mark R. Hillegas, *The Future as Nightmare* (New York, 1967).

Robert L. Jackson, "Zamiatin's *We*," in his *Dostojevskij's Underground Man in Russian Literature* (The Hague, 1958), 150–57.

D. J. Richards, "Four Utopias," *S.E.E.R.* 40 (1961), 220–28.

———. *Zamyatin: A Soviet Heretic* (London, 1962).

Yu. Ryurikov (see part D).

Alex M. Shane, *The Life and Works of E. Zamiatin* (Berkeley, CA, 1968).

Viktor Shklovsky, *Pyat' chelovek znakomykh* [Five renowed people] (n.p., 1927), 43–67.

Darko Suvin, *Od Lukijana do Lunjika* [From Lucian to the lunatic] (Zagreb, 1965), 282–86.

A. Voronsky, *Literaturno-kriticheskie stat'i* [Literary critical essays] (Moscow, 1963), 85–111.

J. White, "Mathematical Imagery in Musil's *Young Törless* and Zamyatin's *We*," *Comparative Literature* 18 (1966): 71–78.

George Woodcock, "Utopias in Negative," *Sewanee Review* 64 (1956), 81–97.

N. Bezdomnyy, "Predtechi sovetskoy 'nauchno-tekhnicheskoy' fantastiki" [Precursors of Soviet "scientific-technological" fantasy], *Russkaya mysl'*[Russian thought] no. 2452 (1966): 2–3.

A. Evdokimov, "Sovetskaya fantastika 1917–1927 godov" [Soviet fantasy, 1917–1937], in *Fantastika 1967* [Fantasy 1967] (Moscow, 1968), vol. III (bibliography).

Boris Lyapunov, "Lyubitelyam nauchnoy fantastiki—Sovetskaya fantastika za 50 let" [For fans of science fiction: Soviet fantasy of the last 50 years], in *Mir priklyuchenii 14* (Moscow, 1968), 687–735 (with bibliography).

R. Nudel'man, "Fantastika, rozhdennaya revolyutsyey" [Fantasy born from revolutions], in *Fantastika 1966* (Moscow, 1967), vol. III, 330–69.

Nonna D. Shaw, "The Only Soviet Literary Peasant Utopia," *S.E.E.J.* 7 (1963): 279–83.

———. "Nation and Superstate in Soviet Utopian Literature," in *Proceedings of the Fourth Congress of the International Comparative Literature Association, Fribourg, 1964*, edited by Francois Jost, 2 vols. (The Hague, 1966), vol. i.

L. M. Polyak, *Aleksey Tolstoy: khudozhnik prozy* [Alexei Tolstoy, Prose artist] (Moscow, 1964).

V. R. Shcherbina, *A. V. Tolstoy* (Moscow, 1956).

N. L. Veksler, *Aleksei Nikolaevich Tolstoy* (Moscow, 1948).

D. 1931–59

Boris Liapunov, *Aleksandr Beliaev* (Moscow, 1967).

K. Andreev, "Knigi o budushchem obshchestve" [Books about future societies], in *Detskaya literatura: 1960 god* [Children's literature 1960] (Moscow, 1961), 33–57.

I. Berezark, "Literatura o budushchem" [Literature about the future], *Zvezda* no. 5 (1960): 200–206.

E. Brandis, *Sovetsky nauchno-fantastichesky roman* [The Soviet science fiction novel] (Leningrad, 1959).

————. V. Dmitrevsky, *Cherez gory vremeni* [Across the hills of time] (Moscow, 1963).

————. *Mir budushchego v nauchnoy fantastike* [The future world in science fiction] (Moscow, 1965).

————. "'Sovremennost' i nauchnaya fantastika" [Modern times and science fiction], *Kommunist* no. I (1960): 66–74.

————. "Mir, kakim my khotim ego videt'" [The world as we wish to see it] in *Vtorzhenie v Persei* [The Perseus invasion] (Leningrad, 1968), 5–31.

L. Cheshkova, "Reka mechty," *Vokrug sveta* no. 2 (1962): 61–64.

V. Dmitrevsky, "Pravo na krylatuyu mechtu" [The right to flights of fancy], *Neva* no. 7 (1958): 201–8.

A. Dneprov, "Nauchnaya fantastika dlya issledovaniya budushchego" [Science fiction for the study of the future], *Molodoy kommunist* [Young communist], no. 8 (1961): 112–19.

Formuly i obrazy—Spor o nauchnoy teme v literature [Formulas and images: Debate on the scientific theme in literature] (Moscow, 1961).

M. Goldsmith, "Soviet Science Fiction," *Spectator* 21 (August 1959).

A. Gromova, "Dvoynoy lik gryadushchego" [The double face of the coming age], *NF—Al'manakh nauchnoy fantastiki* [SF: Almanach of science fiction] I (Moscow, 1964), 270–309.

————. "Na poroge nevedomogo veka" [On the threshold of the unknown century], *Molodaya guardiya* [Young guard] no. 6 (1962): 268–73.

Yu. Kotlyar, "Mir mechty i fantazii" [Fantasy and life], *Oktyabr'* [October] 44 (1967): 194–206.

S. Larin, *Literatura krylatoy mechty* [Literature of the winged dream] (Moscow, 1961).

M. Lazarev, "O tvorchestve I. A. Efremova" [On I. A. Efremova's works], in *Na krayu Oykumeni—Zvezdnye korabli* [In the land of the Oikumens: Star ships], ed. I. Efremov (Frunze, 1961).

Boris Lyapunov, "Fantastika i zhizn'" [Fantasy and life], *Voprosy literatury* [Topics in literature] no. 12 (1959).

V. L'vov, "Velikoe Kol'tso" [The great ring], *Neva* no. 12 (1960).

R. Milch, "Science Fiction in Russia Today," *Riverside Quarterly* 2, no. 3 (1966).

P. Schuyler Miller, "The People's Science Fiction," *Analog* 70 (1962): 150–55.

R. Nudel'man, "Razgovor vo kupe" [Conversation in a train compartment], in *Fantastika 1964 goda* [Fantasy] (Moscow, 1964), 347–67.

O fantastike i priklyucheniyakh [On fantasy and adventure tales] (Leningrad, 1960): E. Brandis, "Puti razvitiya i problemy sovetskoy nauchno-fantasticheskoy literatury" [Paths of development and questions of science fiction]; S. Poltavsky, "O nereshennykh voprosakh nauchnoy fantastiki" [On the unresolved questions of science fiction].

M. Pivovarov, *Fantastika i real'nist'* [Fantasy and reality] (Kiev, 1960).

Yu. Ryurikov, *Cherez 100 i 1000 let* [A century and a millennium letter] (Moscow, 1961).

A. Sinyavsky, "Bez skidok," *Voprosy literatury* no. I (1960): 46–59.

———. "Sovremennyi nauchno-fantastichesky roman" [Contemporary science fiction], in *Puti razvitiya sovremennogo sovetskogo romana* [Development of the contemporary Soviet novel] (Moscow, 1961), 333–50.

V. Sytin, "Otrazhenie mechty" [Reflections of a dream], *Moscow* no. 5 (1961): 206–11.

Peter Yershov, *Science Fiction and Utopian Fantasy in Soviet Literature* (New York, 1954).

Issues of periodicals partly or wholly devoted to science fiction include: *Neva* (1962), no. 4; *Foreign Literature* (1967), no. I; *Soviet Literature* (1968), no. 5.

Red Star: Another Look at Aleksandr Bogdanov

MARK B. ADAMS

Adams, Mark B. "'Red Star': Another Look at Aleksandr Bogdanov."
Slavic Review 48, no. 1 (1989): 1–15.

In recent years, there has been a minor explosion of interest in Aleksandr Bogdanov and other radical Russian intellectuals of pre-Stalinist days. After being in limbo for half a century, their ideas seem almost fresh and vibrant: Set against subsequent Soviet history, their aborted visions of a socialist future seem to give a sense of what might have been. And who knows—in the Gorbachev period, as the Soviet Union sorts out its problems and policies, some of their ideas might enjoy a new lease on life. For these and other reasons, they have recently attracted special interest.

Of course, in Bogdanov's case, there is much to be interested in. Born Aleksandr Aleksandrovich Malinovskii in 1873, Bogdanov trained as a physician in Moscow and Khar'kov, worked briefly as a psychiatrist, and published widely on philosophy, politics, social theory, social psychology, economics, and culture.[1] His early activism in leftist politics led to several arrests, internal exile (1894–95, 1899–1903), and exile abroad (1904–5, 1905–). In 1903 he was one of the original Bolsheviks. Then he published his first philosophical trilogy, *Empiriomonism* (1904–7). Although well received in some circles, this work

---

1 See, for example, Aleksandr Bogdanov, *Kratkii kurs ekonomicheskoi nauki* [On the unresolved questions of science fiction] (Moscow, 1897), *Osnovnye elementy istoricheskogo vzgliada na prirodu* [Basic elements of a historical view on nature] (St. Petersburg, 1899), *Poznanie s istoricheskoi tochki zreniia* [Cognition in historical perspective] (St. Petersburg, 1902), *Novyi mir* [New World] (Stat'i 1904–1905) (Moscow, 1905), *Iz psikhologii obshchestva* [From social psychology], 2nd ed. (St. Petersburg, 1906), *Prikliucheniia odnoi filosofskoi shkoly* [The adventures of a philosophical school] (St. Petersburg, 1908), *Padenie velikogo fetishizma: Vera i nauka* [The fall of a great fetish: Faith and science] (St. Petersburg, 1910), and *Kul'turnye zadachi nashego vremeni* [Cultural tasks of our age] (Moscow, 1911).

occasioned an ideological break with Bolshevism, immortalized in Lenin's acerbic polemic *Materialism and Empiriocriticism*, which attacked Bogdanov for trying to reconcile Marxism with the "idealist" neopositivism of Ernst Mach.[2] Bogdanov then tried his hand at popular fiction, first in *Red Star* (1908), a utopian novel set on Mars, and subsequently in a sequel, *Engineer Menni* (1913); these too received mixed reviews. In 1913, he began setting forth a grand theory of universal structure in a second philosophical trilogy entitled *General Organizational Science (Tectology)* (1913–22).[3] During the Great War, he returned to Russia and served as a military physician. He took no part in the Bolshevik seizure of power in 1917 but was active in the Proletkul't movement until it was disbanded in 1921.[4] Thereafter, according to most biographers, he devoted himself to science. In 1926, Bogdanov founded the Institute of Blood Transfusion in Moscow and the following year published a book on his work there.[5] He died in 1928.[6]

By modern standards, Bogdanov's interests seem remarkably diverse—medicine, psychiatry, blood research, science fiction, Bolshevism, sociology, social psychology, economics, art, philosophy, the philosophy of science. Understandably, most secondary works dealing with Bogdanov have taken a piecemeal approach, focusing on one or another of his pursuits. This approach has produced some remarkable claims about his originality—that he was a founder of cybernetics, that he pioneered organization theory, that he was a profoundly original thinker on science and society, that he was a major philosopher, that he was the founder of Soviet science fiction.[7] Set against

---

2 Aleksandr Bogdanov, *Empiriomonizm* [Empiriomonism], 3 vols. (Moscow and St. Petersburg, 1904–1907); V. I. Lenin, *Materializm i empiriokrititsizm: Kriticheskie zametki ob odnoi reaktsionnoi filosofii* [Materialism and empiriocriticism: Critical notes on a reactionary philosophy] (Moscow: Izdanie Zveno, 1909).

3 Aleksandr Bogdanov, *Vseobshchaia organizatsionnaia nauka* [A general science of organization] (Tektologiia), parts 1–3 (Berlin, Petrograd, Moscow, 1913–29).

4 See Aleksandr Bogdanov, *Sotsializm nauki (Nauchnye zadachi proletariata)* [Socialist science (The scientific tasks of the proletariat)] (Moscow, 1918), *Die Kunst und das Proletariat* (Leipzig, 1919), *Filosofiia zhivogo opyta* [Philosophy of living experience] (Moscow, 1920), and *Elementy proletarskoi kul'tury v razvitii rabochego klassa* [Elements of proletarian culture in the development of the working class] (Moscow, 1920).

5 Aleksandr Bogdanov, *Bor'ba za zhiznesposobnost'* [Sturggle for the viability of life] (Moscow: Novaia Moscow, 1927).

6 The best general discussion of Bogdanov's ideas is to be found in Alexander Vucinich, *Social Thought in Tsarist Russia: The Quest for a General Science of Society, 1861–1917* (Chicago: University of Chicago Press, 1976), 206–30.

7 Such claims are endemic to modern discussions of Bogdanov in both the Soviet Union and the west. For example, a Soviet article depicts Bogdanov as a founder of systems

today's problems and agendas, Bogdanov's work might well seem prescient and inventive. In order to evaluate his originality, however, we must see Bogdanov not in our context but in his own. A case in point is his Martian fiction.

Despite the recent scholarly interest in Bogdanov, most of his publications remain bibliographic rarities. The great exception is his utopian novel *Red Star*, the most popular and accessible of his works. First published in 1908, it was reissued several times in the years following the revolution. A stage version was presented by Proletkul't in 1920, and the novel was subsequently translated into German (1923) and Esperanto (1929).[8] The sequel, *Engineer Menni*, was also popular: First published in 1913, it had appeared in at least six editions by 1923.[9] Following Bogdanov's death, both novels were reissued by the popular science periodical *Vokrug sveta* (1928–29), but they were not republished in the Soviet Union for half a century. Just recently, *Red Star* has appeared in a new Soviet edition of 400,000 copies.[10]

Bogdanov's novels are also his only major works available in English. The translations are quite recent, and their appearance has occasioned new evaluations of Bogdanov's thought. The first English edition of *Red Star* appeared in 1982 in Leland Fetzer's excellent anthology of prerevolutionary Russian science fiction.[11] In his commentary, Fetzer emphasizes the modernity of the novel, noting the "predictions of many technical advances in the future

---

theory: M. I. Setrov, "Ob obshchikh elementakh tektologii A. Bogdanov, kibernetiki i teorii system" [On the lements of A Bogdanov's tectology, cybernetics, and systems theory] in *Uchenye zapiski kafedr obshchestvennykh nauk vuzov goroda Leningrada* [Minutes of the social science faculties of the institutions of higher education in the city of Leningrad]), 1967, no. 8, 49–60. See also the sources listed in Loren Graham's useful biographical article, "Aleksandr Aleksandrovich Bogdanov (Malinovskii)," in *Dictionary of Scientific Biography* (New York: Charles Scribner's Sons, 1970–78) 15 (suppl. 1) (1978): 38–39. This tendency to see Bogdanov's views as highly original and important can be detected even in works that are critical of his ideological failings. See, for example, Dominique Lecourt, "Bogdanov, Mirror of the Soviet Intelligentsia" in Lecourt, *Proletarian Science? The Case of Lysenko*, intro. Louis Althusser, trans. Ben Brewster (London: Humanities Press, 1977), 137–62; this essay was originally published as an introduction to a French anthology of Bogdanov's writings, *La Science, l'art et la classe ouvrière* [Science, art, and the category of innovation], trans. Blanche Grinbaum (Paris: Francois Maspero, 1977).

8 Aleksandr Bogdanov, *Krasnaia zvezda* [*Red Star*] (St. Petersburg, 1908).

9 Aleksandr Bogdanov, *Inzhener Menni* [Engineer Menni] (Moscow, 1913).

10 *Russkaia fantasticheskaia proza XIX—nachala XX veka* [Russian Fantasy of the Nineteenth and Early Twentieth Centuries], Biblioteka fantastiki, vol. 10 (Moscow: Izdatel'stvo Pravda, 1986), 431–568.

11 *Pre-Revolutionary Russian Science Fiction: An Anthology (Seven Utopias and a Dream)*, ed. and trans. Leland Fetzer (Ann Arbor, MI: Ardis, 1982), 71–179.

which cannot fail to impress the reader with their accuracy: radioactive energy, computerized labor statistics, artificial fibers, and rocketry, for example." He also emphasizes "Bogdanov's social prescience," claiming that, in his treatment of human relations, "Bogdanov's words seem strangely prophetic." Fetzer sees *Red Star* as Bogdanov's "opportunity to present an outline of human history, thinly disguised as a history of Mars, from the Marxist point of view, of course," but he dismisses its sequel, *Engineer Menni*, as "inferior to it in every respect."[12]

In 1984, Charles Rougle published a new translation of *Red Star*, together with the first English version of *Engineer Menni* and a poem, "A Martian Stranded on Earth." These translations, bracketed with essays by Richard Stites and Loren Graham, form what must now be regarded as the standard English edition of these works.[13] Stites has provided an excellent introduction to the novels. His opening essay, "Fantasy and Revolution," discusses their historical place in various traditions: science fiction and utopian thought in Russia and the world; scientific and popular views of Mars; Bolshevism; Russian social and political thought; and Bogdanov's intellectual biography. From these contexts, Bogdanov's novels emerge as two minor contributions to seven or eight coherent traditions. From this, it is easy to see how the review of *Red Star* in *Russkoe Bogatstvo* could have dismissed the novel as "trendy, derivative, and unmoving."[14]

What, then, is interesting about Bogdanov's fiction? In his concluding essay, "Bogdanov's Inner Message," Loren Graham expands Fetzer's earlier analysis, arguing that Bogdanov was a "deeply original thinker about the relationship of science and society" who would have "fitted well into one of the university programs formed in the United States and Europe in the late seventies on 'Science, Technology and Society.'"[15] What makes Bogdanov original and modern, in Graham's view, was his recognition that

> even after socialism had been successfully created, civilization would be plagued by a whole series of problems, which we would now probably recognize as problems of "postindustrial societies." Bogdanov was brilliantly prescient in sketching out issues that would face all industrialized

---

12 Ibid., 71–73.
13 Aleksandr Bogdanov, *Red Star: The First Bolshevik Utopia*, ed. Loren R. Graham and Richard Stites, trans. Charles Rougle (Bloomington: Indiana University Press, 1984); hereafter, *Red Star*.
14 Ibid., 12.
15 Ibid., 243.

nations two generations after he first conceived them: the dangers of atomic energy, the problems of preserving the environment, the dilemmas of biomedical ethics, and the shortages of natural resources and food.[16]

According to this reading, Bogdanov was indeed both original and prescient.

Such an interpretation, however, requires two assumptions: First, that these ideas, or their combination, were indeed original to Bogdanov; and, second, that in discussing "contemporary" socialism on Mars, Bogdanov was actually talking about future socialism on Earth. Both assumptions are worth exploring.

Red Star portrays an advanced socialist society established by the indigenous and remarkably humanoid Martians on their home planet, as seen through the eyes of Leonid, a Russian revolutionary visiting from Earth and fresh from the turbulence of 1905. Subtitled "A Utopia," the novel suffers from the drawbacks intrinsic to that genre. The purpose of a utopia is to portray an ideal society, so the reader is lectured about that society endlessly; there must be some literary excuse for all this lecturing, so the chief character is a naïve outsider to whom everything must be explained; and all of this gets boring, so the plot is often thickened with melodrama—a love interest, a mental breakdown, or a murder (Bogdanov employed all three). The sequel, *Engineer Menni*, chronicles how this ideal Martian society came into being.

And what is this ideal society like? It occupies the entire planet of Mars. Its members speak a common language and travel the planet freely, from job to job, at will. It is run by a council, which bases its policies on data from a bureau of statistics. It faces difficult problems, however, notably the exhaustion of the dying planet's energy resources, which is leading the council to contemplate an invasion of Earth.

To contemporary Russian readers, all this must have seemed like a leftist rehash of the works of H. G. Wells. Indeed, *Red Star* can be read in its entirety as a peculiar Russian variant of the Wellsian vision, blending themes from *War of the Worlds* (1898), with Mars as a dying planet, running out of food, and invading the earth; *When the Sleeper Wakes* (1899), with its portrayal of the inevitable but problematic course of social revolution and the class struggle; and *First Men on the Moon* (1901), with its warning about the environmentally damaging effects of human technology and its portrait of a benign and well-organized lunar society alarmed by the energetic aggressiveness and dangerous

---

16 Ibid., 242–43.

disharmony of humankind. Although these scientific romances structured the framework of Bogdanov's novels, the society those novels depict seems most closely to resemble that described by Wells in a nonfictional work entitled *A Modern Utopia* (1905).[17]

In conceptualizing his "modern" utopia, Wells too had to cope with the awkwardness of the genre. In order to avoid the "hardness and thinness" of utopian speculations in which "the blood and warmth and reality of life is largely absent" and whose "common fault is to be comprehensively jejune,"[18] he rejected the novel form in favor of straightforward exposition. Nonetheless, three years before *Red Star* appeared, Wells had already published the view that "no less than a planet will serve the purpose of a modern Utopia"; that the whole world "will surely have a common language"; that there must be "the utmost freedom of going to and fro"; that its population will be "a migratory population beyond any earthly precedent"; that "the Modern Utopia must be not static but kinetic, must shape not as a permanent state but as a hopeful stage, leading to a long ascent of stages"; and that such a society would best be run by an organizational elite, basing decisions on the data generated by a bureau of statistics using the contemporary equivalent of a computer center.[19] Did Bogdanov read Wells's scientific romances and, in particular, his utopia? It seems likely. They were well known and widely published in Europe and even in Russia, where the popular weekly *Vokrug sveta* regularly serialized new works by Wells in Russian translation as soon as they appeared.

It is a truism that a utopia is really about two societies, the one that the author imagines and the real one in which he lives. Since Bogdanov's utopia is on Mars, however, we must distinguish two literary subgenres into which his novel fits. The first is the science fantasy of "class conflict," in which the future of the class struggle is pondered; good examples are Wells's *The Time Machine* (1895) and *When the Sleeper Wakes* (1899), Evgenii Zamiatin's *We* (1920, 1924), Karl Capek's *RUR* (1921), Thea von Harbou's *Metropolis* (1926–27) (as well as the 1926 film by her husband Fritz Lang), and Aldous Huxley's *Brave New World* (1932). Note, however, that all these works are set on a future Earth; other worlds simply do not figure.

Bogdanov's novel is set not on a future Earth, however, but on a present Mars, and this can make a considerable difference in how we interpret it. In

---

17   H. G. Wells, *A Modern Utopia* (London: Chapman and Hall, 1905).
18   H. G. Wells, *A Modern Utopia* (repr., Lincoln: University of Nebraska Press, 1967), 9.
19   Ibid., 11, 17, 35, 47, and 5.

addition to "class conflict" tales, there were also many contemporary "planetary" tales that portrayed a society on another world, often contrasting it with that on the earth. Around the time Bogdanov wrote, Mars was the favored planet for such stories, thanks to the influential contemporary popularizations by astronomer Percival Lowell, notably *Mars* (1895), *Mars and Its Canals* (1906), and *Mars as the Abode of Life* (1908).[20] Examples of such Martian novels are Percy Greg's *Across the Zodiac: The Story of a Wrecked Record* (1880); Kurt Lasswitz's *Auf zwei Planeten* (1897); Wells's *War of the Worlds* (1898); Edwin L. Arnold's *Lieut. Gulliver Jones* (1905), later reissued as *Gulliver of Mars*; and Edgar Rice Burroughs's "Under the Moons of Mars"(1912), reissued as *A Princess of Mars*, the first of a dozen works in his Barsoom series devoted to adventures among the humanoid and not-so-humanoid creatures of the red planet.

In most class conflict tales, the time is the future, and the society depicted is a human successor to today's; by contrast, in planetary stories, the time is now, and the otherworldly society is different from our worldly one in crucial ways. Only Wells managed to generate an impression of the truly alien, but even Lasswitz and Burroughs, who fictively populated Mars with recognizably human types, used their tales to highlight the differences between the two planets. In each work, Earth and Mars share the laws of nature, including the Darwinian struggle for existence and certain laws of history posited by their authors. These common laws of nature, however, do not produce common results: The Martians of each differ from Earthlings because Mars is a different planet—smaller, older, colder, farther from the sun, poorer in resources, and short on water.

Bogdanov's utopia, then, is both a class conflict and a planetary tale. He was not the first to blend these two formats; here, too, Wells led the way. In Wells's *First Men on the Moon* (1901), two Britons travel to the moon through a series of misadventures. There they come upon the Selenites, an intelligent lunar civilization that is essentially an insect hive, with each class biologically fitted to its social function. When the Grand Lunar begins to hear about Earth and its history from the interlopers, however, he becomes anxious about the nearby threat posed by the aggressive and violent character of human society. In many respects, the Selenite society is utopian—it is global, monolingual,

---

20 On Lowell, see L. Leonard, *Percival Lowell: An Afterglow* (Boston, 1921); A. L. Lowell, *Biography of Percival Lowell* (New York, 1935); Brian G. Marsden, "Percival Lowell" in *Dictionary of Scientific Biography* (1973) 8: 520–523; and Michael J. Crowe, *The Extraterrestrial Life Debate 1750–1900: The Idea of a Plurality of Worlds from Kant to Lowell* (Cambridge: Cambridge University Press, 1986), 480–546.

efficient, centralized, and harmonious. But Wells surely does not intend it as a plausible or desirable model for the human future: he is not suggesting that we become an insect hive. Clearly, the lunar society is there, not for emulation, but for comparison, contrast, and commentary.

Did Bogdanov portray his extraterrestrial utopian society for these same purposes? In planetary utopias, after all, the features of otherworldly civilizations are not necessarily intended to apply to the earth. There is no doubt that Bogdanov admires his Martian society as a kind of socialist ideal, but does he seriously propose the Martian present as the earth's future? Graham writes, "One should remember that Mars and Earth in this story are not simply two different planets; they also represent, in accordance with Marxism, the two successive historical epochs of capitalism and socialism."[21] But do they?

Bogdanov's novel contains a remarkable prediction noted by both Stites and Graham. It appears in Sterni's pessimistic speech about the future of socialist revolution on Earth:

> The individual advanced countries where socialism triumphs will be like islands in a hostile capitalist and even to some extent precapitalist sea ... Its character will be perverted deeply and for a long time to come by years of encirclement, unavoidable terror and militarism, and the barbarian patriotism that is their inevitable consequence. This socialism will be a far cry from our own.[22]

Of course, this is a prediction about history and communism, not "science and society." But it raises a nettlesome problem about Bogdanov's intentions, for it demonstrates that in some respects, at least, he envisioned socialism on Earth and Mars as distinctly different.

Which aspects of Martian socialism does Bogdanov see as a product of uniquely Martian conditions? Which aspects are applicable to Earth? To answer these questions, let us turn to Bogdanov's text. The climax of *Red Star* is the debate between two Martians, Sterni and Netti, over the future of Earth. Sterni concludes by calling for its invasion and the eventual elimination of humanity. His justification rests on the differences between Mars and Earth and the consequent superiority of Martian socialism to that which will arise on Earth. Earth "does not recognize any principle of fraternal mutual assistance" and "is terribly

---

21 *Red Star*, 247.
22 Ibid., 113–14.

riven by political and national divisions," he notes, and "this means that instead of following a single and uniform path of development in a single broad society, the struggle for socialism is split into a variety of unique and autonomous processes in individual societies with distinct political systems, languages, and sometimes even races."[23]

It is in this context that Sterni mouths Bogdanov's remarkable prediction, quoted above, about the future of socialism on Earth. A few paragraphs later, he elaborates the same point:

> In many respects this will not be *our* socialism. Centuries of national division, a mutual lack of understanding, and brutal, bloody struggle will leave deep scars on the psychology of liberated Earthly humanity. We do not know how much barbarity and narrow-mindedness the socialists of Earth will bring with them into their new society.[24]

Thus, Sterni's argument is based on the view that socialism on Mars and on Earth will be fundamentally different and incompatible. Because he regards Martian socialism as superior, he concludes that "a higher form of life cannot be sacrificed for the sake of a lower one. . . . There is but one Life in the Universe, and it will be enriched rather than impoverished if it is *our* socialism rather than the distant, semibarbaric Earthly variant that is allowed to develop, for thanks to its unbroken evolution and boundless potential, our life is infinitely more harmonious."[25]

Netti disagrees, not with Sterni's facts, but with his values. On Earth, she says,

> Proceeding through a bitter and difficult struggle from the lowest stages to the higher, this consciousness has finally assumed *human* forms closely related to our own. But these forms are not identical with ours: the history of a different natural environment and a different struggle is reflected in them; they conceal a different play of spontaneous forces, other contradictions, other possibilities of development. . . . Earthlings are not the same as we. . . . They and their civilization are not simply lower and weaker than ours—they are *different*.[26]

---

23 Ibid., 112–13.
24 Ibid., 115.
25 Ibid., 116.
26 Ibid., 116–17.

And what makes them different?

> The struggle for survival is more vigorous and intense there, nature is con-
> tinually creating many more forms of life, but many more of them also
> fall victim to the march of evolution. This cannot be otherwise, because
> the source of life—the sun—provides Earth with eight times more ener-
> gy-giving rays than Mars. ... [Sterni] would drain forever this stormy but
> beautiful ocean of life![27]

She concludes: "The unity of Life is our highest goal, and love is the highest
expression of intelligence!"[28]

Note that Sterni and Netti are arguing about whether socialism on Earth
will be inferior to Martian socialism or simply different—and, hence, whether
the invasion of Earth and the elimination of its humans are justified. To be
sure, Netti sees virtue in diversity and Sterni does not. But both agree on three
points: the conditions on Earth and Mars are very different; this difference
makes their societies, and their socialisms, very different; and neither is a stage
in the other's past or future.

How did the conditions on Mars shape the character of its socialism? The
issue is not taken up further in *Red Star*, a utopia geared to describing the ideal
society, but it is one of the central themes of its sequel, *Engineer Menni*. Fetzer,
Stites, and Graham all dismiss the latter novel as inferior to *Red Star*, but it has
a different and equally important purpose: to chronicle the historical development of Martian socialism. In its foreword, Bogdanov compares the histories of
Mars and Earth, attributing their differences to the role of physical conditions.

> The history of Mars is basically very similar to that of Earthly humanity,
> having followed the same course from the tribal system through feudalism
> to the reign of capital and through it to the unification of labor. This devel-
> opment, however, proceeded more gently and at a slower pace. The natural
> environment on Mars is not as rich as ours; on the other hand, the evolu-
> tion of life there has not demanded the same extravagant sacrifices as on
> Earth. ... Martian humanity developed slower [sic] than ours, but it never
> knew the worst forms of our slavery, the destruction of entire civilizations,
> or the epochs of deep and cruel reaction that we have experienced. ...

---

27 Ibid., 117–19.
28 Ibid., 119.

Why was this so? The natural environment of the planet was poor and harsh, and the experience of thousands of generations built up the dim awareness that it is extremely difficult to restore what has once been destroyed. There was also less discord among people: different tribes and nationalities were more closely related and intercourse among them was easier. The land mass was not broken into separate continents by broad seas and oceans, the mountain ranges were not as high or impassable as on Earth. Also, the weaker force of gravity on Mars facilitated physical movement—all bodies on Earth are two and a half times heavier. The various languages arose from a common source and never became completely distinct. ... Thus people understood each other better and their unity was more profound.[29]

According to Bogdanov, even before the revolution, "a democratic order had been established in all but a few backward countries, but something even greater had been accomplished at the same time, namely, the almost complete cultural and political unification of Mars."[30]

In these passages, Bogdanov takes the view that harsh environmental conditions produce not competition, but cooperation—not an intensification of the struggle for existence between members of the same species, but rather a banding together in the wider struggle for their common existence. In western literature, this idea is usually associated with the "anarchist prince" Petr Kropotkin (1842–1921) and his 1902 opus, *Mutual Aid*.[31] But Bogdanov need not have gotten the idea from Kropotkin. In an important new book, Daniel P. Todes has established that "mutual aid" and similar ideas were quite common among Russian botanists, zoologists, and social thinkers during the late nineteenth and early twentieth centuries.[32]

This characteristic Russian attitude helps us to understand some of the differences between Bogdanov's Martian novels and those of his contemporaries. One of the most popular of these was *A Princess of Mars* (1912) by the American author Edgar Rice Burroughs. The physical Mars he portrayed,

---

29 Ibid., 148–49.

30 Ibid., 148.

31 Peter Kropotkin, *Mutual Aid: A Factor in Evolution* (London, 1902; New York: McClure Phillips, 1902).

32 Daniel P. Todes, *Darwin without Malthus: The Struggle for Existence in Russian Evolutionary Thought* (New York: Oxford University Press, 1989). See also his article, "Darwin's Malthusian Metaphor and Russian Evolutionary Thought, 1859–1917," *Isis* 78, no. 294 (December 1987): 537–51 and the column that it inspired by Stephen Jay Gould, "Kropotkin Was No Crackpot," *Natural History* 97, no. 7 (July 1988): 12–21.

like the one depicted by Bogdanov, fits the standard fin de siècle format—it is smaller, older, colder, poorer in resources, and short on water. On Burroughs's Mars, however, these harsh conditions produce societies truly suited to a planet named for the "God of War": An intensification of the Darwinian struggle for existence has led to a diverse array of ferocious humanoids, resulting in a planet of brutality, barbarism, and cruelty where few offspring manage to survive their first minutes. The very same harsh physical conditions that lead to disunity, intraspecific struggle, and barbarism on Burroughs's Mars, then, produce on Bogdanov's the very opposite: unity, cooperation, and humane planetary socialism.

For Bogdanov, the specific environmental threat that finally brings Martian socialism into being is the shortage of water. *Engineer Menni* takes place at a time when "there was as yet no system of canals, and the whole interior of the continent, about three-fifths of its surface, was devoid of water."[33] This threat leads the hero to conceive "the Great Project"—building the canals—which explains, in turn, why a novel concerned with the historical emergence of Martian socialism centers on three generations of canal-builders.

At the time Bogdanov wrote, there was great public excitement about Mars because that planet's unusually close approach offered the opportunity to observe on its surface what the Italian astronomer Giovanni Schiaparelli had described in 1877 as mountains, seas, and an intricate network of channels—*canali*, a word mistranslated into many languages as "canals." Bogdanov knew Schiaparelli's Greek and Latin terminology for Martian surface features and even mentioned him in the foreword. Did Bogdanov also know, perchance, of Schiaparelli's much discussed article "Life on the Planet Mars," published in Italian (1895) and French (1898), where he had presented these *canali* as evidence of a Fourierist phalanstery? On Mars, Schiaparelli had written, "the institution of collective socialism ought indeed result from a parallel community of interests and of a universal solidarity of citizens" and, as a result, "international conflicts and wars are unknown" there because "all the intellectual efforts which, among the insane inhabitants of a neighboring world are consumed in mutually destroying each other, are [on Mars] unanimously directed against the common enemy, the difficulty which penurious nature opposes at each step."[34] In any case, this planet-wide network of "canals," which suggested

---

33 *Red Star*, 151.
34 Crowe, *The Extraterrestrial Life Debate*, 515. On Schiaparelli, see also Giorgio Abetti, "Giovanni Virginio Schiaparelli," in *Dictionary of Scientific Biography*, vol. 12 (1975), 159–62.

an advanced civilization to many of his contemporaries, became for Bogdanov the great planetary project for survival whose construction stimulated the birth of his utopian socialist society.

In Bogdanov's novels, then, the classic characteristics distinguishing Mars from Earth are the very conditions that led to the essential character of ideal Martian socialism. Although the novels express uncertainty about whether socialism will ever come about on Earth, they are clear on one point: if and when it does come about, it will not be like Martian socialism. This is an important point, for it ultimately governs the way we interpret Bogdanov's novels. We have already twice noted his remarkable prediction that the first socialist state on Earth will be barbarous and chauvinistic, "an island in a hostile sea." Given the humane and harmonious character of the development of Martian socialism, how can this be? It cannot—if Mars is a model for the Terran future. Only if the social histories on Mars and Earth are significantly different does Bogdanov's prediction about Earth makes sense. But how, then, can we read Bogdanov's other descriptions of Martian life as relevant to the earth?

In particular, did Bogdanov really anticipate, as has been claimed, that even a mature socialist society on Earth would have to cope with shortages of water, energy, and other resources? Once again, let us turn to his text. In both novels, Bogdanov repeatedly notes that, in contrast to Mars, Earth is much richer in resources. Furthermore, it gets eight times the solar energy—indeed, we might conclude from the speeches of Sterni and Netti that, if anything, the earth has too much energy for its own good. And what of water? The reason Mars now faces a water shortage, according to Bogdanov, is that "the astronomical age of Mars is twice that of Earth, and for that reason there is relatively little water on the planet" because "in the course of millions of years" it has been absorbed into the planet's crust.[35] By implication, then, Earth will not face a similar shortage for many millions of years, if ever. Clearly, then, Bogdanov does not conceive these shortages as problems that mature socialism will face on Earth. To the contrary, he sees them as some of the harsh, unifying, specifically Martian conditions that helped bring ideal socialism into being! And if Martian socialism is not to be our own, then Bogdanov's depiction of the difficulties of the specifically Martian socialist life does not speak to Earthly futures.

We know that Lenin did not like Bogdanov's novels. Indeed, in a 1913 letter to Maksim Gorkii, he described *Engineer Menni* as "another case of Machism and idealism, but obscured so that neither the workers nor the silly

---

35 *Red Star*, 146.

editors at *Pravda* understood it."[36] This reaction should not surprise us. What was there in the novels for Lenin to like? Bogdanov had clearly argued that the very character of natural conditions on the planet Earth precluded the development of ideal socialism. Indeed, he had openly predicted that the first socialist state on Earth would be isolated, surrounded, barbarous, and chauvinistic. In retrospect, he may have been right. But to a contemporary revolutionary leader such as Lenin, who was trying to orchestrate the revolution and to persuade others of its necessity and virtue, Bogdanov's message could hardly have seemed helpful.

There is a central motif in *Red Star* that makes its author seem distinctly *un*modern. In the passages from Netti quoted above, the Darwinian struggle for existence has been "vitalized" by an almost romantic vision of the unity and energy of "Life." Surely this did not come from Wells; indeed, Netti's sentiments are perilously close to the sort that Wells ridicules in his novels. This aspect of Bogdanov's works has often puzzled his commentators and is sometimes treated as a curiosity largely irrelevant to the rest of his thought. Such a viewpoint is difficult to sustain, however, because Bogdanov's views of life, energy, and blood form a motif central to his intellectual career. Nor is there much puzzle about where such ideas might have come from; to his turn-of-the-century readers, they must have seemed utterly familiar.

Any well-educated contemporary would probably have associated Bogdanov's views of "Life" with the name of Ernst Haeckel (1834–1919). Today, Haeckel is remembered principally for his "biogenetic law," summarized in the familiar dictum "ontogeny recapitulates phylogeny"—the history of the individual repeats, in condensed form, the evolutionary history of the species. In his own day, however, Haeckel was equally renowned for his "Monist philosophy," which conceived of the animate and inanimate as part of a greater unity and of all living forms as genetically interrelated. Both biogenesis and monism found expression in his popular tomes, notably *The Natural History of Creation*, a mainstay of popular Darwinism that was published in eleven contemporary editions and translated into twelve European languages.[37] Equally influential was his popular Monist sermon, *The Riddle of the Universe*.[38] His romantic,

---

36 Ibid., 14.
37 Ernst Haeckel, *Natürliche Schöpfungsgeschichte* (Berlin: Reimar, 1868). For the first English edition, see *The History of Creation*, trans. E. Ray Lankaster, 2 vols. (New York: Appleton, 1876).
38 Ernst Haeckel, *Die Welträthsel: Gemeinverständliche Studien über monistische Philosophie* (Bonn, 1899).

stridently materialistic views on human origins created difficulties for the publication of Russian editions of his works.[39] Nonetheless, many pamphlets by Haeckel were published in Russian translation around the turn of the century and, after 1905, some of his books began to appear in Russian editions.[40]

At the time Bogdanov wrote, Haeckel's monist ideas were certainly well known to educated Russians—and Bolsheviks were no exception. In the final section of *Materialism and Empiriocriticism*, entitled "Ernst Haeckel and Ernst Mach," Lenin drew attention to *The Riddle of the Universe* by the "eminent scientist" Ernst Haeckel, noting:

> The fact that the book was sold in *hundreds of thousands* of copies, that it was immediately translated into all languages and that it appeared in specially cheap editions, clearly demonstrates that the book "found its way to the people," that there are *masses* of readers whom Ernst Haeckel at once won over to his side.[41]

This passage was written in 1908—the year *Red Star* was published.

Did Bogdanov read the works of Haeckel? I know of no direct evidence that he did, but the indirect evidence is compelling. Consider Bogdanov's first philosophical trilogy, *Empiriomonism*. Most commentators have assumed that the monism in this work derived exclusively from the physical chemist Wilhelm Ostwald (1853–1932), who in turn relied on the ideas of Ernst Mach, a connection emphasized by Lenin and most subsequent commentators.[42] In Ostwald's version of monistic nature philosophy, the universe is a manifestation of "Energie" in various forms. Bogdanov was familiar with Ostwald's monism, to be sure, but there is no reason to suppose that it was the sole source of his own. In the popular mind, monism was still most closely associated with Haeckel. It seems unlikely that Bogdanov, a physician, would be familiar with the ideas of the physical chemist Wilhelm Ostwald and not with those of the immensely popular biologist and anatomist Ernst Haeckel.

---

39 See especially his *Anthropogenie*, 5th ed. (1st ed., 1874; Leipzig: Engelmann, 1903), published in English as *The Evolution of Man*, 5th ed. (London: Watts, 1907).

40 For example, see E. Gekkel, *Bor'ba za evoliutsionnuiu ideiu* [Struggle for the revolutionary idea](St. Petersburg, 1909), *Lektsii po estestvoznaniiu i filosofii* [Lectures on natural science and philosophy] (St. Petersburg, 1913), and *Proiskhozhdenie cheloveka* [The descent of man] (Petrograd, 1919).

41 V. I. Lenin, *Collected Works*, 4th ed., vol. 14, 1908 (Moscow: Progress, 1968), 348.

42 Ibid., 226–32 and 269–73, for example.

If there is uncertainty about the source of the monism in Bogdanov's first trilogy, there can be no escaping Haeckel's influence on the second, *Tektologiia* (1913–17). In his mammoth classic *Generelle Morphologie* (1866), Haeckel had coined the word *Tectologie* from the Greek *tekton* (carpenter, builder) or *tektainein* (to build or frame) to name one of the two sciences that together comprise morphology: "Tectologie (oder Strukturlehre): Wissenschaft von der Zusammmensetzung [*sic*] der Organismen aus organischen Individuen verschiedener Ordnung"; and "Promorphologie (oder Grundformenlehre): Wissenschaft von den ausseren Formen der organischen Individuen und deren stereometrischen Grundformen."[43] The eleventh chapter of the book's first volume listed sixty-four "tectological theses" under seven headings: fundamental structure, organic individuality, organic individuums, the interrelations of organic individuums, physiological individuality, tectological differentiation and centralization, and the relation between the parts and the whole.[44]

Bogdanov undoubtedly got the word *tectology* from Haeckel. So far as I can determine, *tektologiia* was not even mentioned in contemporary Russian dictionaries and encyclopedias. Unlike the term *promorphology*, which dealt with the general laws of form and was apparently used somewhat more widely, *tectology* was a term used only in connection with Haeckel's discussion in the *Generelle Morphologie*.[45] Of course, Bogdanov's work went well beyond that of Haeckel, seeking to generalize his morphological principles into a general theory of organizational structure, but in so doing Bogdanov drew heavily on Haeckel's analytical framework.

In basing his understanding of social structure on organic form, of course, Bogdanov was following a time-honored practice. Ever since the eighteenth century, social thinkers had commonly treated society as an "organism" and had based their theories on the latest currents in zoology; their principal differences lay in the model of the organism they used.[46] Bogdanov was one of

---

43 Ernst Haeckel, *Generelle Morphologie der Organismen* [General morphology of organisms], two volumes published as one (Berlin: Georg Reimer, 1866), 1:30.

44 Ibid., 364–74.

45 For example, in the ninth edition of Encyclopedia Britannica, P. Geddes used the term only in reference to Haeckel's division of morphology into "two sub-sciences,—the first purely structural, *tectology*, which regards the organism as composed of organic individuals of different orders; the second essentially stereometric, *promorphology*" (*Encyclopedia Britannica* [1883] 16:842, col. 1). By 1919, *tectology* had found its way into the ninth volume of the *New English Dictionary*, but only as a term coined by Haeckel.

46 See, for example, Herbert Spencer's essay "The Social Organism," in *Essays: Scientific, Political, and Speculative*, vol. 1 (London: William and Norgate, 1868).

many Russian social thinkers of his time who looked to the natural sciences for models in their "quest for a general science of society."[47] Nor was Bogdanov atypical in attempting to create a general organizational theory that applied to everything. Since the mid-nineteenth century, theories like those of Auguste Comte and Herbert Spencer, which encompassed the solar system, biology, society, history, and morality in a single theoretical framework, had been common coin. At the turn of the century—the age of Taylorism and scientific management, of physiological homeostasis and plant sociology, of railroads and electric light and power—it would have been difficult to find any area of activity or discourse where "systems thinking" was not making itself felt.

Another possible source of Bogdanov's view of "Life" was Henri Bergson (1859–1941), whose evolutionary philosophy was tremendously popular and influential among Russian and European intellectuals during the first decade of this century. According to Bergson, life and the universe were evolving toward ever higher stages of complexity, organization, and energy, with each new stage manifesting newly emergent properties. For him, the cause of this evolution was the *élan vital*, a vitalistic energy or impulse that expressed itself by organizing matter into higher and higher states of complexity and consciousness. His vitalistic, holistic, physiological, "energetic" view of evolution, sometimes termed *emergentism* or *Bergsonism*, was expressed in *L'évolution créatrice* (1907), one of the most popular books in Europe at the time Bogdanov wrote. The work was soon translated into both English and Russian and its ideas were well known to most young European intellectuals before World War I.[48]

As a Marxist, Bogdanov might well have preferred to be seen as a follower of Haeckel rather than Bergson; his works are critical of vitalist trends in science and thought. Common to Haeckel's monism and Bergson's emergentism, however, was the view that "Life" was one, that it had a common nature and origin, that all humans were tied to the lowliest worm "by blood," and that "Life" was ever reaching higher levels of energy and organization with higher, newly emergent possibilities and problems. That such views could be shared by the materialist Haeckel, the vitalist Bergson, and the Bolshevik Bogdanov is testimony to the intellectual dialectics of the age: As diverse as contemporaries may have perceived their ideas to be, in retrospect those ideas appear to be mere variations on a theme that preoccupied a bygone time. Something akin

---

47 See, for example, the illuminating discussion in Vucinich, *Social Thought in Tsarist Russia,* especially 206–30.

48 Henri Bergson, *Creative Evolution,* trans. Arthur Mitchell (New York: Henry Holt, 1911); and A. Bergson, *Tvorcheskaia evoliutsiia* [Creative evolution] (St. Petersburg, 1914).

to a blend of monism and emergentism is also the central theme of Bogdanov's poem "A Martian Stranded on Earth," published as a supplement to a 1924 edition of *Red Star*. The poem's early stanzas reiterate the very same differences between Martians and Earthlings emphasized in the novels:

Yes, people—it may seem that the difference is small
Between them and my own Martian race,
But their hearts and their souls are not ours at all,
And I am no friend of their ways.

The harmony of life is outside their ken.
Though their souls swarm with hazy ideas,
The inherited past is the lord of these men;
It has ruled them for so many years. . . .

The difference in nature between them and me
Springs up, and I'm plunged in despair.[49]

The stranded Martian finally becomes reconciled to his exile on Earth by taking a monist view of the unity of all life similar to that expressed in the novel by Netti:

But then I hear Science, whose voice sounds on high
From my home in the sky far away:
"They too are the children of almighty Life,
Your younger blood brothers are they . . ."[50]

First published four years before Bogdanov's death, the poem encapsulates the essential perspectives and tensions of his intellectual life. The ideal, unified, harmonious society he envisioned as emerging from Martian conditions was utterly different from anything possible on Earth, the planet of energy, diversity, and struggle. This dialectical contradiction could be resolved only by the "science" that described the deeper unity: monism. Considering that Bogdanov was a physician turned philosopher, it should not surprise us that his works reflect the leading biological philosophies of his day.

49 *Red Star*, 237–38.
50 Ibid., 238.

The reference to "blood brothers" in this 1924 poem is especially suggestive, since Bogdanov may have intended it literally. In this context, we can see his late researches on transfusion as a natural outgrowth of his earlier thought. His 160-page book on the subject, published in 1927, is often taken as evidence that he had switched from philosophy to biomedical research. It may have met contemporary scientific standards, but this is not a scientific book about transfusion in today's sense —it is not about blood chemistry, the ABO immune system, plasma or platelets, white or red cells. Rather, it is about rejuvenation—*omolozhenie*—a topic of major scientific and popular interest in Europe during the early decades of this century.

In the 1910s and 1920s, Russian investigators carefully monitored foreign research on rejuvenation and published numerous books, pamphlets, and anthologies on the subject, some of which are cited in Bogdanov's work.[51] Of course, such research took many forms, from Il'ia Mechnikov's fascination with yogurt as an aid to longevity, to investigations of the putatively rejuvenating effects of transplanted monkey testicles.[52] Unlike many of his contemporaries, Bogdanov eschews the guts and glands for the blood, a vital fluid whose transfusion, he believed, could rejuvenate the recipient. The originality of Bogdanov's approach, then, lay in the way he sought to link the rejuvenation problem with unrelated contemporary work on blood transfusion. In light of Bogdanov's fascination with the ideas of Haeckel, this link makes sense. What greater embodiment of life's vital energy than blood? What greater demonstration of the unity of life than the vital transfusion of blood from one to another?

---

51 See, for example, *Smert' i bessmertie* [Death and immortality], Novye idei v biologii, Sbornik 3 [New Ideas in Biology, volume 3] (St. Petersburg: Obrazovanie, 1913); N. K. Kol'tsov, *Omolozhenie organizma po metodu Shteinakh* [Rejuvenation of organisms by the Steinach method] (Petrograd: Vremia, 1922); *Omolozhenie: Sbornik statei* [Rejuvenation: A collection of essays], vol. 1 (Moscow and Petrograd: Gosizdat, 1923) and vol. 2 (Moscow and Petrograd: Gosizdat, 1924); and *Problemy starosti i omolozhenie* [Problems of aging and rejuvenation] (Moscow and Petrograd: Gosizdat, 1923).

52 See, for example, Elie Mechnikoff, *Études sur la nature humaine* [Studies in human nature], 2nd ed. (Paris: Masson, 1904), *The Prolongation of Life* (New York: G. P. Putnam's Sons, 1908), and *Etiudy o prirode cheloveka* [Studies in human nature], 5th ed. (Moscow: Nauchnoe slovo, 1917). Mechnikov regarded the "normal" human lifespan as roughly 100 years to 120 years—the very same figure subsequently suggested by Bogdanov. For an example of the contemporary popularity of monkey gland therapy, note the description of Dr. Penberthy in Dorothy L. Sayers's well-known mystery, *The Unpleasantness at the Bellona Club* (London: Victor Gollancz, 1921).

The relation of Bogdanov's 1927 book to his earlier interests is revealed by its title: *Bor'ba za zhiznesposobnost'*.[53] Used to translate the Darwinian phrase "struggle for existence," *bor'ba* was also the word used repeatedly in Bogdanov's novels to describe the struggle of the Martians against their hostile planetary environment. Like that earlier struggle, which brought about Martian socialism, this "struggle for vitality" was envisioned by Bogdanov, not as intraspecific human competition, but rather as a cooperative effort of human life against the harsh forces of nature, an effort in which humans would share their very blood in their common struggle against the forces of decay, degeneration, and death.

Red Star is explicit about this. In a scene set at a hospital, Netti explains that Martians stay young because of "*mutual blood transfusions* between human beings, whereby each individual receives from the other a number of elements which can raise his life expectancy." When asked why the efficacy of this technique has not been recognized on Earth, she suggests that "perhaps it is merely due to your predominantly individualistic psychology, which isolates people from each other so completely that the thought of fusing them is almost incomprehensible to your scientists." By contrast, she notes, "Quite in keeping with the nature of our entire system, our regular comradely exchanges of life extend beyond the ideological dimension into the physiological one."[54]

In this context, Bogdanov's own death in 1928 could hardly have been more fitting, for it drew together the threads of his intellectual life, and it was, as best we can tell, a death he chose. He died at his own Institute of Blood Transfusion during an "experiment" in which he completely exchanged his own blood with that of a certain Koldomasov, a student suffering from both malaria and tuberculosis. According to his son, Bogdanov knew the experiment would kill him. The date was April 7—the day after Stalin had called the Party Central Committee into special session to deal with the Shakhty "conspiracy" of the technocrats, thus initiating the first in a series of Stalinist purge trials that would call to mind Bogdanov's 1908 prediction.[55] As sad as this turn of events must have been to Bogdanov, it must also have confirmed for him that he had been right all along: the ideal, "Martian" socialist vision would not come to pass on

---

53 Bogdanov, *Bor'ba za zhiznesposobnost'*, Institut perelivaniia krovi (Moscow: Novaia Moscow, 1927). *Zhiznesposobnost'* can be translated as "viability," "vital capacity," or "life capacity," but in context, "vitality" best captures Bogdanov's meaning.

54 *Red Star*, 85–86.

55 On the antitechnocratic character of the Shakhty and Industrial Party trials, see the excellent discussion in Kendall E. Bailes, *Technology and Society under Lenin and Stalin* (Princeton, NJ: Princeton University Press, 1978).

Earth. As Graham sagely notes, the "Martian Stranded on Earth" in Bogdanov's poem was Bogdanov himself.[56]

Shortly after Bogdanov's death, as he might well have anticipated, the Russian history from which he felt so profoundly alienated left him and his ideas behind. Now, sixty years later, they are being rediscovered, and modern scholars are busy excavating his legacy. In so doing, we would be wise to approach his writings in an archaeological spirit. When all is said and done, Bogdanov was neither a postindustrial thinker nor a Martian stranded on Earth, but a Russian *intelligent* of the late tsarist period stranded in the postwar world. What separates us from *Red Star* is, simply, most of the twentieth century.

Set not in our context but in his own, Bogdanov seems rather less prescient and original than before, but his thought emerges as more unified and coherent. His novels remain as interesting as ever, of course, but for different reasons: not because he was a deeply original thinker, but precisely because he was *not* a deeply original thinker—because the novels are, as *Russkoe Bogatstvo* noted, "trendy" and "derivative." Bogdanov's originality, such as it was, lay in the unique ways he navigated the flood of ideas washing his intellectual generation—mechanism, vitalism, materialism, organicism, energeticism, emergentism, and monism, Darwinism, Haeckelism, Bergsonism, Machism, Marxism, Bolshevism, Taylorism, Wellsian futurism. Each left its mark on what would later be called "Bogdanovism."[57]

For all their many literary flaws, *Red Star* and *Engineer Menni* give the modern reader an extended glimpse into the mindset of a turn-of-the-century intellectual, a member of one of the more interesting transitional generations in history, a man deeply engaged with the intellectual fashions of his day. To read Bogdanov is to immerse oneself in "the stormy but beautiful ocean" of ideas out of which the intellectual history of our century emerged. Alas, the novels of this promiscuous intellectual dilettante can tell us little about our "postindustrial" future, but they can tell us much about that future's past.

---

56 *Red Star*, 251.
57 See, for example, Lecourt's "Bogdanov, Mirror of the Soviet Intelligentsia," which concludes with a section entitled "Bogdanovism in Soviet Ideology."

Generating Power

ANINDITA BANERJEE

Banerjee, Anindita. *We Modern People: Science Fiction and the Making of Russian Modernity*. Middletown, CT: Wesleyan University Press, 2013. 69–88.

"Communism is equal to Soviet power plus the electrification of the entire country" (*Kommunizm est' sovetskaia vlast' plius elektrifikatsiia vsei strany*). These were the terms in which Lenin reportedly conveyed the Party's approval of the plan forwarded by the newly formed State Commission for the Electrification of Russia, abbreviated as *GOELRO*, in November 1920. Still standing in tall letters above Moscow's central electric station, the slogan remains graven in collective memory as the iconic moment when electric power became the officially designated driving force of utopia. Lenin's pronouncement was striking not because it selected technology as the primary means to shape Russia's revolutionary future. During years of exile in European cities, the Bolshevik leader arrived at the conclusion that the technological foundations of capitalism needed to be appropriated in order to build a twentieth-century workers' state.[1] It is the choice of electrification above all other sectors that seems particularly daring.

While commercial promotion and cheap mass distribution had domesticated and demystified electricity in countries like Germany and the United States by the first decade of the twentieth century, "electrification of the entire country" in the Russian context could only be called a pipe dream. In the West, Thomas Edison's light bulbs and Siemens dynamos changed everyday life, radically affecting the length of the workday, the nature of private and public space,

---

1 Lenin's notebooks from 1908, when he toured Germany, are replete with observations of the changes electrification had wrought in daily life. See V. I. Lenin, *Zapisnye knigi 1907–1917, Polnoe sobranie sochinenii v 45 tomakh* [Notebooks 1907–1917, Collected works in 45 volumes] (Moscow: Gosudarstvennoe izdatel'stvo politicheskoi literartury, 1958), vol. 22.

and the duration and forms of leisure.[2] In contrast, as late as 1919, a commissar of the Bolshevik government noted with trepidation that the number of electric stations in Russia and the United States were 220 and 5,221 respectively, while the consumption of electrical energy in kilowatt-hour per capita was 16 and 500.[3] Even biased retrospective assessments of Russian techno-scientific achievement, such as those found in the *Great Soviet Encyclopedia* of the Stalin era, admitted that "the production and consumption of electricity" remained "one area in which Russia visibly lagged behind until the late 1920s."[4] In a historical study of electrification in Russia, Jonathan Coopersmith notes that even after the First World War had convinced the imperial government to recognize the importance of electrification, efforts to promote and distribute the electrical energy were "extremely slow." After 1917, furthermore, "electricity production dropped sharply and did not gain pre-Revolutionary levels until the mid-1920s."[5] Assessing Lenin's slogan against the objective conditions of electrification in Russia, Stites concludes that it was "a desperate measure to make the economy work and the Soviet regime survive."[6]

Historically, therefore, the great disjuncture between Lenin's vision and the actual state of electrification in Russia was quite evident. Why, then, would his statement about electrification above all others be singled out for immortalization? A closer reading of the famous pronouncement reveals the sources of its unprecedented rhetorical force. Through a particular sleight of signification, the slogan imbued a technology that was virtually nonexistent in everyday Russian life with tremendous symbolic power. The first step in this process was to use the seemingly infallible scientific diction of "equal to" and "plus," which lent the dream of electrification an aura of inevitable prophecy. Far from confirming a self-evident scientific truth, however, the mathematical formula for

---

2 Mark Rose, *Cities of Light and Heat: Domesticating Gas and Electricity in Urban America* (University Park: Pennsylvania State University Press, 1995) and David Nye, *Electrifying America: Social Meanings of a New Technology, 1880-1940* (Cambridge, MA: MIT Press, 1990).

3 L. Dreier, *Zadachi i razvitie elektrotekhniki* [Problems and developments in electrical technology] (Moscow: Gosudarstvennoe izdatel'stvo, 1919), 8.

4 B. A. Vvedensky, "Elektrichestvo" [Electricity], *Bol'shaia sovetskaia entsiklopediia* [The great Soviet encyclopedia], 9th edition, ed. B. N. Vavilov et al. (Moscow: Gosudarstvennoe nauchnoe izdatel'stvo, 1956), 49: 445.

5 Jonathan Coopersmith, *The Electrification of Russia, 1880–1926* (Ithaca, NY: Cornell University Press, 1992), 121.

6 Richard Stites, *Revolutionary Dreams: Utopian Visions and Experimental Life in the Russian Revolution* (Oxford: Oxford University Press, 1989), 46.

communism only served to dissociate electric power from the slow, contingent processes of actual technological development. Placed on the same side of the equation as Soviet authority, electricity became a supplement to ideology, an agent of metaphysical rather than material change. "Electrification of the entire country," consequently, evolved into an indispensable metaphor for erasing the gap between the imperfect present and a future beyond history.

The strategy of conflating two diametrically opposite connotations of electricity within the same mathematical paradigm provides the key to understanding the power of Lenin's slogan. It unerringly taps the very node that made electricity the most marvelous artifact of the scientific and technological revolution at the turn of the twentieth century. Contrary to the dominant scientific principles of the Enlightenment, electricity defied empirical observation and eluded mechanical explanations of energy. Unlike wood, coal, or oil, it was a form of energy rather than a material source of power. Unlike gas or steam, moreover, its production was invisible to the human eye. The epistemological implications of generating electricity, therefore, were just as revolutionary as its physical uses and its potentials for social transformation. The electrifying effect of Lenin's slogan derived from embodying and enacting the very synthesis of matter and mystique that electricity itself represented.

Scholars have interpreted Lenin's call for electrification as the genesis of a unique Bolshevik idiom of technological utopia.[7] This chapter argues that it signaled the culmination rather than the origin of a particular narrative of modernity. The synthesis of electricity's material and metaphysical potentials was not the product of Soviet rhetoric alone. It was codified, popularized, and perpetuated well before the October Revolution and would continue to play a potent role during the actual electrification of Russia in the decade following Lenin's famous pronouncement. Science fiction, a genre seldom associated with politics or policy, provided the crucial discursive site at which the two connotations of electric power were first unified and amplified into a grand paradigm of collective salvation.

This paradigm may be understood through the analogy of an electrical circuit, which consists of a positive pole called the anode and a negative pole called the cathode. In isolation, the two remain inert, but once conjoined they produce a blinding spark. The anode, conventionally labeled the male

---

7 Katerina Clark, for example, calls it the blueprint of the rhetoric promoting five-year-plans of the Stalin era in "Political History and Literary Chronotope: Some Soviet Case Studies," *Literature and History: Theoretical Problems and Russian Case Studies*, ed. Gary Saul Morson (Stanford, CA: Stanford University Press, 1986), 235.

part of the circuit, corresponds to the positivistic understanding of electricity. In the anodic mode, electricity is a rationally explicable source of power that can be mechanically harnessed and used in material ways. The female cathode, in contrast, represents a distinctly nonrational approach toward electricity as an organic or supernatural form of energy. Incommensurable with human cognition and insurmountable by human prowess, electricity in this second mode remains a sacred repository of magic and miracle.

Heidegger's two-pronged model of technology provides a rich framework for assessing why the synthesis of the anodic and cathodic modes electrified the Russian imagination in particular. According to Heidegger, the Greek root *techne* stands for both *instrumentum*, "a means," and *episteme*, "knowing in the widest sense." As the modern usage of the term is limited to the first meaning, technology has become nothing more than a brute instrument for wielding power. This strikingly Fedorovian critique by a philosopher who witnessed the horrors of industrialized warfare in the twentieth century is followed by an explanation of what technology was originally meant to be: a great synthesis of instrumentality with knowledge in the widest sense. Infusing the machine with ways of knowing transforms technology into a source of *poesis*, "something that creates or brings forth."[8]

It is precisely the promise of *poesis*, of generating something new, that imbued Lenin's slogan with tremendous symbolic valence. Pro/creation also provides the paradigm of synthesis through which this chapter reveals the continuities between a rich corpus of electrical fiction and the 1920 call for electrification. The representations of electricity examined in the following sections responded to a particularly gendered view of Russia's relation to modernity. Russia, which constituted the backward, feminine other half of a masculine, advanced West, was correspondingly associated with premodern, nonrational approaches to technology rather than mastery over its mechanical manifestations. The cathodic *episteme* associated with Russia transformed electricity, the primary driving force of modernity in the twentieth century, into something greater than Heidegger's *instrumentum* or Fedorov's prosthesis.

Paradoxically, the physical absence of electric power in everyday Russian life left electricity itself wide open for interpretation. As a result, writers, artists, and thinkers could envision the synthesis of the anode and the cathode in ambitious ways that were unconstrained by the material exigencies of

---

8 Martin Heidegger, "The Question Concerning Technology," in *The Question Concerning Technology and Other Essays*, trans. and ed. William Lovitt (New York: Harper, 1977), 4–5, 12–13.

technological modernization. Science fiction, not surprisingly, became the privileged mode for translating the completed circuit of electrical dreams into a uniquely Russian model of development that I call "ethical modernity." This model invested the material transformations wrought by electric power with a deep social awareness of Russia's own internal schisms between the city and the country; industrial and agrarian economies; and, most significantly, a small urban elite with access to technological comforts and the vast provinces deprived of the benefits of modernity. By the time Lenin issued his call for electrification, science fiction had codified a variety of ethical modernities based on the physics and metaphysics of electric power.

ELECTRIC ORIGINS: ANODE AND CATHODE OF ETHICAL MODERNITY

Long before Thomas Alva Edison's light bulb changed night into day and ignited the imagination of the world, electricity constructed an unusual bridge between scientific knowledge, social awareness, and literary creation in Russia. The historical figure who embodied this bridge was Mikhai Lomonosov, the visionary thinker from the eighteenth century who was canonized as both the father of modern scientific education in Russia and a pioneer of modern Russian poetry. Just as Lenin became the icon of the national electrification drive in Soviet Russia, Lomonosov's name was inalienably bound with the scientific perception of electricity as a tractable natural phenomenon. In a famous plea to develop institutions of higher learning in Russia, Lomonosov, who experimented with capturing lightning just like Benjamin Franklin, used electricity as his primary metaphor. The petition, composed in 1752, was couched in the form of an ode titled "On the Uses of Glass" ("Pis'mo o pol'ze stekla"). Describing the source of energy that best captures the spirit of modern science, he turned to the profound transformation in perceptions of lightning during his own lifetime:

That which stunned the people of antiquity,
That which burns, boils, flows and shines as God's wrath,
And took away devotion from other Gods [. . .]
Others, who at least wished to know what could be wrested from the heavens,
Created Prometheus in their dreams,
Who tore fire away and put it in the hands of the dying.[9]

9 Mikhail Lomonosov, "Pis'mo o pol'ze stekla" [Letter on the uses of glass] in *Izbrannye proiz-vedeniia* [Selected writings], ed. Iu. A. Andreev (Leningrad: Sovetskii pisatel', 1986), 241.

Although Lomonosov counted himself among the "others" in the middle of this passage, his rendition of the Prometheus myth adds an unexpected dimension to the well-known story. The poet redeemed the transgression of Zeus's son, who stole fire from the heavens and handed it to earthly mortals against his father's wishes, by depicting him as an agent not only of progress but also of resurrection. By transforming *molniia*—the Russian term for lightning that traditionally signified both divine power and divine retribution—into a source of life for humanity on the verge of annihilation, Lomonosov imperceptibly introduced a potent cathodic element to the modern project of understanding and subjugating heavenly wrath.

The implications of this synthetic figuration become clear in the seminal essays he published between 1745 and 1756 on the physical science of electricity. In these treatises, he framed the task of bringing the metaphorical fire of the Enlightenment to Russia's dark landscape of backwardness with a socioeconomic imperative that stretched far beyond the confines of university education. Lomonosov combined his discussion of Western-style scientific training in the city with a broad vision of Russia's agrarian countryside, where random vagaries of the weather literally broke the will of peasants already exhausted from hard labor and hunger. Understanding *molniia*, lightning, was therefore the first step toward accessing an eternal fountainhead of energy that would literally bring his starving countrymen back from the dead.[10]

Lomonosov's inimitable fusion of the physics of electricity, social justice modeled on Enlightenment thought, and the spiritual connotations of resurrection made him an iconic figure for later writers and activists such as Alexander Radishchev. Radishchev, whom Catherine the Great personally condemned in 1790 for publishing a searing critique of social inequality in a travelogue titled *A Journey from Petersburg to Moscow* (*Puteshchestvie iz Peterburga v Moskvu*), concluded his observations on the Russian countryside with a biographical sketch of Lomonosov. Echoing d'Alembert's portrait of Franklin, who "tore lightning from the heavens and the scepter from the tyrants," Radishchev militantly called for keeping his legacy alive.[11] By characterizing Lomonosov as someone who "produced flashes of lightning and repelled lashes of thunder," Radishchev

---

10   Mikhail Lomonosov, "Trudy po fizike" [Works in physics] in *Polnoe sobranie sochinenii* [Collected works], ed. S. I. Vavilov (Moscowand Leningrad: Akademiia nauk, 1952), 3: 5, 14, 27.

11   Quoted by Egon Friedell, *A Cultural History of the Modern Age: The Crisis of the European Soul from the Black Death to the World War*, trans. Charles Atkinson (New York: Knopf, 1930–32), 2: 37.

not only conflated the visionary with the mythical figure of Prometheus. His predecessor represented a specifically Russian model of enlightened intellectual whose pursuit of knowledge was not limited to the elite institutions of the city. In Radishchev's view, the fiery urge to instantly improve the lives of the dispossessed set Lomonosov apart from Western pioneers of scientific thought.[12]

Although progressive Russians would continue to venerate the Lomonosovian tradition, a completely different view of electricity took Russian intellectuals by storm in the early nineteenth century. The pendulum swing owed much to the avid interest with which urban Russians followed the trends of life and thought in Western Europe. Starting in 1780, the scientific community and social elite in France, Germany, and Britain became obsessed with Luigi Galvani's discovery that two pieces of dissimilar metals could make a dead frog twitch even in the absence of a source of electricity. Galvani's claim that electricity was of biological rather than physio-chemical origins rapidly acquired a life of its own. Within a year of his discovery, the physician Franz Anton Mesmer advanced the theory that a unified electric field connected the physical world with the human mind, and that thoughts could be manipulated by exposing the body to electrical currents.[13] The most infamous application of Mesmer's theory was the bathtub of shock therapy, where female patients diagnosed as hysterical would receive electric currents to cure their illness. Apart from this particularly feminized form of electric therapy the combined legacies of Galvani and Mesmer generated a plethora of parapsychological and occult understandings of electricity.[14]

---

12 Alexander Radishchev, "Slovo o Lomonosove" [A word on Lomonosov], *Puteshchestvie iz Peterburga v Moskvu* [Journey from Petersburg to Moscow] (Moscow: Khudozhestvennaia literatura, 1964), 203.

13 Franz Anton Mesmer, *Précis historique des faits relatifs au magnétisme animal* [A short history of animal magnetism] (London: Macdonald, 1848), 12. Robert Darnton, in his classic study *Mesmerism and the End of the Enlightenment in France* (Cambridge, MA: Harvard University Press, 1968) surveys the astounding social and intellectual impact of galvanism and mesmerism.

14 See, inter alia, Joseph Ennemoser, *Der Magnetismus, nach der allseitigen Bezeihung seines Wesens* [Magnetism, in historical perspective of its forms] (Leipzig: F. A. Brockhaus, 1819); Casimir Chardel, *Esquisse de la nature humaine expliquée par le magnétisme animal* [A discourse on human nature as explained by animal magnetism] (Paris: Bureau de l'Encyclopédie Portative, 1826); and Jean Amédée Dupau, *Lettres physiologiques et morales sur le magnétisme animal: Une nouvelle theorie et ses applications a la médecine* [Notes on the physiology and morality of animal magnetism: A new theory and its applications to medicine] (Paris: Gabon, 1826).

Encyclopedias, government bulletins, and newspaper articles from nineteenth-century Russia demonstrate that the cult of Galvani and Mesmer had irrevocably converted even the scientific community that Lomonosov had helped to establish. *An Encyclopedic Dictionary* (*Entsikopedicheskii Leksikon*) of 1838 contains a detailed entry on galvanism, written by the physicist E. Kh. Lents.[15] According to a bulletin issued by the Ministry of Education, Lents secured his place at the university by conducting public experiments in electro-psychical phenomena.[16] The eminent scientist F. A. Preobrazhensky published an article in the Petersburg *Journal of Manufacturing and Trade* about a member of the Imperial Academy who had succeeded in constructing a *perpetuum mobile* with galvanism as its driving fuel.[17] The *perpetuum mobile*, an imaginary machine that runs without any visible source of power, added a particularly provocative cathodic dimension to electricity. It was an instrument envisioned by medieval alchemists, who also pursued the elusive goals of fabricating the philosopher's stone, a material created from fire that would turn any base metal into gold, and the elixir of life, which would rejuvenate the dead. The resurrection of the *perpetuum mobile* in conjunction with electric power also imbued it with the potentials of transfiguration and resuscitation.

As evident from Mary Shelley's *Frankenstein*, which is considered to be one of the first texts of modern science fiction, the combination of alchemic transfiguration and galvanic-mesmeric conceptions of electricity resonated particularly well with the ideology and aesthetics of Romanticism.[18] A number of scholars have pointed out, moreover, that the electrifying effect of *Frankenstein* also derived in no small part from the fact that all its so-called scientific components were associated with femininity.[19] Unlike Radishchev, who commemorated Lomonosov as a hyper-masculine modern-day Prometheus,

---

15 E. Kh. Lents, *Entsiklopedicheskii leksikon* [Encyclopedic dictionary], ed. A. Pliusher (St. Petersburg: A. F. Marks, 1838), 123–40.

16 A. Savel'ev, "O trudakh akademika E. Kh. Lentsa v magnito-elektrichestve" [On the works of academic E. Kh. Lentz in electromagnetism], *Zhurnal ministerstva nauki i prosveshcheniia* [Journal of the ministry of science and enlightenment] 5 (1854): 4–5.

17 Quoted in Ibid., 8.

18 Carl Freedman, *Critical Theory and Science Fiction* (Hanover, NH: Wesleyan University Press, 2000), 4–6.

19 See inter alia, Robin Roberts, *A New Species: Gender and Science in Science Fiction* (Champaign: University of Illinois Press, 1993); Jane Donawerth, *Frankenstein's Daughters: Women Writing Science Fiction* (Syracuse, NY: Syracuse University Press, 1997); and Debra Benita Shaw, *Women, Science, and Fiction: The Frankenstein Inheritance* (London: Palgrave, 2000).

Shelley's contemporaries in Russia, Alexander Pushkin and Nikolai Gogol, also turned to its cathodic, alchemic perceptions for articulating the elusive process of literary creation. The terms galvanism, magnetism, and mesmerism thoroughly permeated their vocabularies of aesthetics and affect. In a pioneering exegesis on the dramatic arts called "Theatrical Digressions" ("Teatral'nyi raz'ezd"), composed between 1836 and 1842, Gogol compared the formal features of a play with a perfect machine, but its essence, the ineffable "soul" of the work, with galvanism.[20] Invoking the implementation of mesmerism in psychological treatments, he instructed actors of his famous play *The Inspector General* (*Revizor*) to transfix the audience with a mysterious "shock."[21] Pushkin explained the process of poetic creation through a more elaborate and explicit metaphor in an essay titled "Refutation of Criticism" ("Oproverzhenie na kritiki"), published in 1830. The constituent parts of language, he argued, represented the inert poles of an incomplete circuit, and epiphany occurred when the masculine verb penetrated the feminine noun. As the dead noun came alive, language itself would be reanimated with a "magnetic charge."[22]

The electrical metaphors of Pushkin and Gogol, in turn, closely echoed those used by German Romantics. Both E. T. A. Hoffmann and Johann Wolfgang Goethe interpreted electricity as the tangible manifestation of the Neoplatonic doctrine of innate sympathies. The intimacy and urgency characterizing the Russian writers' representations of creative genius recall Hoffmann's story "The Magnetizer" ("Der Magnetiseur"), published in 1826, in which the protagonist draws out all the rays from inside his beloved and weaves her into his self.[23] Gogol's paradigm of communication and Pushkin's image of language coming alive resonate remarkably with Goethe's pronouncement in 1830 that "We all have some electrical and magnetic forces within us; with lovers this magnetic force is particularly strong."[24] As an incident in Tolstoy's novel *Anna Karenina* demonstrates, electricity continued to be associated with female sexuality and discussed as an occult phenomenon late in the nineteenth century. In a charged moment of ideological and emotional confrontation, the rationalist

20 Nikolai Gogol, "Teatral'nyi raz'ezd" [Theatrical digressions], *Sobranie khudozhestvennykh proizvedenii v 5 tomakh* [Collected creative works in 5 volumes] (Moscow: Akademiia Nauk, 1952), 4:190.
21 Nikolai Gogol, "*Revizor*" [The inspector general], *Sobranie* [Collected works], 4:8.
22 Aleksandr Pushkin, "Oproverzhenie na kritiki," *Polnoe sobranie sochinenii*, 7:185.
23 For commentary, see Christof, *Batteries of Life: On the History of Things and Their Perception in Modernity*, trans. Don Reneau (Berkeley: University of California Press, 1993), 171.
24 Johann Wolfgang von Goethe, *Conversations with Eckerman*, trans. John Oxenford (New York: Dutton, 1930), 190.

hero, Levin, accuses his beloved of indulging in table turning and mediumism. His rival Vronsky retorts, "We acknowledge the existence of electricity, even though we do not know it; why can't you admit there may be other sorts of energy that we have not yet named?"[25]

Science fiction provided the first platform for bringing together the anodic and cathodic, Enlightenment and Romantic approaches to electricity. In 4338, Odoevsky explored the intellectual and cultural implications of synthesizing the Lomonosovian vision of socially conscious modernity with the contemporary cult of Galvani and Mesmer. The most remarkable feature of his work is the presentation, *avant la lettre*, of a distinctly technological understanding of electricity. Long before light bulbs and dynamos made mass electrification a viable idea, Odoevsky's science fiction portrayed a society whose public sphere and private life had been completely transformed by electric power. The physical act of harnessing lightning, which Lomonosov had deferred to an unspecified future, emerged in 4338 as a goal accomplished on a massive scale. St. Petersburg in the novella looks like a "city of lights" (418) with "electric lamps shining through every crystal window" (421). "Galvanostats," balloons powered by electricity, provide public transportation, while the "magnetic telegraph," resembling our contemporary electronic mail, has replaced writing letters (448).

The narrator, who sends dispatches to China about the world's new "center of power" (420, 441) via this futuristic medium, connects energy, political economy, and the spatial history of modernity in an uncannily twenty-first-century diction. In both the literal and figurative sense, the narrative builds up a strong causal connection between electrification, modernization, and geopolitical authority in the future world. While the Orient pays homage to its superior Russian counterpart, Germany and the United States are described as uninhabitable "areas of darkness" (447). Tsungiev explains that these "older civilizations" collapsed at the point when Russia discovered the "power that drives both machines and intelligence" (432).

Electricity, however, also provides the governing metaphor for the particular way in which Russia employs technology in 4338. Tsungiev notes that, unlike Europe, Russia has approached machines in an "Eastern way" (431). Electric power functions not just as the material driving force for its civilization, but also plays a defining role in "improving the moral fiber" of the

25 Lev Tolstoy, *Anna Karenina, Polnoe sobranie sochinenii v 14 tomakh* [Collected creative works in 14 volumes] (Moscow: Khudozhestvennaia literatura, 1951), 8:60.

ruling class and intelligentsia (431). The dual role of electricity in Odoevsky's imagined Russia becomes evident in the central chapter of the novella, where the Chinese visitor is taken to a social gathering in a Petersburg mansion. A collective immersion in magnificent "magnetic baths" provides the high point of the party, whose purpose is to "flush out crass materialism and corrupt thought" (432). Cabinet ministers, scientists, writers, and artists alike emerge from the tubs in an exalted state of consciousness (433). The baths, which in Odoevsky's science fiction exemplify a crucial way in which Russia eschews the frivolous consumerism of Western modernity, are none other than the Mesmeric cabinet tubs used to cure mental illnesses in nineteenth-century Europe.

In Odoevsky's utopia, therefore, dispelling physical darkness and propelling transportation and communication remain meaningless until they are animated with a distinctly cathodic application of electricity. The fusion of its material and epistemological potentials, in fact, constitutes the foundation of an entirely different way of being in the world. This principle, called "New Enlightenment," eschews the notion that rationality alone can serve as the basis of knowledge and action. The elites of St. Petersburg in 4338 explain to the visitor that the mesmeric bath is the ideal instrument for transforming a merely enlightened human being into a product of the New Enlightenment (434).

Odoevsky's philosophical writings provide an elaborate gloss of this intriguing term. In an unpublished essay titled "Electrophysical Phenomena" ("Elektropsikhicheskiia iavleniia"), he welcomed the advent of a technological means through which the modern, scientifically oriented mind could begin to comprehend what lay beyond empirical observation. According to Odoevsky, electricity was the only medium for empirically disproving the opposition between mind and matter, reason and intuition, because it "merges our inner world with the outer environment." "In the highest state of magnetization," he contended, "pure instinct and pure reason come together."[26]

VIRTUAL ELECTRIFICATION: SCIENCE FICTION IN THE AGE OF EDISON

Odoevsky's unique embracement of the anodic and cathodic potentials of electricity remained an isolated instance of visionary thinking for the next two decades. A single innovation, Edison's light bulb, catapulted this novel source of energy into a worldwide object of speculation. Electric power, which promised

---

26 Archives of the National Public Library, St. Petersburg, file 53, folio 39 and file 79, folio 46.

to change night into day, revolutionize communication, and radically affect systems of production and consumption, emerged as the ubiquitous icon of modernity in the last decade of the nineteenth century. The media was instrumental in introducing the term "electricity" to the popular lexicon in Russia. Popular science journals such as *Around the World*, which included Edison's lamp on its cover, and *Nature and People*, which featured a sky filled with electric wires on the cover of an issue in 1895, literally adopted the incandescent bulb as their emblem. An image of the light bulb appeared at the head of a regular column in *Around the World* that reported the latest scientific discoveries and technological inventions. Specialized periodicals soon sprang up to inform the amateur reader about electrical energy. The inaugural issue of *The Journal of Latest Discoveries and Inventions* in 1900 offered two free supplements titled "Electricity as Progress" and "Electricity in Domestic Use." All through the same year, *The Field* carried numerous articles and pictures of the special electricity pavilion at the World's Fair in Paris.

As evident from the examples cited above, the enthusiasm of the Russian media about the transformative effects of electricity closely echoed its Western counterparts. But the resemblance ended there, because electricity did not leave the domain of representation to become an object of everyday life. Coopersmith notes that although individual engineers and investors at various times pushed for adopting the new source of energy, a rigid centralized system of promoting and developing new technologies prevented its application except for a few isolated urban landmarks. In contrast with railways, for example, the imperial government did not deem the generation of electric power strategically important until it was proven otherwise in the First World War.

Consequently, the readers of newspapers and magazines were well aware of electricity's transformative potentials but unable to experience it firsthand. Even as advertisements for incandescent lamps, phonographs, and radios lured the public, the products themselves remained prohibitively expensive. An electric lamp advertised in *The Field* in 1910, for example, cost forty rubles, while an Edison phonography was billed at seventy-five. As for electrification in public space, the limited import of generating equipment and its very selective use failed to dispel the illusion that electric light was as immaterial as electricity itself. An interesting compendium of advertisements from 1900 illustrated the glaring gap between imagining and implementing electric power. Three different varieties of lamps appeared on the same page of *The Field*. The most prominent advertisement, occupying about a quarter-page, declared: "Light for the Twentieth Century: Kerosene Lamp *Orsa*." The next box also touted a kerosene lamp manufactured by a Russian company called the Triumph. Whether in terms of size or strength of rhetoric, the least conspicuous advertisement was for the electric lamp, which was relegated to the very bottom of the page. Even at the threshold of the twentieth century, kerosene remained a far more tangible source of light in Russia's capital city than the foreign miracle of the incandescent bulb.[27]

Borrowing the parlance of our times, it might be said that electricity enjoyed a peculiar virtual existence in Russia. Although the media was flooded with its representations, material manifestations of electric power remained purely hypothetical and deferred to an unspecified future. A comparison with the rapidly changing discourse about electricity in the United States underscores its peculiar status in the Russian context. In 1890, Mark Twain referred to the new source of energy as "a splendid necromancy of modern science." But whereas a mere ten years later the same author could describe how it "lights up the home" and "extends the day long into the night," Twain's epithet of "necromantic science" held true for Russian perceptions of electricity well into the revolutionary period.[28]

Since the "necromantic" aspect of electricity bore little relation to actual developments in technology and industry, Russian magazines and newspapers regaled their curious readers with a panoply of magnetic, galvanic, and mesmeric phenomena readily available at their doorstep. Classified columns announced mesmeric séances, aided by electric shock, organized in the homes of prominent families. The Petersburg Stock Exchange News (Birzhevye vedomosti) carried at least ten daily notices from clinics specializing in electrotherapy for mental problems. In 1899, Nature and People published a report about a certain "Miss Volta," who effected miraculous cures with her "personal electrical aura."[29]

An iconic illustration of virtual electrification may be found on a page containing two articles about electricity in a 1900 issue of The Field. The top half of the page is dedicated to the centennial of a landmark event in the history of science. In 1800, the Italian physicist Alessandro Volta debunked Galvani's claim by constructing the first prototype of storage batteries, proving that electrical energy originated from chemical reactions between bodily fluids and the metal electrodes that Galvani placed on its feet. Right below the story of Volta's

---

27 Niva 32 (1900): 218.
28 Mark Twain's Notebooks and Journals, ed. Frederick Anderson (Berkeley: University of California Press, 1979), 32 and 149.
29 "Miss Volta," Priroda i liudi 4 [Nature and people 4] (1899): 54.

triumph appeared a sizable feature about a pair of magic healers who could not only light cigars and lamps from the "electrical tips" of their fingers, but also bring dead bodies to life.

Imagination, therefore, was the only platform for articulating the possible effects of electrical technology on everyday life. Detailed, elaborate narratives about the projected forms and functions of electricity appeared in the guise of science fiction, whether identified as such or clothed in the mantle of millennial eschatology and modernist manifestos. Electricity in Russia was nationalized through the frame of science fiction long before it could be materially domesticated.

Narratives extrapolating electrical technology attempted to resolve the split in media representations of electricity. An acute awareness of Russia's backwardness, in which kerosene still reigns as the fuel of the impending twentieth century, formed the backdrop of anxiety to the science fictional mode of envisioning the forms and functions of electric power. Consequently, the cathodic representations readily available to the Russian public—Miss Volta, Galvanic healers, shock therapy, and mesmeric séances—constituted an integral part of such speculative portrait. The democratization of electricity—if only virtually—nevertheless conferred a qualitatively different character to science fiction of the post-Edison period as compared to Odoevsky's prescient portrait of an electrically transformed capital city. From the 1890s onward, the Lomonosovian agenda of rural plight returned as a prominent concern, and electrification became as much an instrument of societal reconstruction as epistemic reconfiguration. The orientation of science fiction, correspondingly, shifted overwhelmingly to Russia's vast internal "darkness," its provincial towns and countryside excluded from the urban electrical dream. The cathodic mode, however, was always implicitly present.

Recuperating nineteenth-century figurations of electricity as a vitalist force of creation and healing, science fiction integrated Pushkin and Gogol's models of *poesis* into a new national idiom for the rapidly modernizing twentieth century. While in Odoevsky's work the synthesis of anodic and cathodic applications sustained an ethical class of innovators and administrators, at the cusp of the twentieth century electricity evolved into a consummate means for transfiguring the entire population. Commensurate with this democratic impulse, a new character type emerged as a stock element of science fiction. Electricity became the special area of expertise for a particular brand of Russian scientist or engineer, who, whether by virtue of his background or his chosen field of work, bridged the city and the country, institutional training and populist intuition. Corresponding with the gap between speculation and reality, moreover, this central figure privileged the new synthetic model of knowledge symbolized by electricity.[30]

Ethical and epistemological change became the primary functions of electric power in the realm of the imagination. A story published in 1898 by Konstantin Sluchevsky, a prominent metaphysical poet of the fin de siècle, serves as a representative example of the new kind of electrical science fiction that emerged in Russia during the decade following Edison's invention. "Captain Nemo in Russia" ("Kapitan Nemo v Rossii") employed electricity to articulate an overt literary and ideological response to Western modernity's functional relationship with science and technology. In Sluchevsky's story, Verne's famous hero travels to a remote island on the White Sea, where a Russian is said to have created lush farmlands out of frozen Arctic wastes. What sets Nemo and the protagonist apart is precisely their relation to electricity: while the Frenchman uses electric power only to run his personal submarine, the Russian, literally reincarnating Lomonosov, reinterprets the eighteenth-century visionary's broad view of social transformation within the uniquely Russian understanding of electricity at the turn of the twentieth century. In a striking biographical correlation with the eighteenth-century scientist, Sluchevsky's hero lives on an island close to Lomonosov's hometown, Arkhangelsk. His visionary thinking and scientific activities, however, are shaped by an unprecedented conjuncture between the social consciousness of the Enlightenment and electricity's cathodic perceptions in early-twentieth-century Russia.

Rather than harnessing electricity to satisfy his individualistic wanderlust, the Russian inventor utilizes it for alleviating two existential concerns of the local peasantry, lack of food and the absence of education. As climate control enables local farmers to produce bumper crops during the day and study by Edison's bulbs at night, electricity evolves into a force that simultaneously resurrects the body and kindles the mind. Introducing his gifted assistant to Nemo, the protagonist wryly observes that he is not of French or British origin as the visitor presumes, but "a local peasant, a *samorodok* purer than gold, from the kingdom of darkness and tallow candles."[31] The composite image of electricity

30 The only exception is a popular novel, Vladimir Chikolev's *Electrical Tale: It Never Happened, but It Is Not Imaginary* [*Elektricheskii rasskaz: Ne bylo, no i ne vydumka*] (Moscow: Sytin, 1895), which includes long descriptions of gadgets—obvious extrapolations of those advertised in the press—and constructs a simple portrait of urban comfort.

31 Konstantin Sluchevsky, "Kapitan Nemo v Rossii" [Captain Nemo in Russia], *Sochineniia v 6 tomakh* [Works in 6 volumes] (St. Petersburg: A. F. Marks, 1898), 2:50.

established in the story provides a powerful counterpoint for both stereotypes invoked in the ironic statement: Russia, "dark" and "backward" in European eyes, and its subjects held back by ignorance and superstition. Golden light emitted by incandescent bulbs, the most recognizable icon of modern electrical technology, symbolically purifies both entities.

The two connotations of the term *samorodok* are particularly significant in this context. In the natural sciences, it signifies a metal that can be found in pure form. Slavophiles appropriated the word, which can be literally translated as "self-born," to describe an authentic, non-Eurocentric national identity. The second meaning played a crucial role in repudiating objectivism and discrediting institutional learning derived from the West: as Slavophiles claimed that genuine insight arose from organic connection with the soil, the "self-born" became a particularly valorized repository of situated knowledge. Lomonosov, a fisherman's son, was the first historical figure anointed with this term.[32]

Gold and light in Sluchevsky's story create a direct connection between the *samorodok* and electricity. As his relationship with the miraculous new source of power transcends the hierarchy between the subject and the object, both the human and his source of energy are completely transformed. Rather than remaining a passive force of nature subjugated to serve as mere fuel, electricity manifests its true potentials in the *samorodok*'s hands by alchemically transfiguring him into a substance "purer than gold."[33] Even though "Captain Nemo in

---

32 G. A. Galavanova, ed., *Slovar' sovremennogo russkogo iazyka* [Dictionary of modern Russian] (Moscow: Akademiia nauk, 1962), 13:129.

33 The association of electricity with gold also attests to a new category of speculation about purported parapsychological applications of electricity that came into vogue in Russia in the late 1890s. Alchemy—which means transmutation—involves creating gold by transforming base metals through fire. This ultimate substance, medieval scientists believed, was a panacea for solving all ills including old age and death. The writings of some nineteenth-century parapsychologists who hailed electricity as the magic fire that alchemists had been unable to craft were first translated into Russian in the early 1890s. The celebrated Victorian mesmerist William Carpenter, who contended that electricity would unlock the secrets of transubstantiation, claimed that it could not only turn base metals into gold but also change the body to immortal spirit. Carpenter's book *Mesmerism and Spiritualism Historically and Scientifically Considered* (New York: Appleton, 1890), translated in 1892, created equally wide ripples in popular science journals and "thick" magazines targeted at the discerning intelligentsia. The revival of Galvanic perceptions of electricity, along with the view that it embodied the alchemist's fire, even permeated the discourse of academic journals. *Issues of Philosophy and Psychology* (*Voprosy filosofii i psikhologii*); the prestigious scholarly publication, printed an article on galvanic reanimation in which the author specifically recommends golden electrical circuits (A. A. Glagolev, "Gal'vanizm i bessmertie" [Galvanism and immortality], *Voprosy filosofi i psikhologii* [Questions in philosophy and psychology] 19–20 [1894]: 1–19, 1–26).

Russia" recuperates early-nineteenth-century associations between electricity and alchemy, the older cathodic mode also serves to reconcile the spiritual orientation of Slavophilism with twentieth-century modernity. Originally posited as an organic antithesis to the dehumanizing influence of technology, the *samorodok* develops a life-transforming nonobjective relationship with the primary driving power of the imminent future.

This new reflexive relationship between humanity and technoscience underlies the crucial but unexamined role that electricity played in Nikolai Fedorov's ambitious project for universal salvation. Critiquing the dichotomy between feminized nature (*priroda*) and masculine reason (*razum*), he called for a new nondualistic model of engagement with energy. In Fedorov's view, the fundamental conflict between nature's "blind force" and "humanity rendered helpless by her unpredictability" could be resolved by recognizing the elements as parts of the same organism as humans (2:262).[34] Cultivating an intersubjective relationship between "water, air, fire, and the substance of human bodies" would eradicate famine and flood, striking at the very roots of hunger and disease and paving the way toward immortal life (2:261).[35]

The electrical means to attain this new "cosmic subjectivity" are delineated in the last section of the *Philosophy of the Common Task* in a series of essays tellingly titled "Regulation of Nature" ("Reguliatsiia prirody"). Both the tone and the contents of these essays are overtly science fictional. They extrapolate recent developments in science and technology to describe the radically different forms and functions they will assume in the visionary thinker's novel paradigm of knowledge and action. The last essay in this series eulogizes an unknown nineteenth-century scientist, Nikolai Karazin, as the true progenitor of Fedorov's method. Karazin's portrait is indeed that of a *samorodok*—a provincial visionary from Kharkov whose primary aim was to alleviate the plight of rural agrarian Russia. His plan was to transform electricity in nature—those "waves and lashes that have long astounded the mind and instilled fear"—into a beneficent source of "life-giving rain *that could be commanded at will from the sky*" (2:261, emphasis in text). The objective was to trap atmospheric electricity and use it to fuse hydrogen and oxygen in the air.

What is remarkable about Fedorov's resurrection of Karazin is that he transformed the nineteenth-century scientist's technological proposals into

---

34 N. F. Fedorov, *Philosophy of the Common Task* [*Filosofiia obshchego dela*, ed. V. A. Kozhevnikov and N. P. Peterson (1906–1913; repr. Paris: Homme, 1985)], vol. 2, 262.
35 Fedorov, vol. 2, 261.

a living embodiment of cosmic intersubjectivity. The philosopher laid out an imaginative spatial scheme through which he represented the initial separation and final fusion between humans and elemental energy. "For a long time," mused Fedorov, "humans have helplessly gazed into the atmosphere with its incessant rumblings and upheavals without having a means to participate in the ebb and flow high up in the atmosphere" (2:261). The separation of the earth from the heavens reflects the limited potential of the mind as long as it remains separated from natural matter and energy. Resolution of this impasse requires a series of technological interventions involving electricity. First, balloons powered with electricity—the same "magnetic aerostats" of Odoevsky's fiction—are sent up to trap and store atmospheric power. The balloons are then connected to the earth's surface with "long metallic wires," which in turn fuse with "metallic pipes for transferring electrically-generated rain" to arid farmland (2:261).

The scenario conjures up a striking landscape of multiple umbilical cords between the vast cosmos and the mortal inhabitants of the earth (2:263), in which electrical energy literally incarnates a new connection of fertile benevolence between nature and humanity. A closer examination of Fedorov's proposal also reveals the dialectics between anodic and cathodic approaches to electricity. While atmospheric energy remains untapped, it represents the feminine mysterious persona of nature, inaccessible to human reason and indeed a source of fear and flood. The transformation of this mysterious entity into a fountainhead of resurrection requires masculine anodic rationality to overcome its alienation. The wires and pipes connecting Heaven and Earth also resemble an electrical circuit whose poles have been finally conjoined, leading to a colossal outburst of new life.

ELECTRIFYING MODERNISM: THE VITALIST ALCHEMY OF SCIENCE FICTION

Eschatological thought, however, was not the only sphere in which the anodic and cathodic potentials of electricity were synthesized into a powerful narrative of overcoming death. A pair of unusually correlated speculative texts—one written by an obscure popular author, the other by a founder of the Symbolist movement—envisions electricity as a combined conduit of physical immortality and psychic transfiguration in the imminent future. The popular writer Vladimir Shelonsky interwove the two aspects in a science fictional novel titled *In the Future World* (*V mire budushchego*), published in 1892. This work is modeled on a traditional *voyage imaginaire* with one crucial difference: the spaceship that transports an eclectic group of scientists and philosophers to the North Pole runs on electric power. Such a substitution of the magic carpet with a futuristic machine is hardly remarkable, but a matrix of spiritual allusions transforms this tale of adventure on an electric ship into a uniquely Russian allegory of folk chiliasm. The protagonists choose electricity as the only force strong enough to match the ultimate objective of their quest, *Polnoch'* or the "Midnight Land." According to scholars of utopian folklore, the term originated in a sixteenth-century legend of fugitive Old Believers who wandered about in Siberia looking for an undiscovered section of the Arctic where nobody ever grew old.[36] By enabling humans to reach this mythic space, electricity evolves into a technological means to achieve immortality. Like Sluchevsky and Fedorov, the author ascribes the conception of the project to a Russian *samorodok* incarnating a synthesis of sophisticated scientist and peasant magus. He solves the problem of constructing a battery that can store enough energy to last the duration of the journey; after much trial and error, the protagonist receives a dream revelation that gold is the only appropriate medium for trapping and transporting electric power.[37]

Shelonsky's narrative is remarkably similar to the only experiment of Andrei Bely, the Symbolist poet and literary theorist, in writing science fiction. Bely's story, published in 1904 and titled "Argonauts" ("Argonavty"), is set in the twenty-third century. The plot consists of a perilous journey in an electrical spaceship. Its passengers call themselves "Argonauts"—an obvious allusion to the myth of Jason seeking the Golden Fleece—and choose a peasant-engineer who also possesses prophetic powers as the leader of the group. He uses gold to construct and propel the fantastic vessel, trapping large amounts of electricity in its shining scales. After many trials and tribulations, the group arrives at a magical space in which their bodies turn into golden rays and their minds leave the material world to connect with the transcendental noumenon. The story also contains an autobiographical subtext that transforms it into an epistemological and aesthetic manifesto. It renders that quest of the literary group "Argonaut," which Bely founded, into an inimitable synthetic form of science fiction.[38]

---

36 A. Klibanov, *Narodnaia sotsial'naia utopia v Rossii: period feodalizma* [Folk utopia in Russia: The feudal period] (Moscow: Nauka, 1977), 231.

37 Vladimir Shelonsky, *V mire budushchego* [In the world of the future] (Moscow: I. D. Sytin, 1892).

38 Andrei Bely, "Argonavty" [Argonauts], *Rasskazy* [Stories] (Munich: Fink, 1979), 30–41.

Shelonsky and Bely's works operate on the same set of motifs developed in Sluchevsky's fiction and Fedorov's philosophy: the unique relation of the *samorodok* to electricity, gold as both the conduit of electrical energy and the alchemical means of transubstantiation, and resurrection as the goal of electrification. Bely's story, however, restores the vital connection between language, electricity, and life first articulated by the Romantics. Read as an allegory of a literary movement, "Argonauts" introduces a novel connotation to electricity as an indispensable element of *zhiznetvorchestvo* or life-creation—a term Russian modernists used to convey their goal of transforming life through art. Synthesizing Pushkin and Gogol's imagery of electricity with the new democratizing impulses of Sluchevsky and Fedorov's extrapolations results in a new vision of art in modern Russia: an electrical force unleashed from the rarefied atmosphere of urban elitism that would become a potent medium for changing the entire society.

In contrast with Bely, however, some Russian modernists were obsessed with the rapid domestication of electricity in the West. Rather than reinterpreting it for the audience at home, they bemoaned the profanation of a mysterious cosmic force in the name of progress. The most prolific science fiction writer among this group, Valery Bryusov, predicted an apocalyptic moment in the near future when the irrational cathodic "essence" of electricity would wreak vengeance upon humanity blinded by the material comforts provided by its technological manifestations.[39] On the eve of the First World War, Bryusov published an ominous story titled "Rebellion of the Machines" ("Vosstanie mashin," 1914) that thematized the imminent implosion of society. The world erupts into mayhem when the appliances and electrical grids citizens depend upon develop a "diabolic logic" of their own and take over. In images that explicitly invoke the Romantic conception of electricity, domestic artifacts such as light bulbs, telephones, and radios begin to personify and respond to the humans' repressed anxieties.[40] A "nervous explosion" (100) destroys both the topography and the equilibrium of a society organized into interconnected "power zones"(101).

---

39 In real life, Bryusov retained a paranoid fear of the invisible occult powers of electricity. Vladislav Khodasevich noted that he always switched the lights off before exiting a room ("Bryusov," *Sobranie sochinenii v 4 tomakh* [Moscow: Soglasie, 1997], 4:32).

40 Valery Bryusov, "Vosstanie Mashin" [Rebellion of the machines], *Povesti i rasskazy* [Novellas and short stories], ed. T. M. Muguev (Moscow: Sovetskaia Rossiia, 1983), 103. Subsequent references in parentheses.

While Bryusov conceived of an electrical discharge as deadly rather than liberating or resurrecting, many of his contemporaries enthusiastically adopted the image of an electric spark instantly destroying the existing order of things and transfiguring the consciousness of the people. The term "electrifying" appeared in Russian journalism in 1917 as a metaphor for the unrest consuming intellectuals and proletariat alike. "The political atmosphere is electrified," wrote Nikolai Shelgunov, a public intellectual and leftist activist, on the eve of the Revolution; "everyone's heightened consciousness will explode into a single electric discharge."[41] Not surprisingly, *razriad*, the Russian term for an electric discharge, became a favored metaphor of the Futurist movement in Russia. Unlike the Symbolists, Futurists did not regard the contested connotations of electricity— agent of apocalypse, medium of resurrection, facilitator of superior lighting and communication—in separate and mutually exclusive categories. Like the Italian Futurist Filippo Marinetti hailing "the reign of Holy Electric Light come to liberate Venice from venal moonshine,"[42] they adopted electricity *in toto* as the most potent embodiment of the movement's epistemological, social, and aesthetic agenda.

The shock of an electric current conveyed particularly well the mortal blow Futurists wished to deliver to existent hierarchies. More radical members of the movement, such as Khlebnikov, declared that such a shock would remove detritus of the past, purge the present of its falsehoods, and provide the necessary prelude to a future utopia in which electricity would play a constructive role in reorganizing both material life and human cognition. Khlebnikov developed this theme by synthesizing positivistic and mystical perceptions of electricity in a completely new paradigm. Rejecting the classical myth of Prometheus that underlies representations of electricity from Lomonosov's poetry to the science-fictional *samorodok*, he turned to archetypal Slavic beliefs for articulating its valence and functions in the Russian context. According to A. N. Afanas'ev, the pioneering folklorist whose commentaries exerted a decisive influence on Khlebnikov's imagery, lightning was long perceived to be the divine agent that generated the universe from chaotic matter: the God Perun is believed to have animated and spiritualized the earth's dead flesh by touching it with his sword of heavenly fire.[43] Accordingly, Khlebnikov eschewed the modern term "electricity" in favor of the archaic *molniia*, meaning lightning.

---

41 Nikolai Shelgunov, *Vospominaniia* [Reminiscences] (Moscow: Gosudarstvennoe izdatel'stvo [State publishing], 1923), 122.

42 Filippo Marinetti, *Selected Writings*, trans. R.W. Flint (New York: Noonday, 1972), 63.

43 A. N. Afanas'ev, *Poeticheskie vozzreniia slavian na prirodu* [Slavic poetic perspectives on nature] (Moscow: Indrik, 1995), 1:125–35.

In a letter to fellow Futurist Alexei Kruchenykh, Khlebnikov defined electric power as the reincarnation of primordial lightning. He outlines its tremendous potential for reconstituting not just material life but logos itself. Futurist language, Khlebnikov contends, is an "electrical discharge" (*razriad*) because it breaks down stratifications of "high" and "low," "literary" and "folk" diction.[44] This formulation of electricity as a force for synthesizing Russia's estranged internal halves adds a radical dimension to the linguistic symbolism of Bely's science fiction. Whereas the Argonauts posited electricity as a technologically mediated source of energy, Khlebnikov rejects the mantle of modernity altogether. The archaism *molniia* penetrates false signifiers of literary language and elevated diction to become the agent for restoring language to the primordial Slavic persona. This hypothesis is borne out by the invocation of Pushkin—also recuperated by Bely—in the same letter. Khlebnikov contrasts his own understanding of electricity with that of Pushkin, "for whom electricity merely translated foreign words into Russian" (367).

The possibilities opened up in the letter to Kruchenykh are fictionalized through a narrative poem composed between 1915 and 1921—a period beginning before the Revolution and ending after the Civil War—in which electricity is transformed into an elaborate cosmogonic myth. Faithful to his assertion that the new form of energy will peel away layers of false consciousness and generate a national persona authentic to its core, the poet makes a radical break from its prior representations as an agent for ameliorating existing ills of the modern age. Instead, he constructs an original framework of space-time within which lightning brings about *poesis*.

Khlebnikov's poem "Lightning Sisters" ("Sestry molnii"), which has received practically no critical attention, represents an especially powerful isntance of his inimitable proclivity for folding back the present to an as-yet-uninitiated past.[45] He splits and feminizes the ancient deity Perun into twin "lightning sisters," who become "the only Gods" of the future: "I am God / And you will not have / Other Gods / Except myself."[46] The story of creation revolves around the premise that a radical transformation of the environment—

---

44 Velimir Khlebnikov, "Neizdannye proizvedeniia" [Unpublished works], ed. N. Hardziev and T. Grits, *Sobranie sochinenii* [Collected works] (Munich: Fink, 1971), 4:367. Subsequent reference in parentheses.

45 For an extensive evaluation of Khlebnikov's treatment of time, see Raymond Cooke, *Velimir Khlebnikov: A Critical Study* (Cambridge: Cambridge University Press, 1987), 104–60.

46 Velimir Khlebnikov, "Sestry-molnii" [Lightning sisters], *Sobranie sochinenii* [Collected works], ed. Dmitrii Chizhevsky et al. (Munich: Fink, 1968), 2:157.

such as that posited by a Marxist revolution—would remain meaningless until their "talking sword" kindles the language and spirit (158). Lightning is the power animating the New Soviet Man, who is portrayed as both a technician and a poet. His mechanical or artistic creations remain lifeless until fired by the electric spark of inspiration. Lightning is the feminine "muse" that injects life into unborn words and vast future construction sites that only exist as blueprints in the imagination (170).

It is obvious that Khlebnikov did not literally abandon tropes of modernity such as literary language or technology. but instead of recognizing them as already accomplished facts, his myth of the future imbues the very concept of modernity with an aura of immanence, whose masculine power cannot be phenomenologically manifested without the feminine cathodic element. It is also important to note that the poet both appropriates and subverts preexisting narratives to develop his original approach to electrical *poesis*.

Fedorov's fingerprints, for example, are visible throughout "Lightning Sisters." The poem reiterates the philosopher's gendered dualism between man and nature as well as his spatial dichotomy in the opening image of the sisters, "perched at the top / of long green stalks" (155) and looking down on a landscape of human bodies and human tasks waiting to come to life. Like Fedorov, Khlebnikov identifies modern humanity as a male entity, a "warrior" (159) embodying the incomplete consciousness of the anode. Reason, which blinds him in the *Common Task*, is the element that lightning seeks to shear away: "Fear the dullness of reason! / I will clothe the [naked] one / Who has been deceived by Reason" (156). In an earlier version of the poem, Khlebnikov explicitly invokes the Fedorovian aim of employing electricity to "fertilize" the agrarian heartland with rain: "I'll run after the harvest / ... We rejuvenate and freshen" (381). But the final version transcends the philosopher's ultimate objective of bringing back to life the dead forefathers of all humanity.[47] Khlebnikov's "lightning sisters" do not purport to bring those who are already dead back to life; instead, their cosmos is unborn, waiting to be animated by the cathodic feminine creative impulse.

Khlebnikov's feminization of electricity stands out in the very masculinist cult of the machine, associated with Futurism. His choice to represent a dual female body as the primary source of *poesis*, however, can be traced back

---

47 For immortality in Fedorov's philosophy, see Irene Masing-Deliv, *Abolishing Death: A Salvation Myth of Russian Twentieth-Century Literature* (Stanford, CA: Stanford University Press, 1992), 76–104.

to an earlier mode of representation. At the cusp of the twentieth century, the exciting new source of power provided a rich metaphorical source for articulating divergence from the norm of carnal, heterosexual love. Vladimir Solov'ev, for example, depicted sexual sublimation not as bodily intercourse, but as a "fusion of opposites yielding light."[48] The Symbolist poet Zinaida Hippius amplified this formulation in her 1901 poem, "Electricity" ("Elektrichestvo"). Structured in the form of an electrical circuit, it initially depicts the anode and the cathode standing for unresolved dichotomies not just between positives and negatives but also flesh and spirit, death and life, the past and the present. Their coming together at the end of the poem constitutes at once an explosive orgasm—denoted by *razriad*, the same term as electrical discharge and catharsis—and transcendence. The spark causes instantaneous death to the parts of the circuit, but also ushers in the blinding light of life after death.[49] Scholars who have delved into Hippius's ambiguous sexuality refer to the poem as a particularly bold instance of cross-gendering, despite the perceived dichotomy of the male and female poles of the circuit.[50] Khlebnikov's triadic conception of the twin lightning sisters and the lone "warrior" complements the complicated sexual permutations of Hippius's Symbolist poetics.

Like a number of avant-garde writers and artists, Khlebnikov committed himself after 1917 to devising utopian projects meant to be translated into reality. Electricity forms the basis of the most elaborate of his plans. A series of housing and education projects, "Homesteads from the Future" ("Kol iz budu-shchego," 1918–21), which the poet composed after the long-awaited catharsis of the October Revolution had already taken place, represent electricity as a consummation of physical power and spiritual energy, a spectacular result of the contact between masculine human endeavor and the feminine heavenly spark of lightning. The landscape of Russia in the future is dotted with transformers and radio towers, monumental structures of electrical technology that also serve as anthropomorphic totems. Bridging Heaven and Earth through "hairs of lightning," the gigantic markers of electric power serve as conduits for Perun's divine logos. Electricity operates in this fictional reality as the metonym for internationalist egalitarianism brought about by a successful synthesis of its material and metaphysical functions: power stations and radio towers not only

---

48 Quoted in Ibid., 116.

49 Zinaida Hippius, "Elektrichestvo" [Electricity], *Stikhotvoreniia* [Poems], ed. L. A. Nikolaeva (St. Petersburg: Akademicheskii proekt, 1999), 111.

50 Olga Matich, *Paradox in the Religious Poetry of Zinaida Gippius* (Munich: Fink, 1972), 112–13.

disseminate light and information in Khlebnikov's utopia but also serve the more abstract function of transforming the consciousness. They fuse hitherto disparate units of society into a harmonious "universal soul."[51]

In the chaos and privation following the October Revolution, the science fictional synthesis between the anodic and cathodic connotations of electricity remained one of the few "real" repositories of hope for the nation's eventual recovery and progress. Despite—or perhaps because of—the continued absence of electricity from everyday life, its imagined potentials for saving Russia and its subjects only gained in strength. The worst years of War Communism was when the government first began to valorize mass electrification. Bolshevik rhetoric about instantly modernizing Russia, therefore, betrays more synergy with than divergence from the science fictional extrapolations discussed in this chapter. Acutely conscious of this inversion between reality and representation, Khlebnikov added a comment to "Lightning Sisters" in 1920 declaring that "electricity is now the only real force that can conquer tears."[52]

GOELRO ELECTRIFICTION: SCIENCE FICTION'S SYNTHESIS OF SALVATION

In the economic and social devastation following the Civil War, while the actual production of electricity plummeted, the synthesis of its anodic and cathodic perceptions continued to thrive in political manifestos and literary production. Artists and writers' responses to Lenin's slogan demonstrate that both GOELRO and its architect were seamlessly absorbed into the epistemic and figural continuum explored in the previous sections. Two examples from the visual arts illustrate this point.

Lenin stands in the foreground of both Gustav Klustis's painting *Electrification* from 1920 and Pavel Filonov's *GOELRO* from 1930 against the canvas of an electrified world. His representation, however, is far from realistic. Both portraits recuperate the tremendous potentials of synthesizing the anodic and cathodic perceptions of electricity that were perpetuated and popularized through science fiction and its allied cultural discourses over the three preceding decades. Rendered in a distinctly Suprematist mode, Klustis's depiction of "electrification" foregrounds the transformation of the mortal leader into a gigantic

---

51 Velimir Khlebnikov, "Kol iz budushchego" [Homesteads from the future], *Sobranie sochinenii* [Collected works], 4:294.
52 Khlebnikov, "Sestry molnii," 168.

superhuman. It is significant that even though the technological infrastructure of electrification—the anode—is prominently featured in the painting as a gigantic transformer, it is nevertheless subservient to the human transfigured by electricity's cathodic power. Filonov's portrait, composed a decade later, complicates the connection between electricity and modernity even further. In a mode reminiscent of the science fictional associations between electric light, gold, and the alchemical transubstantiation of base flesh into pure energy, Lenin's body becomes one with the red-and-gold landscape presumably illuminated by electric power. The painting also invokes Fedorov's projects of eliminating the duality between subject and object, and Khlebnikov's vision of immanent modernity powered by the lightning sisters. Electric light, making the Futurist's imagined buildings transparent and shattering the division between inner and outer space, also penetrate the leader, the first child of the Revolution.

The most sophisticated engagement with GOELRO, however, may be found in the science fiction of Andrei Platonov. An engineer by training, Platonov began his involvement with the Bolshevik electrification plan at the level of local politics. He spent many years in the early 1920s electrifying the countryside around Voronezh, his hometown in the Tambov region. Platonov's first response to Lenin's slogan reflects the sensibility of the *samorodok* peasant-engineer of science fiction to perfection. In 1921, Platonov composed a pamphlet titled "Electrification" ("Elektrifikatsiia") to be distributed in the local party cell. Rhetorical and representational strategies of the ostensibly "informational" essay belong squarely in the continuum examined in this chapter. The pamphlet describes in epiphanic tones how electrification will bridge the rift between town and country, radically improve both industrial and agricultural labor, and change the quality of life for workers and peasants alike. Simultaneously, it describes the Revolution as a mystical cosmic event, a lightning discharge (*razriad molnii*) that has changed the world. Along with expressing hope that electricity will save historically deprived sections of Soviet society, Platonov also proclaims that it is the new instrument for uplifting the consciousness of its most deprived citizens. Not only would electrification provide shorter working days and domestic comfort to workers and peasants, but also produce a complete change in the indefinable "essence," *sut'*, of the proletariat.[53]

In contrast, Platonov's fictional accounts of electrifying rural Russia offer a chilling deconstruction of the Bolshevik project. While the task of producing energy ex nihilo, literally out of nothing, stands at the center of his early short

---

53 Andrei Platonov, *Elektrifikatsiia* (Voronezh: Proletarskaia literatura, 1921), 3 and 9.

stories "Markun" (1921) and "Thoughts of Satan" ("Satana mysli," 1922), whose Fedorovian paramaters Thomas Seifrid explores in some detail, it is Platonov's late science-fiction story "The Homeland of Electricity" ("Rodina elektrichestva") published in 1926, that engages directly with GOELRO.[54]

"Homeland of Electricity" is set in the ruinously dry summer of 1921 among Russian peasants located literally in the middle of nowhere. Although Platonov adopts a "realistic" locale and time, it is that very chronotope that provides a perfect frame for critically enacting utopia. Inhabitants of the Russian village, ravaged by war and famine to the extent that their bodies are literally shrinking, are ready to receive any succor available. Paradoxically, the lack of equipment and information—the village is simply allotted a broken-down generator with no fuel supply—places them in a pre-GOELRO time warp when electricity simply did not exist in its mechanical manifestation. Their perceptions and representations of electrification, therefore, are rendered through a rich spectrum of metaphors not from contemporary propaganda but pre-Revolutionary science fiction. Platonov depicts the villagers' assessments of electricity in palpable intertextual connection with earlier representations of the mysterious energy. The generator represents an animate, supernatural, feminine being, and Party rhetoric becomes an object of superstitious faith. Women compare the nonfunctioning dynamo with a miracle-working icon of the Madonna, a heavenly intercessor mitigating drought and famine and restoring the fecundity of the earth; men assign it the status of a Red Worker sent by the authorities to "correct" their ideological orientation.[55]

The peasants interpret the Bolshevik leader's pronouncement literally as magic incantation rather than policy statement. "Now life will be mighty and beautiful, and there will be eggs for everyone" (45), the village head sings, paraphrasing the promise of the Hymn to the Third International: "Now life will be mighty and beautiful, and there will be bread for everyone." Folk chiliasm, rather than revolutionary zeal or technological knowledge, lies at the basis of this eccentric association of electrification and eggs. Equipped only with a broken dynamo and no fuel, famine-ravaged peasants fail to understand that electrification is meant to revolutionize agriculture. Instead, they regard the nonfunctioning generator as a repository of life in its most cosmic manifestation.

---

54 Thomas Seifrid, *Andrei Platonov: Uncertainties of Spirit* (Cambridge: Cambridge University Press, 1992), 50–55.

55 Andrei Platonov, "Rodina elektrichestva" [Homeland of electricity], *Izbrannye proizvedeniia* [Selected works], ed. M. A. Platonova (Moscow: Ekonomika, 1983), 42 and 46. Subsequent citations of this source appear in parentheses within the text.

Eggs represent the fountainhead of creation in Slavic folk belief, in which the world is said to have originated from a "cosmic egg" in pre-Christian mythology; the symbol later evolved into the colorful eggs of Resurrection shared at paschal celebrations.[56] The song grotesquely reverses the potential of cosmic regeneration with which science fiction ranging from Sluchevsky's "Kapitan Nemo" to Fedorov's and Khlebnikov's philosophical fantasies imbued electricity. The narrator-protagonist of Platonov's story, a mechanic summoned from town to help the villagers, represents a similar mockery of the *samorodok*-hero. Caught in the rift between language and reality, his subjective perceptions begin to literalize the paradox of rural electrification.[57] Full of official zeal, he arrives at the village only to find himself in a parallel universe. At first, he is skeptical about the villager's adorations of the generator, but in the absence of infrastructure, he begins to accord it the same anthropomorphic or deistic status. In order to provide the necessary energy for starting the dynamo, he first attempts to fuel it with grain liquor—a profane waste of the plentiful "bread" promised in the Third International—and then coaxes out his own "vital energy" to start the recalcitrant machine (*mashina* in Russian is grammatically feminine). Following the directives of the local council, he attempts to educate the villagers about the new-fangled source of energy. But scientific, mechanistic explanations completely fail their purpose, and the protagonist finally resorts to the same metaphysical terms as Futurists in an earlier era. Citing folkloristic myths of creation, he sums up the definition of electricity: "It is *molniia*, lightning . . . the spirit of the Gods."

---

56 Afanas'ev, *Poeticheskie*, 2:227.
57 Coopersmith documents that this was a stated principal goal of GOELRO, 163.

Imagining the Cosmos: Utopians, Mystics, and the Popular Culture of Spaceflight in Revolutionary Russia

ASIF A. SIDDIQI

Siddiqi, Asif A. "Imagining the Cosmos: Utopians, Mystics, and the Popular Culture of Spaceflight in Revolutionary Russia." *Osiris*, Second Series 23 (2008): 260–88.

By taking a pair of steps, I crossed over the threshold from one epoch to another, into the space [era].[1]

—Mikhail Popov, organizer of the world's first interplanetary exhibition, on what it felt like to step into the display hall, 1927

S pace achievements represented an important marker of Soviet claims to global preeminence during the Cold War. In books, movies, posters, and songs, Soviet authorities sang the glories of their space program; cosmonauts and artifacts toured the world using rhetoric that conflated mastery of space with mastery of nature. During and after the Cold War, both Russian and Western historians underlined the connection between the Soviet space program and Marxist fascinations with technology.[2] These accounts located the

---

1 Sergei Samoilovich, *Grazhdanin vselennoi (Cherty zhizni i deiatel'nosti Konstantina Eduardovicha Tsiolkovskogo)* [Citizen of the universe (Outline of the lfie and work of Konstantin Eduardovich Tsiolkovsky] (Kaluga, 1969), 181.

2 William Shelton, *Soviet Space Exploration: The First Decade* (New York, 1968); James E. Oberg, *Red Star in Orbit* (New York, 1981); William P. Barry, "The Missile Design Bureaux and Soviet Piloted Space Policy, 1953–1974" (DPhil diss., University of Oxford, 1995); David Easton Potts, "Soviet Man in Space: Politics and Technology from Stalin to Gorbachev (Volumes 1 and 2)" (PhD diss., Georgetown University, 1992).

social and cultural origins of the Soviet space program as part of the project of modernization, secularism, and "progress." When the first young hero cosmonauts flew into space in the early 1960s, Soviet commentators repeatedly depicted them as emblematic of a modern and technologically sophisticated Russia, overtaking the West. Furthermore, unlike American astronauts who thanked God for their successes, Soviet cosmonauts were explicitly atheistic; one of the first cosmonauts, the young Gherman Titov, famously declared on a visit to the United States that during his seventeen orbits of the earth, he had seen "no God or angels," adding that "no God helped build our rocket."[3] And in the 1970s, when the Soviets launched their first cargo ship to a space station, they named it simply *Progress*.

Through lenses of modernity, secularism, and progress, historians typically traced back the history of the Soviet space program to the "patriarch" of Soviet cosmonautics, Konstantin Tsiolkovskii, who in 1903 produced the first mathematical substantiations that spaceflight was possible. According to this deeply engrained story, the Bolsheviks recognized the value of his work after the Russian Revolution, honored him with many awards, and made him a national treasure. To the Bolsheviks, Tsiolkovskii's ideas were a perfect vehicle for catapulting Russia into the modern technological age of Ford and Taylor. Soon, inspired by Tsiolkovskii, young men and women joined together to build rockets. The Soviet government supported them and, in 1933, sponsored the creation of a national institute to build rockets. The intellectual and engineering groundwork that they created eventually bore fruit a quarter century later with the launch of *Sputnik*, the world's first artificial satellite.[4] The received story, built on a series of willful distortions, masked a set of complex social and cultural processes, particularly the ways in which social and cultural factors outside state sponsorship—besides popular Marxist rhetoric about the role of technology—enabled the project of space exploration in the Soviet Union.

In the late 1920s and early 1930s, Tsiolkovskii's ideas on space exploration fed enormous popular interest in the cause of cosmic travel in the Soviet Union. With little or no support from the state, amateur and technically minded enthusiasts formed short-lived societies to discuss their interests and exchange information.[5] Some put up impressive exhibitions displaying the visions of the

---

3 "Titov, Denying God, Puts His Faith in People," *New York Times*, May 7, 1962.

4 Nicholas Daniloff, *The Kremlin and the Cosmos* (New York, 1972); James Harford, *Korolev: How One Man Masterminded the Soviet Drive to Beat America to the Moon* (New York, 1997).

5 For an international perspective, see Asif A. Siddiqi, "Nauka za stenami akademii: K. E. Tsiolkovskii i ego al'ternativnaia set' neformal'noi nauchnoi kommunikatsii" [Science

major prognosticators of the day such as Tsiolkovskii, the American Robert Goddard, and the Romanian-German Herman Oberth. In the popular media, advocates wrote about the power of technology to improve and remake Russian society. On the cultural front, the science fiction of Aleksei Tolstoi, the paintings of the Suprematists and the Amaravella collective, and Iakov Protazanov's famous interplanetary movie *Aelita* all engaged mystical and spiritual ideas of the place of humanity in the cosmos. These embryonic artistic, philosophical, and cultural explorations were important not only because they underlined an interest in the power of modern science but also because they disseminated ideas about space travel that were not simply about technology or modernization.

In a number of important ways, the space enthusiasts represented a counterexample to the more prominent elements of Soviet scientific and technical intelligentsia of the period. The two groups shared a few common traits. Both possessed a reverence for knowledge about the natural and material world. They exhibited an ambivalence between reason and faith, the former represented by an aspiration for modernization and the latter by a weakness for mysticism. Finally, although few of the space enthusiasts were revolutionary in the way that many Russian intelligentsia self-identified, the space obsessed saw themselves as the vanguard of a new era; the resistance they faced from public quarters for their utopian leanings emboldened their self-image as revolutionary and iconoclastic actors.

Yet two major characteristics distinguished the *kosmopolity* from the burgeoning Soviet scientific and technical intelligentsia. First, the space obsessed could claim no formal education in the natural sciences; their "higher" knowledge was often the result of informal schooling or, at best, mediocre institutions. Second, they embraced an anti-elitist stance that led them to actively engage with the popular culture of the day. In fact, their very embrace of more popular and populist forms of communication contributed as much to their estrangement from the orthodox scientific community as their lack of formal educational identifiers, the autodidact Tsiolkovskii being the quintessential embodiment of this alienation. Revisiting the noise that these space enthusiasts generated—which spanned the revolutionary divide of 1917—opens a critical window into the discursive strategies used by marginal scientific actors in revolutionary Russia to advance seemingly outlandish scientific ideas. Theirs was

beyond the walls of academic: K. E. Tsiolkovsky and his alternative network of informal scientific communication], *Voprosy istorii estestvoznaniia i tekhniki* [Issues in the history of science and technology] no. 4 (2005): 137–54.

the curious case of a demographic who strongly identified with the mainstream scientific and technical intelligentsia while being almost completely alienated from them.

Their cause, space exploration, was a small but important part of the wild cultural explorations of the New Economic Policy (NEP) era of the 1920s; it stemmed from both ideological oppositions and unions. Two intellectual strands contributed to the birth and sustenance of the 1920s space fad: technological utopianism and the mystical tradition of Cosmism. The former (seemingly modern, urban, international, materialist) clashed and meshed with the latter (superficially archaic, pastoral, Russian, spiritual), creating a complex ideological context for popular interest in spaceflight. If the language of technological utopianism has retained its place in the received history of Russian space travel, the role of Cosmism has been all but obscured. Recovering the "hidden" history of the Cosmist roots of Soviet space travel underscores how advocates of interplanetary flight from the early Bolshevik era navigated the entire spectrum between extreme technology fetishism (such as the amateur student societies) and extreme occult fascinations (the Biocosmists). The most important bridge between these two seemingly contradictory worldviews was Konstantin Tsiolkovskii, the patriarch of Russian space travel.

TECHNOLOGICAL UTOPIANISM

Russian utopian thought, which has a history long predating Bolshevism, Marxism, and indeed the nineteenth century, encompassed everything from overtly secular ideas to explicitly theological conceptions, and from monarchist ideals to anarchist visions. Already before the revolution of 1917, Russian utopian philosophy incorporated both Marxist notions and twentieth- century modernist ideals of science and technology. The revolution, however, allowed technological utopian visions to move from the wisp of dreams to the arena of *possibility*. After 1917, an ostensibly secular brand of millenarianism entered the picture.

The richest expressions of this meeting of sensibilities between utopia, technology, and possibility occurred during the NEP years, when the country moved through a rapid economic recovery that fostered what Sheila Fitzpatrick called "an upsurge of optimism among the Bolshevik leaders."[6] Notwithstanding harsh conditions in the cities, the urban population continued to grow through

---

6 Sheila Fitzpatrick, *The Russian Revolution*, 2nd ed. (Oxford, 1994), 113.

the 1920s due to peasant migration into the cities and massive demobilization following the end of the civil war. Despite one million unemployed in 1924, wages finally began to rise the same year, and the standard of living for the average factory worker—someone like the tireless space crusader Fridrikh Tsander—began to improve noticeably. With urban renewal accelerating and the first fruits of the revolution appearing, people conjured up old dreams of utopia in new and experimental ways. In his indispensable study *Revolutionary Dreams: Utopian Vision and Experimental Life in the Russian Revolution*, Richard Stites has described the many ways in which a wide spectrum of actors, from the poorest peasant to the most influential member of the intelligentsia, invoked, debated over, wrote about, and often rejected utopia.[7] From ritual to religion, mannerisms to machines, and art to architecture, utopian thought pervaded Soviet society at all levels. The utopian discussions of the period were not monolithic; in fact, their very contradictions and illogic often gave the social experimentation a rich and expansive tenor.

In the 1920s, technology played a major role in the social conjuring, debating, and enabling of utopias. Prominent voices of the scientific and technical intelligentsia, as well as Bolshevik leaders, engaged in this discourse, and indeed, their pronouncements reflected the same types of tensions between naïveté and pragmatism emblematic of broader NEP culture. Lenin's fascination with the rapid electrification of Russia, industrial Taylorism, and the construction of modernized railroads in Russia were certainly all practical, but they also carried with them an underlying idea that technology itself was a possible panacea.[8] Beyond his oft-quoted phrase "communism equals Soviet power plus the electrification of the entire country," Lenin had an almost evangelical view of the role of electricity, and technology in general, as if it had the power to transform nation and culture. H. G. Wells, after interviewing Lenin in 1920, wrote, "Lenin, [who] like a good orthodox Marxist, denounces all 'Utopians,' has succumbed at last to Utopia, the Utopia of electricians."[9] Even as Lenin

---

7   Richard Stites, *Revolutionary Dreams: Utopian Vision and Experimental Life in the Russian Revolution* (New York, 1989). See also Paul Josephson, "'Projects of the Century' in Soviet History: Large-Scale Technologies from Lenin to Gorbachev," *Technology and Culture* 36 (1995): 519–59.

8   For Lenin's personal role in plans for Soviet electrification, Taylorism, and railroads, see Jona-than Coopersmith, *The Electrification of Russia, 1880–1926* (Ithaca, NY, 1992), 153–55; Anthony Heywood, *Modernising Lenin's Russia: Economic Reconstruction, Foreign Trade, and the Railway* (Cambridge, UK, 1999); and Kendall E. Bailes, "Alexei Gastev and the Soviet Controversy over Taylorism, 1918–24," *Soviet Studies* 29 (1977): 373–94.

9   H. G. Wells, *Russia in the Shadows* (New York, 1921), 158–59.

underlined "the need to dream," he was also unforgiving of those who shied away from the harsh realities of practical action. In the prerevolutionary days, Lenin had been consistently critical of utopian socialists as well as the Populists for their unrealistic goals.[10]

Lev Trotskii (Leon Trotsky), another hardheaded revolutionary few would characterize as being impractical, also spoke rather uncritically of the powers of science and technology. In his 1923 tract *Literature and Revolution*, Trotskii wrote that because of the revolution, "[t]he shell of life will hardly have time to form before it will burst open again under the pressure of new technical and cultural achievements." Under the twin spells of science and utopia, Trotskii conjectured that advances in medicine would create a new "superman," able to "rise to the heights of an Aristotle, a Goethe, or a Marx."[11] Maksim Gor'kii (Gorky), one of the most important cultural commentators of the day, who held Konstantin Tsiolkovskii in very high esteem, frequently spoke of technology as miraculous and a panacea to the world's ills; he coined the phrase "an area of miracles" to speak of the power of science.[12]

Stites and others have pointed to the Russian interest in aviation, which held a much broader fascination for the Soviet populace in the 1920s than did spaceflight, as reflective of "a kinetic metaphor for liberation." Aviation represented a mixture of modernity and liberation that proved irresistible to many leading Bolsheviks. They appropriated its symbolic meanings to encourage and inculcate ideas about a new world and used it to bridge the literal and metaphorical gaps between urban and rural masses.[13] Yet although flight served as a metaphor for liberation, and perhaps even emancipation, it had some basis in the reality of the 1920s; both in Soviet Russia and the rest of the developed world, most urban citizens had seen pictures or drawings of airplanes if not an actual machine flying over their heads.

10 The "need to dream" quotation is from V. I. Lenin, *Polnoe sobranie sochinenii: Izdanie piatoe* [Complete collected works, 5th edition], vol. 6 (Moscow, 1959), 171–72. For Lenin and utopianism, see Stites, *Revolutionary Dreams* (cit. n. 7), 41–46; Robert C. Tucker, "Lenin's Bolshevism as a Culture in the Making," in *Bolshevik Culture: Experiment and Order in the Russian Revolution*, ed. Abbott Gleason, Peter Kenez, and Richard Stites (Bloomington, IN, 1985), 25–38; Rodney Barfield, "Lenin's Utopianism: State and Revolution," *Slavic Review* 21 (March 1971): 45–56.

11 Leon Trotsky, *Literature and Revolution* (Ann Arbor, MI, 1975).

12 Bernice Glatzer Rosenthal, "Political Implications of the Occult Revival," in *The Occult in Russian and Soviet Culture*, ed. Bernice Glatzer Rosenthal (Ithaca, NY, 1997), 390.

13 Richard Stites, "Utopias in the Air and on the Ground: Futuristic Dreaming in the Russian Revolution," *Russian History/Histoire Russe* 11, nos. 2–3 (1984): 236–57.

The dream of spaceflight in the 1920s differed in two significant ways from the concurrent interest in aviation. First, spaceflight, which was also about liberation from the earth, pushed the physical limits of emancipation beyond conception, past the boundaries of the visible skies. Second, spaceflight was entirely a discourse of fantasy: voyages beyond the atmosphere had no precedent or template. Liberation and fantasy in one shape or other are common to most utopian dreams, but by extending liberation (into space) and pushing utopian speculations beyond reality (into fantasy), the spaceflight discourse was infused with a "universal" (in both senses of the word) appeal that aviation lacked. For a brief period in the 1920s, spaceflight was the most potent manifestation of the "fantasy of liberation" and indeed may be seen as a "liberation of fantasy." The speculations about spaceflight would not have been possible without the promise of new twentieth-century technology that made the utopias of liberation and fantasy attainable. As one single force—a combination of technology, fantasy, and liberation—spaceflight promised what aviation could only offer in part: total liberation from the signifiers of the past—social injustice, imperfection, gravity, and ultimately, the earth.

COSMISM

Technology, fantasy, and liberation also figured prominently in a parallel set of ideas known as Russian Cosmism that has fed into a nationalist discourse in present-day Russia.[14] In the early twentieth century, Cosmism resonated strongly in some Russian intellectual circles as a corpus of philosophical thought about the evolution of both humanity and the universe and the relationship between the two.[15] The philosophy influenced many famous Russian intellectuals in the 1920s. They included Bolshevik ideologues, scientists, writers, philosophers, poets, artists, and architects, who gathered in Moscow and Kaluga, Tsiolkovskii's hometown, to discuss its attributes. Cosmism's intellectual

---

14 For links between modern Russian Cosmism and post-Soviet Russian nationalism, see James P. Scanlan, ed., *Russian Thought after Communism: The Recovery of a Philosophical Heritage* (Armonk, N., 1994), 26–28.

15 For only a sampling of works on Russian Cosmism since the late 1980s, see L. V. Fesenkova, ed., *Russkii kosmizm i sovremennost'* [Russian cosmism today] (Moscow, 1990); Svetlana Semenova, "Russkii kosmizm" [Russian cosmism], *Svobodnaia mysl'* [Free thought] no. 17 (1992): 81–97; Semenova and A. G. Gacheva, eds., *Russkii kosmizm: Antologiia filosofskoi mysli* [Russian cosmism: Anthology of philosophical thought] (Moscow, 1993); O. D. Kurakina, *Russkii kosmizm kak sotsiokul'turnyi fenomenon* [Russian cosmism as sociocultural phenomenon] (Moscow, 1993).

foundations comprised a hodgepodge of Eastern and Western philosophical traditions, theosophy, Pan-Slavism, and Russian Orthodox thinking.[16] The outcome was a nationalist and often reactionary philosophy that continues to attract the attention of many Russian intellectuals.

Tsiolkovskii served as a key contributor to the canon of Cosmism, but the most important worldview that fed into twentieth-century Cosmism stemmed from the writings of Nikolai Fedorovich Fedorov (1828–1903), the eccentric philosopher whose works influenced many, including Dostoevskii (Fyodor Dostoevsky), Gor'kii, and Tolstoi (Leo Tolstoy).[17] While working as a librarian at the Rumiantsev Library in Moscow, Fedorov developed his infamous *Filosofiia obshchego dela* (Philosophy of the common task), the most enduring and notorious of his many works.[18] Described by one Western biographer as "one of the most profound, comprehensive, and original ideas in the history of Russian speculation," Fedorov's doctrine, published after his death in 1906, was about "the common task" of all humanity, to resurrect the dead.[19] Fedorov's mission stemmed from a distinctly theocratic view of the universe in which he saw Christianity as primarily a religion of resurrection, an idea that attracted both Dostoevskii and Tolstoi. He believed that humanity's moral task was to emulate Christ and make bodily resurrection possible. Mass resurrection would finally eliminate the artificial boundaries among the "brotherhood" of humanity, that is, between previous and current generations. In other words, none of the ills of society could be solved without devising a solution to the inevitability of death. He argued that using all of the resources at its disposal, including science and technology, humanity should engage in a quest to reas-

16 For the best English-language meditation on Russian Cosmism as a historical process, see Michael Hagemeister, "Russian Cosmism in the 1920s and Today," in Rosenthal, *Occult in Russian and Soviet Culture* (cit. n. 12), 185–202.

17 Those said to be influenced by Fedorov included writers (Dostoevskii, Gor'kii, Odoevskii, Pasternak, Platonov, Tolstoi), political thinkers (Bogdanov, Lunacharskii), poets (Khlebnikov, Maiakovskii, Zabolotskii), painters (Filonov), architects (Mel'nikov), heliobiologists (Chizhevskii), and scientists (Tsiolkovskii, Vernadskii). For a description of the Moscow-based Fedorovtsy (supporters of N. F. Fedorov) in the 1920s, see Michael Hagemeister, *Nikolaj Fedorov: Studien zu Leben, Werk und Wirkung* [Nikolai Fedorov: Studies in his life, works, and activities] (Munich, 1989), 343–62.

18 Fedorov devotees independently printed and distributed 480 copies of the original in 1906. A second volume was issued in 1913. His writings have been collected in A. G. Gacheva and Svetlana Semenova, eds., *N. F. Fedorov: Sobranie sochinenii v chetyrekh tomakh* [Nikolai Fedrov: Collected works in 4 volumes], 5 vols. (vols. 1–4 and supplement) (Moscow, 1995–2000).

19 George M. Young Jr., *Nikolai F. Fedorov: An Introduction* (Belmont, MA, 1979), 7.

semble the corporeal particles lost in the "disintegration" of human death. In an ideal utopian setting ("as it ought to be"), Fedorov believed that there would be no birth and no death, only the progressive reanimation of the deceased millions from history.[20]

Two aspects of Fedorov's "philosophy of the common task" related to Cosmism in general and to voyages into space in particular. First, to achieve his ultimate goal of "liberation from death," Fedorov called for restructuring human society and its natural environment, which for him included not only the earth but the entire universe. In the early postrevolutionary era, the idea of "regulating nature" by taking absolute control over it resonated deeply with the scientific and technical intelligentsia, who, infected by Bolshevik claims of remaking the social universe, were also interested in remaking the natural one.[21] Second, Fedorov believed that humans from Earth would have to travel into the cosmos—to the moon, the planets, and stars—to recover disintegrated particles of deceased human beings that are spread throughout the universe. Once the bodies of the deceased were reconstituted (in forms that might not resemble humans), the resurrected would then settle throughout the universe. In his *Philosophy of the Common Task*, Fedorov wrote, "[The] conquest of the Path to Space is an absolute imperative, imposed on us as a duty in preparation for the Resurrection. We must take possession of new regions of Space because there is not enough space on Earth to allow the coexistence of all the resurrected generations."[22]

Fedorov's ideas of restructuring humanity and the cosmos, especially the supreme role of science and technology in this transformation, anticipated Tsiolkovskii's writings, which are sprinkled with the Promethean urge to remake everything that surrounds us. Many historians have claimed that

---

20 Summarized from Fedorov works collected in vols. 1 and 2 of Gacheva and Semenova, *N. F. Fedorov* (cit. n. 18).

21 The famous Russian geochemist Vladimir Vernadskii, who shared these views (although he probably never heard of Fedorov), headed the Commission for the Study of the Natural Productive Forces (KEPS), a body whose goals encompassed such transformative projects as harnessing solar and electromagnetic forces for the good of Russian society. Kendall E. Bailes, *Science and Russian Culture in an Age of Revolutions: V. I. Vernadsky and His Scientific School, 1863–1945* (Bloomington, IN, 1990). Remarkably, Bailes never once mentions Vernadskii's interest in Cosmism. For Vernadskii and Cosmism, see G. P. Aksenov, "O nauchnom odinochestve Vernadskogo" [The scientific isolation of Vernadsky], *Voprosy filosofii* [Issues in philosophy] no. 6 (1993): 74–87.

22 Jean Clair, "From Humboldt to Hubble," in *Cosmos: From Romanticism to the Avant-Garde*, ed. Jean Clair (Munich, 1999), 25; Young, *Nikolai F. Fedorov* (cit. n. 19), 182–83.

Fedorov inculcated Tsiolkovskii with his ideas about space travel. During his brief stay in Moscow as a teen in the 1870s, Tsiolkovskii had indeed met daily with Fedorov, who worked at a Moscow library. Fedorov played a critical role in supporting the young student in his struggle to learn more about the natural sciences. As Tsiolkovskii later remembered, "It is no exaggeration to say that for me he took the place of university professors."[23] Yet, those who suggest that Fedorov may have influenced Tsiolkovskii to take up the cause of spaceflight are certainly mistaken. Throughout his life, Tsiolkovskii himself maintained that during his tenure of study under Fedorov, the two never discussed space travel although both had independently begun thinking of the possibility by this time.[24]

In parallel with his more technical writings, Tsiolkovskii issued numerous short monographs, beginning in the late nineteenth century, that touched on the philosophy of cosmic travel. These two strands, the technical and the philosophical, intertwined and influenced each other throughout his life, and although his philosophical writings are less well known than his technical ones, they form a corpus of work that exceeds in size his combined works on aeronautics, rocketry, and space travel.[25] Tsiolkovskii brought a messianic

---

23 Konstantin Altaiskii, "Moskovskaia iunost' Tsiolkovskogo" [Tsiolkovsky's youth in Moscow], *Moscow*, no. 9:176–92 (1966), on 181.

24 The legend that Fedorov pointed Tsiolkovskii in the direction of space travel probably originated from scientist Viktor Shlovskii in his "'K' in 'Kosmonavtika ot A do Ia'" ["C" in "Cosmautics A–Z"], *Literaturnaia gazeta* [The literary gazette], April 7, 1971. See also V. E. L'vov, *Zagadochnyi starik: Povesti* [The enigmatic old man: Novellas] (Leningrad, 1977). Many Western and Russian authors, without any evidence, make a direct causal connection between Fedorov and Tsiolkovskii. Michael Holquist, "Konstantin Tsiolkovsky: Science Fiction and Philosophy in the History of Soviet Space Exploration," in *Intersections: Fantasy and Science Fiction*, ed. George E. Slusser and Eric S. Rabkin (Carbondale, IL, 1987), 74–86; Holquist, "The Philosophical Bases of Soviet Space Exploration," *Key Reporter* 50 (Winter 1985–86): 2-4; and Vladimir V. Lytkin, "Tsiolkovsky's Inspiration," *Ad Astra* (November–December 1998): 34–39.

25 Especially through the 1920s, during the height of the "space fad," Tsiolkovskii's output on philosophical topics increased dramatically. He self-published such works as *The Wealth of the Universe* (1920), *The Origins of Life on Earth* (1922), *Monism of the Universe* (1925), *Reason for Space* (1925), *The Future of Earth and Humanity* (1928), *The Will of the Universe: Unknown Intelligent Forces* (1928), *Love for Oneself or the Source of Egoism* (1928), *Intellect and Passion* (1928), *The Social Organization of Humanity* (1928), and *The Goal of Stellar Voyages* (1929). All of these works, and others unpublished during his lifetime, have been compiled into one volume: L. V. Golovanov and E. A. Timoshenkova, eds., *K. E. Tsiolkovskii: Genii sredi liudei* [K. E. Tsiolkovsky: A genius among men] (Moscow, 2002). For the best analysis of Tsiolkovskii's philosophical works, see V. S. Avduevskii, ed., *K. E. Tsiolkovskii: Kosmicheskaia filosofiia* [K. E. Tsiolkovsky: Cosmic philosophy] (Moscow, 2001), 370–472.

and transformative vision to the cause of spaceflight that mimicked some of
Fedorov's ideas about immortality and cosmic unity. He also drew upon occult
thought rooting back to German philosopher Carl du Prel, who was famous
for drawing a link between cosmic and biological evolution, that is, that
Darwinian natural selection acted on planetary bodies just as they acted on
living organisms.[26] In Tsiolkovskii's worldview, the occult, theories of evolution, and Christianity existed without contradiction. At a fundamental level,
Tsiolkovskii was a religious thinker whose life was an attempt to reconcile the
scientific views of nature that seemed to contradict his strong faith in Christ. As
such, he expended a great deal of energy explaining biblical events with the aid
of contemporary science.

Like Fedorov, Tsiolkovskii believed that humanity's place in the universe
depended on two related ideas, monism and panpsychism. He described both
of these concepts in *Monizm vselennoi* (Monism of the universe), a brochure he
self-published in 1925 that would be his most complete statement of cosmic
philosophy. According to his version of monism, all matter in the universe,
including organic matter, is made out of a single substance, has the same structure, and obeys the same set of laws. He explained panpsychism as the belief
that all matter is made up of "atoms of ether," even smaller than "regular" atoms,
which are in and of themselves *living organisms* or "happy atoms."[27] When
these atoms combine in different ways, they produce different living beings
with differing abilities. Because these ether atoms are indestructible, there is no
such thing as true death as the atoms can be reconstituted in different combinations from the one that gave life to a specific human being.[28]

For all their "progressive" ideas about the role of science and technology
and human expansion of space, Fedorov and Tsiolkovskii had a darker side to

26 For a sympathetic analysis of the differences between Fedorov and Tsiolkovskii's philosophies, see V. V. Kaziutinskii, "Kosmizm i kosmicheskaia filosofiia" [Cosmism and cosmic
philosophy], in *Osvoenie aerokosmicheskogo prostranstva: Proshloe, nastoiashchee, budushchee* [The conquest of aero-cosmic space: Past, present, and future], ed. B. V. Raushenbakh
(Moscow, 1997), 139–44.

27 K. E. Tsiolkovskii, *Monizm vselennoi* [Monism of the universe] (Kaluga, 1925). Tsiolkovskii's
ideas were not original; they were heavily influenced by the ideas of such German thinkers
as Gottfried Leibniz and Ernst Haeckel.

28 In *Volia vselennoi* [Will of the universe], a brochure published in 1928 in Kaluga, Tsiolkovskii
wrote, "Death is one of the illusions of a weak human mind. There is no death, for the existence of an atom in inorganic matter is not marked by memory and time—it is as if the latter
does not exist at all." K. E. Tsiolkovskii, "Volia vselennoi," in *K. E. Tsiolkovskii*, Golovanov
and Timoshenkova (cit. n. 25), 228–29.

their vision. Fedorov's "common task" had a distinctly totalitarian tinge as it did not allow choice in the equation, that is, he argued humans would *have* to participate in his project without exception. Tsiolkovskii's view of the search for human perfection also reflected his firm belief in eugenics; he advocated the extermination of imperfect plants and animal life and called for a "battle against the procreation of defective people and animals."[29] In a piece finished in 1918, he wrote:

> I do not desire to live the life of the lowest races [such as] the life of a negro or an Indian. Therefore, the benefit of any atom, even the atom of a Papuan, requires the extinction also of the lowest races of humanity, and in an extreme measure the most imperfect individuals in the races.[30]

This view of space travel, which combined the search for human perfection, racial purity, and occult thinking, provided the fundamental impetus to Tsiolkovskii's more mathematically inclined meditations on rocket flight into outer space. Tsiolkovskii seamlessly combined his fascinations with technology and the occult into a fully formed weltanschauung. Yet to much of his audience in the 1920s—especially those young and technology-minded students who were inspired to dream of space travel—his goal of space travel fit nicely with prevailing Bolshevik rhetoric connecting technology with modernity. The technophiles, in fact, believed that by avoiding Tsiolkovskii's mystical invocations, they could construct a vision of space travel that directly countered antiquated notions of the cosmos as part of an epistemology of superstition and folktales. In forming societies to argue their cause, they saw in space travel a vehicle for creating a new world of machines and men.

TECHNOLOGICAL UTOPIANISM: THE COSMIC SOCIETIES

Most of the men and women who organized cosmic societies in the 1920s did so without any material support or encouragement from the state. They did, however, absorb official discourses on the role of technology as a panacea for all social ills in new, postrevolutionary Russia. Space advocates saw in space exploration (and its corollary, rocketry) a manifestation of the cold hard

29 K. E. Tsiokovskii, "Liubov' k samomu sebe, ili istinnoe sebialiuboe," in *K. E. Tsiolkovskii,* Golovanov and Timoshenkova (cit. n. 25), 378–402, on 401.

30 K. Tsiolkovskii, "Etika ili estestvennye osnovy nravstvennosti" [Ethics, or the natural basis of morality], in *K. E. Tsiolkovskii,* ed. Avduevskii (cit. n. 25), 82.

power of rationality, science, and mathematics to move society ahead on the path of "progress" and "modernization." Several technology-enraptured (and short-lived) societies coalesced during the period of the space fad. Of these, the most important and influential was the Moscow-based Society for the Study of Interplanetary Communications (Obshchestva Izucheniia Mezhplanetnykh Soobshchenii, OIMS), formed in 1924. It was not only the first group in the world to effectively organize for the cause of space exploration but also the first to build a domestic and international network around the idea. The history of the organization, a combination of serendipity, willful devotion, and eventual loss of momentum due to indifference from the state, illustrates the ways in which technological utopianism inspired a few to bring an esoteric idea to many.[31]

The society emerged during the first intense wave of public fascination with spaceflight in the spring of 1924, set off by a story in the newspaper *Izvestiia* under the headline "Is Utopia Really Possible?" about the recently published meditations on spaceflight written by the foreigners Oberth and Goddard.[32] Spurred to promote a Russian source for such ideas, the sixty-six-year-old Tsiolkovskii immediately republished his own prerevolutionary works on spaceflight. Almost overnight the Soviet media began to devote considerable attention to the cosmos. News and rumors of Oberth and Goddard's exploits, the publication of Aleksei Tolstoi's new space fiction novel *Aelita*, and the "Great Mars Opposition" of August 1924—when Mars and Earth were closer to each other than in hundreds of years—fed an explosion of public interest in space. In one lengthy *Pravda* article ("Voyage into Cosmic Space"), the author narrated the new history of space exploration, harking back to Leonardo da Vinci, Cyrano de Bergerac, Jules Verne, and H. G. Wells. The history naturally culminated with the works of Tsiolkovskii, Oberth, and Goddard. Palpably excited by the optimism of the times, the writer concluded, "[W]ithin a few years, hundreds of heavenly ships will push into the starry cosmos."[33]

31 For a detailed account of the society, see Asif A. Siddiqi, "Making Spaceflight Modern: A Cultural History of the World's First Space Advocacy Group," in *The Societal Impact of Spaceflight*, ed. Steven J. Dick and Roger D. Launius (Washington, DC, 2007), 513–37.

32 "Novosti nauki i tekhniki: Neuzheli ne utopiia?" [Scientific and technological news: Is it utopia?], *Izvestiia VTsIK*, October 2, 1923.

33 M. Ia. Lapirov-Skoblo, "Puteshestviia v mezhplanetnye prostranstva" [Journeys in interplanetary space], *Pravda*, April 15, 1924. For Goddard's prominent role in the space fad, see Asif A. Siddiqi, "Deep Impact: Robert Goddard and the Soviet 'Space Fad' of the 1920s," *History and Technology* 20, no. 2 (2004): 97–113.

The media frenzy over space exploration in early 1924 might have faded away had it not been for some resourceful young men and women. In April 1924, about a dozen students at the prestigious Zhukovskii Military Air Engineering Academy's Military-Science Society (VNO) set up a Section on Reactive Motion to exchange ideas about rockets.[34] In compiling a list of goals, the section touched on all the key strategies that would characterize the ensuing space fad, from its technical side (building rockets), to outreach (lectures, publications, and bookstores), to building a community (by interesting others in the same topics), to opening a channel to the West (by collecting media from overseas), to acknowledging the artistic medium as a possible way to educate and popularize (by branching into film).

The section first organized a public lecture. One of the section leaders, Morris Leiteizen, whose father was a famous prerevolutionary Bolshevik, asked a family friend, Mikhail Lapirov-Skoblo, to do the honors. Lapirov-Skoblo, thirty-five years old and a rising member of the reconstituted postrevolutionary technical intelligentsia, had been briefly acquainted with Lenin. After the latter's death, he served as deputy chairman of the Scientific-Technical Department of the Supreme Council of the People's Economy (VSNKh, or Vesenkha), a body tasked with supervisory duties over applied research and development in Soviet industry. He also headed *Pravda*'s department of science and technology.[35] Tsiolkovskii's recently published works so inspired Lapirov-Skoblo that he wrote the first well-researched expositions on space travel in the postrevolutionary era in *Pravda* and other publications.[36]

Lapirov-Skoblo's lecture, held on the evening of Friday, May 30, 1924, was a resounding success. Tickets sold out two days earlier; on the day of the talk, the organizers were forced to call for the police to control the mass of people who wanted to attend. Attendees eagerly bought up all the utopian literature on space travel on display—H. G. Wells's *War of the Worlds*, Russian science fiction from Aleksei Tolstoi and Aleksandr Beliaev, and books by the popular science writer Iakov Perel'man. Lapirov-Skoblo's lecture, titled "Interplanetary

---

34 The leading VNO student members included V. P. Kaperskii, M. G. Leiteizen, A. I. Makarevskii, M. A. Rezunov, and N. A. Sokolov-Sokolenok., r. 4, op. 14, d. 197, ll. 32–33, Archive of the Russian Academy of Sciences (hereafter cited as ARAN), Moscow.

35 When Lenin supervised the formation of the State Commission for Electrification of Russia (GEOLRO) in 1920, he tapped Lapirov-Skoblo to represent the Vesenkha on GOELRO. For a biography, see r. 14, op. 14, d. 197, ll. 30–30b, ARAN.

36 For his other articles, both titled "Puteshestviia v mezhplanetnye prostranstva," see *Molodaia gvardiia* [Young guard], 1924, no. 5, and *Khochu vse znat'* [I want to know everything], 1924, no. 3:140.

Communications (How Modern Science and Technology Solves This Question)," may have been the first exposition on space exploration in Russia open to the general public. His lecture was a typical example of the rhetoric of the technological utopian space advocates; he linked the idea of spaceflight with both modern technology and the future of a new Bolshevik Russia, a nation he believed had left behind its roots in tradition, backwardness, and peasant life. He concluded by calling on the Soviet populace to build rocket engines to "transform into reality the centuries-old dream of flight into space."[37]

Following Lapirov-Skoblo's talk, section members invited the audience to sign up to form the core of a public society, thus opening up membership to laypeople outside the Zhukovskii Academy. While the complete list of 179 names has been lost, the surviving pages give a sense of these people. Of the 121 names preserved, 104 were men. The majority of the members (68) were young, between the ages of twenty and thirty. In terms of professions, a total of 96 members, that is, roughly 80 percent, were evenly split between students and workers. A smaller number identified themselves as "scientific workers," "writers," or "scientists and inventors."[38]

Grigorii Kramarov, elected to chair the new society's "presidium," recalled forty years later that no one had any illusions that the Soviet Union would soon be sending men into space. He remembered that "in the work of the society [we] all saw one more possibility to aid the Motherland, to aid in the building of socialism." Instead of building rockets, the society would bring science and technology to the masses. Its members were "convinced that the society's work would contribute to the preparation of cadres, who in the future would create the economic and scientific and technical base for solving the greatest problems."[39] They paid lip service to the notion that technology would improve social conditions in revolutionary Russia. In a speech to factory workers, Fridrikh Tsander, one of the principal activists in the society, spoke of the many benefits to be gained from space travel: of "senior citizens [who] will find

---

37 For the transcript, see r. 4, op. 14, d. 194, ll. 49–62, ARAN. For recollections of attendees, see r. 4, op. 14, d. 197, ll. 35–8, ARAN; G. Kramarov, *Na zare kosmonavtiki: K 40-letiiu osnovaniia pervogo v mire obshchestva mezhplanetnykh soobshchenii* [At the dawn of the space age: On the 40th anniversary of interplanetary communication] (Moscow, 1965), 25–28.

38 R. 4, op. 14, d. 196, ll. 6–21, ARAN; V. M. Komarov and I. N. Tarasenko, "20 iunia—50 let so vremeni sozdaniia v moskve obshchestva izucheniia mezhplanetnykh soobshchenii (1924g.)" [20 June: 50 years since the establishment of the society for interplanetary communication in Moscow], *Iz istorii aviatsii i kosmonavtiki* [From the history of aviation and spaceflight] 22 (1974): 75–82; Kramarov, *Na zare kosmonavtiki* (cit. n. 37), 28.

39 Kramarov, *Na zare kosmonavtiki* (cit. n. 37), 50.

it much easier to maintain health in [space]," of the "inhabitants of Mars ... [whose] inventions could help us to a great extent to become happy and well off," and of "astronomy, [which] more than the other sciences, calls upon man to unite for a longer and happier life."[40] When critics attacked their views for being utopian, the members responded by calling their opponents "conservative," thus locating supporters and detractors of space exploration within a binary world; one was either modern ("with science and technology") or traditional (against "progress").[41]

Throughout 1924, the society held numerous lectures and debates in Moscow, Leningrad, Kharkov, Ryazan, Tula, Saratov, and elsewhere, introducing the idea of space exploration to a huge audience beyond technology fetishists. But despite their many successes—including one near-riotous event in October 1924, when the Moscow horse militia had to be called out to control unruly crowds interested in rumors of a rocket launch to the moon that year—lack of state support proved to be the society's undoing. In late 1924, when the society petitioned the administrative department of the Moscow city council to register the organization officially, the city council rejected the application on the grounds that the society had "insufficient scientific strength among its members."[42] The society's members also had to deal with less committed members, who were unable to sustain interest in the face of both the widespread poverty of the times and the possibility that space exploration was decades away. Society head Kramarov remembered that the most common question from the audience after each lecture was "How quickly would flight to the planets be accomplished?"[43] When it became clear that travel into space was years, if not decades, away, the "accidental members" dispersed quickly, leaving only a handful of the truly dedicated to pursue the cause. Eventually, even the faithful had to come down to earth; most, such as Tsander, had little time to devote to activities that did not provide money for living. Valentin Chernov, for example, remembered later that his job as a violinist forced him to

---

40 See F. A. Tsander, "Doklad inzhenera F. A. Tsandera a svoem izobretenii" [Address of engineer F. A. Tsander on his invention], in *Iz nauchnogo naslediia* [Scientific legacy] (Moscow, 1967), 10–14.

41 V. Chernov, "Raketa na lunu" [Rocket to the moon], r. 4, op. 14, d. 194, ll. 1-3, ARAN.

42 R. 4, op. 14, d. 197, l. 19, ARAN. Tsander later confirmed that the lack of "scientific workers" among members of the "board of directors"—i.e., Tsander, Leiteizen, Kaperskii, Rezunov, Chernov, Serebrennikov, and Kramarov—was a source of dissension that contributed to the society's dissolution.

43 Kramarov, *Na zare kosmonavtiki* [At the dawn of the space age], (cit. n. 37), 56.

abandon the society.[44] Like many utopians, the society was unable to sustain a vision beyond the short term.

TECHNOLOGICAL UTOPIANISM: THE MEDIA

Dissemination of celebratory ideas about space travel during the NEP era depended greatly on the existence of vibrant popular scientific media, which directly equated technology with modernization and societal benefit.[45] The journal *Khochu vse znat'* (I want to know everything), published by the Leningrad-based newspaper *Rabochaia Gazeta* (Working gazette), for example, set out to "[help] readers in developing a material understanding of the world" and to "familiarize readers with the newest achievements in modern science and technology" that would benefit the revolution.[46] Publishers, both private and public, found that scientific titles were particularly popular among urban masses. Jeffrey Brooks notes that "publishers had difficulty keeping up with the demand for works in popular science," which "comprised a fifth of [all] titles published from 1921–27."[47] By the mid-1920s, biweekly and monthly journals devoted to popular science were ubiquitous on newsstands and included both new and older publications.[48] The partially independent Leningrad-based publisher P. P. Soikin, which published the journals *Mir prikliuchenii* (World of adventure), *Priroda i liudi* (Nature and people), and *Vestnik znaniia* (Journal of knowledge), played an influential role in the popularization of science through the second and third decades of the twentieth century. Having

---

44 Ibid., 51–52. Tsander, in his autobiography, notes that "the lack of published material and of spare time did not permit us to work intensively." "Autobiography of Friedrich Arturovich Tsander, Mechanical Engineer," in N. A. Rynin, *Rockets*, vol. 2, no. 4, of *Interplanetary Flight and Communication*, trans. T. Pelz (Jerusalem, 1971), 187.

45 For a view on the role of popular science in the postrevolutionary period, see James T. Andrews, *Science for the Masses: The Bolshevik State, Public Science, and the Popular Imagination in Soviet Russia, 1917–1934* (College Station, TX, 2003).

46 Advertisement for *Khochu vse znat'* in inside cover of various issues of *Vestnik znaniia* [Herald of knowledge].

47 Jeffrey Brooks, "The Breakdown in Production and Distribution of Printed Material, 1917–1927," in Gleason, Kenez, and Stites, *Bolshevik Culture* (cit. n. 10), 159, 168–69.

48 Popular science journals included *Bor'ba mirov* (The worlds' struggle), *Khochu vse znat'* (I want to know everything), *Krasnaia nov'* (Red virgin soil), *Mir prikliuchenii* (World of adventure), *Nauka i tekhnika* (Science and technology), *Pioner* (Pioneer), *Priroda i liudi* (Nature and people), *Tekhnika i zhizn'* (Technology and life), *Tekhnika—molodezhi* (Technology for youth), *Vestnik znaniia* (Journal of knowledge), *V masterskoi prirodi* (In nature's workshop), *Vsemirnyi sledopyt* (Universal detective), and *Znanie—sila* (Knowledge is power).

published Lenin's first legal work in prerevolutionary times, Soikin remained one of the few imperial-era publishing concerns allowed to operate during the NEP years.[49] Although private publishers were producing only about 5 percent of all copies of books in 1925, Soikin carved out a dominating niche in the popular science market that remained unchallenged until complete nationalization of the press in the post-NEP era. Circulation of *Vestnik znaniia*, one of Soikin's most popular monthlies, for example, increased from 25,000 in 1925 to 75,000 by 1931.[50] Such publications were widely available via bookstores such as Leningrad's Nauka i Znanie (Science and Knowledge), one of the largest in the city, which catered exclusively to scientific and applied scientific titles. Its catalog in 1928 boasted around 7,000 titles from "all branches of [scientific and technical] knowledge."[51]

Space and space-related topics constituted a significant, although by no means major, slice of the popular science literature. Based upon an in-depth search through the popular science literature in early twentieth-century Russia, my research suggests that the number of articles on spaceflight published between 1923 and 1932 (inclusive), the key years spanning the space fad, amounted to nearly 250 articles and more than thirty books. Compared with the other pressing topics of the day, this output did not represent a great number, but that so many works on space exploration were published on such an arcane subject is in and of itself a striking result.[52] By comparison, in the United States, only *two* nonfiction monographs on spaceflight appeared in the same period. Only in Germany, the single Western nation with a vocal spaceflight community, were there comparable levels of media attention.[53]

The content of popular science media suggests that readers were not merely passive receptors of information on spaceflight. Brooks has noted that Soviet newspapers during the NEP era contained three spheres of discourse:

---

49   A. M. Admiral'skii and S. V. Belov, *Rytsar' knigi: Ocherki zhizni i deiatel'nosti P.P. Soikina* [Knight of books: Sketches from the life and work of P. P. Soikin] (Leningrad, 1970).

50   Publication runs are from the back pages of *Vestnik znaniia* in 1925 and 1931.

51   From commercial advertisements in the back covers of various popular science magazines in 1928.

52   Asif A. Siddiqi, "The Rockets' Red Glare: Spaceflight and the Russian Imagination, 1857–1957" (PhD diss., Carnegie Mellon University, 2004).

53   For the two American monographs, see Robert H. Goddard, *A Method of Reaching Extreme Altitudes*, Smithsonian Miscellaneous Collections, vol. 71, no. 2 (Washington, DC, 1919); David Lasser, *The Conquest of Space* (New York, 1931). For the German space fad, see Michael J. Neufeld, "Weimar Culture and Futuristic Technology: The Rocketry and Spaceflight Fad in Germany, 1923–1933," *Tech. Cult.* 31 (October 1992): 725–52.

explanatory, interactive, and informational.[54] The dialogue over spaceflight in popular science journals echoed these divisions. Both *Nauka i tekhnika* (Science and technology) and *Vestnik znaniia* had forums for interacting with readers. The former, under the banner "Correspondence with Readers," published more than two dozen responses to readers' letters per issue. Inquiries and comments came from all over the country: Moscow, Rostov-on-Don, Voronezh, Leningrad, Krasnodar, Voznesensk, Kharkov, Grozny, Kiev, Taganrog, Donbass, and elsewhere. *Vestnik znaniia* had a similar section titled "Living Communication," which published numerous editorial responses to readers' letters on various topics. The transformative, beneficial, and modernizing aspects of space travel were rarely, if ever, questioned in the exchange of ideas.

Many readers asked where to get materials on space, a service that the journals provided repeatedly, pointing out not only articles on space published in the journals' own pages but also those published elsewhere.[55] Some of the responses provided information while others clarified ambiguous topics. To comrade A. Semenov from Leningrad, for example, *Nauka i tekhnika* used a drawing to illustrate the changing distances between the planets. In some cases, the journal editors displayed a distinctly pedantic attitude to its readers, implying that lack of scientific and technical knowledge about space travel was indicative of ignorance about the modern world. For example, *Nauka i tekhnika* chastised comrade Pavliuchenko from Aleksandrovka for his "bewilderment" about movement through space in the absence of matter to push against.[56] On occasion, the journals acknowledged the "many numbers of questions to the Editors" on the topic; *Vestnik znaniia* claimed that numerous readers of the journal were dissatisfied with short articles on space travel and demanded complete books on the topic.[57] Some readers' communications required special attention.

54 Jeffrey Brooks, "The Press and Its Message: Images of America in the 1920s and 1930s," in *Russia in the Era of NEP: Explorations in Soviet Society and Culture*, ed. Sheila Fitzpatrick, Alexander Rabinowitch, and Richard Stites (Bloomington, IN, 1991), 231–52.

55 "Pred'iaviteliiu bileta avio-loterei ser. 008, no. 10220 (Baku)" [Holder of the avia-lottery ticket serial number 008, 10220 (Baku)], *Nauka i tekhnika* no. 34 (August 19, 1927): 35; Ia. I. Perel'man, "Mezhplanetnye polety" [Interplanetary flights], *Vestnik znaniia* no. 4 (1928): 254; and "Tov. Miklashevskomu (Moscow)" [To Comrade miklashevsky (Moscow)], *Nauka i tekhnika* no. 23 (June 9, 1928): 31.

56 "Tov. A. Semenovu (Leningrad)" [To Comrade Semenov (Moscow)], *Nauka i tekhnika* no. 47 (November 18, 1927): 28; "Tov. Pavliuchenko (d. Aleksandrovka)" [To Comrade Paviluichenko (village of Alexandrovka)], *Nauka i tekhnika* no. 14 (April 1928): 30. For an answer to a similar question, see "L'vovu" [To L'vov], *Vestnik znaniia* no. 2 (January 1931): 127.

57 "Ot redkatskii" [From the editors], *Vestnik znaniia* no. 11 (1928): 551.

Vestnik znaniia returned comrade Iosifov's manuscript, "The Importance of the Planet and Its Satellites in the Solar System," with several points explaining why his conclusions were "absolutely incorrect." In the same readers' section, comrade Goldenveizer conjectured about the unpleasant sensations space travelers might experience in a vessel, some of which had been discussed by Tsiolkovskii, Noordung, and others.[58] In one case, when a reader anticipated Fermi's paradox in relation to the possibility of space travel, *Vestnik znaniia* devoted a full article with responses from prominent writers, including Tsiolkovskii and Iakov Perel'man, to the question "Is Interplanetary Communications Possible?"[59] According to the writers, the answer was a resounding "yes," but only because modern science and technology would make it possible.

The Cosmopolitans

Beyond societies and publishing, space advocates of the 1920s also used the medium of the *vystavka*, or "display," to publicize their cause. Through exhibits, enthusiasts were able to let their visions run free in more creative ways than was possible via lectures or publications. By exposing the possibility of space travel for the first time to thousands, they served a very important role during the space fad. Unlike the technological utopians who organized or wrote, exhibition organizers represented a constituency that embraced certain mystical ideas about spaceflight. In their lexicon, Tsiolkovskii assumed near-messianic status in a cause that was equal amounts of fetishizing of technology and speculation about human evolution. Recovering the history of the exhibitions underscores how in the 1920s, the line between lunar aspirations and lunacy was often invisible and that the lexicon of technological utopians was frequently indistinguishable from those who were mystically minded.

In 1925, a group of spaceflight enthusiasts organized a small exhibition of spaceflight-related artifacts in Kiev.[60] Although the exhibit remained open for less than three months, its success prompted one of its organizers,

---

58 "I. T. Iosifovu" and "Podp. Goldenveizeru," in *Vestnik znaniia* no. 19 (October 10, 1931): 1004.

59 "Vozmozhny li mezhplanetnye soobshcheniia?" [Are interplanetary communications possible?] *Vestnik znaniia* no. 4 (1930): 152–53. Fermi's paradox describes the seeming contradiction of our galaxy being more than a billion years old—and therefore possibly full of alien life—but humanity's having no contact with them.

60 The only detailed documentary evidence on the exhibition are three letters from Fedorov to Tsiolkovskii describing the works of the Kiev Society, written in August–September 1925. Fedorov to Tsiolkovskii, August 16, 1925, Kiev, r. 4, op. 14, d. 195, ll. 10–12, ARAN.

Aleksandr Fedorov, to join with the Moscow-based Association of Inventors (Assotsiatsiia Izobretatelei-Izobretateliam, AIIZ) to open the world's first international exhibition on space travel in 1927.[61] The AIIZ, a forum for amateur enthusiasts to discuss their interests in science and technology, had recently created the Sector for Propaganda and Popularization of Astronautics to promote the cause of spaceflight.[62] The sector's leading members included a motley crew of self-described inventors: a pilot, a former convict, a student, a technician, a librarian, and Fedorov.[63] Obsessed with Tsiolkovskii, the idiosyncratic Fedorov found a shared cause in his fellow exhibition organizers, who, like Fedorov, seemed to see the old man in overtly evangelical terms. In one letter to Tsiolkovskii, Fedorov wrote that he considered himself "fortunate to work under the leadership of creative great ideas, a thinker of our times and a preacher of great inconceivable truths!"[64]

Having organized the previous exhibition in Kiev, Fedorov suggested to the sector that it host a major exhibition of space artifacts in Moscow. The idea was to construct models of rockets and spacecraft conceived by the leading Soviet and foreign theoreticians of the day and display them with information for curious visitors. The association planned to display many of Tsiolkovskii's publications on spaceflight in one place—a library of sorts that they called the "smithy of all inventors."[65] The exhibition, which would also commemorate the tenth anniversary of the great October Revolution, would be augmented by a publicity blitz on space travel, including lectures in dozens of locales in and around the capital city. The ragtag band of organizers united in their zealous belief in the power of "invention" and "inventors" and held up Tsiolkovskii as some sort of "prophet" of a new era, "superior even to Edison."[66]

61 The literal translation of AIIZ is "Association of Inventor-to-Inventor," but the society was commonly known as the Association of Inventors.
62 R. 4, op. 14, d. 198, l. 41, ARAN. The precise word they used was *zvezdoplavaniie*, which literally translates as "stellar dynamics" in the same way that *vozdukhoplavaniie* means "aerodynamics." The closest English word is "astronautics," a term that Belgian writer J. J. Rosny invented. Other sections in the AIIZ included one for "culture-propaganda," one for language, and one for developing a universal language.
63 The "organizational committee" of the AIIZ's astronautics sector included G. A. Polevoi (pilot), I. S. Beliaev (former convict), A. S. Suvorov (student), Z. G. Piatetskii (technician), and O. V. Kholoptseva (librarian). R. 4, op. 14, d. 198, ll. 1–2, ARAN.
64 Fedorov to Tsiolkovskii, September 7, 1926, Moscow, f. 555, op. 4, d. 641, ll. 1–5, ARAN.
65 Efofbi [O. V. Khloptseva, pseud.] and Polevoi to Tsiolkovskii, February 5, 1927, Moscow, f. 555, op. 3, d. 198, ll. 6–8, ARAN.
66 Efofbi to Tsiolkovskii, December 3, 1928, Moscow, f. 555, op. 3, d. 199, ll. 5–6, ARAN.

Although Soviet-era accounts focused solely on the organizers' fascination with modern technology, Fedorov and his associates were inspired not only by the products of modern engineering, but also by a mystic calling. They referred to themselves as "cosmopolitans" (*kosmopolity*), a word derived from the term *cosmopolite* ("citizen of the world"), and their cause as "cosmopolitanism" (*kosmopolizm*).[67] Unlike many other technically minded popularizers of space exploration in the 1920s who carefully ignored Tsiolkovskii's spiritually oriented works about Cosmism and human destiny, the exhibition organizers embraced them, deifying Tsiolkovskii as a preacher, a visionary, the father of cosmopolitanism. They embraced the "master's" vision of animate matter and monism and believed in the importance of their efforts as part of a big evolutionary leap for all of humanity. In several effusive communications to Tsiolkovskii (the "first honorary captain rocket-mobilist") in late 1927, the organizers referenced Leibniz's worldview on monism and underscored the power of inventors to "find the resources for human immortality"—the foundation of the Cosmist view of the universe.[68] Their rationale for space exploration had as much to do with equating technology with modernization as with a self-important and mystical notion of human destiny that harked back to the nineteenth century.

The exhibition, unimaginatively named the "World's First Exhibition of Models of Interplanetary Apparatus, Mechanisms, Instruments, and Historical Materials," opened on April 24, 1927, not far from what is now Maiakovskii Square at number 68 (now 28) Tverskaia Street, one of Moscow's biggest thoroughfares. Open to the public for two months, the exhibition had an elaborately designed entrance with a huge display of an imagined planetary landscape, designed and built by Arkhipov, placed behind a large pane of glass. Part of the display, somewhat incorrectly called "Lunar Panorama," showed a hypothetical planet with orange soil and blue vegetation crisscrossed by straight canals. A giant silver rocket descended from the starry sky while a voyager in a spacesuit (made of plywood) stood at the edge of a crater. Organizer Mikhail Popov

---

67 AIIZ to Tsiolkovskii, January 21, 1927, Moscow, f. 555, op. 3, d. 198, ll. 1–1ob, ARAN. Although nearly identical, the word *kosmopolizm* differed in meaning and etymology from the pejorative term *kosmopolitizm* that party ideologues used in the late 1940s to describe a "decadent" and "bourgeois" lifestyle during the late Stalin years. The latter word was first introduced into public discourse in January 1949. *Kosmopolit* was probably derived from the early seventeenth-century French word cosmopolite, as in a "citizen of the world."
68 Efofbi to Tsiolkovskii, December 7, 1927, Moscow, f. 555, op. 3, d. 198, ll. 34–34ob, ARAN; AIIZ to Tsiolkovskii, December 18, 1927, Moscow, f. 555, op. 3, d. 198, ll. 38–38ob, ARAN.

described the feeling of entering the exhibition: "By taking a pair of steps, I crossed over the threshold of one epoch to another, into the space [era]."[69]

Although state organs ignored the show, it succeeded resoundingly with the public. According to the organizers, in two months, between 10,000 and 12,000 people visited the exhibition. Visitors included schoolchildren, workers, service employees, artists, scientists, policemen, and such luminaries as poet Vladimir Maiakovskii.[70] Visitors, who were invited to record their impressions in a book of comments, were both effusive and candid. One person, who signed as "Gorev," wrote, "Our mind is not accustomed to all the 'wonderful and unknown' which literally was [sic] seen and heard, as if in a dream, yet we understand that this is not a fantasy but a completely feasible idea supported by the achievements of science and engineering." Another person, an artist from the Third State Cinematographic Studio, recommended that "it would be desirable that our inventors achieve the first landing on the moon." One of the most captivated visitors was S. G. Vortkin, a reporter from the most important workers' news daily, *Rabochaia Moscow*, who wrote, "I am going to accompany you on the first flight. I am quite serious about this. As soon as I heard what you had done, I tried in every way to make certain that you would take me with you. Please do not refuse my request."[71]

Spaceflight in Art and Culture

The degree of popular Soviet fascination with space in the 1920s is also underlined by how deeply it resonated in the various art forms of the day. From literature to film to painting to poetry to architecture to language, clusters of artists produced works that reflected their belief that cosmic travel was an inevitable part of their future. A small sampling of this vast output—Tolstoi's novel *Aelita*, Protazanov's movie of the same title, Malevich's Suprematist paintings, and the Amaravella group's artwork—highlights some of the key dimensions of this cultural discourse. On the surface, artists with a spiritual-flavored view of the cosmos may have been disengaged from the modernist technologically minded utopians, but in fact they were linked by a network united in the cause of space exploration. And like their more "scientifically minded" space-enthusiast

---

69 Samoilovich, *Grazhdanin vselennoi* (cit. n. 1), 181.
70 "Vospominaniia Z. G. Piatetskogo," r. 4, op. 14, d. 198, l. 38, ARAN; "Vospominaniia O. V. Kholoptsevoi," r. 4, op. 14, d. 198, l. 11, ARAN.
71 Comments from Rynin, *Rockets* (cit. n. 44), 205–6.

colleagues, the artists produced their populist work largely isolated from the elite Soviet scientific and technical intelligentsia of the NEP era.

Literature

The most widely disseminated media for communicating ideas about space exploration was *nauchno-fantastika* (literally, "scientific-fantasy"). Although many historians have explored the various dimensions of Soviet science fiction in the early decades of the twentieth century, its use of space as a plot or philosophical device has remained largely unscrutinized.[72] Space fiction, which constituted about one-fifth of all Soviet science fiction in the postrevolutionary period to World War II, was remarkable for its disproportionate social resonance given the subgenre's low numbers. To some degree, most of the space-related works reflected the same characteristics of the broader science fiction literature, that is, almost all such works were technologically optimistic and can be divided into adventure stories (*krasnyi pinkerton*, or "red detective") and future utopias. Richard Stites's claim that "[Soviet] science fiction was a striking example of revolutionary discourse because of its total vision of communist life and its treatment of 'revolutionary dreams'" was also true for the smaller subset of space fiction.[73] Although the stories were less about social than technological revolution, the prevailing mood of revolution allowed the latter to be conflated with the former.

The most famous Soviet science fiction novel of the 1920s, Aleksei Tolstoi's *Aelita: Zakat Marsa* (Aelita: Sunset of Mars), first published in serialized form in 1922–23, remains the most famous *space* fiction work of the period.[74] It also perfectly encapsulated the contradictory themes of space advocacy in the 1920s. In the story, an engineer and a soldier voyage to Mars, where the latter incites a proletarian revolution among the bourgeois Martians. Aelita is the queen of Mars who falls in love with the Red Army soldier. On

---

72 For general reviews of early Soviet science fiction, see Darko Suvin, "The Utopian Tradition of Russian Science Fiction," *Modern Language Review* 66 (1971): 139–59; A. F. Britikov, *Russkii Sovetskii nauchno-fantasticheskii roman* [The Russian and Soviet science fiction novel] (Leningrad, 1970); Patrick L. McGuire, *Red Stars: Political Aspects of Soviet Science Fiction* (Ann Arbor, MI, 1985).

73 Stites, *Revolutionary Dreams* (cit. n. 7), 167–68.

74 The novel was originally published in three serialized parts in the journal *Krasnaia nov'*. In 1923, it was published as a stand-alone novel as *Aelita (Zakat Marsa)* (Moscow, 1923).

one level, the novel incorporates many elements of postrevolutionary utopian science fiction: a bourgeois enemy, a socialist revolution, modern science and technology, adventure and romance borrowed from Edgar Rice Burroughs, and utopian dreaming. Yet *Aelita*'s narrative also has hints of mysticism, especially ideas infused with theosophy and ancient anthroposophic ideas, not dissimilar to Fedorov and Tsiolkovskii's Cosmist views of the universe.[75] Defending his position from critics who blamed him for being too "emotional" in the novel, Tolstoi wrote, "Art—an artistic creation—appears momentarily like a dream. It has no place for logic, because its goal is not to find a cause for some sort of event, but to give in all its fullness a living piece of cosmos."[76] His use of the lexicon of panpsychism suggests a link to the mystical side of Tsiolkovskii and the Cosmists.[77]

Aelita, despite its invocation of space travel, or maybe because of its Cosmist overtones, was a novel less about looking forward than looking to the past. Although regarded as the most important Soviet science fiction novel of the period, *Aelita*, Halina Stephan rightly claims, "concluded rather than inaugurated a literary tradition." Yet, the technologically minded spaceflight enthusiasts of Tolstoi's day avoided the mysticism and found it futuristic since the novel was the first of the period that used a rocket for interplanetary travel. Members of the Moscow Society for the Study of Interplanetary Communications were so taken by Tolstoi's use of the rocket that they considered using the story to develop a film script —a project that was brought to fruition by others.[78]

75 Halina Stephan makes a similar point. Stephan, "Aleksei Tolstoi's *Aelita* and the Inauguration of Soviet Science Fiction," *Canadian-American Slavic Studies* 18 (1984): 63–75.
76 Tolstoi quoted in Ibid., 72–73.
77 See also Ian Christie, "Down to Earth: *Aelita* Relocated," in *Inside the Film Factory: New Approaches to Russian and Soviet Cinema*, ed. Richard Taylor and Ian Christie (London, 1991), 97–98; Rosenthal, introduction to *Occult in Russian and Soviet Culture* (cit. n. 12), 25.
78 Leiteizen to Tsiolkovskii, May 4, 1924, Moscow, f. 555, op. 4, d. 356, ll. 2–3, ARAN. In addition to *Aelita*, Aleksandr Bogdanov's *Krasnaia zvezda* (Red star) enraptured space enthusiasts of the period. Less about spaceflight than about an idealized Communist utopia on the planet Mars, the novel has also been seen by some scholars as a warning on how socialism might take on distinctly totalitarian tones if sufficiently militarized. The Society for the Study of Interplanetary Communications evidently established communication with Bogdanov in 1924, interested in his idea of using atomic power to propel spaceships. Space enthusiasts were less likely to explore Bogdanov's philosophical arguments than his technological vision; both parties shared a view of technology as autonomous, positive, and liberating. Loren R. Graham, "Bogdanov's Inner Message," in *Red Star: The First Bolshevik Utopia*, ed. Loren R. Graham and Richard Stites (Bloomington, IN, 1984), 241–53.

Film

The movie version of Tolstoi's *Aelita* appeared soon after publication of the print version and was directed by Iakov Protazanov, the Russian film director of prerevolutionary fame.[79] Released officially in September 1924 at the peak of the space fad, *Aelita* has since been hailed as the most important Soviet science fiction movie of the interwar era. It also contributed enormously to the popularization of spaceflight in Soviet culture in the 1920s. For example, interest in the movie after its release drove up attendance numbers at interplanetary talks sponsored by space societies such as the OIMS. The film also established a new standard for Soviet cinema, if not in quality, then certainly in popularity and hype. Weeks of intense advertising campaigns in *Pravda* and *Kino-gazeta* (Movie gazette) preceded its release, while airplanes dropped thousands of leaflets announcing the opening over Voronezh.[80] Tickets for the opening shows sold out, and the size of the crowd on opening night prevented even Protazanov from attending.

Protazanov, who, like Tolstoi, had only recently returned to the Soviet Union from exile, engineered a significant transformation in Tolstoi's relatively conventional novel, producing a remarkable movie that not only mirrored and telescoped many prevailing social concerns of the NEP-era in movie form but also critiqued Tolstoi's novel itself. With the help of scriptwriters Aleksei Faiko and Fedor Otsep, Protazanov reimagined Tolstoi's original account of the voyage to Mars as a dream in the mind of the protagonist Los'.[81] The so-called revolution on Mars—which occupies only one-fourth of the film—is riddled with ambiguities that do not demarcate strictly along bipolar lines (capitalist–communist, benevolent–exploitative); nothing is really what it seems. Here, Los' is not simply a one-dimensional caricature of the new Soviet man but rather a man living in and mirroring the contradictory realities of NEP life.

---

79 M. Aleinikov, *Iakov Protazanov: O tvorcheskom puti rezhisera* [Iakov Protzanov: On the creative path of a filmmaker], 2nd ed. (Moscow, 1957); Aleinikov, *Iakov Protazanov* (Moscow, 1961); Ian Christie and Julian Graffy, eds., *Protazanov and the Continuity of Russian Cinema* (London, 1993); Denise J. Youngblood, "The Return of the Native: Yakov Protazanov and Soviet Cinema," in Taylor and Christie, *Inside the Film Factory* (cit. n. 77), 103–23.

80 The movie was produced by a new multinational company, Mezhrabpom-Rus', a joint Russian-German company that combined Mezhrabpom (International Workers' Aid), a Berlin-based relief organization and Rus', a Russian production company formed in 1918. Richard Taylor, *The Politics of the Soviet Cinema, 1917–1929* (Cambridge, UK, 1979), 74.

81 Faiko and Otsep made changes to the original plot with Tolstoi's agreement. Aleinnikov, *Iakov Protazanov* (cit. n. 79), 32. Most Western sources incorrectly list his name as "Otsen" instead of the correct "Otsep."

In the movie *Aelita*, Protazanov sought to produce an "impartial" work, so the negative response surprised him. By and large, the state media criticized the film. In fact, the movie caused so much controversy that as late as 1928, newspapers and journals were still engaged in attacking the movie for being "alien to the working class," for its "petty bourgeois ending" because Los' returns to the domesticities of marriage, and for being "too Western."[82] Although many critics wrote off *Aelita* as a misstep in Protazanov's long career, it was an incredibly popular film; it did, after all, feature evocative acting, exotic scenes in interplanetary space, a glamorous princess, and women in provocative costumes. Grigorii Kramarov, the head of the OIMS, later underscored how "the book and film played a significant role in strengthening interest towards interplanetary communications and contributed to the development of activities of our Society."[83] Among those deeply affected by the hoopla over *Aelita* was ten-year-old Vladimir Chelomei; forty-five years later, as general designer of the Soviet space program, he named a new project of his, a huge space complex to send the first Soviet cosmonauts to Mars, *Aelita*.[84]

Art

Besides *Aelita*, both the novel and the film, other Russian works of art crossed the lines dividing technology and mysticism. Some scholars have claimed connections between the Russian avant-garde and Cosmism, arguing that the universal views of Nikolai Fedorov deeply influenced artistic personalities such as Vasilii Kandinskii, Kazimir Malevich, and Pavel Filonov.[85] But these connections were neither monolithic nor consistent. No single movement encapsulated the contradictions of the Soviet space fad better than did the Suprematists. Mentored by one of the legendary artists of the Russian avant-garde, Malevich, the Suprematists exemplified the duality and ambiguity of the

---

82 Youngblood, "Return of the Native" (cit. n. 79), 111–12; Youngblood, *Soviet Cinema in the Silent Era, 1918–1935* (Ann Arbor, MI, 1985), 30–32. For a list of reviews, see Aleinikov, *Iakov Protazanov* (cit. n. 79), 408. For Protazanov's comment about being "impartial," see page 31 of Aleinikov's study.

83 Kramarov, *Na zare kosmonavtiki* (cit. n. 37), 19–20.

84 Asif A. Siddiqi, *The Soviet Space Race with Apollo* (Gainesville, FL, 2003), 745–54.

85 Iurii Linnik, *Russkii kosmizm i russkii avangard* [Russian cosmism and the Russian avant-garde] (Petrozavodsk, 1995); Michael Holquist, "Tsiolkovsky as a Moment in the Prehistory of the Avant-Garde," in *Laboratory of Dreams: The Russian Avant-Garde and Cultural Experiment*, ed. John E. Bowlt and Olga Matich (Stanford, CA, 1996), 100–117.

space fad, cutting across not only mysticism (Cosmism) and science (space technology) but also the time and politics of the imperial and Bolshevik eras.

Suprematism as an organized movement of Russian and Soviet artists developed in the mid-1910s by extending and rejecting many of the foundations of Cubism. It reached its peak right after the October Revolution and then expanded into other media (principally architecture) in the early 1920s before losing direction late in the decade. Malevich had unveiled Suprematism at an exhibition of futurist art in 1915, with works that in their geometric shapes and colors completely dispensed with representations of conventional space and perspective. The paintings acquired a peculiarly compelling nature by the juxtaposition of colors and shapes that conveyed a continuum of space and time rather than self-contained and defined objects or ideas. Malevich himself called his work the "nonobjective world," that is, a perception of the environment's distilled spaciousness.[86]

Such an approach naturally led many Suprematist artists to eulogize first aviation and then ultimately the cosmos as the ultimate environment of spaciousness. In their paintings, such as Boris Ender's *Cosmic Landscape* (1923), space—both cosmic and otherwisebecame an integral part of the composition instead of "filler" in more traditional artistic creations. Malevich expressed interest in the most modern frontiers of art and science and technology, and he spent many years in pursuit of what he called the "science of art." He firmly believed in the power of technological "progress" and, like many other intellectuals of the day, supported the perfection of nature via artificial means. Malevich wrote, "I shall make my whole state comfortable and convenient, and, what is more, I shall convert other states and eventually the whole globe to my comfort and convenience."[87] His writings show an undeniably technologically utopian gloss, sprinkled with flirtations with anarchist ideas. Some scholars have suggested that Malevich, like many other Russian intellectuals, was captivated by mysticism and theosophy. For example, Igor Kazus claimed Malevich was "the first Russian artist to take note of [Fedorov's views of the universe, and] placed [them] at the base of Suprematism."[88] Malevich's many writings and works,

---

86 Larissa A. Zhadova, *Malevich: Suprematism and Revolution in Russian Art, 1910–1930* (London, 1982), 49–50.

87 Serge Fauchereau, *Malevich* (New York, 1993), 27.

88 Quotation from Igor A. Kazus, "The Idea of Cosmic Architecture and the Russian Avant-Garde of the Early Twentieth Century," in Clair, *Cosmos* (cit. n. 22), 194. John Golding also notes that "Malevich had ... fallen under the spell of other occultists and pseudo-scientists fascinated with ideas about the fourth dimension, which had already been disseminated

however, suggest that his works were attempts to merge some of the disparate ideological underpinnings of modernity and spiritualism, that is, technological utopianism and mysticism.

Malevich's interest in spatial ideas beyond Earth first manifested themselves after 1916. As he wrote to a friend, "Earth has been abandoned like a worm-eaten house. And an aspiration towards space is in fact lodged in man and his consciousness, a longing to break away from the globe of the earth."[89] Paintings at the time show geometric forms (usually squares or rectangles) with hollowed-out spaces and stretched drops of color, drenched in white light that highlighted things unimaginable on Earth, that is, without reference to any form of nature. There was literally no up or down. Malevich's engagement with spatial ideas in the cosmic sense reached a zenith in 1917–18, during the height of the revolutionary years and just after the first major references to space travel appeared in the media. In 1919, he explicitly articulated the notion that Suprematism itself could be part of the project of space exploration:

> Between [Earth and the Moon], a new Suprematist satellite can be constructed, equipped with every component, which will move along an orbit shaping its new track. ... I have ripped through the blue lampshade of the constraints of color. I have come out into the white. Follow me, comrade aviators! Swim into the abyss. I have set up the semaphores of Suprematism. I have overcome the lining of the colored sky. ... Swim! The white free abyss, infinity is before you.[90]

Some of Malevich's paintings from this period, such as *Suprematism* (1917) and *Drawing* (1918), depict objects not dissimilar to what we might today call space stations or futuristic cities in the cosmos. Malevich, of course, never alluded to them as such, and most certainly would not have known about such things given that few people in the world had yet articulated similar ideas in print. Yet the paintings show a remarkable understanding of the basic concepts of space travel, particularly the idea of space stations, and predate similar artistic visions that were common in Soviet popular science journals and pulp

---

by the turn of the century." Golding, *Paths to the Absolute: Mondrian, Malevich, Kandinsky, Pollock, Newman, Rothko, and Still* (Princeton, NJ, 2000), 62. See also Igor A. Kazus, "Cosmic Architecture and the Russian Avant-Garde," *Project Russia* 15 (undated): 81–88. For a compelling and convincing counterargument, see Zhadova, *Malevich* (cit. n. 86), 59.

89   Quoted in Zhadova, *Malevich* (cit. n. 86), 124n39.

90   Ibid., 57.

fiction of the 1920s. Malevich's fascination with the cosmos peaked around 1918 with his attempts to achieve an absolute spaciousness with pure whiteness, a white light of infinity that he represented in perhaps his most extreme avant-garde experiment, *White Square on White* (1918).

Like Malevich's works, many of his protégés' works hinted at a Fedorovian or Cosmist view of space. The case of the Society of Easel Painters (OST), which included a number of Malevich protégés, perfectly encapsulated the tensions between technological utopianism and Cosmism in the Soviet space fad of the 1920s. Like many in the Soviet avant-garde, the OST were taken with the wonders of technology and believed that art should mirror and interpret technological advancement in both mechanistic and abstract ways. Artists such as Vladimir Liushin, who produced *Station for Interplanetary Communications* (1922), seemed wholly beholden to the power of the machine to benefit society.[91] Yet Ivan Kudriashev, a Malevich protégé, eventually gravitated to a different view of the cosmos. Unlike other artists, Kudriashev had a direct connection to the space advocacy community: his father, a model builder, had been employed by Tsiolkovskii to build some of his conceptions. The younger Kudriashev accompanied his father on a visit to see the old man and translated Tsiolkovskii's technical terms for the model builder.[92] Kudriashev's philosophy, underlined in messianic essays about the expansion and settlement of humanity throughout the solar system, suggested a closer emotional affinity to Fedorov's mystic ideas than to earlier Suprematist works. Other Malevich followers, Lazar Lissitzky and Georgii Krutikov, explored a new type of architecture designed for "flying cities." These ideas stemmed not only from a fascination with space but also from the utilitarian view that because living space on the earth was limited, one had to devise other spaces for habitation, a distinctively Fedorovian view of life.[93]

The most striking example of artistic fascination with space resulting from the meeting between the artistic avant-garde and the philosophy of Cosmism was in the work of the informal Soviet artists' group known as Amaravella. The self-contained contradictions characteristic of Russian Cosmist philosophy

91 Vladimir Kostin, *OST (Obshchestvo stankovistov)* (Leningrad, 1976); John E. Bowlt, "The Society of Easel Artists (OST)," *Russian History/Histoire Russe* 9, nos. 2–3 (1982): 203–26.
92 Kostin, *OST* (cit. n. 91), 24–6; Zhadova, Malevich (cit. n. 86), 129n19.
93 S. O. Khan-Magomedov, "Proekt 'letaiushchego goroda'" [The flying city project], *Dekorativnoe iskusstvo* [Decorative arts] no. 1 (1973): 30–36; Kazus, "Idea of Cosmic Architecture and the Russian Avant-Garde" (cit. n. 88), 196–97.

characterized their work: although they advocated a universal and cosmic consciousness to life and art, their art reflected deeply national influences (such as medieval Russian art), and their philosophy followed the tradition of a nationalist Russian approach to the cosmos, best underscored by many of Fedorov's followers. Superficially, the group aspired to combine the most modern aspects of both science and art, the progenitors of a long tradition during Soviet times, but on a deeper level, theirs was the lexicon of both "rational" and "irrational" science, of both modern and archaic art.[94]

Petr Fateev, a thirty-two-year-old painter, formed and led the original Amaravella around 1922. It reached a stable membership of a few energetic and inspired artists such as Viktor Chernovolenko, Aleksandr Sardan, Sergei Shigolev, and Boris Smirnov-Rusetskii by 1927–28, when the name Amaravella was coined, apparently derived by Sardan from a Sanskrit word meaning "bearing light" or "creative energy." The group, which operated as a commune, explored a remarkably wide range of ideas and approaches to art based on the members' nebulous philosophical ideas about cosmic harmony. Sardan, who was also a professional musician, produced compositions that were combinations of sound, painting, and architecture. His works such as *Sound in Space* (1920), *Lunar Sonata*, and *Cosmic Symphony* (both 1925) tried to represent the "sound" of architecture through vivid colorful hues that aspired toward a cosmic (aural) harmony. Other works such as *Earth, Ocean, Space* (1922) and *Cosmic Motive* (late 1920s) addressed his philosophical views, some of them borrowed from eastern philosophies, while *From the Moon to Space Way* (1930) and *Earthly Beacon and Signals from Space* (1926) elucidated technical ideas. The group exhibited their works several times, including once in New York in 1927, when six of Sardan's paintings were displayed at an exhibition organized by the Russian avant-garde artist Nikolai Rerikh. Rerikh, in turn, served as a link to the "other" space advocate community, centered on Tsiolkovskii: he befriended Aleksandr Gorskii, an influential Cosmist and occultist who himself moved to Kaluga, Tsiolkovskii's adopted hometown, in the 1930s.[95]

---

94 For survey of the vast literature on the union of science and art in the Soviet Union, see the special issue of *Leonardo* 27, no. 5 (1994), under the banner "Prometheus: Art, Science, and Technology in the Former Soviet Union."

95 Iurii Linnik, *Amaravella: Put' k pleiadam; Russkie khudozhniki-kosmisty* [Amaravella: Path to the Pleiades: Russian cosmist artists] (Petrozavodsk, 1995), 82–145; Linnik, "Amaravella," *Sever* no. 11 (1981):108–14.

Linking Communities: Biocosmists

At the very extreme of the continuum from technological utopianism to Cosmism were those who were fully engaged in a spiritual and sometimes occult-like interest in space exploration. In the early 1920s, the most explicit mark of Cosmism's imprint emerged through scientific, cultural, and artistic icons such as Vladimir Vernadskii (the geochemist), Vladimir Zabolotskii (the poet), and Maksim Gor'kii (the writer) but also via short-lived groups such as the Anarchist-Biocosmists. The group (also known as the Biocosmist-Immortalists) coalesced in 1921 after the state's crackdown on anarchists following the funeral of famous Russian anarchist Petr Kropotkin. When the authorities arrested an anarchist group named the Universalists, a new collective, the Anarchist-Biocosmists, replaced them; adherents pledged their support to the Bolsheviks but also announced their goal of initiating a social revolution "in interplanetary space."[96] The group, which had factions in both Moscow and Petrograd, briefly published a journal, *Bessmertie* (Immortality), under the banner "Immortalism and Interplanetarianism." In their manifesto, issued in 1921, they announced several goals, including victory over space ("not air navigation ... but cosmic navigation"). They declared the two basic human rights to be the right to exist forever and the right to unimpeded movement in interplanetary space. Inspired by Fedorov's ideas, they wanted to abolish death, colonize the universe, and then resurrect those who had already died.[97] Just after Lenin's death, the Anarchist-Biocosmists published an official statement in *Izvestiia* arguing that all was not lost as the "[workers] and the oppressed all over the world could never be reconciled with the fact of Lenin's death."[98]

Devotees of Cosmism and Fedorov's philosophy were connected to the technological utopian spaceflight community via a network that highlighted the fine line between science and mysticism. Tsiolkovskii, someone who was equally

---

96 For the original Biocosmist manifesto, see A. Sviator, "Biokosmicheskaia poetika," in *Literaturnye manifesty ot simvolizma do nashikh dnei* [We: The novel, novellas, stories, plays, essays, and memoirs], ed. S. B. Dzhimbinov (Moscow, 2000), 305–14, on 305.

97 "Deklarativnaia rezoliutsiia," *Izvestiia VTsIK*, January 4, 1922. The Biocosmists unsuccessfully tried to recruit such prominent scientists as Eugen Steinach and Albert Einstein. Michael Hagemeister, "Die 'Biokosmisten'—Anarchismus und Maximalismus in der frühen Sowjetzeit," in *Studia slavica in honorem viri doctissimi Olexa Horbatsch*, ed. Gerd Freidhof, Peter Kosta, and M. Schutrumpf, vol. 1, pt. 1 (Munich, 1983), 61–76; Hagemeister, "Russian Cosmism in the 1920s and Today" (cit. n. 16), 195–96.

98 A. Sviatogor, N. Lebedev, and V. Zikosi, "Golos anarkhistov," *Izvestiia VTsIK*, January, 27 1924.

at ease writing about propellant masses as about victory over death, was naturally the most obvious and important link between the two sides.[99] There were other, more famous links. During the one-hundredth anniversary of Fedorov's birthday, Maksim Gor'kii, a devotee of Fedorov's, famously declared in an interview in *Izvestiia* that "freedom without power over nature—that's the same as freeing peasants without land."[100] It is less well known that Gor'kii, who also believed in the search for immortality, considered Tsiolkovskii to be an important scientific and philosophical thinker. During his exile, the writer had heard of Tsiolkovskii via the latter's 1925 work *Prichina kosmosa* (Reason for space), a meditation on humanity's spiritual calling to go into space. Although Gor'kii intended to visit Tsiolkovskii in Kaluga upon his return to the Soviet Union in 1928, the two never met. Tsiolkovskii, however, sent Gor'kii many of his brochures on Cosmist philosophy, and they evidently resonated deeply with the writer; Gor'kii sent a well-publicized congratulatory letter to the "interplanetary old man" (as he liked to call Tsiolkovskii) on his seventy-fifth birthday in 1932.[101]

Even at the extreme of mysticism, people remained connected with the technological utopians. One well-known Biocosmist member, Leonid Vasil'ev, who was also a respected researcher of telepathy, maintained a friendship with Aleksandr Chizhevskii, the young intellectual and well-known Cosmist who wrote extensively on the relationship between cosmic factors (such as sunspots) and social activity on Earth. Chizhevskii lived in Kaluga briefly and later wrote a massive memoir on his relationship with Tsiolkovskii.[102] Chizhevskii also holds a special place in the history of Soviet space exploration: he wrote the famous German-language introduction for the 1924 Tsiolkovskii monograph that effectively set off the Soviet space fad of the 1920s, enrapturing the technological utopians who wanted to build rockets to bring the Soviet Union into the modern world.[103]

---

99 Tsiolkovskii also communicated with an international association, devotees of a philosophy similar to Russian Cosmism, known as the Association Internationale de Biocosmique, based in Lyon, France. Ass. Int. Biocosmique to Tsiolkovskii, [illegible but probably April 16, 1934], Lyon, f. 555, op. 3, d. 200, ll. 12-3, ARAN.

100 A. Gornostaev, "N. F. Fedorov," *Izvestiia*, December 29, 1928.

101 Gor'kii to Tsiolkovskii, n.d., 1932, n.p., f. 555, op. 4, d. 183, l. 1, ARAN. For Gor'kii and Tsiol kovskii in general, see G. Chernenko, "Sorrento —Kaluga —Moscow," *Nauka i zhizn'* no. 6 (1972): 46–48.

102 A. L. Chizhevskii, *Na beregu vselennoi: Gody druzhby s Tsiolkovskim; Vospominaniia* (Moscow, 1995).

103 Alexander Tshijewsky, "Anstatt eines Vorworts," preface to K. E. Tsiolkovskii, *Raketa v kosmicheskoe prostranstvo* (Kaluga, 1924), unnumbered preface page.

Utopia Abandoned?

The political, social, and cultural climate dramatically changed in the Soviet Union between the early 1920s, when the fad began, and the early 1930s, when the fad ended. The combined repercussions of the Cultural Revolution, the First Five-Year Plan, and nationwide collectivization completely transformed much of Soviet society. For those involved in scientific or technical work, the Shakhty trial and the Industrial Party affair redefined, with tragic consequences, the boundaries of "proper" behavior and expression. Party ideologues purged out of influential positions a huge number of old specialists, especially those with roots in prerevolutionary times.[104] They also removed "old influences" from the editorial boards of several popular science journals. The government absorbed P. P. Soikin's semiprivate publishing company, perhaps the most important promoter of space-related themes, and changed the profiles of several of its former journals. Although science popularization still remained a very important project for Bolsheviks, the tenor of outreach changed. The journal *Priroda i liudi*, for example, changed its name to *Revoliutsiia i priroda* (Revolution and nature) to reflect the explicitly utilitarian, socialist, and applied nature of its message. Its stated goal was now to popularize "technology for the masses." Similarly, the elite Academy of Sciences, although disconnected from the populist space fad, underwent a process of "Bolshevization" that significantly limited its independent voice in matters of science so that it could refocus attention to applied, rather than fundamental, science.[105]

The rise of the state (both government and party) as a ubiquitous and inescapable force in society at the turn of the 1930s profoundly affected the indigenously maintained space fad. In particular, the Bolshevik Party's effort to realign scientific and technical work in the country for socialist reconstruction proved decisive. After an explosion of media attention at the turn of decade, by 1933, the space fad was nearly over. The metamorphosis was striking. In 1931, the press published nearly two dozen articles on spaceflight; in 1932, less than a dozen; the following year—when there were no private popular science journals left—no more than a handful. The same journals that had popularized utopian discussions about space travel now devoted more attention to technical knowledge applicable to

---

104 Kendall E. Bailes, *Technology and Society under Stalin: Origins of the Soviet Technical Intelligentsia, 1917–1941* (Princeton, NJ, 1978).

105 Michael David-Fox and György Péteri, eds., *Academia in Upheaval: Origins, Transfers, and Transformations of the Communist Academic Regime in Russia and East Central Europe* (Westport, CT, 2000); Andrews, *Science for the Masses* (cit. n. 45), 130–34.

workers on the shop floor. Linking science to industrial productivity marginalized many seemingly outlandish ideas such as space exploration. Societies, exhibitions, media, and art on the topic either disappeared or mutated into new forms.

A few spaceflight supporters from the 1920s were casualties of the Great Terror, although it is important to underscore that none suffered *because* of their advocacy of space travel. Cosmist philosopher N. A. Setnitskii lost his life in the late 1930s, while Tsiolkovskii's friend Aleksandr Chizhevskii was arrested in 1940 and eventually spent sixteen years in domestic exile. In 1939, the People's Commissariat of Internal Affairs (NKVD) shot Morris Leiteizen, former secretary of the Society for the Study of Interplanetary Communications and the son of an old Bolshevik who had been a friend of Lenin's. Mikhail Lapirov-Skoblo, one of the earliest advocates for spaceflight in the 1920s, also fell to the purges. After a very distinguished career as a vocal spokesperson for the Soviet scientific and technical intelligentsia, he was arrested in 1937, sentenced in 1941, and died in confinement in 1947 while working at a battery factory.[106]

Artists and writers also fell during the upheavals of the Cultural Revolution and the Great Terror. During the former, the Suprematists came under attack from the Association of Russian Revolutionary Painters (AKhRR) as part of a general move to discredit the artistic avant-garde.[107] Similarly, the Proletarian Writers' Association launched a campaign that discredited the genre of science fiction, calling the style a distraction to the problems at hand. By 1936, the government included *Aelita* on its list of banned movies; the NKVD arrested some science fiction writers in the late 1930s while the government removed even Jules Verne from children's literature. Soviet science fiction did not recover from the resultant consequences until the Khrushchev era.[108]

Most space advocates, however, survived. They successfully embraced the discursive shift from indefinite utopia to definite industrialization by changing their strategies. Popularizers and enthusiasts altered their lexicon rather than changing their vision. Many, for example, refocused their attention from rockets flying in space to the purer engineering problem of "reactive motion." Through

106 Semenova, "Russkii kosmizm" (cit. n. 15), 96–97; Roy Medvedev, *Let History Judge: The Origins and Consequences of Stalinism*, rev. ed. (New York, 1989), 444; E. N. Shoshkov, "Lapirov-Skoblo Mikhail Iakovlevich," in *Repressirovannoe ostekhbiuro* (St. Petersburg, 1995), 137.

107 Fauchereau, *Malevich* (cit. n. 87), 31–33.

108 McGuire, *Red Stars* (cit. n. 72), 13–15; Peter Kenez, *Cinema and Soviet Society, 1917–1953* (Cambridge, UK, 1992), 144; Britikov, *Russkii Sovetskii nauchno-fantasticheskii roman* (cit. n. 72), 137.

the 1920s, interplanetary travel had always been connected to the development of reactive motion, that is, with rocket and jet engines. In the early 1930s, however, activists and enthusiasts disconnected reactive motion from interplanetary travel and connected it with more realistic goals that were part of the prevailing state culture of aviation. Although most space advocates never stopped aiming for outer space, they redefined the problem into smaller chunks, the first step being "conquering the stratosphere" using the principle of reactive motion. Stratospheric flight literally and metaphorically lowered the ceiling of ambition while locating the original idea of space exploration within prevailing aviation culture. Reactive motion implied a real engineering problem with real solutions; it also held immediate utility as such a principle could be used to propel airplanes. Many enthusiasts in Europe had already demonstrated the possibility. The limits of possibility moved downward from the cosmos to the clouds.

CONCLUSIONS

From the perspective of the Soviet state, the space fad was of no importance. During its existence, no major party or government official was involved in the activities of either the technological utopians or the mystically minded space advocates. The relatively loose controls over social, cultural, and economic activity during NEP allowed the ideas of space activists to flourish without notice or support from the party and the government. Trotskii's single public comment on the space fad was derisive and cautionary. In a section on proletarian culture and art in *Literature and Revolution*, he argued:

> Cosmism seems, or may seem, extremely bold, vigorous, revolutionary and proletarian. But in reality, Cosmism contains the suggestion of very nearly deserting the complex and difficult problems ... on earth so as to escape into the interstellar spheres. In this way Cosmism turns out quite suddenly to be akin to mysticism ... [and may] lead some ... to the most subtle of matters, namely to the Holy Ghost.[109]

Interest in space, he argued, would lead enthusiasts from the useful to the useless and from science to religion—what Lenin had scorned as the opiate of the masses. Trotskii's comment (disingenuously?) avoided underscoring the connection between science and religion, represented in the space fad

---

109 Trotsky, *Literature and Revolution* (cit. n. 11), 211.

by the technological utopians and the mystics, respectively. Both rationales contributed in wholly different ways to the defining of the contours and flavor of the space fad in the 1920s but both also shared many deep-rooted rationales.

The most important contribution of the technological utopians—such as the societies and the popular media—was to link the cause of spaceflight with science and technology. Prior to the 1920s, in the public imagination, space exploration was part of the discourse of fantasy, speculation, and often mysticism. In the 1920s, by linking spaceflight with the sciences and suggesting that space travel was entirely plausible by means familiar to most people, the spaceflight advocacy community brought such ideas into the realm of possibility and the "rational." The link with science, which the Bolsheviks believed provided the way to modernization, also equated spaceflight with "being modern." After the late 1920s, spaceflight became, like aviation, one manifestation of the self-reflexive notion of twentieth-century modernization.

The approach of the technological utopians differed in important ways from that of their fellow Cosmists. Where technology-inspired space advocates looked to a future of many unknown possibilities for humanity, Cosmists looked to the past (the dead) as way station to a singular goal: the reanimation of humanity into a single universal organism. If the former tied their dreams of space exploration (however implausibly) with the modernizing exigencies of the day, the latter were not interested in modernization but the evolution of the species. It is tempting to argue that the tension between these seemingly contradictory ideas provided the charge for the creative outpouring on space exploration in the 1920s; or that both the "old" and the "new" appeal were necessary for mass interest in such an arcane idea as spaceflight. Such assertions would, however, be impossible to test since they raise counterfactual, rather than factual, questions.

A more analytically valuable perspective would be to view the two sensibilities as not altogether incompatible, especially as the boundaries between the two were not always clear. The nearly invisible web of connections via friendship or acquaintance that linked disparate believers in the cause of space travel muddled distinctions between the differing rationales for space travel. Sometimes cold science and ill-defined mysticism existed in the same breath. The artists who emerged from the Suprematist umbrella embodied this duality without contradiction; they worked within the most avant-garde of artistic traditions—materialistic, forward thinking, urban—yet infused their work with Fedorovian views from the late nineteenth century rooted in a pastoral and antimaterialistic aesthetic.

Technological utopianism and Cosmism shared a number of basic elements: both were utopian, both relied on the notion that humanity needed complete control over nature, and both afforded technology a prominent role in the realization of their ultimate goal of transforming society. In their language and iconography, technological utopians spoke with the same evangelical tones as their spiritual compatriots. Like the Cosmists, utopians were obsessed with the future imperatives of humanity and paid fealty to technology, travel, and Tsiolkovskii. In advocating the science of space exploration in the 1920s, "believers" not only used the language of mysticism—the most obvious meeting point between science and religion—but also shared many of the same rationales, goals, and ideologies.

The case of spaceflight culture in the experimental climate of the NEP years provides a striking case in which the demarcations between science and mysticism were at best nebulous. Writing about Bolsheviks' fascination with technology, Anthony J. Vanchu noted that "while science and technology had the power to demystify religion and magic, they themselves came to be perceived as the locus of magical or occult powers that could transform the material world."[110] In effect, science and technology became a new cosmology in the Marxist-Bolshevik-Leninist context of the interwar years; they were both alternatives to religion and religions themselves. Spaceflight was one vibrant example of this conflation.

Through the decades after the 1930s, Soviet space advocates altered their strategies to fit the needs of practical science and industrialization. Still utopian, they abandoned the mystical for the technological. By the time that cosmonaut Titov declared that he had not found God nor angels in outer space, the religion of space travel could be distilled down to modernity, secularism, and progress. But statements such as Titov's obscured an alternate history of the Soviet space program that harked back to the 1920s, discarded and lost through much of the Soviet era. Titov's willful disengagement of Christ from the cosmos underscored the irony that his achievement had been made possible largely because of people such as Tsiolkovskii who had set out to do the exact opposite, that is, to integrate the mystical and the technological; the modern rocket with its new Communist cosmonaut was conceived as much in a leap of faith as in a reach for reason.

---

110 Anthony J. Vanchu, "Technology as Esoteric Cosmology in Early Soviet Literature," in Rosenthal, *Occult in Russian and Soviet Culture* (cit. n. 12), 205–6.

Part Two

Russia's Roaring Twenties

Soviet Science Fiction of the 1920s: Explaining a Literary Genre in its Political and Social Context

DOMINIC ESLER

Esler, Dominic. "Soviet Science Fiction of the 1920s: Explaining
a Literary Genre in its Political and Social Context." *Foundation*
39, no. 109 (Summer 2010): 27–52.

INTRODUCTION

Although the USSR witnessed a remarkable efflorescence of science fiction in the 1920s, this early period has received little attention beyond Russia's borders. Dividing the genre into six broad categories, this essay examines the literary characteristics of 1920s Soviet sf and links these to the wider social and political context. Many of the texts discussed are only available in Russian, although English translations are referenced when possible.

Sf was present in Russian literature before the 1917 revolution, although it had yet to achieve a firm foothold. According to Suvin, only around twenty-five original Russian sf works were published in the twenty years before 1917,[1] the most significant of which was Alexander Bogdanov's *Red Star*, a

---

1 Darko Suvin, *Metamorphoses of Science Fiction* (New Haven, CT: Yale University Press, 1979), 252.

novel inspired by the failed 1905 revolution.[2] After the 1917 revolution, radical creative experiments reflected the rupture experienced in all areas of life. In literature, groups of writers united by artistic and ideological attitudes engaged in a fierce conflict to be recognised as the true cultural representatives of the Soviet Union. On this battlefield, where innovation was regarded as a necessity rather than an advantage, sf held an unusual position. Although sf did acquire its own dedicated champions, the genre was dispersed across a spectrum of journals and publishing houses and adopted by a wide range of authors who had already made their names in the literary mainstream.

The popularity of sf during this period can only be understood by considering the strong elements of scientific and technological utopianism that were so integral to contemporary revolutionary ideology. Marsh writes that "Science and technology have always figured prominently in Soviet literature as a direct consequence of the dominant position which they occupy in Soviet society,"[3] and the elevation of science was evident from the first moments of the USSR. In the postrevolutionary period, the social transformation of mankind could not be imagined without comparative scientific progress: "The Bolshevik envisaged that the creation of a radically new society would entail the transformation not simply of people's minds, but of the natural landscape."[4] Leon Trotsky's *Literature and Revolution* (translated 1991) demonstrates the level to which this faith in science had permeated all the way to the top echelons of the Communist Party. In what Stites describes as "an extraordinary endorsement of the experimental utopianism that characterized the 1920s,"[5] Trotsky soberly envisages a future where social improvements, such as the liberation of women, seem to be overshadowed by burgeoning scientific capabilities which will permit not only the biological improvement of the human organism but also the rearrangement of the entire surface of the earth.

Of all the literary genres that arose during the 1920s, sf was perhaps the most suitable to realise these utopian dreams. If sf arose as a literary reaction to

---

2 Alexander Bogdanov, *Red Star* (1908), trans. Charles Rougle (Bloomington, IN: Bloomington University Press, 1984).

3 Rosalind J. Marsh, *Soviet Fiction since Stalin: Science, Politics, and Literature* (London: Croom Helm, 1986), 5.

4 Roger Cockrell, "Future Perfect: H. G. Wells and Bolshevik Russia, 1917–32," in *The Reception of H.G. Wells in Europe*, ed. Patrick Parrinder and John S. Parrington (London: Thoemmes Continuum, 2005), 74.

5 Richard Stites, *Revolutionary Dreams: Utopian Vision and Experimental Life in the Russian Revolution* (Oxford: Oxford University Press, 1989), 168.

the nascent scientific worldview within Europe at the beginning of the twentieth century, "with its sweeping social changes and its unveiling of the promises and threats of modern technology," this worldview was particularly resonant with the Soviet regime.[6] Sf's willingness to part from conventional reality made it appealing at a time when "traditional realism was simply an obstacle in the path of the construction of Lenin's communist utopia,"[7] and it was more suitable than other literary avenues of the fantastic because it emphasised self-help rather than resorting to any external magical aid. Its flexibility made it suited to a wide range of purposes and, as the "literature of discontinuity," sf was particularly relevant in the aftermath of the revolution,[8] as Zamiatin notes:

> Life itself has lost its plane reality: it is projected, not along the old fixed points, but along the dynamic coordinates of Einstein, of revolution. In this new projection, the best-known formulas and objects become displaced, fantastic, familiar-unfamiliar. This is why it is so logical for literature today to be drawn to the fantastic plot, or to an amalgam of fantasy and reality.[9]

In short, Soviet writers discovered in sf a ready-made literary vehicle capable of carrying some of the most important issues of the political and social context. Zamiatin called for Soviet writers to replicate the achievements of H. G. Wells, while Trotsky sought a "Soviet Jules Verne" who "would be able to captivate the literate workers and rural proletariat with the majestic perspective of social construction."[10]

Native authors were quick to rise to the challenge. According to Kats, the first contender was Aristarkh Obolyaninov, who worked on the editorial board of the émigré journal *The Coming Russia* in Paris beside Alexei Tolstoi. Obolyaninov received a government invitation to return to the USSR after the Berlin publication of his 1921 novel *Red Moon*, which follows the Soviet scientist Vorontsov and his daughter Anna on a scientific expedition to the moon,

---

6 Patrick Parrinder, ed., *Science Fiction: Its Criticism and Teaching* (London: Routledge, 2003), xi.

7 R.C. Kats, *Istorija sovetskoj fantastiki* (St. Petersburg: St. Petersburg State University Publishing House, 2004), 9.

8 James Gunn, "Towards A Definition of Science Fiction," in *Speculations on Speculation*, ed. James Gunn and Matthew Candelaria (Oxford: The Scarecrow Press Inc., 2005), 8.

9 Y. Zamyatin, "The New Russian Prose," in *A Soviet Heretic*, trans. Mirra Ginsburg (London: Quartet Books, 1991), 105.

10 Kats, *Istorija sovetskoj fantastika*, 9–10.

where they manage to transform an imperial war between rival governments into a civil war along strict Bolshevik principles.[11] Alexei Tolstoi's similar triumphant return to his homeland on the strength of his sf novel *Aelita*, at roughly the same time, emphasises the high regard that the Soviet regime held for sympathetic sf.

Soviet sf even had its own dedicated literary group, the long-forgotten *Red Selenite*, which was subsidised by the State Publishing House. Kats argues that this group became "practically the most influential writers' faction" during the first decade of the Soviet Union, at one time close to the leadership of the Communist Party, and there were even rumours that *Red Selenite* owed its creation to Lenin himself.[12] In 1921, *Red Selenite* began publication of an almanac called *Selena*, the first installment of which had a circulation of 100,000 copies, a very large number if we consider that a popular magazine such as *Universal Detective*, which also occasionally published sf, achieved 100,000 copies only in 1929, after starting in 1925 with 10,000.[13] By 1926 and 1927, *Selena* was being published six times a year, and the authors that appeared in the almanac included Platonov, Beliaev, and Zamiatin. If Gernsback's *Amazing Stories*, which began in 1926, was the first English-language magazine entirely devoted to sf, then it is possible that *Selena* may have been the first magazine entirely dedicated to the genre in the world. For the time being, sf had acquired the blessing of the Soviet regime.

The Physicality of Contact

According to Mark L. Brake and Neil Hook, "It is in attempts to institute a physicality of contact that the science fiction of the early twentieth century dwells"—the vast, impersonal and sometimes abstract vistas of recent science were only comprehensible through the concrete representation of their relationship to the individual.[14] This "physicality of contact" is a useful way to consider the works of Konstantin Tsiolkovsky and Vladimir Obruchev, both of whom were primarily scientists and adopted sf as a medium through which to inculcate knowledge and passion for science in the reader, rather than

---

11 Ibid., 12–14.
12 Ibid., 7.
13 Patrick L. McGuire, *Red Stars: Political Aspects of Soviet Science Fiction* (Ann Arbor: University of Michigan Research Press, 1985), 12.
14 Mark L. Brake and Neil Hook, *Different Engines: how science drives fiction and fiction drives science* (London: Macmillan, 2008), 87.

opting for equations, diagrams, and theory, and neither was very interested in literary elements such as character and plot. Scientific accuracy remained of the utmost importance. Kats refers to Tsiolkovsky's particular dislike for implausible sf,[15] and Obruchev expressed the same sentiments: "A good science-fiction novel must be plausible; its reader must be convinced that all the events described could take place in certain circumstances, that there is nothing supernatural about them."[16] It is largely due to this rigid attitude that their sf has not aged well. Much of the science described in their works seems banal, while those theories which have since been discredited are only of historical interest.

Although Tsiolkovsky is commonly described as a sf writer, his writing barely achieves many of the qualities expected of "fiction." His sf career began with "On the Moon," a light-hearted "story" published in a Moscow magazine in 1892 and which epitomizes his approach.[17] An unnamed man wakes up to discover he is on the moon and that he has been fortunate enough to have been transported with a physicist who is able to explain the peculiarities of their environment. There is no pretense at character or plot; the two men merely delight in testing their new capabilities.

Like "On the Moon," Tsiolkovsky's best work, *Beyond the Earth*,[18] is solely concerned with presenting the latest scientific developments to a mass audience in a way that is simple and easy to relate to, although the scientific horizons of the latter are exponentially wider. Six men—an Italian, Gallileo; a German, Helmholtz; a Frenchman, Laplace; an English man, Newton; an American, Franklin; and a Russian called Ivanov—gather in a high Himalayan castle in the year 2017 and dedicate their lives to science after being "driven into seclusion by disillusionment with people and the pleasures of life."[19] Having developed the necessary super-fuel, the scientists put their minds to the task of sending a rocket into space and, once free of the earth, travel to the moon while subsisting on vegetables grown in special hydroponic greenhouses that exploit the unshielded light of the sun.

---

15 Kats, *Istorija sovetskoj fantastika*, 27.
16 Vladimir Obruchev, *Plutonia: An Adventure through Prehistory* (1924), trans. Brian Pearce (London: Lawrence and Wishart, 1957), 10.
17 Konstatin Tsiolkovsky, "On the Moon" (1892), in *Call of the Cosmos*, ed. V. Dutt (Moscow: Foreign Languages Publishing House, 1962), 10–51.
18 Konstatin Tsiolkovsky, *Beyond the Earth* (1920), trans. Kenneth Syers (London: Pergamon Press, 1960).
19 Ibid., 17.

Tsiolkovsky describes a utopian vision of the future which has much in common with the dedicated sf utopias to which we will soon turn. Earth is at peace under the guidance of a global congress. There is a common set of laws and a world language; war has been eradicated and the aversion to bloodshed has led to the disappearance of meat from mankind's diet. The availability of various types of aircraft has made cargo transport and personal travel cheap and easy. Science, technology, and culture have all advanced immeasurably but, although the world has entered an unprecedented period of happiness, these improvements have resulted in an unconquerable problem: the rapid growth of the population.

For Tsiolkovsky, only space can provide the necessary environment for the perfect, sustainable human society. It holds resources sufficient for all of man's needs, and weightlessness has a wide range of benefits, especially for the old and the sick. Moreover, life in space will encourage the evolution of the human organism, as humans find ways to adapt themselves. Tsiolkovsky's vision stretches far enough into the future to encounter the death of the sun, a scale on which even the possibility of migrating to distant solar systems is not out of the question: "do not forget that mankind is immortal and 12,000 [years] is no great matter, so even if those suns and their planets may not be our inheritance they may well be the heritage of mankind as a whole."[20] Paradise cannot be achieved by a static society trapped on Earth—man must leave his home. Tsiolkovsky advocates space travel, not merely in the name of science itself, but as a fundamentally necessary step in the long-term future of mankind.

Beyond the Earth is heavy with scientific arguments, simplified explanations and statistics, and the reader is regularly provided with scientific lectures. Yet the work achieves a lightness by virtue of its enthusiasm and optimism for the future.

Obruchev's two sf novels, *Plutonia* and *Sannikov's Land*, look to the distant past rather than to the future, dealing with palaeontology rather than astronautics.[21] Obruchev had literary pretensions not possessed by Tsiolkovsky, and viewed his novels in the tradition of earlier works such as Jules Verne's *Journey to the Center of the Earth* and Arthur Conan Doyle's *The Lost World*, both of which Obruchev criticises for their implausibility. In keeping with the spirit

---

20 Ibid., 39.
21 Vladimir Obruchev, Земля Санникова (1926), adapted by P. H. Collin (London: George G. Harrap, 1968).

necessary in literature is difficult to sustain in a "perfect" environment. Yet this is more than a merely formal problem. By reducing the future to a harmony peaceful yet simultaneously monotonous, a kind of living death, the sf utopia threatens to undermine itself. The destruction of the individual and his or her own personal thoughts and feelings anticipates the dissolution, not just of the harmful aspects of contemporary life, but of those altruistic desires that lead to the utopia in the first place. Evidence of this ambivalence can be found even in Mayakovsky's strident satire, where, besides disease and alcoholism, "harmful" habits such as dancing, poetry-reading and even love have been eradicated; in this environment it is hard not sympathise with Prisypkin: "What did we fight for? Why did we shed our blood, if I can't dance to my heart's content— and I'm supposed to be leader of the new society!"[34] Sometimes this crucial issue is openly articulated. In *The Discovery of Riel*, it is realized as a dichotomy between the home planet of Riel (Geliy's alternate consciousness) and Paon, the equivalent of Mars, where a population of artists and scientists has consciously decided not to tame nature or to impose a universal perfect society. On Paon the people are less happy but more talented; the existence of pain and suffering makes life seem even more valuable. Thus, when Riel makes his discovery— that an atom of *onteyit* contains a world that seems to be Earth, a world riven by war and violence—the reader is forced to question whether this world is entirely undesirable.

There were other, more threatening aspects of the utopia that were sufficiently important to a new sf subgenre: the dystopia. The first Soviet dystopia was Evgeniy Zamiatin's seminal *We*, which took themes current in contemporary utopias and pushed them to what Zamiatin considered to be their inevitable limits.[35] *We* is not anti-Soviet—he considered himself to be more revolutionary than contemporary Bolsheviks—but warns against the dangers of the eschatological "end of history" inherent in the utopian ideal. *We's* Unified State has constructed itself on entirely rational principles, ensuring equality and the strictly regulated distribution of work and resources. Yet this future has become so mechanized that it has come to oppose those elements of human life that appear *irrational*, and therefore destabilising, such as art and love. The individual has become almost entirely dehumanized, known by number rather than name. Public and private spheres have merged, yet the result is a panopticon-like landscape founded on fear and suspicion rather

34 Mayakovsky, *The Bedbug*, 43.
35 Evgeniy Zamyatin, *We* (1924), trans. Clarence Brown (London: Penguin, 1993).

than the joyous collective mind of *The Coming World*. The final stage of this process is a medical operation to remove the imagination, after which there is no significant difference between man and machine.

We is not the only example of a Soviet sf dystopia from the 1920s. Another is Andrei Marsov's "Love in the haze of the future,"[36] a story that shares enough characteristics with *We* to perhaps be a direct response to that novel (although Marsov's story has humorous elements absent in the earlier work). The world of the 46th century is a Great Republic governed by the Soviet of World Reason, whose agents are identified by numbers rather than names. The working week has been reduced to just one hour, and the population of the world spends its free time relaxing in marvelous tropical gardens created from the coastal strips. Cities proliferate with ray-emitting machines that open each individual's subconscious for inspection, ensuring a crime-free society and the victory of the collective. Yet again, the regime has attempted to eliminate love, although, unlike *The Coming World* or *We*, there is no scientific solution to the problem.

In literary terms, the dystopia provided greater possibilities than the utopia. Neither *We* nor "Love in the haze of the future" is split between the present and the future, both using other methods to manifest this division. Information and comparison is embedded into the very structure of *We*: the novel's narrator, D-503, is writing a diary that will accompany an intergalactic expedition to seek alien life, and must explain the particularities of the Unified State. It is significant that conflict in the dystopia, in both a dramatic and a literal sense, comes from *within* the future society. Opposition to the repressive regime in both *We* nor "Love in the haze of the future" takes the form of an irrepressible surge of "atavistic" thought and behaviour, an atavism that clearly represents twentieth-century values rather than those of prehistoric man. This device allows a comparison of the future with the present without transporting a character across time and space.

World Catastrophes

However powerful utopias might have been on an ideological level, it was evident that they were lacking in popular appeal and drama. In fact, there was a strong belief in the 1920s that literature was missing something important. The writer Lev Lunts, speaking for a movement called the Serapion Brothers who

---

36 Andrei Marsov, "'Ljubov' v tumane buduschego" (1924), in various ed., *Венецианское Зеркало* (Moscow: Russkaja Kniga, 1999), 199–220.

called for Soviet versions of Wells, Verne, Kipling, Stevenson, and Dumas, put it pointedly: "What shines in the novella of recent times? Exquisite speech and magnificent refined style. Or: subtle psychology, surprising types, rich ideology. But there is no entertainment. It's boring. Boring."[37] This opening was filled by "revolutionary adventures" that played explicitly on the political and social context. The heroes were workers, the villains, capitalists. For these novels, Nikolai Bukharin suggested the term *red detective* or *red Pinkerton*. According to Robert Russell, the *red detective* fell into two main categories: sf and detective or thriller fiction.[38] However, the *red detective* was often a mix of both genres. Novels such as Ilya Ehrenburg's *The D.E. Trust* (1923)—the letters stand for "Destruction of Europe"—and the first and most popular *red detective*, *Mess-Mend* by Marietta Shaginian,[39] adopted sf themes such as near-future settings or fantastical weaponry. Sometimes the *red detective* would become a fully fledged work of sf in its own right, a subgenre that Suvin calls the "catastrophe novel" because it inevitably concludes with the breakdown of society before pausing on the threshold of a triumphant socialist world order.[40] In this section, I will consider two such works, both by Alexei Tolstoi: *The Garin Death Ray* and "The Union of Five."[41]

The Garin Death Ray and "The Union of Five" share certain important characteristics. In the eponymous Garin, a Russian engineer has discovered a way to channel light via a "hyperboloid" to create a superpowered laser capable of dissecting or incinerating any material in its path. Using this ray, Garin intends to incise a giant hole in the earth's crust, extracting unimaginable quantities of liquid gold with which he will create his own paradise on Earth: a dictatorship stretching across all the continents. The "Union of Five," a manipulative group of industrial capitalists, has a similarly nefarious scheme. Like Garin, these men occupied an unpopulated island from which they intend to launch a series of 200 missiles at the moon, splitting off some of its surface and causing global chaos, in the midst of which they will buy up all the devalued stocks and businesses to become rulers of the world. Neither plan is fulfilled, however: in both works the villains inadvertently initiate a global socialist revolution,

---

37 Lev Lunts cited in Robert Russell, "Red Pinkertonism: An Aspect of Soviet Literature in the 1920s," *Slavic and East European Review* 59, no. 3 (1982): 386–412, 390.

38 Ibid., 390.

39 Marietta Shaginian, *Mess-Mend* (summary) (1923–24), http://www.sovlit.com/mess-mend, last accessed February 26, 2011.

40 Suvin, *Metamorphoses*, 254.

41 Alexei Tolstoi, *The Garin Death Ray* (1925), trans. George Hanna (Moscow: Foreign Languages Publishing House, 1955); "Sojuz pjati," in various ed., *Собрание сочинений: Том четвертый* (Moscow: State Publishing House, 1958), 7–45.

transforming the world into a society peacefully impervious to capitalist criminality. *The Garin Death Ray* fits more securely into the category of *red detective* or "catastrophe novel." It is easy to trace the generic conventions and ideological themes that Tolstoi has inserted into a sf framework almost identical to that of "The Union of Five": a convoluted chase across Europe, violent action scenes, and a patriotic Bolshevik opponent to foil Garin's plans and inspire the workers, rather than an automatic conversion to socialism: "Everything that leads towards the establishment of Soviet power throughout the world is good," argues the hero, Shelga. "Everything that hinders it is bad."[42]

Both works are driven by the ideological Soviet opposition between communism and capitalism, a common feature of the *red detective*: "[The social space of these fantastic worlds] is always split, antagonistically polarized by the conflict between gigantic and irreconcilably hostile powers ... the global nature of this conflict is emphasized by the planetary scale of the plot's space, completely filled with this explosive conflict."[43] On this scale the safety of the Soviet Union is not subordinate to the safety of mankind. Informed by the violence of recent wars, the entire Earth may become a battlefield on which the fighting may achieve a particularly brutal level. This is realized vividly when Garin uses his weapon to explode an aniline factory near a small town in Germany, killing everyone within miles. Both texts depict a world on the edge of an apocalypse instigated by hostile capitalist forces, and this threat is specifically realized through science and technology.

Yet they also emphasize the marvels of the scientific age. In "The Union of Five," man has already travelled to the moon, and there is a direct reference to the Martian expedition of Engineer Los in Tolstoi's earlier *Aelita*. And in *Garin*: "At a time when the dialectics of history had led one class to a destructive war and another class to insurrection, when cities were burning ... in that monstrous and titanic decade the amazing minds of scientists gleamed here and there like torches."[44]

However, science is not necessarily driven by an altruistic urge to do good. The individual scientist does have the potential to help mankind—"An enlightened, disciplined mind is the holy of holies, the miracle of miracles"—but not

42 Ibid., 223.
43 Rafail Nudelman, "Soviet Science Fiction and the Ideology of Soviet Society," trans. Nadya Peterson, ed. Robert Philmus and Darko Suvin, *Science Fiction Studies* 16, no.1 (1989): 38–66, 40.
44 Tolstoi, *Garin*, 100.

all scientists are enlightened.[45] Some, such as Engineer Korvin of "The Union of Five," use their talents for personal gain, and even those that are enlightened might have their work turned against mankind. The end result of the scientist's labor depends not on his own intentions but on he who has the power to possess and control them. All that the "amazing minds of science" seem to have produced under the influence of capitalism are monstrous weapons and other threats: "the chimneys of the factories where poison gas, tetryl and other hellish products were being manufactured on a world-wide scale, products that deprived the local people of all zest for historical reminiscence [and], probably, for life itself."[46] It is no longer possible to place blind trust in the grand narrative of scientific progress.

It is important to note the specificities of Garin's plan for world domination. After separating a select group of people for breeding purposes, the remains of mankind will be rendered unthinking slaves by a minor skull operation. The chosen ones will become "a beautiful and refined race ... with new organs of thought and sensation. While communism is dragging all humanity behind it to the heights of culture I will do it in ten years."[47] Although Garin's vision is described as "the logical end of imperialism,"[48] its resemblance to the dystopian nightmare of We is striking. Tolstoi's earlier Aelita also questioned the assumptions of scientific optimism, emphasizing—according to Leninism-Marxism—a natural and inevitable social progression toward the happiness of mankind. Yet despite this frequent pessimism, Tolstoi occasionally offers us moments that express a sense of transcendence:

> Once more Earth will warm up unceasingly from atomic disintegration in order to again burst as a tiny star. Such is the cycle of terrestrial life. There has been an infinite number of these cycles and an infinite number of them is yet to come. There is no death. There is only eternal renewal.[49]

Soviet Space Stories

Although many examples of the red detective and its close relatives have survived, we have only a few early Soviet examples of the internationally popular sf subgenre of space opera, which proliferated in American pulp magazines

---

45 Ibid., 102.
46 Ibid., 177.
47 Ibid., 225.
48 Ibid., 282.
49 Ibid., 256.

of the 1920s and '30s and, while receiving little respect, helped to establish sf as a genre. Working from Wilson Tucker's well-known 1941 definition of space opera—"the hacking, grinding, stinking, outworn spaceship yarn, or world-saving for that matter"—Gary Westfahl suggests three crucial attributes. Space opera must have a spaceship, and "journeys through uncharted realms, mysterious stuff separating safe harbours"; it must be an exciting adventure, driven by conflict and violence; and it is formulaic and mediocre, generating endless repetitions of itself.[50]

Although I have been unable to find any secondary literature dealing specifically with the topic of Soviet space opera, Nikolai Mukhanov's little-known novel *Blazing Abysses*, which describes a war between Earth and Mars in the year 2923, shows it clearly existed.[51] After fifty years of peace between the two planets, a secret, influential group called the Soviet of Five, who seek political and cultural hegemony over all inhabited planets in the solar system, have driven the ruling council of Mars into declaring war on Earth. The ensuing conflict provides the background for the adventures of Ronye Ono-Beru, 200-year-old head of all the technical forces of Earth, and Geniy Oro-Mosku, the young chief of the terrestrial interplanetary fleet. Geniy's brother-in-law, the Martian poet Gro Fezera-Mar, is the secret leader of the Soviet of the Five and the mastermind of their plans for domination. Geliy and Ronye's exploits lead them to Mars, whose inhabitants live deep underground beside subterranean rivers and lakes, and then back to Earth, where, although the war has been won, the indefatigable Gro continues to lay his schemes.

Interspersed throughout the action are descriptive passages fleshing out the earth of *Blazing Abysses*. The planet is united under a Soviet Federation and is experiencing a time of peace. Physical labor has been eradicated, and the existence of mankind has been improved by a host of changes, such as the establishment of a global common language, the invention of miniature personal flying apparatuses, "radio-baths," and the replacement of solid meals with food-pills (the population has to chew a special kind of putty to stop their teeth falling out). Most of these novel developments are mentioned only once and have no real purpose other than scenic. The novel returns more frequently to the miracle-element *nebuliy*, the discovery of which has allowed

---

50 Wilson Tucker, writing as Bob Tucker, cited in Gary Westfahl, "Space Opera," in *The Cambridge Companion to Science Fiction*, ed. Edward James and Farah Mendelesohn (Cambridge: Cambridge University Press, 2003), 197–208.

51 Nikolai Mukhanov, *Pylajushchie bezdny* (1924), in *Derevjannaja koroleva* (Moscow: Russkaja Kniga, 1999), 291–491.

space travel (engineless ships propelled by electrons), the establishment of colonies on the moon, the realignment of the earth's axis, but also the construction of weapons of unthinkable power: "*Tau-rays*, achieving a speed of 200,000 kilometres per second, reducing any intercepted material to atomic dust."[52]

The fascination with monstrous weaponry is linked to the monumental scale that is a key aspect of the novel, and is not infused with pessimism in the manner of *The Garin Death Ray*. According to Mendlesohn, the "sense of wonder"—an appreciation of the sublime, whether natural or technological—is the one immediately recognizable narrative of science fiction, rarely approached in "mainstream" literature.[53] The "sense of wonder" was an important element of space opera, as Brake and Hook note: "Massive in scale, its square jawed heroes rescuing scantily clad and screaming heroines, it could at worst reduce a reader to tears of frustration through bad plotting, superficial dialogue and hoary schemes. At its best it opened the vistas of the imagination to the possibilities of the universe."[54] Consequently the scale of things is often unimaginable: Ronye's son, the superhuman, ingenious Ken, has invented a machine powerful enough to move planets from their orbits, and the novel's final twist is a rogue meteor, larger than the sun, that threatens both Earth and Mars.

The utopian future of *Blazing Abysses* emphasises scientific and technological, rather than social, development. Factories produce "almost everything that is necessary for man's happiness."[55] Other than a passing mention that children are the property of the federation, earth's society receives little attention. Yet the weight of the Soviet context is still manifest: Geliy is from Moscow, ancient Siberia is "the centre and soul of modern technology."[56] More significant is the transformation of the interplanetary war into a Martian civil war. The Soviet of Five and their secret supporters turn out to be members of a dispossessed Martian class known as the "largomerovs," the descendants of former imperial rulers, great dynasties, and those wealthy Martians whose fortunes were nationalized when Mars became a federation—class enemies according to

---

52 Ibid., 298.
53 Farah Mendlesohn, "Introduction: Reading Science Fiction," in *The Cambridge Companion to Science Fiction*, ed. Edward James and Farah Mendlesohn (Cambridge: Cambridge University Press, 2003), 1–12, 3.
54 Brake and Hook, *Different Engines*, 92.
55 Mukhanov, *Pylajushchie bezdny*, 306.
56 Ibid., 306.

Bolshevik doctrine. The largomerovs are the only barrier to the unification of Earth and Mars in a common culture and humanity.

However, the novel's ideological dimension is stated lightly and is always subservient to the needs of the plot, with no greater weight than any of the technological background details. Significantly, Geliy's rivalry with Gro is not realized along ideological lines but according to individual passions such as love, hate, vengeance—in *Blazing Abysses*, the emotions are as monumental as the weaponry. The novel gains its impetus through the juxtaposition of personal adventure story against a wider background of war and peace. In contrast to the dedicated utopias, the novel manages to find room for plot, however lurid. Its structure permits continual extension, and there is always room for another adventure or subplot. *Blazing Abysses* moves swiftly and episodically, in short, bite-size chapters, frequently slipping backwards to retell the same events from another perspective, and its division into three larger parts further emphasizes its serial nature. The false climax of the end of the war merely leads into the threat of the comet and the potential resurgence of the tenacious Soviet of Five in the novel's final third.

It will be evident by now that *Blazing Abysses* fits the basic type of space opera described by Tucker; the only significant respect in which it departs from this model is by limiting the range of its action to the earth and Mars. In this it reflects the smaller scale of early Soviet sf in general. The only example that I have discovered of travel beyond the edge of the Solar System in 1920s Soviet sf is a colonial expedition described in *The Discovery of Riel*.

Although *Blazing Abysses* is the sole example of fully-fledged space opera I have found, a consideration of Nikolai Aseyev's "The Executed Earth"—a space opera in miniature—will be enough to suggest the existence of a wider body of shared sf concepts and themes.[57] The peace of the solar system has once more been disrupted by an unprovoked Martian attack on Earth, although Martian's intent is vague and inconsistent: "Mars's sun had gone out, and they were left to choose between slowly fading away or victoriously conquering a neighbouring source of warmth and light."[58] This time the attack is an expression of the coarse Martian will in general rather than that of a villainous minority. While Mars pummels the earth's surface with its missiles, the Great Pilot descends into the caves of the mountain of Eternal Wills, where, with the

57 Nikolai Aseyev, "Rasstreljannaja Zemlja" (1921), in various ed., *Живая мебель* (Moscow: Russkaja Kniga, 199), 451–55.
58 Ibid., 452.

Inventor, he alters the earth's orbit and sends it hurtling towards their enemies. The subterranean location of this laboratory mirrors that of Ken's machinery in *Blazing Abysses*. Approaching Mars, the earth's champions neutralize the Red Planet with a mysterious but supremely power weapon.

Although the basic materials of space opera are present, "The Executed Earth" is distinguished by its vague, epic quality. The date is unspecified, and little is described of the future earth apart from the mandatory existence of a world Soviet, this time divided into North and South Communes. Instead, the story invites an allegorical interpretation, which is clearly emphasised by two nameless characters and metaphorical weaponry: "The first missile of compressed will was fired from Mars."[59]

Alexei Tolstoi's *Aelita* described an adventure to Mars with a very different orientation.[60] After *We*, *Aelita* has become perhaps the best known Soviet sf work of the decade, aided by the influential 1924 film adaptation. *Aelita* certainly did not, however, "[begin] the tradition of Soviet utopian literature," as Kosack writes.[61] *Aelita* is an unusual and awkward mix of romantic, symbolic, mystical, and ideological elements, combined with themes borrowed from earlier sf works. The novel has much in common with the space opera, yet its heavy ideological leaning renders it a very particular example of this type, and highlights the potentially transformative effects of the Soviet context upon sf. The novel's most obvious predecessor is Bogdanov's *Red Star*. While Bogdanov utilized the Martian setting to construct the kind of utopian society that he wanted to see on Earth, Tolstoi reversed this conceit by creating a tsarist-era Mars on which the revolution can only be induced with the help of socialists from Earth.

Aelita's plot is sparse. In St Petersburg, the engineer Los, grieving over his dead wife, has built a rocket that can travel to Mars within ten hours. His traveling partner is Gusev, a lively and experienced Red soldier. Once on Mars, Los falls in love with Aelita, daughter of Tuscoob, the Martian Supreme Engineer. Meanwhile, Gusev discovers that the seemingly peaceful Martian society is actually strictly stratified and that the workers of the great city of Soatsera are preparing to rise up against their cruel masters, led by Tuscoob. Gusev joins the

---

59 Ibid., 455.
60 Alexei Tolstoi, *Aelita* (1922–23), trans. Lucy Flaxman (Moscow: Foreign Languages Publishing House, no date).
61 Wolfgang Kosack, *Dictionary of Russian Literature Since 1917*, trans. Maria Carlson and Jane T. Hedges (New York: Columbia University Press, 1988), 422.

revolt with enthusiasm, becoming the leader of the weak-willed Martian rebels, but the workers are defeated and Gusev and Los forced to flee back to Earth.

Aelita is largely a rather cynical propaganda exercise to ease Tolstoi's return to the Soviet Union. Even in synopsis, the similarities of its plot with that of Obolyaninov's *Red Moon* will be apparent. It is full of plot holes and inconsistencies, and includes a lengthy, irrelevant chapter revealing that men from long-lost Atlantis arrived on Mars millennia earlier and mingled with the local population. It is evident that Tolstoi often aims for atmosphere and emotional impact rather than detail, particularly with regard to the symbol of Aelita calling for Los over the radio waves between the planets: "Aelita's voice, the voice of love and eternity, the voice of yearning, reached him across the universe."[62] This image, combining romantic emotion and technology, was particularly resonant for Tolstoi. It appears more than once in his sf, playing an even more important part in the film adaptaion of *Aelita* (the screenplay of which was written by Tolstoi himself), and appearing in *The Garin Death Ray*: "That same night, over the dark sea, over sleeping Europe, over the ancient ash-heaps of Asia Minor, over the dust-covered thorns of the sun-dried vegetation of Africa's plains, radio waves carried the voice of a woman."[63]

Kern is correct to write that Tolstoi "equipped his Mars with an assortment of science fiction features and a minimum of thought."[64] To begin with, there is a strange dissonance inherent in the classical, almost pastoral descriptions of Martian architecture and art, which rely on terrestrial equivalents: "shapes and ornaments ... curiously like those of the Etruscan amphoras."[65] Then there is the piecemeal Martian technology, which excels in some areas while lagging in others, featuring advanced aircraft but not spaceships or cars. This lack of innovation did not pass unnoticed in the 1920s. Zamiatin writes: "In his latest novel, *Aelita*, Tolstoi attempted to transfer from the mail train to the airplane of the fantastic, but all he managed was to jump up and plop back on the ground with awkwardly spread wings, like a fledgling jackdaw that has fallen out of its nest (daily life)."[66]

However, it must be said that there was nothing unusual in the portrayal of Martians as essentially human, in mind and body: this convention is followed

---

62 Tolstoi, *Aelita*, 276.
63 Tolstoi, *Garin*, 147.
64 Garry Kern, "Aelita," in *Survey of Science Fiction Literature: Vol. 1* (Epping, UK: Bowker Publishing Company, 1979), 28–32, 31.
65 Tolstoi, *Aelita*, 71.
66 Zamyatin, "New Russian Prose," 102.

in both *Red Star* and *Blazing Abysses*. In fact, Tolstoi devotes more effort than either Mukhanov or Bogdanov to populating his Martian landscape with other creatures, even if they are only decorative: "Strange prickly-looking balls scudded aside and leapt into the tentacled undergrowth."[67]

A large part of the book's drama comes from the opposing personalities of Los and Gusev. Gusev's warmongering, cheerful super-Bolshevik is compared positively to Los, who is introverted and helpless. Yet their characters are not constant, and alter in proportionate measures to the ideological needs of the plot. On earth, Gusev seems to be as tormented by his experience of war as Los is by the loss of his wife: "He had nightmares—he would suddenly gnash his teeth, mutter, sit up, breathing hard, his face and chest dripping with sweat. Then he would go back to sleep, waking up next morning depressed and restless."[68] However, once on Mars: "Having flown across space and landed in ninth heaven, he was as much at home in it as he had been on Earth. He slept like a babe. His conscience was clear."[69] In contrast, Los does not start out as an ineffectual dreamer. He is described in a similar traditionally masculine manner to Gusev: "A broad-shouldered man of medium height emerged from the scaffolding. His thick crop of hair was white, his face young and clean-shaven, with a large handsome mouth and piercing, light-grey, unblinking eyes."[70]

One of the significant areas in which *Aelita* differs from the space opera type is in its dichotomy of love and war. *Blazing Abysses* embeds love and personal relationships within its wider plot, while *Aelita* depicts love as a shameful, effeminate emotion that impedes rather than inspires bravery. The novel loses a large part of its momentum as it strains to incorporate the increasing ideological weight, the sense of adventure with which it begins is gradually lost, and the plot collapses when the heroes return to Earth. The end result is surprisingly ambiguous, however. First, because the Martian revolution is ultimately unsuccessful. Second, because Los, his rocket, and Soviet science itself are treated with disdain. While one of the original aims of the expedition had been to demonstrate Soviet superiority to the West—the project is sponsored by the Soviet government—both the USSR and the wider world seem to have lost interest. Paradoxically, *Aelita* ends up undermining its own sf foundation, the very reason it had been so fascinating.

---

67 Tolstoi, Aelita, 57.
68 Ibid., 36.
69 Ibid., 79–80.
70 Ibid., 12–13.

In spite of all its flaws, it is not hard to see why *Aelita* was popular within the Soviet Union. Rather than depict far-future adventures such as those of *Blazing Abysses*, the novel restages the Russian Revolution in a way that Soviet readers could relate to directly. Instead of a hairless superman who bathes in radio waves and lives on foodpills, Gusev is a contemporary Bolshevik hero, whose attitude, however exaggerated, reflects important aspects of the Soviet context. Even Zamiatin begrudgingly commends the soldier: "The only figure that is alive, in the usual Tolstoyan fashion, is the Red Army soldier Gusev. He alone speaks, all the others recite."[71] Almost a century later, however, Gusev's proclamations verge on parody: "Hallo, Comrades Martians! [*sic*] We bring you greetings from the Soviet Republics! We've come to make friends with you!"[72]

Science and the Soviet Union

Tolstoi was not the only author to question the futuristic visions depicted in contemporary Soviet sf. In this section, we will examine the work of another two authors who, in their own ways, questioned the dominant scientific optimism. Both were unusual in adopting the contemporary or near-future USSR as an imaginative location, rather than the distant future or an alien planet, and both experienced the hostility of the Soviet regime. The first, Andrei Platonov, is not usually associated with sf. Platonov produced several short stories quite different from anything else published during the 1920s. We will consider three of these here—"Descendants of the Sun," "The Lunar Bomb," and "The Ether Tract"—which deal with the same themes and form a loose trilogy explicitly acknowledged within "The Ether Tract," when, during a visit to a grave at the "House of Remembrance" the narrator notes the memorial urns of the three central scientist-protagonists.[73]

Platonov's heroes are all scientists or engineers attempting to overcome the physical laws of the universe. Their goals are usually set very high, Peter Kreizkopf's plan to travel to the moon in "The Lunar Bomb" being the least

71 Zamyatin, "New Russian Prose," 102.

72 Tolstoi, *Aelita*, 97.

73 Andrei Platonov, "Descendants of the Sun" (1922), in *Worlds Apart*, trans. Elliott Urday, Alexander Levitsky, and Martha T. Kitchen, ed. Alexander Levitsky (London: Overlook Duckworth, 2007), 584–87; "The Ether Channel" (1928–30), in *Worlds Apart*, trans. Elliott Urday, Alexander Levitsky, and Martha T. Kitchen, ed. Alexander Levitsky (London: Overlook Duckworth, 2007), 591–615; "The Lunar Probe" (1926), in *Worlds Apart*, trans. Elliott Urday, Alexander Levitsky, and Martha T. Kitchen, ed. Alexander Levitsky (London: Overlook Duckworth, 2007), 587–91.

impressive. Vogulov, of "Descendants of the Sun," plans to utilize the vast explosive power of his "ultralight" super-fuel to control the climate by rearranging the surface of earth. In "The Ether Tract," Mikhail Kirpichnikov leads a project to dig a vast vertical shaft in the Siberian tundra which will tap into the thermal energy of the earth, while Kirpichnikov's colleague, Isaac Mathieson, develops a method of controlling machinery by thought alone and Kirpichnikov's son Egor discovers how to increase the size of any matter by feeding it a concentrated beam of "ether"—an omnipresent atmosphere of dead electrons.

Platonov's stories all strive to realize the spirit of that particularly Soviet scientific utopianism: the transformation of man through transformation of the world itself. Trotsky's words are particularly relevant to Platonov's sf: "Man will change the course of the rivers, reshape and remove mountains and he will lay down rule for the ocean. Most likely, thickets and forests and grouse and tigers will remain, but only where he commands them to remain."[74] "The Ether Tract" claims that only the USSR provides the right environment for this transformation: "As an intelligent and honest man, having graduated from a tile-making workshop, [Kirpichnikov] knew that outside socialism scientific work and technological revolution are impossible."[75] Yet this Soviet bias is not consistently reflected in any of the stories, all of which depict an altruistic internationalism and a global era in which "The passion for knowledge [has become] a new organic sense for man, just as demanding, incisive, and rich as the faculty of sight or love."[76] Rather than passively observing the universe and accepting its nature, man is filled with the confidence that it is possible to realize his will: "The radio's electromagnetic waves were whispering through the atmosphere and the interstellar ether, the challenging words of Man— the builder. Ever more insistently, unbearably, thoughts and machines were penetrating unknown, unconquered, rebellious matter and molding it into Mankind's slave."[77]

However, these optimistic views of a scientific future are continually undermined by unresolved ambiguities. As Seifrid writes: "Far from depicting ... unqualified victory, [the stories] tend to portray science as failing,

---

74 Leon Trotsky, *Literature and Revolution*, trans. Rose Strunsky (London: Redworlds, 1991), 280.
75 Andrei Platonov, "Efirnyj trakt" (1928–30), in various ed., *Derevjannaja koroleva* (Moscow: Russkaja Kniga, 1999), 63–128, at 76.
76 Platonov, "The Ether Channel," 592.
77 Platonov, "Descendants of the Sun," 584.

or at least attaining partial success over the cosmos."[78] Man's increasingly extreme attempts to master the world are inseparable from the proportionate dangers that they incur. Vogulov's ultralight poses a threat to the entire planet: "The Carpathians had resettled themselves in closer proximity to the stars."[79] Kreizkopf does not return from the moon. And Mathiesson's experiments displace the constellation of Hercules while inadvertently bringing meteors crashing to earth. These failures are reiterated in "The Ether Tract" when Mikhail Kirpichnikov's thermal tunnel uncovers the remains of an advanced prehistoric species of humanity, the Aiuna, who were destroyed by their own experiments, despite which Egor Kirpichnikov successfully recreates their technology at the end of the story.

The progression of history seems to be cyclical and inevitable, and yet there is something glorious in the attempt. The frenzied attempts of mankind to change their world give life a new meaning. Life is harsher but more worthy; the struggle with nature has created an epic humanity driven by proportionately monumental emotions and desires: "man began to die in the heat of his labors, to write books celebrating pure courage, to love as Dante had loved, and to live not years but rather days. And man did not regret this."[80] In this milieu, the "sense of wonder" becomes life's driving force. While Kreizkopf hurtles towards the moon, he transmits: "Announce that I am at the source of earthly poetry: someone on Earth guessed the existence of the Star symphonies and, inspired, wrote poems."[81]

If Platonov's sf offers an ambiguous view of the transformational powers of science, that of Mikhail Bulgakov is consistent in its pessimism. Bulgakov's novellas, *The Heart of a Dog* (written 1925, published 1968) and *The Fatal Eggs* (1925), are the only examples of Soviet sf considered in this essay that explicitly criticize the Soviet regime.[82] Rather like a Soviet-era Gogol, Bulgakov passed by mere surrealism in favour of sf and, eventually, fantasy. The author was evidently familiar with the genre. His works reveal a clear debt to Wells, explicitly so in *The Fatal Eggs*: "Vladimir Ipatyich, the heroes of H. G. Wells are

---

78   Thomas Seifrid, *Andrei Platonov: Uncertainties of Spirit* (Cambridge: Cambridge University Press, 1992), 51.

79   Platonov, "Descendants of the Sun," 585.

80   Ibid., 586.

81   Platonov, "The Lunar Probe," 589.

82   Mikhail Bulgakov, *The Heart of a Dog*, trans. Michael Glenny (London: Vintage, 2005); *The Fatal Eggs*, trans. Mirra Ginsburg, in *The Fatal Eggs and Other Soviet Satire* (London: Quartet Encounters, 1993), 53–133.

nothing compared to you. And I had always thought his stories were no more than fairy tales ... Do you remember his Food of the Gods?"[83]

Both works foreground a single similar sf theme. *The Heart of a Dog* describes the transplant of a human brain and testicles into the body of a stray, which subsequently turns into a man. But the organs were extracted from the corpse of a Communist sympathizer, and the resulting creature cannot be taught to behave in a mature manner and causes havoc. *The Fatal Eggs* depicts the misapplication of a newly discovered type of light that causes biological organisms to grow monstrously. Having requisitioned an invention that exploits this phenomenon, the government attempts to rejuvenate the USSR's chicken population, which has been decimated by a savage epidemic. However, bureaucratic bungling results in the wrong eggs being hatched, releasing giant snakes, crocodiles, and ostriches across the Russian countryside.

This Frankenstein theme emphasizes the dangers of meddling with nature, although the particulars of the lesson vary. *The Heart of a Dog* suggests that it is impossible to improve the human race through science, and perhaps unnecessary: "Will you kindly tell me why one has to manufacture artificial Spinozas when some peasant woman may produce a real one any day of the week?"[84] On the other hand, *The Fatal Eggs* demonstrates the perils of the misuse of science.

Both stories place the individual scientist in stark contrast to the Soviet regime and the general populace. Far from encapsulating the spirit of the age, the scientist is shown to have no sympathy with the new regime, in which science is given little respect or freedom. Both scientists, Preobrazhensky (*The Heart of a Dog*) and Persikov (*The Fatal Eggs*), are almost the same age, 60 and 58, and are world-famous men who have considered departing from the USSR altogether. Both have experienced the scarcities of the new regime in an identical, material way—the loss of rooms urgently needed for their work—and consider the postrevolutionary period to be an unnatural aberration. In spite of their flaws—Preobrazhensky is a snob, Persikov is an introvert with no social skills—they have considered the new era from an analytical perspective and found its claims inconsistent with reality, as Preobrazhensky argues:

> You can't sweep the dirt out of the tram tracks and settle the fate of the Spanish beggars at the same time! No one can ever manage it, doctor—and above all it can't be done by people who are two hundred years

83 Bulgakov, *The Fatal Eggs*, 65.
84 Bulgakov, *The Heart of a Dog*, 108.

behind the rest of Europe and who so far can't manage to do up their own
fly-buttons properly![85]

Far from providing an environment in which science can flourish, the new
regime is considered to be *incompatible* with science. "You do not know how
the amphibians differ from the reptiles?" Persikov asks his students. "It is
simply ridiculous, young man. The amphibians have no pelvic buds. None. Yes,
you ought to be ashamed. You are probably a Marxist?"[86] Unlike the govern-
ment-sponsored projects of Platonov's sf, science in Bulgakov's novellas takes
place far from official organs. Preobrazhensky can only fund his attempts to
improve the human race by running a medical practice that provides special
regenerative surgery. His talent in the latter, which is particularly useful in matters of sexual health, brings him powerful friends who rely upon him but who
know nothing of his greater goals. Similarly, although Persikov works for a state
university, the men in the Kremlin seem to be the last know about his discovery.
When they do take an interest, it is only to save face on the world stage, and
even then the vital equipment for Persikov's experiments can only be obtained
from abroad.

Professional Science Fiction

By the end of the 1920s, Soviet sf had ceased to attract authors of all back-
grounds that were interested in exploiting the genre and had begun to acquire
its own dedicated practitioners. The first professional sf author in Russia was
Alexander Beliaev, an invalid whose works are still read with much affection
in Russia today. Beliaev was prolific and influential enough for his work to be
considered on its own. The author published at least seventeen sf novels and
scores of short stories, for the first time raising the possibility of a Soviet sf writer
whose range might equal that of Wells. In fact, Wells personally congratulated
Beliaev during his 1934 visit to Leningrad: "They differ favourably from the
novels of the Western writers. I am even a little bit envious of their success!"[87]
Beliaev's oeuvre is far too large to consider in its entirety; we will concen-
trate on certain important themes that distinguished his sf from that of his

---

85 Ibid., 40.
86 Bulgakov, *The Fatal Eggs*, 56.
87 Maria Kozyreva and Vera Shamina, "Russia Revisited," in *The Reception of H. G. Wells in
    Europe*, ed. Patrick Parrinder and John S. Parrington (London: Thoemmes Continuum,
    2005), 48–62, at 57.

contemporaries. Among Beliaev's works are examples of stories written in the educational style of Tsiolkovsky and Obruchev, such as "Above the Abyss,"[88] in which the narrator is hypnotized into believing that gravity has been reversed and mankind is spinning into space. There is also an example of a highly ideological novel, *The Struggle in Space*, which amalgamates the usual far-future technological speculation of the utopia with a devastating war between America and the Pan-European and Pan-Asiatic Unions of Soviet Republics. However, these kinds of sf are in the minority beside his adventure novels.[89]

Beliaev's two most popular works, *Professor Dowell's Head* and *The Amphibian*, are representative of his work in the second half of the decade.[90] The first, set in 1920s Paris, concerns a nefarious scheme by the scientist Kern, whose colleague, Dowell, has developed a miraculous technique to reanimate the human head after death. Once a suitable body is available the head can be reattached and the individual granted a new life. Rather than allow Dowell to announce his discovery to the world, Kern keeps Dowell's disembodied head hidden in his laboratory and forces the more talented scientist to dictate scientific theories which Kern passes off as his own. *The Amphibian* describes the adventures of Ichthyander, a young Argentinian man who is given fish-gills by his "father," the scientist Salvator, which allow him to survive underwater. Once discovered, Ichthyander's abilities make him a natural target for the machinations of local pearl-gatherers and the enmity of the local Christian leaders.

The emphasis on biological science is one of the defining features of Beliaev's sf, and demonstrates his debt to Wells. However, unlike Bulgakov, Beliaev imbues his sf with an optimistic glow. Science is always innately beneficial, and although some might try to turn it to their own desires they are always defeated in the end. It is particularly significant that Beliaev gives little space to questions of ethics, an ambivalence that is particularly conspicuous in the treatment of Salvator, whose work is the transplanting of animal parts into unwitting children. Yet, when Salvator is called before a court in the final moments of *The Amphibian*, the issue is realized as an oversimplified conflict

---

88 Alexander Beliaev, "Nad bezdnoi" (1927), in *Science Fiction and Adventure Stories by Soviet Writers*, ed. E. Krichevskaya and N. Ostroumova (Moscow: Progress Publishers, no date), 32–52.

89 Alexander Beliaev, *The Struggle in Space* (summary) (1928), http://www.sovlit.com/space.html, last accessed 26/02/2011.

90 Alexander Beliaev, *Professor Dowell's Head* (1925), trans. Antonia W. Bouis (New York: Macmillan Publishing Co. Inc., 1980); *The Amphibian* (1928), trans. L. Koleshnikov (Moscow: Foreign Languages Publishing House, no date).

between secularism and religion. Salvator argues that the principal and only victim in the case is God himself. Other works, such as the short story "The Devil's Windmill," in which the scientist Wagner discovers a way to employ severed human limbs as powerful machines, similarly reduce any opposition to science to mere superstition.[91] In general, however, Beliaev does not let matters of science and ethics get in the way of the main element of his novels, which is plot. Of all the authors considered in this essay, Beliaev most of all subordinates sf's "sense of wonder" to other requirements of plot, and, if *The Amphibian* and *Professor Dowell's Head* are driven by conventional themes of romance and adventure that seem strangely incongruous beside the scientific issues, it is largely because they are aimed at a younger readership. This also explains the mild nature of the scientific descriptions, which never approach Bulgakov's gruesome images.

Beliaev's sf is also set apart by setting. Avoiding the future, Mars, and even Russia itself, Beliaev opts for contemporary foreign locations, refusing even to place any Russian or Soviet characters within his plots (although the "Professor Wagner" series takes place in Russia, there is almost no sense of location, and the eponymous scientist is given a non-Russian name). Minor ideological confrontations sometimes arise in *The Amphibian* and *Professor Dowell's Head* that are recognisable expressions of the Soviet context, such as Salvator's following statement: "No, I could not make Ichthyander—and other Ichthyanders—public property in a country where greed and the struggle for survival turn the greatest discoveries into something evil, only adding to the amount of human suffering."[92] Yet, other than regularly undermining religion, there is no constant ideological line. Although Beliaev would portray Americans entirely negatively in *The Struggle in Space*, one of the heroes of *Professor Dowell's Head* is Dowell, an American who came to Paris during WWI to be a surgeon. The foreigner and the foreign landscape have become elements of the fantasy, rather than devices to demonstrate the decadence and degradation of the capitalist world, as in *The Garin Death Ray*.

The combined effect of these qualities is a notable reduction of the horizons of sf. Conflicts are always localized; protagonists are always struggling for the sake of personal relationships and love rather than acting as spokespeople for monolithic constructions such as "the workers." And the consequences

---

91 Alexander Beliaev, "Chertova mel'nica" (1929), http://lib.ru/RUFANT/BELAEW/hel-mill.txt, last accessed February 26, 2011.

92 Beliaev, *The Amphibian*, 266.

of the scientific breakthrough in question are always obscured. There is no scientific-technological, or even social, revolution, because Beliaev has severed the connection between scientific progress and Soviet ideology.

Concluding Remarks

Soviet sf flourished in the 1920s because it was ideally suited to support the emphasis upon science and technology that was an integral tenet of Bolshevik utopianism. Part of its attraction was that it was flexible enough to be adapted to a wide range of needs. At times sf was exploited to realize the projected results of the revolutionary doctrine: the overwhelming predominance of utopian themes indicates sf's close relationship with the contemporary climate. At other times sf offered an ambiguous assessment of Soviet scientific optimism, although the genre could also be utilized to explicitly undermine the new regime by attacking this cherished tenet.

However, Soviet sf output began to decline sharply from 1927 and, other than a rise in the immediate prewar years, was generally lower and more sporadic throughout the 1930s and 1940s.[93] All of the major sf writers of the earlier part of the 1920s left the genre. Some, such as Zamiatin, departed from the USSR entirely, while others, such as Itin, were oppressed by the regime. Even writers such as Tolstoi, whose work continued to be well received, turned their back on sf. *Selena* was forced to cease publication in 1928, the almanac's regular names only briefly able to find homes in other publications.

What had caused this rapid reversal in the regime's attitude to sf? McGuire offers four possible reasons: that sf ran contrary to the general European literary trend of "realist objectivity" after World War I; that the escapist nature of sf was simply a distraction from the actual physical problems of building socialism; that sf was lumped together with other ideologically suspect literary movements; that much of sf was perceived to be either ideologically naïve or anti-Soviet.[94] These reasons are useful but avoid the broader picture. The crucial factor is that the end of the 1920s witnessed the rise of Stalinism and the tremendous transformation of the political and social context of the USSR. In this new environment, all arts rapidly lost whatever freedom they may have had and became subservient to the increasingly totalitarian state, although the reductive pressures of Stalinism and imminent Socialist Realism were

---

93 McGuire, *Red Stars*, 18.
94 Ibid., 14–15.

particularly damaging to a genre that reveled in the freedom to overcome the usual boundaries of time and space. The regime's new, limited, and linear vision of the future left little room for imagination, and its attitude to science itself altered sharply, curtailing the spirit of broad scientific optimism and discouraging individual speculation and international dialogue.[95] Emergent Stalinism, with its narrow, unassailable vision, would not tolerate alternative versions of the future.

It was not until after Stalin's death that Soviet sf began to recover from these blows. Censorship eased slightly, and, with the success of the early space program, both technological utopianism and sf experienced a renaissance. This change was heralded in 1957, the year of Sputnik's launch, by the publication of Ivan Yefremov's *Andromeda*, an encyclopaedic depiction of the earth in the fifth millennium, combining high adventure and romance with space travel, aliens, a range of technological speculations, and a properly fleshed out interplanetary communist society.[96] Three years later Gagarin successfully made man's first trip into space. The second golden age of Soviet sf, dominated by the Strugatsky brothers, was about to begin.

---

95 Graham, Loren R., *Science in Russia and the Soviet Union: A Short History* (Cambridge: Cambridge University Press, 1993), 122.

96 Ivan Yefremov, *Andromeda: A Space-Age Tale* (1957), trans. George Hanna (Moscow: Progress Publishers, 1980).

The Plural Self: Zamiatin's *We* and the Logic of Synecdoche

ELIOT BORENSTEIN

Borenstein, Eliot. "The Plural Self: Zamiatin's *We* and the Logic of Synecdoche." *The Slavic and East European Journal* 40, no. 4 (1996): 667–83.

Evgenij Zamiatin's most famous work begins with an implicit paradox: his biting satire of utopian collectivism is entitled "We" ("My"), and yet the first word of the novel proper is the title's antithesis: "I" ("Ja"). The precarious relationship of the individual "I" to the collective "we" is so striking that even the narrator, D-503, whose perceptions of his own dilemma are limited by his initial blind faith in the One State, is painfully aware of it. One might easily conclude that the "I/We" dichotomy is either a simple vehicle for Zamiatin's anti-collectivist stance, or an extended parody of the collectivist pretensions of proletarian writers.[1] I would argue, however, that Zamiatin's inquiry into the nature of the self is far more subtle: in *We*, Zamiatin reveals the problem of selfhood to be a problem of language. The entire novel can be seen as a challenge to the linguistic and philosophical assumptions on which D-503's initial "state-sanctioned" conception of the self is based: the logic of synecdoche and the possibility of "wholeness" or "integration." When forced to explain to his imaginary readers the nature of his relationship to the One State, D-503 repeatedly asserts that his "I" has value only when it is a synecdoche for "we": an "I" that protests its independence is no more viable than a severed finger.[2] D-503's

---

1 "We" was the pronoun of choice for the poets of the "Proletarian Culture" and "Smithy" movements. For a discussion of Zamiatin as a response to proletarian poetics, see Carden, Dolgopolov, Doronchenkov, Etkin, Heller ("La Prose" 219; "Zamiatin" 147–55), and Lewis and Weber.

2 Evgenij Zamiatin, *My: roman, povesti, rasskazy, p'esy, stat'i vospominaniia,* comp. E. B. Skorospelova (Kishinev: Lit. artistike, 1989), 68. All references to the text use this edition. All translations are my own.

predilection for synecdoche is apparent throughout his journal, and can be seen as a natural outgrowth of both the novel's subject matter and the mathematician narrator's unplanned detour into the terra incognita of poetic language. But the prevalence of synecdoche, which can be considered to include not only such striking images as D-503's self-description as a germ or phagocyte within the larger body of the One State, but also his persistent translation of human events into formulas involving fractions, must be considered in the larger context of the One State's ideology.[3]

In his *Grammar of Motives*, Kenneth Burke extends synecdoche beyond its standard dictionary definition ("part for the whole, whole for the part, container for the contained, sign for the thing signified, ... cause for effect, effect for cause"[4]) to the realm of philosophy: Burke identifies the "'noblest synecdoche,' the perfect paradigm for all lesser usages" in metaphysical models that assert the "identity of 'microcosm' and 'macrocosm.'" Such doctrines, which treat the individual as "the replica of the universe, and vice versa," are the "ideal synecdoche, since microcosm is related to macrocosm as part to whole, and either the whole can represent the part or the part can represent the whole." Burke also finds a similar synecdochic pattern in "all theories of political representation, where some part of the social body ... is held to be 'representative' of the society as a whole."[5] The political ramifications of synecdoche are easily exploited in the totalitarian context, and, as Burke's definition suggests, this exploitation works on more than one level: both the leadership of society by a fuhrer or a "conscious vanguard" and the individual's societal role as "cog in the wheel" or "worker bee in the hive" rely on synecdoche. In the context of the novel, the logic of synecdoche holds a dual appeal for Zamiatin's narrator: not only does it elucidate the hierarchy of the collective over the individual, but it is also quite seductive for a mathematician who continually (and unmathematically) attempts to prove, rather than disprove, by example.

D-503's identity crisis, which involves the discovery of an apparently distinct and separate self of which he had been previously unaware, arises when the introspection required by writing leads him to follow the ideology

---

3 Neither synecdoche nor the fragmentation of the self are limited to the novel *We*. Readers of his short story "The Cave" (1922) will recall that the protagonist is torn between his "old" self and his "caveman" self (325); Zamiatin's "In the Boondocks" ("Na kuličkax") prominently features the motif of "human pieces." It is in the novel *We*, however, that Zamiatin explores these themes most thoroughly.

4 Burke, Kenneth. *A Grammar of Motives* (Berkeley and Los Angeles, 1969), 507–8.

5 Ibid., 508.

of synecdoche to its logical conclusions. The fundamentally hierarchical One State employs synecdoche to create a model in which the microcosm of the individual not only represents but is subsumed by the collective. But, as Burke notes, synecdoche implies "an integral relationship, a relationship of convertibility, between ... two terms."[6] When D-503 becomes conscious of himself as a "self," he unwittingly seizes upon the "identity of 'microcosm' with 'macrocosm'" implied by his synecdochic connection to the One State and creates an identity that, like the "we" of the One State, is plural. The "I" discovered by D-503 can never by an indivisible integer, but is instead subjected to endless fractioning and fragmentation. Like the "we" of the One State, D-503's "I" must function not only as a whole, but as the sum of its parts.

Certainly, one is tempted when analyzing Zamiatin's novel to look at *We* as the narrator himself envisions his story: the conflict between D-503, the loyal State cipher, and D-503, the passionate and irrational rebel.[7] Yet to focus on this struggle, so reminiscent of a medieval morality play, is to examine the problem of which D-503 is most conscious; in effect, by following D-503's lead, we take on the role of the implied reader whom he addresses throughout the text. Rather than viewing the novel in terms of a split into two discrete personae,

---

6 Ibid., 508.

7 Such interpretations are most often found in studies that treat *We* in the context of other "dystopian" or "anti-utopian" novels. See, for example, Beauchamp (93), Richards (222–23), Sicher (386), and Warrick (70–71). Often such interpretations are expressed in the language of humanism: Alexandra Aldridge, noting D-503's "frantic search for identity" (70), cites Robert Elliott's assertion that D-503 is "struggling to become human" (Aldridge 71). Robert Louis Jackson finds that the "tragedy" of D-503's story is that "the conflict of two 'I's,' of reason and instinct is never resolved in a new synthesis" (154). Margaret Mikesella and Jon Suggs state that "only through acknowledging this buried self can D-503 achieve autonomy" (92). For a decidedly anti-humanist view on this aspect of Zamiatin, see Mary Ellen Brooks's Maoist reading of Zamiatin and Solzhenitsyn. Gary Rosenshield, refuting the idea that D-503 "oscillates from one personality extreme to the other," or that there is a "regular progression the course of the novel from the old to the new self," finds that the novel presents "a personality the warring sides of which are engaged in an uninterrupted struggle for supremacy" (55). Most recent criticism, however, rejects a straightforward division in D-503's psyche. Barratt notes that the "conflict within D between his 'old' and 'new' self," the "growth of D's artistic spirit" is "more apparent than real" ("Revolution" 367–58). Using Jung as his point of departure, Collins sees the entire novel as a representation of the disparate aspects of D-503's psyche (71). Though his analysis is quite sophisticated, it still relies on an agonistic model in which the "eventual victory of the true Self" is, if not the outcome of the novel, at least a possibility (78). The most complex approach to the problem of the self in *We* deals with issues of authorship, and is developed by Beehler, Cooke ("Manuscript"), Csicsery-Ronay, Edwards, Morson, and Rosenshield, and Štriedter. Their contributions are examined below.

we must instead analyze the two radically different states of consciousness through which the narrative is filtered. By mediating the action through a consciousness that continually swings from dissociation (multiple selves) to solipsism (one self creating and encompassing all others), Zamiatin calls the very possibility of the stable self into question. Though these two mental states are superficially antithetical, the difference between the breakdown of the unitary self into its component parts (dissociation) and the insistence that any Other is only an extension of one's own subjectivity (solipsism) is, for Zamiatin, merely a matter of perspective. Each case recapitulates the One State's model of the synecdochic self, in which a monolithic voice arises from the combination of constituent parts. Both cases can be represented by an integer that is the sum of a set of fractions. Yet just as I-330, the mouthpiece for Zamiatin's ideas on entropy and revolution, asserts that there is "no final integer," and therefore no permanent social revolution, the oscillation between solipsism and dissociation suggests that there is no final, essential "Self," and that the very idea of the whole, undivided integer (and the concomitant ideology of integration so essential to the One State) is illusory.[8] There is no "Self" in this text, nor can there be; instead, there are only parts that pretend to speak for an illusory whole.

As many critics have observed, D-503's status as an anonymous member of the monolithic collective is challenged the moment he puts pen to paper.[9] By calling on its citizens to portray the glory of the One State for the sake of the less-enlightened denizens of far-off worlds, the proclamation in the *State Gazette* compels the narrator to become aware of his synecdochic relationship to the State. D-503 cannot write about his position within the collective "we" without adopting a rhetorical stance that is, at least formally, outside of its confines. Unlike the anonymous voice of the *State Gazette*, which never uses the first person singular, D-503 cannot speak for the One State as the One

---

8 In his close reading of the first entry of We, Andrew Barratt identifies the "vocabulary of integration" as an essential component of the State's ideology ("First Entry" 103). Michael Beehler offers an excellent critique of Zamiatin's rhetoric, charging that Zamiatin's "dialectics relies upon the figure of the integer, the whole, unambiguous, countable entity that can be rigorously distinguished from other equally clear and well-defined entities" (54). Though he uses this observation to analyze the problem of the individual and the status of writing, Beehler's focus on the totalitarian desire to purge both the text and the state of superfluous "noise" does not lead him to question the ontological status of the self in Zamiatin's novel.

9 See, for example, Jurij Štriedter: "D-503 has to communicate his message to other worlds ... For this purpose he has to imagine their 'linguistic consciousness.' Thus, discovering the possibility of the 'words of others,' he discovers, gradually and slowly, his own 'word.'"

State; he can only speak as a part on behalf of the whole. Any perceptions provided by D-503 can only paint a portrait of the One State from within: when D-503 looks in the mirror, he sees D-503, rather than the entire One State. Though this paradox would appear to be simply formal, it provides the immediate impetus for the oscillation between dissociation and solipsism as the novel proceeds. Indeed, the journal's initial entry, in which the "we"-centered discourse of the *State Gazette* sets the "I" of D-503's narrative in sharp relief, gives the first indication of the connection between language and D-503's mental state. The first time D-503 refers to himself as "I," he appears to "know his place": he asserts that he is not writing, but copying ("Ja prosto spisyvaju"). Moreover, the words he quotes were not "written" but "printed" ("napečatano"): the monolithic discourse of the One State betrays no origins.[10] But after D-503 has fulfilled his duty and copied this lengthy excerpt, he turns his attention to himself: "Ja pišu eto-i čuvstvuju: u menja gorjat ščeki."[11] D-503's second sentence begins, like his first, with the word "ja," but the self-deprecation of the first sentence is replaced by self-consciousness. Tellingly, his verb "pišu," which describes his activity, prompts another verb "čuvstvuju," which calls attention to the writing "ja" as a thinking, feeling subject. His awareness of himself as a writer becomes an awareness of himself as a physical body: the words of the *State Gazette*, which command him to write, inevitably direct his attention inward.

This sudden self-consciousness finds an appropriate metaphor in Entry 11: his growing reflexivity on paper is "mirrored" by his dismay upon looking at his reflection closely for the first time. Just as D-503 will eventually express shock that such strange and irrational words spring forth from his pen, so too does he fail to identify completely with the "outsider" he sees in the mirror. Before he began writing, D-503 presumably had at least a rudimentary sense of correspondence between his "I" as linguistic subject and the physical body of the number D-503. By Entry 11, however, this connection has broken down. D-503's examination of himself in the mirror "for the first time in [his] life" ("pervyj raz v žizni") leads to a rejection of his image: "s izumleniem vižu sebja, kak kogo-to 'ego.'" As he gazes in the mirror, D-503 grows certain that the man

---

10 Štriedter sees the novel as the narrator's "polemical dialogue" with the "authoritarian, unique, and absolute word" of the "Unique State" (188). In his Bakhtinian reading, Streidter claims that the novel demonstrates "how, in an established totalitarian Unique State, the individual can rediscover himself through his linguistic consciousness and how the plurality or polyphony of reality can be rediscovered and become manifest ... through the creation of the novel" (189).

11 Zamiatin, *My*, 10.

in the mirror is "an outsider, alien to me, I have met him for the first time in my life. And I am real, and I am not him" ("postoronij, čužoj mne, ja vstretilsja s nim pervyj raz v žizni. A ja nastojaščij, ja—ne—on"[12]). D-503's experience with the mirror is essentially schizoid, reinforcing the sense that the D-503 who looks in the mirror is not the same D-503 who looks back.

Even more striking is the fact that D-503 switches allegiances from the spectator to the man in the mirror without even seeming to be aware that he has done so; initially, D-503 describes the man in the mirror as the "I that is he" ("Vot ja-on"), and proceeds to describe this man as though he were a third person. But when he looks into the mirror image's eyes in an attempt to figure out what hides behind them "there" ("tam"), suddenly the narrator's "I" now refers to man in the mirror:

> И из «там» (это «там» одновременно и здесь и бесконечно далеко) – из «там» я гляжу на себя – на него, и твердо знаю: он … – посторонний, чужой мне, … А я – не – он …[13]

By the time this passage is finished, D-503 is literally no longer himself, for the "I" that narrates the journal has aligned itself with the image that is initially rejected as an exterior "him." This transition is not only easily lost on the reader, but has apparently escaped the attention of the narrator as well: what appears to be a straightforward rejection of an alien self at the end of the paragraph is actually a denial of the subject who was narrating when the paragraph began. Nonetheless, the narrator continues as though no such change has taken place.

Once again, the pronominal confusion sparked by the mirror scene can be viewed as a more explicit textualization of the alienation inherent in the writing process. The subject's casual abandonment of the speculative D-503 for the man in the mirror resembles one of D-503's narrative strategies that is as subtle as it is pervasive: the identification of the narrating "I" with both the subject of recollected events ("At that moment I sensed my Guardian Angel behind my back"[14]) as well as with the D-503 who sits at his desk and writes about what has occurred. Though the gap between the two D-503's might appear purely formal, in the case of a narrator who constantly regrets the feelings he experienced only moments ago, the ability to casually recreate a previous

---

12 Ibid., 43.
13 Ibid., 43.
14 Ibid., 47.

(and antithetical) state of mind entails still more dissociation. The man who looks in the mirror (here, D-503 as writer) is obliged to merge his "I" with that of the D-503 whose image he examines (that is, the "hero" of the events recalled, as it were, "in tranquility"). When recalling emotions of which he is now ashamed, the narrator does not take advantage of the passing of time to distance himself from his past experience; on the contrary, the regretful "I" who writes the journal entries quite effortlessly recreates the alien "I" who experienced the events he describes. Each retelling of the past obliges D-503 to become his "other self" all over again. Just as the narrative "I" unconsciously switches sides as D-503 looks in the mirror, so too does the narrator unwittingly become the "alien I" that is the focus of his description; in each case, subject and object switch roles without knowing it. The mirror scene shows why one cannot accept D-503's own characterization of his dilemma as a split between two warring selves: D-503 is only capable of describing those aspects of the problem of which he is aware. When he reflects on his dilemma, he cannot help but oversimplify it.

The mirror scene, however, is a rare moment when D-503 can observe his other "self" as though they were completely separate entities; usually he envisions his dissociation in terms of a container whose hidden contents are forcing their way to the surface. Thus in the very first entry D-503 resorts to a peculiar comparison: his feelings resemble those of a woman who first feels the pulse of a "small, blind little person" within her ("ešče krošečnogo, slepogo čelovečka"). The result is a double consciousness: "Èto ja i odnovremenno—neja."[15] Andrew Barratt has connected this "small, blind little person" with D-503's imaginative or irrational self; this passage, then, provides a preview of the conflict that will develop between the two D-503's.[16] While this argument is persuasive, we must nonetheless examine the structure of the imagery as well as its content. In the space of one short entry, D-503 shifts between two metaphors of self: first he is only a small unit encompassed by a larger group ("Ja, D-503, stroitel' Integrala,—ja tol'ko odin iz matematikov Edinogo Gosudarstva"[17]), then he himself is the containing entity. Both metaphors are based on the body as an organizing principle: in each case, the body is the container of constituent elements. The body of the One State is sketched only later in the narrative, such as in D-503's description of the masses as a "million-headed

---

15 Ibid., 11.
16 Andrew Barratt, "The First Entry of *We*: An Explanation," *The Structural Analysis of Russian Narrative Fiction*, ed. Joe Andrew (Keele: Keele University Press, 1984), 108.
17 Zamiatin, *My*, 10.

body" ("millionogolovoe telo"[18]) in Entry 22 or a "million-armed body" ("millionorukoe telo") in Entry 3.[19] Here, it is alluded to only when D-503 declares his willingness to tear out part of himself and lay it "at the feet" ("k nogam") of the One State, an admittedly conventional figure of speech that, were it not for subsequent developments, would hardly merit our attention. But the similarities of the two "bodies" show that D-503, though soon to become a past master at metaphor, can only create a sense of individual self through analogy to the larger, more familiar "Self" of the One State. The smaller "self" (or "body") of D-503 becomes a miniature replica of the macrocosmic "body" of the society at large. Thus when the narrator's "self" dissociates into smaller "selves," D-503 ironically resembles the State in its hypostasis of the collective "body politic"; when D-503 imagines that even the external world is a subset of his own consciousness, he mimics the hegemonic aspirations of the authoritarian "we."

Both D-503's dissociation and his solipsism are parodies of the rational equations he uses to describe the number's relation to the One State. They put the lie to the supposed infallibility of mathematics: if the same formula (the whole = the sum of its parts) can be used to describe both extremes of D-503's consciousness, then something has been left out of the equation. When he plays apologist for the regime, however, D-503 cannot bring himself to abandon the elegant logic of the part's mathematical relationship to the whole (the logic of synecdoche). By using mathematics, D-503 casually dismisses the loss of ten "numbers"[20] during an accident on the launch pad: "Desjat' numerov—eto edva li odna stomillionnaja ast' massy Edinogo Gosudarstva."[21] As he develops his skills as a writer, however, D-503 turns to deceptively simple metaphors to encode and to demonstrate this basic formula. Thus, in Entry 20 he uses the metaphor of a scale:

> И вот – две чашки весов: на одной грамм, на другой тонна, на одной «я», на другой «мы», Единое Государство. Но ясно ли: допускать,

---

18 Ibid., 83.

19 Ibid., 16.

20 It is perhaps no accident that D-503's cold calculations contain, as Leighton Brett Cooke has discovered, a mathematical error: he is off by two decimal points, and thus underestimates the value of the ten men (Leighton Brett Cooke, "Ancient and Modern Mathematics in Zamyatin's *We*," in *Zamyatin's We: A Collection of Critical Essays*, ed. Gary Kern (Ann Arbor, MI: Ardis, 1988), 156).

21 Zamiatin, *My*, 71.

что у «я» могут быть какие-то «права» по отношению к Государству, и допускать, что грамм может уравновесит тонну – это совершенно одно и то же. Отсюда – распределение: тонне – права, грамму – обязанности; и естественный путь от ничтожества к величию: забыть, что ты – грамм и почувствовать себя миллионной долей тонны ... [22]

D-503's reasoning is, here as elsewhere, pure sophistry, dependent on the choice of a convincing metaphor rather than a well-developed argument. But the very mathematics that underlies D-503's justification of the One State is also nothing more than an aptly chosen metaphor, an attempt to transform the novel from story to story problem. The underlying assumption that mathematics has some bearing on the relationship between the individual and the collective is never tested through rational proof. Like most stories, it requires the willing suspension of disbelief: it can only be accepted on faith. Thus D-503 is closer to the essence of his beliefs when, after launching into a comparison of the "million-headed" body of the One State to the joyous existence of molecules and atoms, he deliberately simplifies his explanations for his "primitive" readers in Entry 22: "'My'—ot Boga, a 'Ja'—ot d'javola."[23]

That D-503's conception of the part's relation to the whole might be faulty is underscored by the mistakes he makes in the mathematical calculations in which he, one of the State's most valuable mathematicians, should presumably be proficient. In his excellent study of the use of mathematics in Zamiatin's novel, Leighton Brett Cooke shows that the One State and its supporters are "mathematically naive and often ignorant."[24] When D-503 calculates the chances of his being assigned to the very auditorium I-330 tells him to find, he divides the number of auditoriums (1500) by the total population of the One State (10,000,000), and determines that the chances were 3 in 20,000.[25] As Cooke points out, however, this equation is incorrectly formulated: rather than dividing the number of auditoriums by the population, D-503 should have divided 1 (D-503's auditorium) by 1500 (the total number of auditoriums in the One State).[26] Cooke uses this mistake as one of many examples of the State's mathematical weakness; for the purposes of the present study, however, the significance is not that D-503 has committed a mathematical error. Rather,

22 Ibid., 75.
23 Ibid., 83.
24 Cooke, "Ancient and Modern Mathematics," 151.
25 Zamiatin, *My*, 18.
26 Cooke, "Ancient and Modern Mathematics," 156.

it is the nature of the error that is revealing: he substitutes the entire population of the One State for himself. He has confused the whole with the part.

Thus D-503, who initially celebrates minute anonymity within the collective body of the One State, cannot maintain a stable sense of his relationship to the greater whole. D-503's ideological lapses are mirrored by a linguistic "slippage" that is fundamentally connected with identity: D-503's confused sense of his "I" is abetted by the constant redefinition of the term "we." Like all pronouns, both terms are inherently ambiguous "shifters" whose referent depends entirely on context. When referring to himself and the State, O-90, or I-330, he has no choice but to use the same word: "we." Only rarely does D-503 explicitly distinguish the collective "we" from the merely plural "we": "my vse" and "my vdvoem." His first romantic encounter with I-330 (Entry 10) resembles a rite of passage in reverse, in which D-503 leaves the larger, social sphere for incorporation within a smaller, intimate "nation of two." He has already passed the first test by neglecting to report I-330 to the authorities; now he is in a liminal state: "Ja byl otrezan ot mira —vdvoem c nej."[27] His choice of words reinforces his exclusion from the One State's "body politic" by prefiguring his later formulation of individualism as a severed finger ("ja otrezan," čelovečeskij palec, otrezannyi ot ruki"[28]). At the same time, it introduces the opposition between "my vse" and "my vdvoem."

D-503 cannot remain on his own, "cut off," for long, however. In his affair with I-330, he manages to submerge himself just as thoroughly (but just as ambiguously) as he has within the collective self of the One State. When he joins with I-330, however, it is not to form a new, metaphorical "body"; rather, both he and I-330 are repeatedly described as vessels for a common essence that flows back and forth between them. In a transparent reversal of standard sexual imagery, their first kiss is described as an opening of D-503's body: "v menja vlit glotok žgučego jada." The resulting intoxication turns D-503 into glass ("Ja stal stekljannym") allowing him to see the two different "I"'s within him.[29] On the surface, it would seem that the pregnancy metaphor of Entry One has come to fruition in Entry 10: the "other" D-503 has come out of its shell, which has now cracked and begun to break ("skorlupa treščala, vot sejčas razletitsja v kuski"[30]). This initial encounter, however, proves to be only a tease. When D-503 consummates his passion in Entry 13, the boundaries between

---

27 Zamiatin, *My*, 40.
28 Ibid., 68.
29 Ibid., 42.
30 Ibid., 42.

Self and Other are completely broken, with curious results. Just the touch of her shoulder causes him to realize that "we are one, it flows into me from her" ("my odno, iz nee perelivaetsja v menja"). As they walk, he repeats his identification with I-330 in a phrase that parodies the earlier marching of the entire state in Entry Two: "My šli dvoe—odno." Now he envisions the two of them (who are, we recall, one) as contained within the womb of the world, which is itself an "immense woman."[31] Thus far his identification with I-330 (and subsequent submergence within yet another containing entity) does nothing to suppress D-503's ego; far from it, he becomes convinced that "it's all for me: the sun, the fog, the pink, the gold—for me … " ("vse—dlja menja: sol'nce, tuman, rozovoe, zolotoe—dlja menja … "[32]). D-503's relationship with I-330 is one of constant submergence and aggrandizement, as is his relation with the world of the One State: when they finally make love, he is "poured into her" ("ja vlilsja v nee"), and the rest of the world disappears: "ne bylo Edinogo Gosudarstva, ne bylo menja." This total loss of self is transformed at the moment of climax to an identification of himself with the universe: "ja—vselennaja."[33]

D-503 is most comfortable and secure when he can inscribe himself within just such an enclosing (and sheltering) entity: though being part of I-330 or part of the One State does not prove a lasting solution to his preoperative identity crisis, his acceptance of his own role as a constituent element provides him with a temporary illusion of wholeness. Once again, this is a trick of perspective: as a part of the larger group, D-503 might seem minute and insignificant, but his relative smallness makes him appear indivisible. D-503 is himself aware that he is more likely to experience fragmentation when he is alone: Мне было жутко остаться с самым собой – или вернее, с этим новым, чужим мне, у кого только будто по странной случайности был мой номер: Д-503.[34] Salvation from both loneliness and fragmentation is offered by the fish-like Ju, who expresses her willingness to abandon the children entrusted to her by the State and stay with D-503, who is "also a child" ("Vy —tože ditja"). Significantly in a novel where maternity is repeatedly identified with enclosure (Entry 1; O-90's focus on her pregnant womb), the motherly Ju is capable of temporarily restoring D-503 to wholeness: Она быстро обклеила всего меня улыбками – по кусочку на каждых из моей трещин – и я почувствовал себя

---

31 Ibid., 50.
32 Ibid., 51.
33 Ibid., 52
34 Ibid., 33.

приятно, крепко связанным.[35] D-503, whose realization of metaphors is at times almost Majakovskijan, manages to elaborate the image of his "breakdown" to the extent that he imagines the possibility that someone might metaphorically put the pieces of D-503 back together.

The unstable nature of D-503's sense of self is the inevitable by-product of an unending process which, like the struggle between entropy and energy described by I-330, never results in a final synthesis. Both D-503's solipsism and his dissociation are the apparent results of his growing awareness of himself as an author. As Jurij Štriedter observes, D-503's attempt to communicate with other worlds necessitates the imagination of the "linguistic consciousness" of his intended readers, the discovery of "the possibility of the 'words of others.'"[36] Cooke comes to similar conclusions, emphasizing the importance of "confession, self-reflection and much digression" to D-503's "chosen genre," as well as the "continual estrangement" from his accustomed worldview that this genre requires.[37] D-503's obligation to imagine an addressee he cannot possibly know is an act of supreme imagination that cannot leave him unchanged.

Though Štriedter looks to Baxtin's conception of the novelistic genre's inherent dialogism to explain D-503's identity crisis, we must still remember that D-503 only realizes he is writing a novel as his writing progresses; initially, he sees his work only as a journal. D-503 turns to this form only because his mathematician's pen "is incapable of creating the music of assonance and rhyme" ("Moe privyčnoe k cifram pero ne v silax sozdat' muzyki assonansov i rifm[38]"). Though D-503 laments that his journal has begun to resemble an adventure novel,[39] the gap between his intention and his result can also be viewed in terms of poetry: instead of producing the outward-looking "odes" commanded by the One State, D-503 produces extended lyric poetry in prose. D-503's use of the lyric mode is paradoxically consistent with his goal of describing his (and the State's) life to an unknown audience. His task is reminiscent of Osip Mandel'štam's description of the relationship between the lyric

---

35 Ibid., 79. This is the third time D-503 refers to Ju's smiles as a "bandage" ("plastyr'") that can cover his wounds; the other two occasions are in Entries 18 and 19 (pages 69 and 71).

36 Jurij Štriedter, "Three Postrevolutionary Russian Utopian Novels," in *The Russian Novel from Pushkin to Pasternak*, ed. John Garrard (New Haven, CT: Yale University Press, 1983), 187.

37 Leighton Brett Cooke, "The Manuscript in Zamiatin's *We*," *Russian Literature* 17 (1980): 372, 374.

38 Zamiatin, *My*, 10.

39 Ibid., 68.

poet and his readers in his 1913 essay "On the Addressee" ("O sobesednike"): for Mandel'štam, the poet is like a swimmer who seals a description of his fate in a bottle and tosses it into the sea. Though the swimmer cannot address his letter to a concrete individual, the letter nonetheless has an intended reader: "Pis'mo, zapečatannoe v butylke, adresovano tomy, kto najdet ee. Našel ja. Značit, ja i est' tainstvennyj adresat."[40] Here one recalls D-503's frustration as he tries to imagine his reader: "Kto vas znaet, gde vy i kto."[41] For the work to have any power, the implied reader must always be distant and unknown, but there must nonetheless be an addressee: "Net liriki bez dialoga."[42] In an earlier article on Francois Villon, Mandel'štam elaborates on the demands his art puts on the poet: "Liričeskij poet po prirode svoej,—dvupoloe syščesto, sposobnoe k beščislennym rassceplenijam vo imja vnutrennego dialoga."[43] Baxtin's approach to the novel as a polyphonic genre draws our attention to the multi-voicedness of Zamiatin's text, but Mandel'štam's discussion of the interior dialogue and the unknown addressee is particularly well-suited for an examination of D-503's experience of this multi-voicedness as it encroaches on his work.[44] Like the lyric, the journal is a genre that demands both self-reflection and the creation of an imaginary, usually individual reader; here we should recall the common adolescent practice of naming one's journal as if it were a person (such as Anne Frank's "Kitty" or Zlata Filipović's "Mimi"). Even when no name is given to a journal, the internal dialogue inherent in the genre reveals itself when the writer addresses himself in the second person, as does D-503 in Entry 34: "Voz'mi sebja v ruki, D-503"[45]).

Though D-503 usually addresses his readers as if they were completely exterior to him, the boundary between them and the narrator is remarkably fluid. D-503 and the readers do not so much share personality traits as pass them back and forth. If D-503's creation of his readers initially entails the imagination of himself as something alien, these readers then serve as the perfect receptacles for any subsequent incongruities in D-503's own personality. Thus he begins to project all unsettling aspects of his own existence onto his readers, who are by definition alien and savage: "I ne vo mne iks (ètogo ne možet

---

40 Osip Mandel'štam, *Proza* (Ann Arbor, MI: Ardis, 1983), 17.
41 Zamiatin, *My*, 21.
42 Mandel'štam, *Proza*, 21.
43 Ibid., 5.
44 For a comparison of Mandel'štam theory of dialogue with that of Baxtin, see Boym (118–19, 125–26).
45 Zamiatin, *My*, 121.

byt')—prosto ja bojus', čto kakoj-nibyd' iks ostanetsja v vas, nevedomye moi citateli."[46]

As D-503 insists on a growing identification between himself and his unknown readers, he subjects them to the very fragmentation from which he is suffering, and which was both the cause and result of the readers' "existence." In his appeals for understanding, he asks his readers to imagine that they, too, are experiencing dissociation (Entries 5 and 16). By Entry 20, the narrator has divided his readers into opposing camps whose differences correspond to the split D-503 perceives within himself:

> Вы, ураниты, – суровые и черные, как древние испанцы, мудро умевшие сжигать на кострах, – вы молчите, мне кажется, вы – со мною. Но я слышу – розовые венеряне – что-то там о пытках, казнях, о возврате к варварским временам. Дорогие мои, мне жаль вас – вы не способны философски-математически мыслить.[47]

Though this division by planet obliges D-503 to paint a more elaborate picture of his unseen readers, it nevertheless creates a near-total identification of the readers with the narrator. If all of his readers understood him, they would resemble only that aspect of D-503 that happens to have the upper hand at the moment. By imagining opposition on the part of a portion of his readers, D-503 implies that the Venusians would support the "hairy man'"who is struggling for primacy in the narrator's consciousness. Thus each side of D-503 can claim the solidarity of one faction of the readership; each side has the comfort of knowing that it forms yet another "we" with some of the readers.

If the creation of the "readers" is an intrinsic part of D-503's growing dissociation, his opposing trend toward solipsism can be seen as an attempt to incorporate other members of the One State within himself, often with the help of his imaginary audience. On a number of occasions D-503 expresses grief at the thought that he has been cast out of the million-armed body of the State. By experimenting with solipsism, D-503 is essentially toying with the possibility of reestablishing this lost comradeship, but on his own terms. In effect, he recapitulates the mission of the Integral by trying to "integrate" those around him into his aggrandized "I"; having unintentionally cut himself off from the enclosing presence of the One State's "we," he attempts to take on the State's monologizing role for himself.

---

46 Ibid., 22.
47 Ibid., 76.

D-503's first moment of solipsism comes, appropriately enough, right after his first entry in the journal. In the initial entry, the process of writing had obliged him to look inward, to the point where he actually imagined another human being contained within him. In the second entry, D-503's extended praise of the glories of "our" regimented existence suddenly gives way to self-consciousness:

> . . . будто не целые поколения, а я – именно я – победил старого Бога и старую жизнь, именно я создал все это, и я как башня, я боюсь двинуть локтем, чтобы не посыпались осколки стен, куполов, машин . . . [48]

The first part of his statement could be rationalized away as merely an example of D-503's synecdochic logic gone haywire: as a part of the whole, D-503 can feel individual pride for a collective victory. But D-503's identification of himself as the creator, as well as his Majakovskijan portrayal of an enormous, towering body, cannot be explained in terms of his zeal for the One State. Instead, D-503's solipsism reveals itself to be a product of the act of writing. The above citation is made in the context of D-503's "estranged" perception as a chronicler for an unknown audience. His brief sensation of godliness is preceded by the statement that on this day (the day after he started his journal), he saw his world "as though I were seeing it just then for the first time in my life" ("kak budto tol'ko vot sejčas pervyj raz v žizni"[49]).

On other occasions when D-503 affirms what T. R. N. Edwards has called "an almost Berkeleian sense of himself . . . as the creator of the reality he records,"[50] he entertains the idea by juxtaposing his fellow numbers (who presumably have an existence exterior to D-503) with his imaginary readers (who presumably do not). Curiously, it is the readers who emerge as the more "real" of the two groups. D-503 asserts the fictionality of his fellow numbers and the reality of his readers when he feels that the other characters do not recognize his importance. Offended that the old woman who keeps watch at the Ancient House assumes that he must have come looking for I-330, D-503 writes in Entry 21:

> И что за странная манера – считать меня только чей-то тенью. А может быть, сами вы все – мои тени. Разве я не населил вами эти страницы

---

48 Ibid., 13.
49 Ibid., 12.
50 T. R. N. Edwards, *Three Russian Writers and the Irrational: Zamyatin, Pil'nyak and Bulgakov* (Cambridge: Cambridge University Press, 1982), 73.

– еще недавно белые четырехугольные пустыни. Без меня разве вы
увидели вас все те, кого я поведу за собой по узким тропинкам строк?[51]

The premise of D-503's logic is that the readers are *a priori* real, and that
inclusion in the text of the journal is the essential criterion for reality.[52]
When one examines Zamiatin's novel as metafiction, D-503's statement
is absolutely correct: none of the novel's characters would be known to us,
the readers, if D-503 had not written about them in his journal. Since their
status is derivative of D-503's own narrative existence, one can, indeed, call
the other characters his "shadows." The novel, however, is a psychological
narrative at the same time that it is metafictional; as D-503 puts it, the journal
is a "seismograph" that sketches the curve of "even the most insignificant of
[his] brain's waverings" ("daže samyx neznačitel'nyx mozgovyx kolebanij"[53]).
In *We*, the metafictional aspects of the narrative are inevitably the expression
of a solipsistic consciousness.

D-503's solipsism both leads to and results from Zamiatin's most incisive
critique of traditional notions of the subject: the fetishizing of the self in the
object of D-503's physical text. The journal becomes both the physical embodiment of D-503's psyche and the "objective" source of knowledge to which
D-503 turns in order to validate any given information or hypothesis. The text's
dual function as representation of both absolute truth and D-503's subjective
impressions is inherently self-referential and solipsistic: for D-503, the notes he
writes eventually usurp the State's role as unquestionable authority. The entry
that most clearly establishes the text's role is also, perhaps not coincidentally,
the one in which Zamiatin's ideas on entropy and energy are explained to D-503
by I-330: both Zamiatin's philosophy of infinite revolutions and the problem of
the self-referential text are integral parts of the novel's inquiry into the problem of identity. Painfully aware of his authorial role, D-503 begins Entry 28
with yet another address to his readers, to whom he acknowledges his "duty."[54]
But when he describes his discussion with I-330, his relationship to the text
is that of a reader rather than author. When D-503 calls the rebels' plans to

---

51 Zamiatin, *My*, 77.
52 Long before this passage, D-503 has already characterized reality as a text. In Entry 3, he
     tells his readers, "perhaps you have read the great book of history only up to the page our
     ancestors had reached 900 years ago" (15). Cooke notes several instances of D-503's use of
     textual imagery to describe the world ("Manuscript" 377–78).
53 Zamiatin, *My*, 22.
54 Ibid., 100.

overthrow the State "madness" ("bezumie"), I-330 counters with D-503's own words:

> Надо нам всем сойти с ума – как можно скорее сойти с ума. Это говорил кто-то вчера. Ты помнишь? Там ...
>
> Это у меня записано. И следовательно, это было на самом деле.[55]

I-330 unintentionally appeals to D-503's vanity not once, but twice: she cites his own words to dismiss his argument, and this in turn causes D-503 to compare her citation with the text of his journal in order to confirm its truth. Now the text, which he earlier characterized as a "seismograph" of his brain's activity, has become an unimpeachable source.

For D-503, author of the journal, to become D-503, reader of the journal, involves yet another dissociation: the representation of D-503's own consciousness is treated as though it were the work of another. This split is, of course, made complete after D-503 undergoes the Operation. After providing a brief description of the weather (i.e., objective reality), D-503's first written words after the Operation constitute a denial of authorship: "Neuželi ja, D-503, napisal èti dvesti dvadsat' stranic?"[56] Yet before the Operation, D-503 repeatedly considered the journal either an extension or the essence of himself: in an earlier entry D-503 cannot bring himself to burn the manuscript, which he calls "this torturous—and perhaps dearest—piece of myself" ("ètot mučitel'nyj—i možet byt' samyj dorogoj mne—kusok samogo sebja"[57]). Structurally, D-503's identification with his manuscript is a variation on his earlier obsession with the individual's synecdochic relation to the State: where D-503 had earlier been merely a limb or a cell in the body of the One State, now his journal is a piece of D-503's consciousness. Here we have the complete identification of macrocosm with microcosm: D-503 decides that he has invested his entire self into the manuscript. In Entry 33, D-503 takes (premature) leave of his readers, to whom he has "shown [his] entire self" ("pokazal vsego sebja"[58]).[59] When he decides to kill Ju in Entry 35, he rolls up his manuscript into a tube and stuffs it

---

55 Ibid., 102.
56 Ibid., 142.
57 Ibid., 104.
58 Ibid., 120.
59 D-503's propensity to identify himself with the written word extends even beyond his own manuscript. When Ju hands him a letter he assumes to be from 1-330, D-503 is "completely projected onto the envelope" (69).

into a pipe, turning his journal into a murder weapon: "pust' ona pročtet vsego menja—go poslegnej bukvy."[60]

As might be expected in such a self-referential work, D-503's confusion about the status of his writing is prefigured by a story he retells in his manuscript: the story of the savage and the barometer. In Entry Four, a speaker summarizes a story that had been recently discovered during an archeological dig. The tale is about a savage who notices that every time a barometer points to the word "rain," rain does, indeed, fall; the savage, having deduced that the barometer is the cause of the rain, later drains out enough mercury so that the barometer will once again show rain. Zsuzsa Hetényi considers the speaker's interpretation of the story a metaphor of revolution;[61] yet when examined in the light of D-503's own confusion about representation and reality, the story of the savage and the barometer seems to have more to do with D-503 than with any historical models. Like the savage, D-503 confuses cause and effect: having started to write in order to represent reality, he eventually views his manuscript as the source of existence rather than merely its depiction. Both the savage and D-503 are deceived by synecdoche: they confuse the symbol with the object that it represents, the effect with the cause. Significantly, after D-503 has completely distorted the connection between his manuscript and his world in Entry 28 by citing his text as proof, he notices in the following entry that the barometer reading does not correspond with the actual weather: the barometer has dropped, but there is still no wind.[62]

Only after the Operation does the problem appear to be resolved, and yet the solution is no less parodic than D-503's earlier attempts at self-construction. The new D-503 starts his entry with, appropriately enough, a report on the barometer reading, which now, apparently, is in perfect sync with the actual weather. He now rejects the subjective impressions recorded in the previous 39 entries: what once comprised his entire inner life ("all of me") no longer has any connection to D-503. The hierarchy of "My" over "ja" has returned with a vengeance, as shown by the novel's penultimate

60 Zamiatin, *My*, 127.
61 Zsuzsa Hetényi, "O dikarjax XX veka: Ob odnom aspekte sootnošenija ponjatij revoljucii, gosudarstva i cerkvi v romane 'My' E. I. Zamiatina" [Savages of the twentieth century: On an aspect of the relationship between the meaning of revolution, the state, and the church in E. I. Zamyatin's novel *We*], *Studia Slavica Academiae Scientiarum Hungaricae* 33, nos. 1–4 (1987): 269–276, 273.
62 Zamiatin, *My*, 106.

sentence: "Bol'še: ja uveren—my pobedim."[63] What better word could have been chosen to show the supremacy of the collective at the end of the novel than *pobedit'*, a verb whose lack of a first person singular form leaves no room for the possibility of an individual victory? If Zamiatin's novel draws any conclusion at all about the nature of the self, it is the existentialist notion that "existence precedes essence." Here we must recall the aphorism casually pronounced by I-330 in Entry 28: "Čelovek—kak roman; do samoj poslednej stranicy ne znaeš', čem končitsja."[64] Ironically, even the stabilization of D-503's personality mimics the creation of the society in which he lives: the One State was made possible only by excluding unacceptable elements behind the Green Wall. D-503 finally becomes a stable, integrated self only after the excision of those parts of himself that caused his self-consciousness to develop.

---

63 Ibid., 143.
64 Ibid., 101.

Science Fiction of the Domestic: Iakov Protazanov's *Aelita*

ANDREW J. HORTON

Horton, Andrew J. "Science Fiction of the Domestic: Iakov Protazanov's *Aelita*." *Central Europe Review* 2, no. 1 (January 10, 2000): http://www.ce-review.org/00/1/kinoeye1_horton.html.

Iakov Protazanov's film *Aelita*[1] (1924) has gone down in history with the interesting honor of being the first Soviet science fiction film. Critics have most vividly remembered its expensive Martian scenes with futuristic and Constructivist sets and costumes by Alexandra Ekster and Isaak Rabinovich and the infamous passage where the protagonists start a proletarian revolution on Mars. However, it is only really in the last decade that it has been understood that film is rather at odds with its reputation, and in reality it is neither science fiction nor a prorevolutionary film.

The majority of the film is set in Moscow, where the action begins, develops, and has its ultimate resolution. What action does occur on Mars is eventually shown to have been illusory and a result of hero's dissatisfied imagination, giving an end feeling of it being more of an anti-climatic non-science-fiction film if anything. Furthermore—as we shall see—the film may be pro-Communist but it has a decidedly anti-revolutionary feel about it, which goes in some way to explain the failure of the film with critics at the time. Aside from doubts about the film's commitment to the revolution, contemporary filmmakers were scathing about the film's alleged continuity with the bourgeois cinema of the Tsarist age.

---

1   Iakov Protazanov's *Aelita* is available on DVD and VHS from Amazon.com. Note that both items are in North American and Canadian formats.

Despite heavy criticisms at the time from official Soviet critics, *Aelita* emerges today (largely due to a pioneering reading of the film by Ian Christie) as a highly complex film that holds as many breaks with prerevolutionary cinema as it has continuities.[2] It engages with a number of themes and styles and attempts to bring them together within a sophisticated plot which comments on the social, political and historical reality of 1920s Russia, as well as providing audiences with a ripping yarn.

To bring these themes together Protazanov employs a series of interlinking metaphors centring around images of differing times, differing spaces, journeys between these spaces, substitution and doubling, building and change, and oppositions between domestic life and fantasy. It is within this context that the film draws on the realm of science fiction—not as an end in its own right, but as part of Protazanov's rich metaphoric language to talk about earth-bound affairs.

Aelita: The Plot

The film covers the years 1921–23 and is thus set in the period of Lenin's New Economic Policy (NEP)—the relaxation of the principles of Communism to allow small-scale capitalism in order to revitalize the postwar Russian economy. The film starts with the arrival of a mysterious and undecipherable radio message around the world. Los, the hero of the film, and his colleague Spiridonov are just two of many radio engineers around the globe to receive the message.

Los—an individualist dreamer and a hangover from the bourgeois intellectual classes—starts to think about the sender of the message. The action then switches to Mars, where we are introduced to Aelita, daughter of Tuskub, the ruler of a futuristic totalitarian state in which the oppressed working classes are put into cold storage when they are not needed. Aelita uses a new telescope to view life on Earth, and soon focuses on Los.

While the strange Earthling fills her dreams, Los becomes increasingly obsessed with the mysterious message and in turn fantasises about Aelita watching him. His marriage starts to crumble and his wife seemingly starts to fall for the charms of an aristocratic and opportunistic crook called Erlich (which means "honest" in German). As Los perceives his marriage falling apart

---

2   I. Christie, "Down to Earth: Aelita Relocated," in *Inside the Film Factory: New Approaches to Russian and Soviet Cinema*, ed. R. Taylor and I. Christie (New York: Routledge, 1991), 80–102.

so he becomes evermore drawn to the mysterious messages and away from his wife, Natasha. As a result of his dissatisfaction, he decides to accept a job as a civil engineer on a dam construction project in Eastern Russia, taking him away from home.

Meanwhile, Erlich schemes with his wife to rob Los's colleague, Spiridonov, and Kravtsev (a buffoonish amateur detective with almost Benny Hill–type qualities) starts to investigate the Erlichs. In the course of his bungled detective work, he comes to the conclusion that Spiridonov is part of the ring.

Spiridonov in fact emigrates to the West, and when Los returns home and shoots his wife a fit of jealousy over her supposed infidelity, he decides to disguise himself as his fellow engineer. Now back in Moscow and his wife out of the way, he can resume his obsession with Aelita. To reach her, he builds a spacecraft which he had designed with Spiridonov.

Los takes on Gusev, a revolutionary bored with his marriage to his doting wife, as a crew member and takes off for Mars, unaware that Kravtsev is on board investigating the person he believes to be Spiridonov. On Mars, Los and Aelita are joyfully united in an embrace, but Aelita momentarily becomes Natasha in Los's eye and he is seized by guilt. Aelita, who has also murdered to be with her beloved, and the Earthlings are then imprisoned by the dictatorial Tuskub.

Gusev manages to rouse their fellow imprisoned workers into a revolutionary fervor, and Aelita offers to lead the revolution. Gusev correctly smells a rat in a royal wanting to lead an anti-monarchist coup, but is too late to prevent what he suspects. Aelita uses the revolution to overthrow Tuskub and establish her own totalitarian regime. Horrified, Los wrestles with Aelita, now his foe, on a staircase, but when he succeeds in pushing her off to her death, he sees it is in fact Natasha he has been grappling with.

This confusing state of affairs is explained when Los awakens from a dream and finds himself on a station platform at the point shortly after he shot Natasha. The mysterious Martian message is revealed as being a fragment from an advertisement for tires which has become lodged in Los's mind. Disturbed by his dream and the image of Natasha, he returns to the scene of his crime and finds that in fact his shots missed Natasha and she is still alive. He is able to banish his jealousy and the two are reunited. The scene is witnessed by Gusev and Masha, who, concerned about Los's state of mind, have followed him from the station where the couple met him. Erlich, meanwhile, gets a bizarre and ironic comeuppance by being accused of the murder of Spiridonov by the bungling Kravtsev.

As well as a happy ending in personal and moral terms, there is also a political one too: Los rejects his bourgeois and individualistic personal project of building a spacecraft and decisively realises he has to engage with social duty. Tearing the plans from their secret hiding place and thrusting them into the fire he announces to Natasha, "We have different work to do."

The Symbolism of Time

In the course of the film, time moves forward and progress and improvement are shown in action. As such, forward movement of time and more abstractly "the Future" are equated with improvement. Scenes at the start of the film show squalor, dysfunctionality, and chaos—on the trains, at the refugee checkpoint, and in the housing shortages and the opportunist criminality of "NEP men."

Later scenes illustrate how Lenin's NEP policies were effectively dealing with the post-civil war economic and social disorder. The refugee checkpoint has no more work for Natasha and the orphanage where Natasha later works is peaceful and harmoniously efficient. Law and order is enforced; the NEP man Erlich is arrested (albeit for a crime he never committed and that never even happened); and the trains are more orderly. This outward social progress is mirrored in Los's personal life: his renewed commitment to his wife and to working for society and not just for his own personal ends.

In between, Protazanov uses images of building and rebirth to illustrate the process. Los works on a hydroelectric plant and then is later shown constructing his spaceship, and the orphanage is an unashamedly sentimental diversion from the main course of the plot just to use it as a symbol for the youthful regeneration in society. Images of modernity and efficiency abound from the opening sequence of electrical arcing, showing the power of industrial modernization, to the rather more wasteful technological heights of Los's craft. A variety functions of Soviet life are shown to be running smoothly, with theatrical productions and parades to demonstrate and to celebrate this.

The plot, although in essence temporally linear in nature, contains some flashback sequences to the Past. "The Past" here is the past of prerevolutionary times. "The Past," however, for Protazanov, as indeed for anyone in Russia immediately after the Revolution, takes on more than just a difference in temporal setting. It is inextricably linked to ideology, representing all the negative features of the Tsarist regime; including the sort of bourgeois attitudes of individualism that would allow a man to waste his energies on research into projects of no use to rebuilding society, such as research into space travel.

The Past, though, is not something the characters are protected from by fact of its temporal removal from them. It leaks through the barrier of the Revolution and into the chaos of the NEP world to infect them. This is most obviously illustrated in the character of Erlich, and when Spiridonov emigrates he tells Los in a postcard "The past turned out to be stronger than I."

Los is caught in a similar struggle. Significantly, Los later disguises himself as Spiridonov and the two characters are played by the same actor (Nikolai Tsereteli), both factors serving to emphasize the similarities in ambivalent attitudes in the characters to former values. Los, however, is to win his battle.

As well as Los acting as a double for Spiridonov, he also acts as a double for Protazanov himself. The director was already important before the Revolution and would still be worthy of a place in the cinema history books had his career ended in 1917. Like many in the Russian film industry (who were largely middle- or upper-class, and therefore supported the Tsarist "Whites") he emigrated after the Revolution, working in Paris and Berlin.

His return to Russia after the Civil War was an enormous triumph for the new regime, who were able to make much political capital out of his return to the fold. He had continued to make films while in voluntary exile and was establishing a reputation as a major European director. He must have been aware that in returning to Russia he would have been turning his back on international success and a part of him may well have wondered what would have happened if he had stayed in the West. Certainly, he appeared to have remained wedded to the Past to some extent, since he retained a preference for using film crews with pre-revolutionary experience.[3]

It is interesting to note that the film *Aelita* is loosely (very loosely in fact[4]) based around a novel by the same name by Alexei Tolstoi, a relative of the great Russian writer Lev Tolstoy and an upper-class émigré who—like Protazanov—also returned to Soviet Russia.

As such Los, the "'bourgeois specialist' ostensibly committed to the Revolution, but still emotionally, perhaps unconsciously, unadjusted to the new order,"[5] is also a double of Protazanov and Tolstoi. Similarly, Protazanov's experience of being caught between East and West is played out in the film as well.

---

3 D. Youngblood, "The Return of the Native: Yakov Protazanov and Soviet Cinema," in *Inside the Film Factory: New Approaches to Russian and Soviet Cinema*, ed. R. Taylor and I. Christie (New York: Routledge, 1991), 103–123.

4 Christie, "Down to Earth," 87–88; Alexei Tolstoi, *Aelita* (1923) (Firebird Publications, 1987).

5 Ibid., 91.

The Symbolism of Location

Just as the past is used to signify a different attitude, so the different spatial elements in *Aelita* play a similar function. Several locations in the film are depicted or referred to, all carrying a distinct meaning relating to a particular mental attitude. Journeys between these locations can be seen as not just spatial but ideological, and as having the nature of an odyssey of personal discovery. The concept of travel even emerges from the mysterious message the radio stations receive when at the end we find out that it is from an advertisement for car tires.

Mention has already been made of Spiridonov's journey to the West. Here the overlap between spatial and temporal meaning is strong as can be seen in Spiridonov's postcard to Los. The West holds the same values as the Past.

If the West corresponds to the Past, then the East corresponds to the Future. It is the place where the rebuilding of Russia is to take place, like the hydroelectric plant where Los goes to console himself for six months and finds the inner strength to go back to his wife. It is the place where Gusev and Masha are heading for as they wait at the station at the end of the film. It's seen as a place involving participation in life, society and its regeneration, and since it is also the Future we are not presented with any problems that might occur there.

This contrasts with Moscow, which is the home of the bourgeois Los and his wife Natasha and the place where they get caught up in the strife which results in Los's individualistic dreams that lead him astray from the true Communist cause. Moscow could be seen as the Present, the time of immediate concern, containing the problems that need solving in the context of the film.

More positive aspects of Moscow's character come out in its depiction as the scene of domestic life. It could easily be argued that this is one of the central pillars of meaning in *Aelita*. The whole film plots Los's dissatisfaction, rejection and eventual reconciliation with domestic life and shows how his inability to run his personal life overflows into inability to interact with society and fulfil the goals of Communism. Full realization of this theme, though, comes only in comparison with Moscow's anti-domestic counterpart—Mars.

Reasserting the Domestic

Before analyzing further the symbolism of Mars it is worth taking a small detour to consider why Protazanov should chose this theme of domestic life as one of his central themes. That he wanted to use his film to praise marriage and domesticity might now seem a rather twee concept in today's terms.

In the early 1920s things were not so clear cut, though. Aleksandra Kollontai, the Communist radical feminist, had already published her collected essays on sexual relations under the title *Novaya moral i rabochii klass* (New Morality and the Working Class, 1918).[6] In this book, she advocated a view of "love-play" that loosened the image of traditional monogamy (although her critics have, admittedly, exaggerated her writings and events in her personal life to discredit her feminist philosophy).

Also at this time, common-law relationships were given the same legal strength as full marriages, partly as a matter of revolutionary principle to overthrow the old bourgeois morality and partly to recognise the reality as it stood—common-law relationships were already a fact.

Soviet males were delighted with this new sexual order and as a result the fluidity and casualness of relationships increased dramatically. This process was assisted by the revolutionary mood and the disjointed nature of postwar NEP society and the disruption to prewar relationships that the turmoil of war had caused. One unfortunate side effect was that many Soviet women found themselves swiftly rejected when they became pregnant.

Assaulted both by male opportunism and revolutionary feminist ideology, conventional relationships were on the decline and the burden on the state increased as the number of orphans and absent fathers who refused to pay alimony mushroomed. This was aggravated by the fact that adoption was made illegal in 1918. As a result of the Revolution, the First World War, the Civil War, and the new notions of morality, there was such a large number of orphans (7 million in 1921) that the state was unable to cope and "gangs of homeless children, viscous and undomesticated ... infested squalid city slums."[7]

It must have seemed to any observer arriving from abroad at that time—as Protazanov had done—that, however noble the concept of sexual freedom and the creation of new less repressive notions of family units as revolutionary ideals may have been, it was ruining the very fabric of society and a return to traditional family and society values was called for.

---

6 Aleksandra Kollontai, *Selected Articles and Speeches* (New York: International Publishers Co., 1984).

7 R. Stites, *The Women's Liberation Movement in Russia: Feminism, Nihilism, and Bolshevism 1860–1930* (Princeton, NJ: Princeton University Press, 1978), 346–391, which gives a fuller (and fascinating) treatment of the subjects of the "Reasserting the domestic" section of the article.

Mars: The Anti-Domestic

Analyzing Mars we can see it is Los's refuge from the world of hard practical problems—making a relationship, a marriage, and society work. Dissatisfied with the prosaic qualities of domestic life resulting in his relationship with Natasha, he seeks a higher more exalted form of love. Aelita is a queen, and her appearance contrasts markedly with Natasha's, with Aelita looking like a classical statue with hard sculpted hair and a marble-white face, moving in slow, gracious but somewhat stiff movements. Even Aelita's very name suggests a classical sort of detachment.

Natasha, however, is portrayed by Protazanov as the more attractive of the two. Her face is radiant and framed by soft wispish curls and her movements free and natural. To emphasise Protazanov's approval of her, she is a committed Communist and engages actively with society to help others; she works is at a refugee checkpoint and then an orphanage and participates in voluntary events in her spare time. Natasha—in contrast to Aelita—is a distinctly Russian name.

Natasha as well as getting heavily involved in public-spirited activities is also devoted to their domestic life. She is frequently shown in a domestic setting whereas Mars in general, and Aelita in particular, exhibits no such domestic acts as eating, cooking, or caring for people. Even when Tuskub sleeps he does so in a very un-room-like setting; indeed, the atmosphere is more like that of a public space such as a square or a park. A direct contrast is made by adjoining shots of the regal Aelita with Natasha hard at work washing.

As well as contrasting differences in the two women, these scenes show how in Los's mind Aelita is, in effect, the result of his opinions of Natasha and a substitution for her. Later this substitution is stressed still further when Aelita becomes Natasha, first when the former is embraced by Los and secondly when Los tries to push Aelita off the staircase.

Los's fantasies totally enthrall him. Aelita, already composed of everything which Los isn't happy in Natasha, is depicted as being formed in accordance with the fantasies of male domination in a relationship which seems almost narcissistic and adolescent; she is naïve and manipulable, she needs to be taught by Los how to kiss; she is obsessed by his image and desperate to try and see him; she is prepared to sacrifice herself for him, putting herself in danger for him and even murdering to get to him.

Mars: Out of Time

Whereas Moscow, East, and West can easily be equated with a temporal meaning, Mars stands curiously resistant to being placed on this axis. The appearance is futuristic, with Ekster and Rabinovich's famed set designs and costumes. Even the technology shows evidence of being far ahead of Earth with the capacity to freeze and unfreeze people and an interplanetary telescope with impressive resolution.

With this degree of advancement, a Utopia might be expected but the political mood turns out to be definitely medieval, with a harshly hierarchical militarised feudal system, devoid of emotion, in operation. The whole atmosphere is caught between sheer idealistic hypermodernity and its harsh angularity and oppressive qualities.

The world of this fantasy is so strong that Los is able to project a whole scenario of him going to Mars into a dream. The ridiculousness of the whole journey is shown by the fact that all the characters on the journey are in disguise: Los as Spiridonov, Gusev as a woman (his own clothes having been hidden by Masha as a vain attempt to prevent him from voyaging to Mars) and Kravtsov pretending to be what he aspires to—a detective.

The journey is achieved by means of the spacecraft that Los has built. The vehicle seems to have not very much in common with modes of transport, the interior being easily mistaken for an ordinary room in a flat. The domesticity of the situation is emphasized by the household items around the room, such as a table and chairs, and by the resemblance of the high-tech gadgetry to ordinary household plumbing. In addition, the three characters act out such domestic scenes as packing a suitcase when they are preparing to leave the spaceship.

Revolution: Vent of Restlessness?

For Los, the trip to Mars is a regression into fantasy as escape from married life and this too can be extended to Gusev (although Los's later awakening implies Gusev's marital problems may never have actually occurred). While Los is the bourgeois central character, Gusev is the proletarian hero. Soldier, accordionist, Bolshevik, and founder of four Soviet Republics, Gusev suffers from the same discontent with married life that plagues Los.

Masha, like Natasha, is cast as a caring domestic person and this is emphasized by her job as a nurse. The extramarital element Gusev needs in his life, though, is not erotic fantasy as with Los but action and excitement; in short—revolution.

This, superficially a device in the plot to get a Bolshevik on Mars with Los to start a revolution, is a crucial part of the film's central meaning. The implication is two-fold: first, that revolution interferes with domestic life, and secondly that revolution is the expression of male restlessness and dissatisfaction with a stable personal life. This could be read as a damning indictment of the men such as Lenin and Stalin who had led the October Revolution and who still led Soviet Russia. *Aelita*, taken to its logical conclusion, would therefore imply that the leaders of the Revolution were unstable men with unsuccessful personal lives, an inability to relate to society, and perhaps childishly shallow visions of human relationships.

Further criticism of revolution ensues as Gusev's Martian uprising unfolds. Revolution is shown to be susceptible to manipulation as Aelita uses it to overthrow Tuskub and set up her own regime. Hovering between the lines just waiting to be read is the inference that the causes of the October Revolution had been portrayed and Russia was once again under a form of repressive dictatorship acted out for the personal gain of the leaders.

For Los, Aelita's seizing of the revolution for herself is a personal disaster and the revolt on Mars shows up the hollowness of his fantasies. Aelita, the supposedly innocent, manipulable and tameable, turns out to be scheming, manipulative and untameable. She isn't even herself and is revealed to Los as the substitution for Natasha that she really is, all of which proves to Los that he is as unable to sustain the fantasy as much as it is unable to sustain him. Personal fantasy is no substitute for engaging with reality.

He returns to the real world and rushes back home where, to his delight, he finds that he has not killed Natasha after all and his reconciliation with her and with reality can begin. The revolution on Mars has dissolved from the real world and we are left unsure about whether we should even be concerned about the failure of this uprising that we've seen. In reality it never happened, but its failure still delivers clear signals about revolutions and their limitations. The suggestion that Mars might be an Aesopian device to represent Russia is reinforced by color associations—the red planet and the Red country.

Aelita: A Film Before Its Time?

If *Aelita* is not a science-fiction film, then what can we say about it? Clearly, it is a film that brings together a number of subtextual readings and is just as adventurous in the scale of its underlying elements as it is in terms of the different acting styles and plots it tries to combine. It is not about Mars but life in Russia in general and Moscow specifically. It is a portrait of a man's erotic escapism and how this effects not just his ability to function within a relationship and within society.

The film praises domesticity and married life at a time when society was experimenting with the nature and meaning of relationships and debating their role in a revolutionary society. It is a film that looks to rebuilding, consolidation, progress and the future and rejects revolution as an unachievable Utopian ideal open to hijack. Undoubtedly in this respect Protazanov saw the future of Russia lying not with revolution but with evolution.

This is also, however, a film with a strong personal element. Protazanov, son of a merchant and recently returned from a long period abroad, can be seen to be personified in Los, the man caught between the Past and the Future, and also as representing Alexei Tolstoi, the author of the film's nominal source.

While many critics at the time were disappointed with *Aelita* and sneered at its ideology, its extravagant expense, its lack of formal experimentation, its appeal to a mass market, its mixture of genres and its inability to become a prototype for future Russian filmmakers, Protazanov in the long term proved to have predicted the winning side on many of these points.

Audiences were far more appreciative of Protazanov's cinema than that of, say, Sergei Eisenstein or Dziga Vertov. As Stalin started to put his personal stamp on cinema, the formal experimentation that had prevailed in *Aelita*'s day was cast out in preference to the sort of mass-appeal that Protazanov wanted, not just in *Aelita*, but all his films. This led Protazanov to produce more films than any of the experimentalists, such as Eisenstein, or Vertov, over the next ten years.

Although the dream device in the plot was much criticized at the time, Protazanov effectively refuted his critics by using a similar dream device later in his film *Tommy* and by the 1940s it had become a standard of Western cinema for psychological effect and today the device is so common it is considered a cliché.

Although science fiction would not immediately take off in the Soviet Union as a film genre, it had an important effect outside of the country, inspiring Fritz Lang's *Metropolis* (1926) both with its sets and costumes and ist distopian view of a futuristic society. Furthermore, Protazanov's treatment of science fiction was to become mirrored in later Soviet "science-fiction" works such as Andrei Tarkovsky's *Stalker* (1979) and Aleksandr Sokurov's *Dni zatmeniya* (Days of the Eclipse, 1989), both of which also stripped away the science-fiction elements of the novels on which they were based in order to focus more on earth-bound moral and philosophical issues. It is also interesting to note that both the later films also follow *Aelita*'s lead in being nominally based on a work of fiction which is so substantially reworked that the film becomes almost totally independent of the book save for the character names and a few plot characteristics.

The ideas Protazanov held on the nature of relationships also came to prevail in Russian thinking. By the end of the 1920s, discussions on "new morality" were over and there was a strong call among Russian people for a return to older family values, an opinion that enabled Stalin to introduce marriage laws at least as harsh as those in place before the Revolution.[8]

Aelita was never rehabilitated, though, perhaps because of its attitude to revolution. The film, in this respect, predicted too well for the authorities, and by the time the 1930s had come many Russian citizens would have undoubtedly found Protazanov's insinuations on the destructive and corrupting powers of revolution to be all too accurate.

Many of the ideas in this article arose from discussions of *Aelita* with Julian Graffy of the School of Slavonic and East European Studies, London, and without his input this article would not have been possible.

---

8 Ibid., 387.

Eugenics, Rejuvenation, and Bulgakov's Journey into the Heart of Dogness

YVONNE HOWELL

Howell, Yvonne. "Eugenics, Rejuvenation, and Bulgakov's Journey into the Heart of Dogness." *Slavic Review* 65, no. 3 (2006): 544–62.

> The important man plunged his hands dressed in slippery gloves into jars, pulled out brains, a stubborn man, a persistent one, searching for something all the time, cutting, examining, squinting, and singing "Toward the sacred banks of the Nile ... "
>
> —final sentence from *Heart of a Dog*

On May 24, 2005 the science section of the *New York Times* ran an article on Cornell University's collection of pickled human brains, the remainder of a once 600-brain repository.[1] At the end of the nineteenth century, anatomists cut into these brains, hoping to unlock the secret of why one brain produces a genius, another produces you or me, and yet another produces a criminal. Comparing the anatomy of different brains led to nothing, and over time the collections of brains housed by scientific organizations in Philadelphia, Tokyo, Paris, and Moscow mostly disappeared. The basic question, of course, has not disappeared: we still do not know how the brain—a vast collection of neurons—produces the mind, the unique phenomenon of human consciousness. Although our knowledge of the physical and cognitive processes that take place in the brain is exponentially more complex than it was in Mikhail Bulgakov's

---

1 Peter Edidin, "In Search of Answers from the Great Brains of Cornell," *New York Times*, May 24, 2005, section F.

time, the link between the physical brain and our irreducible humanity (which is represented as "heart" in *Heart of a Dog*) is as elusive as ever.

In this article, I propose a new reading of *Heart of a Dog*, one that takes seriously Professor Preobrazhenskii's claim that his real interest is "eugenics, the improvement of the human species."[2] The Professor's eugenics project is not limited to a cosmetic, physical improvement of human subjects; it anticipates urging humankind toward a higher stage of intellectual and spiritual development as well. Therefore, when he mistakenly transforms a dog into a man instead of a more intelligent dog, he considers the experiment an abject failure because the new man "no longer has a dog's heart, but a human one, and the vilest one you could find."[3] This does not deter the Professor from further research; on the contrary, at the end of the book he is still searching for the mysterious mechanism that connects the secrets of the brain to the secrets of the heart. The science that makes rejuvenation procedures and genetic engineering possible is no longer as fictional as it was in Bulgakov's time, thus, an analysis that highlights the novel's exploration of how science, politics, and ideology interact is long overdue. I propose that the novel's enduring significance lies not in its overworked interpretation as an anti-Soviet satire or as a warning against scientific hubris.[4] Rather, it remains a brilliant exploration of the conundrum of where nature meets nurture in efforts to enhance humankind.

---

2 Bulgakov, *Heart of a Dog*, 104.

3 Ibid., 105.

4 I am indebted to the many previous critical studies of Bulgakov's novella for their various insights. I do not agree with the two lines of thought that dominate existing interpretations of *Heart of a Dog*, however. Cold War–inspired critics did not dwell on the novella's scientific theme, obscured as it was by the presence of subversive political satire, which they were eager to find in a piece of banned Soviet literature. Most other critics have cast Preobrazhenskii as a mad scientist in the Frankenstein tradition, one who unleashes forces he himself cannot control. See, for example, Ellendea Proffer, *Bulgakov: Life and Work* (Ann Arbor, 1984); A. C. Wright, *Mikhail Bulgakov: Life and Interpretations* (Toronto, 1978); and Diana Burgin, "Bulgakov's Early Tragedy of the Scientist-Creator: An Interpretation of *Heart of a Dog*," *Slavic and East European Journal* 22, no. 4 (1978): 494–508. While there is ample evidence for the importance of political satire and the condemnation of scientific hubris in the novella, taken together the two approaches yield unsatisfactory contradictions. If one sees in the novel a thundering anti-Soviet tirade, then Preobrazhenskii, as the most forceful and articulate voice of this tirade, must be viewed in a positive light. To cast him as a sinister scientist is difficult when it is clear that Bulgakov has enormous sympathy for his formidable protagonist, whose views on society, political reform, and Soviet housing committees he largely shares. On the other hand, if one views with horror the elitist Professor's dangerous dabbling in sex gland grafts and trans-speciation, then Bulgakov's intent to create an anti-Soviet broadside is called into question.

Soviet Eugenics

The rise and fall of the Russian eugenics movement in the 1920s forms the social and intellectual backdrop for Bulgakov's story about the creation of a New Soviet Man. Many of Russia's most prominent early twentieth-century biologists—the real-life peers of Bulgakov's fictional protagonist—had a great deal of faith in the power of biology to transform our understanding of human nature and, with it, our blueprints for social progress. In their eugenic aspirations, these scientists participated in some of the same kind of radically utopian thinking as prerevolutionary philosophical proponents of human regeneration and resurrection.[5] The focus here will remain on the 1920s, the time in which Bulgakov wrote his two satirical science novels (*Heart of a Dog* and *Fatal Eggs*). Not incidentally, it was also the historical moment in which Bolshevik policy-makers and Soviet scientists tried to find a common ground for creating the New Soviet Man.

Although there is little evidence to suggest that Vladimir Lenin was at all interested in the emerging science of genetics before the revolution, once the revolution had been accomplished, it became immediately clear to most Bolshevik leaders that resolving the nature-nurture debate was an issue of some urgency. Andrei Siniavskii later described the situation succinctly: "The Revolutionary flag read: 'everything anew.' But to create the 'new man,' a single revolutionary leap forward was not enough."[6] The architects of the revolution were confronted with the problem of constructing this new man, one who would be psychologically, physically, and culturally at home in the radically different society envisioned by communism. In *Literature and Revolution*, Lev Trotskii wondered whether "the proletariat has enough time to create a 'proletarian' culture?"[7] Trotskii was not alone in his doubts about how the new man might be created in a single generation if culture, science, and psychological habits are transmitted over many generations. Clearly, the challenge of creating new men and women out of existing human material—out of a population, moreover, that, according to Marxist dictates, had been enslaved for centuries—remained on the table throughout the 1920s.

---

5 The essays in Irina Paperno and Joan Delaney Grossman, eds., *Creating Life: The Aesthetic Utopia of Russian Modernism* (Stanford, 1994) foreground the uniquely Russian modernist impulse to literally transform artistic, mystical, and religious ideals into real life. Philosophers like Nikolai Fedorov and Vladimir Solov'ev called for projects that would make metaphors about "eternal life" and "universal love" into scientific and social realities.

6 Andrei Siniavskii, *Soviet Civilization: A Cultural History* (New York, 1990), 114.

7 Leon [Lev] Trotsky, *Literature and Revolution* (New York, 1957), 184.

At first, it seemed that beneficial changes in the biological composition of a given society, in tandem with needed social reform, could lead to the rapid advancement of humankind. Russia's leading biologists realized that a link— however tentative and abstract—might be made between genetics, which involved fundamental research on the inheritance patterns of fruit fly populations, plant varieties, and poultry breeds, and "eugenics," which implied a promise that biology would produce practical applications that would improve the overall health of society. Ideally, biology could be shown to pull in the same direction as Bolshevism. The popular press seemed to have agreed: in the early 1920s, lay readers could choose from a plethora of books and journal articles explaining our evolutionary origins, the biological bases of behavior, the effect of hormones on personality, and other biosocial ideas.[8] The journal of the Russian Eugenics Society published articles with the following titles, any of which would fit into the intellectual universe of Bulgakov's Professor Preobrazhenskii: "On the Methods of Physically Improving Posterity," "Birthrate Pattern of the Moscow Intelligentsia," "About the Connection between Character and Evolution."[9]

The founding fathers of the Russian eugenics movement were biologists of the prerevolutionary generation, trained in Europe and dedicated to fundamental research in Mendelian and population genetics. They offered no concrete suggestions on how to apply the existing knowledge of genetics (still far

---

8 See Mark Adams, "The Soviet Nature-Nurture Debate," in *Science and the Soviet Social Order*, ed. Loren Graham, (Cambridge, MA, 1990). Adams cites letters from the Petrograd publisher M. V. Sabashnikov to Iu. A. Filipchenko, in which Sabashnikov inquires about "books with a materialist approach to man and nature that he felt would appeal to political authorities" (98). Eric Naiman also emphasizes the vitality of the public discourse connecting biomedical and social topics in the 1920s. A good example is the discussion carried out in the popular press about the endocrine system, which some authors "used ... to explore the real meaning of the term 'soul' ... or as proof that God did not exist." Eric Naiman, *Sex in Public: The Incarnation of Early Soviet Ideology* (Princeton, NJ: Princeton University Press, 1997), 143. This kind of biosocial discourse was effectively cut off in the 1930s and did not return to the Soviet press again until the 1970s, when a few journals began to publish censored versions of essays on sociobiology by V. R. Dol'nik, V. P. Efroimson, and others.

9 See articles by V. P. Osipov, "K voprosu o merakh fizicheskogo ozdorovleniia potomstva" [On the measures of physical well-being through the generations], *Russkii evgenicheskii zhurnal* [The journal of Russian eugenics] 3, no. 1 (1925): 37–45; A. V. Gorbunov, "Rozhaemost' moskovskoi intelligentsii po dannym ankety russkogo evgenicheskogo obshchestva" [Fertility of the Moscow intelligentsia in the Russian eugenic society survey data], *Russkii evgenicheskii zhurnal* 6, no. 1 (1928): 3–53; and Ia. Ia. Roginskii, "Uchenie o kharaktere i evoliutsii" [Lessons on character and evolution], *Russkii evgenicheskii zhurnal* 6, no. 2 (1928): 65–106.

from complete) to effect changes in the population; they simply advocated more research. In the long run, though, their eugenic perspective was visionary: in the future, biology would unlock the keys to perfecting human nature and human society. One of the founders of the Russian Eugenics Society, Nikolai Konstantinovich Kol'tsov, articulated the appeal of the eugenic vision to a modernizing, secularist society. In a lead article for the society's inaugural journal bearing the title "Uluchsheniie chelovecheskoi porody" (Improving the human race), he points out that every progressive revolution in human history has been motivated by the ideal of improving and enhancing humankind, from the cult of beauty that inspired the civilization of ancient Greece, to the highest ideals of Christianity, which, after two thousand years "are still not attainable."[10] He places biology at the vanguard of a new stage in our cultural evolution, as the source of knowledge that will finally bring the goal of improving human life within our reach. Preobrazhenskii's eugenic rhetoric in *Heart of a Dog* mimics the article's title, when he tells Bormental', "I was concerned with something else altogether—eugenics, the improvement of the human species!" (*Ia zabotilsia o sovsem drugom, ob evgenike, ob uluchshenii chelovecheskoi porody*).[11]

Ultimately, though, Bolshevik policymakers in positions of power needed more concrete measures. By the time it became clear that "idealistic" eugenics had no immediate solutions to the country's social and health problems, the demise of the Soviet eugenics movement was already imminent.[12] After all,

---

10 N.K. Kol'tsov, "Uluchsheniie chelovecheskoi porody" [Improvement of the human species], *Russkii evgenicheskii zhurnal* 1, no. 1 (1922): 1.

11 I have not been able to determine whether Bulgakov had specifically read Kol'tsov's programmatically titled article. Given Bulgakov's decision to use the popular topic of rejuvenation surgery to motivate his plot, it is even more likely that he would have seen Kol'tsov's edited volume *Omolozheniie* (Moscow, 1923). As a former medical student, and as the relative of several doctors, Bulgakov knew scientists of Kol'tsov's generation socially and translated his acquaintance with their milieu into the deeply felt portrayal of Preobrazhenskii. Thus, in Preobrazhenskii-the-scientist we find the quirks of a very three-dimensional man (one who addresses a political tirade to "the hapless cardboard duck which hung upside down from the sideboard," 36). These quirks convincingly inhabit the two-dimensional figure of Preobrazhenskii-the-wizard who plays a more symbolic role in the novel.

12 An invaluable overview of the rise and fall of the Soviet eugenics movement can be found in Mark Adams, "Eugenics as Social Medicine in Revolutionary Russia," in *Health and Society in Revolutionary Russia*, ed. Susan Gross Solomon and John F. Hutchinson (Bloomington, IN: Indiana University Press, 1990). In recent years, Russian historians have used opened archives to produce a fuller account of the nexus between genetic science and social issues in the early Soviet years. See, for instance, a forthcoming cultural history of the Soviet eugenics movement by Vasilii Babkov (Moscow, manuscript in preparation).

most of its founders and active researchers were primarily interested in the fundamental problems of chromosomal inheritance and population genetics, problems that defined new disciplines in the throes of discovery, but were far from producing applied results. The Russian eugenicists were political liberals harboring only a grudging willingness to come to a mutually beneficial accommodation with the new regime. Increasingly, they were viewed as dangerous technocrats, elitists with bourgeois sympathies, theoreticians with more interest in fruit flies than in improving the proletariat. Still, before the complete demise of the eugenics movement, a younger cohort of Marxist eugenicists attempted to reformulate the possibilities of biosocial improvement with neo-Lamarckian logic. Their logic went as follows: if at least some hereditary traits can be acquired under conducive environmental conditions, then ameliorating changes in the social structure will prompt the appearance of desirable traits, which will then be passed down to the next generation. This idea, popularized by the Viennese biologist Paul Kammerer, was influential among Marxist philosophers who tried to reconcile eugenics with socialism in the mid-1920s. Kammerer argued that Mendelian genetics left us beholden to the past, whereas Lamarckism would allow us to take control of our own future.[13] As we shall see, this idea comes into play in Bulgakov's portrayal of Bormental', whose optimism about the implications of the Professor's experiment is fueled by his teleological notion of evolutionary progress.

By 1930, the "Great Break" in cultural policy associated with Stalinism had set a new course in the biological sciences as well. "Bourgeois" genetic science was officially disavowed, and eugenics was condemned as a pernicious intellectual import from the west. Bolshevik ideologues had settled on an interpretation of Marxism-Leninism that would lead ultimately to a strictly "nurturist" view of human nature. This view, which holds that human nature is purely a social product, by implication infinitely malleable and beyond biological constraints, is the one that was subsequently enforced in the Soviet Union up until its collapse in 1991.[14] Until the inauguration of Stalin's first Five-Year Plan,

---

13 Paul Kammerer, *The Inheritance of Acquired Characteristics* (New York, 1924).

14 Note that this view is still hotly defended in some circles. In Russia, as late as 1992, Nikolai Dubinin's *Istoriia i tragediia sovetshoi genetiki* [The history and tragedy of Soviet genetics] (Moscow, 1992) singles out the biosocial theories of V. P. Efroimson, M. E. Lobashev, B. L. Astaurov, and P. F. Pokitskii for hostile attack. By taking the work of these geneticists out of context, Dubinin implies that their belief in biological contributions to certain ethical and psychological phenomena is equivalent to "anti-humanist eugenics . . . the basis of racist, fascist ideology" (324).

however, different parties were actively elaborating both the "nature" and the "nurture" explanations of human behavior. The coexistence, for a time, of both explanatory paradigms complicated early Bolshevik efforts to understand how to go about creating the New Soviet Man. Thus, *Heart of a Dog* is Bulgakov's response to one of the most exciting, intellectually stimulating, and politically complicated issues of his day: he devises a plot that centers around a eugenic experiment; he places his main protagonists at different points of the contemporary spectrum of biosocial thought, and he deploys four narrative points of view, each of which embodies voices that were important in the nature-nurture dialogue of his time.

A Menippean Satire of Nature and Nature

In *Heart of a Dog*, a brilliant Moscow biologist, Filip Filippovich Preobrazhenskii, lives and works in a spacious seven-room apartment. He employs a cook (Dar'ia Petrovna) and a housekeeper (Zina) and is accompanied in his professional endeavors by his scientific disciple and devoted assistant, Dr. Bormental'. Preobrazhenskii has thus far been able to retain his "excessive" square footage because he is a world-renowned specialist in rejuvenative surgery and counts among his patients some of the most important and influential members of New Economic Policy (NEP) society.[15] In the winter of 1924, the Professor lures a stray mutt ("Sharik") off the Moscow streets and uses him in an unprecedented operation. The Professor transplants the pituitary and the testes of a recently deceased man into the dog, and soon the dog is fully humanized. He walks, talks, looks, and thinks like a man. Unfortunately, he is an appalling

---

15 With NEP (1921–1928) Lenin hoped to jumpstart the country's devastated economy by temporarily allowing some private economic activity. Entrepreneurs in certain market sectors were able to flourish, and it is this class of nouveaux riches that Bulgakov pokes fun at in the depiction of Preobrazhenskii's clients. Interest in rejuvenating organ transplants was hardly native or unique to Russia in the 1920s, however. The most famous and notoriously successful purveyor of sexual rejuvenation in the United States was "Doctor" John Brinkley. Brinkley ran a lucrative business transplanting the sex glands of Toggenburg goats into an unending stream of male clients who were convinced by Brinkley's claims that the procedure would cure impotence and reinvigorate the whole endocrine system. At his peak in the 1930s, Brinkley was a fabulously wealthy man whose political connections reached to the White House. See also Arnold Kahn, "Recovering Lost Youth: The Controversial and Colorful Beginnings of Hormone Replacement Therapy in Aging," *Journal of Gerontology: Biological Sciences* 60A, no. 2 (2005): 142–47; and Erica R. Freeman, David A. Bloom, and Edward J. McGuire, "A Brief History of Testosterone," *Journal of Urology* 165, no. 2 (February 2001): 371–73.

human being, who displays just about every vice that might particularly offend his patron. Much of the novel's humor derives from the clash between the Professor's cultivated, erudite demeanor and the new man's brash and crude barbarity. There is a darker undertone to the odd couple comedy that ensues when a scientific genius has to live with his own botched experiment, however. The time is 1925, well into the postrevolutionary decade, and tolerance for the remnants of the old bourgeoisie is waning. The man-dog is crafty enough to figure out how he can use the politicized atmosphere of the times to denounce his benefactor and free himself from the rules the latter imposes. As the situation worsens, Bormental' abandons his original faith in the dog's reformation and threatens to murder Sharikov. Preobrazhenskii rejects this option and instead performs a reverse surgery, which turns the man back into a dog, and a fairly lovable mutt at that.

The events of the novel take place in the space of a few weeks, from mid-December 1924 to late January 1925. The setting is precisely defined as Prechistenka and Obukhov Streets in Moscow; fantastic events intrude into this recognizable neighborhood, however, and the dates correspond symbolically to dates of religious significance in the Russian Orthodox calendar. The mayhem that ensues when Sharik-the-dog turns into Sharikov-the-human provides a broad platform for the novel's satirical targets and sets the stage for a more serious and ambiguous exploration of the philosophical questions that dogged (bad pun!) the Bolshevik project of creating a New Soviet Man. Thus, *Heart of a Dog* exhibits in miniature form all the generic attributes of a Menippean satire that Bulgakov would also employ in his later masterpiece, *The Master and Margarita*.

Menippean satire interpolates topical humor directed against contemporary social mores with significant philosophical or metaphysical themes. The Menippean satirist saturates his satirical-philosophical vision with erudite detail. In order to support and amplify the worldview presented in the work, its characters embody set stations and attitudes, rather than presenting well-rounded psychological portraitures. To recognize *Heart of a Dog* as a form of Menippean satire is useful, insofar as it encourages us to consider the novel's main characters as representative types interacting in a kind of tragicomic symposium, where the question at stake is no less than the nature of human nature and the prospect of radical social transformation. The novella's three protagonists represent three different possible ways of understanding the biological potential of human beings. Sharik represents a consistently "biologizing" view of human nature that holds out little hope for radical reconstruction through nurture; Bormental' represents a neo-Lamarckian view of biosocial forces that links progressive evolution to positive environmental changes; whereas Professor Preobrazhenskii represents a strictly genetic view of inheritance (evolutionary change is the result of random, unpredictable mutations), complicated by an overarching allegiance to the eugenic project of improving humankind through a more advanced knowledge of biology. All three viewpoints clash directly with the dogmatic environmentalism represented by the young communist activists who form the housing committee. By "environmentalism" I mean a strictly "nurturist" approach to shaping human behavior. In this view, human beings are essentially tabulae rasae, and it is our environment—family, peers, social training, physical surroundings—that scripts our values, inclinations, and behaviors. This reading intentionally sharpens the line between representative viewpoints in order to arrive at a better understanding of the whole (which ultimately eludes neat divisions).

The Dog: Biology Is Destiny

To show one way in which Bulgakov brings this point of view to bear on his theme, we need look no further than the stray dog's monologue in the first and second chapters. When Bulgakov adopts the dog's perspective for extended passages of the narration, he does not limit himself to what the dog might know. Instead, for comic effect, he endows his canine character with rather sophisticated medical knowledge ("I can easily contract pneumonia . . ."), sharp class consciousness (he distinguishes between cooks for the gentry and "those nobodies from the Soviet of Normal Diet"), and surprising worldliness (the dog remarks that Frenchmen eat everything with red wine). Therefore, it is all the more striking that the dog has one quirk of perception that is entirely consistent with his species identity. Presumably, the difference between animal and human consciousness lies in the degree to which the latter breaks free of innate programming and instinctual patterns to develop a free personality that transcends biology. The dog Sharik, however, assumes simple innateness in human character and motivation, perverting class consciousness into biological determinism on the basis of breeding. In Sharik's opening monologue, the behavior of human beings is so closely correlated to their outward appearance, that character itself is explained as just another expression of physical type. When a cook throws scalding water at the stray dog, the dog understands this cruelty as an inevitable expression of the cook's physical type: "What harm did I do him? . . . The greedy brute! Take a look at that mug of his sometimes—it's wider than it is long. A crook with a brass jowl."[16] That the dog sees character and behavior as essentially another expression of innate biological endowment is repeated and explicitly reinforced a few pages later, when Sharik spots the Professor. "A gentleman. Do you think I judge by the coat? Nonsense. Many proletarians are also wearing coats nowadays. ... No, it is the eyes I'm talking about. When you look at the eyes, you can't mistake a man."[17] In Sharik's view, at least, the Professor would be a gentleman even without his coat; his breeding shows through in his eyes.

It is not until the epilogue, after a clandestine surgery that converts Sharikov into a dog again, that Bulgakov returns to Sharik the narrative style and point of view he possessed in the opening monologue. Now Sharik suffers from occasional headaches, but he explicitly dismisses the clearly local, environmental cause: "True, they've slashed up my whole head for some reason, but it'll heal before my wedding. It's not worth mentioning."[18] Instead, he attributes his malady to his genes: "I'm absolutely convinced there was something shady in my ancestry. There must have been a Newfoundland. She was a whore, my grandmother, may she rest in the Heavenly Kingdom."[19] In short, the dog's voice is consistently (not to mention humorously) biologizing. If animal behavior is determined by instinctual patterns that are, by definition, hereditary, then from a dog's point of view, human behavior is also ultimately an unfolding of innate propensities, which are inherited in more or less the same way as eye color and height.

Housing Committee: Social (Re)construction

At the opposite extreme from the notion that "biology determines destiny" is the notion that environment does. Bulgakov could still make fun of this approach and its results in *Heart of a Dog*, because the trajectory of Soviet environmentalism had not yet reached its conclusion in a political correctness enforced by punishment. The scenes in which the Professor is tormented by the housing committee and appalled by the rapidly Bolshevized Sharikov ridicule the notion that human beings can be reformed by their environment alone. For example, the housing committee is made up of what appear to be four young men. The unisex, utilitarian simplicity of their clothes and manners presumably reflects

---

16 Bulgakov, *Heart of a Dog*, 1.
17 Ibid., 5.
18 Ibid., 122.
19 Ibid.

the egalitarian consciousness represented by the victorious proletariat. They insist on being called "comrades" instead of "gentlemen," but their request that the Professor do his part in promoting social equality by giving up his rooms is rendered in convoluted, half-assimilated bureaucratese: "We've come to you after a general meeting of the tenants of this house which went into the question of consolidating the tenancy of the apartments."[20] Clearly, Bulgakov shares his protagonist's sense of irony and distaste when confronted with the products of the new society's cultural imprinting. He also presents a challenge to the belief that a qualitatively "new man" can be created by changing the environment of the "old man." The Professor perceives that people have indeed changed within the new cultural environment—but only for the worse. He also perceives the areas of human behavior and personality that are still influenced by biology and seemingly immune to cultural remolding. When confronted by the housing committee, he demands to know whether the "peach-complexioned one" is a man or a woman. "Blushing violently," she admits to being a woman.[21] When one of her male colleagues also turns a vivid red "for some unknown reason" during this interchange, one implication is that gender—and sexual attraction between the genders—cannot be erased by environmental dictate; rather, it is part of human nature.

Bormental': Evolution in a Positive Direction

There are, of course, many facets to Charles Darwin's theory of evolution, not all of them equally compatible with early twentieth-century yearnings for social utopia. Bormental' is a Baltic German whose father was an examining magistrate in Vilno. Thus, he shares with his mentor politically disadvantageous class origins, an appreciation of fine cognac, and a rational, secular belief in science as the key to ameliorating the human condition. There are also significant differences between the two. Bormental' is a generation younger than his mentor, who was already fifty-two years old at the time of the revolution.[22] Bormental' was doubtless just beginning his career as a scientist when his well-appointed father presumably fell from grace at the time of the Bolshevik takeover. Like many of his generation, he may have initially resisted the policies of the new regime, especially out of loyalty to his prerevolutionary intellectual mentors.

---

20 Ibid., 25.
21 Ibid., 24.
22 Ibid., 104.

Yet, Bormental' is ready to object that the Professor "take[s] too dark a view of things"[23] in his vehement rejection of everything the Bolsheviks have done. When the Professor demands to know why "the proletarian [cannot] leave his galoshes downstairs instead of tracking up the marble,"[24] Bormental' displays his sympathetic awareness of class inequities by reminding his mentor that the proletarian does not even own any galoshes. It is not hard to see how Bormental' can combine a rational faith in science with a "fellow traveler's" willingness to work within the parameters of the new regime, which, after all, shared with its scientists a secular, rationalist belief in science and technology as the panacea for problems facing the new society. In the end, Bormental' will stand by his uncompromising scientist-mentor, but his initial reaction to the dog's transformation is colored by his desire to see biology and the ideals of Bolshevism coincide.

Bormental''s scientific journal represents a distinct change of narrative perspective. His case history begins with an objective record of dry scientific observations: "Laboratory dog. Approximately two years old. Breed—mongrel. Name—Sharik. Fur—thin, shaggy, grayish brown, mottled."[25] With each subsequent entry, however, the events that Bormental' records become more and more difficult to fit within the existing framework of scientific knowledge. Bormental' ignores the warning signs inherent in his own disjointed prose, which Bulgakov represents visually as a hysterical mess. Parts are in pencil, some phrases are triple underlined, others are in violet ink, and certain entries are stained with inkblots. Each inkblot graphically denotes the point at which Bormental' retreats from the metaphysical implications of his own dawning realizations. After all, in Bormental''s conscious mind, the experiment is a stunning success. Preobrazhenskii's experiment proves that through science, mankind has the power to rush up the evolutionary ladder, even skipping a few rungs. What has been achieved by grafting the pituitary and testes onto the dog is, in Bormental''s triple-underlined phrase, "complete humanization."[26] If science has found the key to transforming a dog into a man, surely it can use similar methods to transform a lesser man into a greater one.

To be sure, the new man retains certain canine features. Sharikov has a visceral dislike of cats and the appalling habit of snapping at fleas with his teeth. His short stature, sloping brow, and bad posture (as if still yearning to walk

---

23 Ibid., 34.
24 Ibid., 35.
25 Ibid., 56.
26 Ibid., 60.

on all fours) can also be attributed to his canine heredity; in fact, Bormental'
assumes this is the case. He includes in his scientific notes a sketch of the dog's
paw gradually lengthening into a man's foot and notes with scientific pleasure that the dog is losing most of his hair and retaining only "thin and silky"
strands on his head. From Bormental"s point of view, the dog's appearance is
proof of the progressive direction of evolution (from dog to man). Bormental',
seems to be influenced by this line of thought: man is the blood relative of the
dog, as Il'ia Mechnikov so memorably suggested in his 1909 speech honoring
the fiftieth anniversary of Darwin's *On the Origin of Species*.[27] We are all part
of one magnificent chain of evolution. What was latent in the dog at a lower
evolutionary level (for instance, the power of speech) has been "released" by
the successful operation.[28] Bormental"s scientific optimism reaches its apogee
in his response to the dog's rapid assimilation of human speech. "The grafted
pituitary has opened a speech center in the canine brain, and the words have
burst out in a stream. In my view, what we see is a resuscitated and expanded
brain, and not a newly created one. Oh, the marvelous confirmation of the
theory of evolution! Oh, the greatest chain of evolution from dog to the chemist Mendeleyev!"[29] The problem is that Sharikov, as a particular example of
the miraculous leap from animal to man, opens his mouth initially and primarily to spew out obscenities. The reader laughs, the Professor is appalled, and
Bormental' is caught between the scientific thrill of hearing language emerge
from this new species and horror at the kind of language that emerges.

It should come as no surprise that the miracle of language and the
enigma of where it comes from should take on such importance in the further

---

27 Note that Mechnikov's portrait hangs on the wall of the Professor's waiting room until the
    unruly Sharik smashes it in a rampage that precedes his operation. Mechnikov's study of
    comparative pathology helped put the older notion of a "great chain of being" onto firmer
    scientific footing. In 1908, Mechnikov won the Nobel Prize for work that showed that the
    immune defenses in higher organisms show traces of their evolutionary origins in more
    primitive animals. Evidence that higher organisms retain structural features of the lower
    organisms could be interpreted philosophically as a validation of the "unbroken chain of
    evolution" that leads from animal to man. Indeed, in his 1909 speech Mechnikov empha-
    sized that the study of comparative pathology had shown us that "man is a blood relative of
    the animal world." See Alexander Vucinich, *Darwin in Russian Thought* (Berkeley: University
    of California Press, 1988), 281.

28 In this view, no fundamental, mysterious divide uniquely separates Homo sapiens from the
    rest of the animal world. This concept is also explored (and rejected) in Osip Mandel'shtam's
    poem of the same period "Lamarck." In the knowledge of good and evil, Mandel'shtam
    implies, we are unique and have stepped off the evolutionary scale.

29 Bulgakov, *Heart of a Dog*, 63.

characterization of Sharikov.[30] The question of the origin of language—specifically bad language—echoes the larger question already posed about what combination of biological and cultural programming determines the individual human being's behavior in society. One of the ways in which Russian intellectuals could interpret Darwinian evolution so that it retained a positive teleological direction was to invoke neo-Lamarckian ideas about the possibility of the biological inheritance of acquired characteristics. Sharikov has indeed "inherited" most of the characteristics his human "parent" had *acquired* during his lifetime as a balalaika-playing, hard-drinking, skirt-chasing newly urbanized peasant. Klim Chugunkin, the deceased (in a drunken brawl) donor of the pituitary and testes used in the experiment, spoke mostly in obscenities. The transfer of Chugunkin's substandard language to his laboratory prodigy complicates Bormental's attempts to reconcile directed evolution with social improvements. Bormental' attributes Sharikov's spontaneous linguistic vulgarity to habits picked up in his previous life's environment: "During his canine existence, Sharik's brain accumulated a mass of concepts. All the words he used in the beginning were gutter words. He heard them and stored them in his brain."[31] Here's the rub: if Sharikov has essentially inherited the nasty characteristics acquired in his former existence, then the promise of a progressive eugenics promoting the proletarian class is thrown into doubt.

---

30 The theories of Bulgakov's near contemporary, the Soviet linguist Nikolai Iakovlevich Marr (1864–1934) might have influenced the direction of Bulgakov's satire as much as the delicious temptation of translating the Pygmalion story, with its valorization of elitist values, to the inverted world of a socialist cultural revolution. Already prior to the revolution, Marr had arrived at his idea that all human languages can be traced back to a single universal proto-tongue. After the revolution, he found an easy compatibility between his original sociolinguistic leanings and Marxist doctrine. He proposed that language mirrors class consciousness, like any other superstructure. He went so far as to suggest that the languages of the economic underclass—whether French, German, Russian, or Chinese—should have more in common with each other than with the corresponding upper-class language spoken by the elite of each language group. In short, Marr suggested that if the economic base of a society changes—as it had most dramatically in Russia—then language will change, too. Bulgakov pokes fun at the problem that this theory—which reigned supreme in the 1920s—posed for the zealous proponents of socialist rebuilding. *Heart of a Dog* presents a world in which the Russian language seems to be strained to the breaking point: the Professor speaks with elevated correctness and constantly sings verses from Giuseppe Verdi's operas under his breath; the housing committee members speak in an incomprehensible new language of Soviet bureaucratese; and Sharikov continues to swear with gusto, even as he assimilates bureaucratic jargon to manipulate his advantage.

31 Bulgakov, *Heart of a Dog*, 64.

It was precisely this kind of argument that brought about the demise of the neo-Lamarckian eugenics movement in the Soviet Union. In a 1925 pamphlet attacking Lamarckianism, Iurii Aleksandrovich Filipchenko, one of the founders of the Russian eugenics movement, turned the promise of a "proletarian" eugenics on its head: "If acquired characteristics are inherited, then, obviously, all representatives of the proletariat bear in themselves the traces of all the unfavorable influences which their fathers, grandfathers, and a long series of distant ancestors have suffered over many, many years."[32] Along the same lines, one could argue that if the capacity for language is biological, how should one treat evidence of an innate linguistic backwardness in the very class one is trying to promote to the vanguard of national identity?[33] If, on the other hand, language is an entirely social phenomenon, something learned from one's parents and peers, why does the influence of a supremely proper linguistic milieu have no influence on Sharikov's speech habits? Finally, the problem of language proves to be a powerful illustration of the futility of applying existing eugenic solutions to create the New Soviet Man. The unfortunate choice of Chugunkin illustrates why any class-based eugenics program designed to promote the proletariat will dissolve in a fatal paradox. Bad stock will most likely produce bad offspring, as in the case of Sharikov. Only good stock will (possibly) create desirable offspring, and nature herself takes care of ensuring a supply of "desirable offspring" on her own, without the intervening hand of science. As Bormental' attempts to comprehend Sharikov's recalcitrance, "who swore tenderly and melodiously, his tongue twisting over the obscenities,"[34]

---

32 Quoted in Adams, "Eugenics as Social Medicine in Revolutionary Russia," 213. Iu. A. Filipchenko (1882–1930) received his doctorate in zoology and comparative anatomy in 1917 and was soon promoted to professor of zoology at Petrograd University. Filipchenko was an indefatigable teacher, organizer, and promoter of genetic research in Petrograd. His view of eugenics—which he avidly promoted in the college curriculum and in popular books—was based on a strictly Mendelian understanding of how traits are inherited. Therefore, he understood eugenics as having to do with the promise of scientific research to improve human lives (what today we might call "medical genetics"), but he had no patience for any suggestion that hereditary traits can be acquired through the influence of the external environment.

33 One view of linguistic origins is essentially biological, as evidenced in the implicit meaning encoded in our ideas about "native speakers" and the "mother tongue." T. P. Bonfiglio, unpublished manuscript. If the innateness of our capacity for language somehow extends to an "innate" aptitude for the language of our forbears, then Sharikov has inherited his "native" capacity for Russian from Klim, and he presumably sucked in the sounds of *mat* along with his mother's milk (he was born a street mutt).

34 Bulgakov, *Heart of a Dog*, 99.

the reader is reminded of Liza Doolittle (Galatea) succumbing to Henry Higgins's (Pygmalion's) regime of speech improvement. Bulgakov's treatment of the Pygmalion theme is intentionally ambiguous. When Sharikov refuses to be "cultured" by either his bourgeois caretakers or his Bolshevik handlers, we are reassured by the tenacity of human nature, which finds a loophole for free will despite the best efforts of both scientists and social activists to engineer a more perfect world. It is Bulgakov's scientist hero, Preobrazhenskii, who most fully embodies this view of human nature.

Preobrazhenskii: The Biologist as Woland

When the omniscient narrator takes over and describes the new man as others see him, the vector of evolution described by Bormental' is reversed. As we have seen, in Bormental''s journal (chapter 5), Sharikov is represented as a lower species on his way to becoming a higher one. In the next chapter, Sharikov appears to us as a degenerate who is descending, rather than ascending, the putative ladder of evolution. When the Professor summons Sharikov to his office, he finds "a short man of unpleasant appearance . . . leaning against the door-jamb, one leg crossed over the other. The hair on his head was coarse and stood up like shrubs in a badly cleared field, and his face was covered with stubble. His forehead was strikingly low. The thick brush of hair began almost directly over the black tufts of his shaggy eyebrows."[35] In this view the finger of heredity is also present, but it is pointed at the theory of the "criminal type" popularized by the Italian psychiatrist Cesare Lombroso in the late nineteenth century. Lombroso studied the physical traits of criminals and declared that he had found certain innate atavisms that were common to most of them. In the early twentieth century, Lombroso's idea was amplified by other theorists, who argued that the various unhealthy manifestations of modern civilization could actually cause evolution to reverse its course (which was falsely assumed to be progressive) and produce individuals with atavistic or degenerate features.[36] We soon learn that Bulgakov's scientist-protagonist rejects all teleological notions of evolution (whether progressive or degenerate). Preobrazhenskii's reputation as a wizard is predicated on the atmosphere of anxiety in which he operates, however. The demand for the Professor's rejuvenation surgeries can

---

35   Ibid., 68.
36   For a full discussion of the intersections between Russian literary culture and early twentieth-century psychiatric theory in Russia, see Irina Sirotkina, *Diagnosing Literary Genius: A Cultural History of Psychiatry in Russia, 1880–1930* (Baltimore, 2002).

be seen as the inverse reflection of a general atmosphere of decadence and anxiety about decay. His wealthy patients are clearly unmoored from the previous era's class structure and moral certainties, and their quest for (sexual) youth renders them almost grotesquely animalistic. In general, metaphors of decadence, degeneration, and devolution dominate the descriptions of NEP-era excesses. Paradoxically, in Russia of the 1920s, metaphors of degeneration coexisted and sometimes coincided with the Bolshevik rhetoric of the newness, strength, and health of dawning socialist society.[37]

The utopian rhetoric of transfiguration that colors the tone of Preobrazhenskii's and Bormental''s discussions—*improving the human race!*—conveys the powerful appeal eugenic solutions held for a society that had lived through devastating demographic upheavals. As the NEP era dawned at the beginning of the 1920s, years of war, famine, epidemics, and displacement caused by the revolution and civil war had taken a drastic toll on the population. Not only had the country lost a significant percentage of its population but also, in both urban and rural settings, the face (literally) of the population had changed. Accounts of the day are often framed by the discourse of degeneration and reverse evolution. Bulgakov's *Notes of a Country Doctor*, which he worked on throughout his first year as a writer in Moscow (1921) reflect a sense of biological crisis that belies any easy optimism about bringing enlightenment to the masses. In one story, the peasants' stubborn ignorance and their resistance to the doctor's efforts lead to the spread of degenerative diseases like syphilis. Other stories amplify the theme of biological and cultural inertia that will reappear in a single memorable line in *Heart of the Dog*, when Professor Preobrazhenskii exclaims "no one can succeed in this, and least of all a people who being generally behind Europeans by some 200 years are still not even sure of how to button up their own pants."[38] The idea that society needed to

---

37 Bulgakov depicts the recipients of sex gland grafts as sexual maniacs indulging in grotesque excess (one old man relishes visions of being flocked by naked young women every night; a female patient in her fifties keeps up with her ardent young lover, etc.). Yet as Naiman points out in his chapter, "The Discourse of Castration," in *Sex in Public*, early Soviet interpretations of rejuvenation therapy were enthusiastic for reasons that were antithetical to Bulgakov's satirical portrayal. In the Soviet press, rejuvenation was tied to the sublimation of sexual energies, presumably into the healthy work of building socialism. So, for instance, a procedure that involved tying the vas deferens to prevent ejaculation was assumed to have a rejuvenating effect because it prevented vital secretions from being spent externally and redirected them internally to the benefit of the whole organism. Also, this procedure would obviously prevent the man from being the cause of (unwanted) pregnancy.

38 Bulgakov, *Heart of a Dog*, 37.

be "improved" was so pervasive in the postrevolutionary decade that it seems to have left its mark on almost every discipline. Geneticists sought to unravel the mechanisms of heredity and the secrets of transmitting "good" qualities; physiologists turned their attention from drooling dogs to investigating higher mental function in humans; psychiatrists openly discussed the possibility of setting up "genius farms" to protect the fragile psyches of the most brilliant people. Even geochemists, led by Vladimir Vernadskii, developed the utopian concept of a "noosphere" that both elevates mankind's responsibility for his environment and implicitly provides a blueprint for the future shape of a better humanity.

In this context, Professor Preobrazhenskii emerges in a different light than when we see him as the literary caricature of the "mad scientist." His evil doings shrouded in darkness as he pulls brains out of jars, he is illuminated by hell-fire when he plunges ahead with the dog's operation. These portentous scenes emerge from one layer of the work's narrative structure, one in which fantastic imagery and science fictional motifs are dominant. Yet it can be argued that *Heart of a Dog* continually resists being relegated to the farcical and fantastical realm of allegory. Instead, the science fictional layer of the novel is coextensive with the very real world of scientific debates that occupied intellectuals, health officials, and policymakers in NEP-era Moscow. Preobrazhenskii is an exaggerated portrait of his nonfictional contemporaries in the scientific world, for whom the research agenda of broadening our understanding of heredity and the philosophical goal of bettering humanity through science were not at all opposed. Some have suggested that the portrait of Preobrazhenskii was inspired by Bulgakov's uncle, a leading gynecologist who lived in a six-room apartment on Obukhov Lane.[39] It seems equally plausible that his unusual name and patronymic were inspired by the ubiquitous Iu. A. Filipchenko, who published new books popularizing eugenics in each of the first four years after Bulgakov's move to Moscow.[40]

---

39 Several sources have noted that Bulgakov's uncle, N. M. Pokrovskii, had also complained to the authorities that his living space was being reduced. See, for example, Milne, *Mikhail Bulgakov*, 62; Haber, *Mikhail Bulgakov*, 275.

40 Iu. A. Filipchenko, *Chto takoe evgenika* [What is eugenics] (Petrograd, 1921); Filipchenko, *Kak nasleduiutsia razlichnye osobennosti cheloveka* [How human traits are inherited] (Petrograd, 1921); Filipchenko, *Puti uluchsheniia chelovecheskogo roda: Evgenika* [Ways of improving the human race: Eugenics] (Petrograd, 1924); and Filipchenko, *Frensis Gal'ton i Gregor Mendel'* [Francis Galton and Gregory Mendel] (Moscow, 1925).

In the climactic turning point of *Heart of a Dog*, Preobrazhenskii seizes upon the difference between rejuvenation and the goal of eugenics. Although the fiercely intelligent, visionary Preobrazhenskii is best understood in the context of the Russian eugenics movement, the specifics of the dog's operation are based on early twentieth-century notions of hormonal rejuvenation. The Professor's technical rationale for the dog's operation is elliptic: he claims that once he had succeeded in "extract[ing] the sex hormone from the pituitary," he wanted to "perform a little experiment."[41] The design of the Professor's medical experiment, and the reason it fails as a social experiment, does not make sense outside the context of early endocrinology and rejuvenation theories. At the beginning of the twentieth century, scientists began to speculate, on the basis of new experimental evidence, that chemical secretions, rather than nerve activity, might be responsible for most physiological activities. These internal chemical secretions could affect every cell in the body; indeed, their importance to all life functions was reflected in the neologism coined in 1905 to describe them: *hormone*, from the Greek word "arouse to activity."[42] Bulgakov's scientist-hero believes he has located the seat of hormonal production and distribution in the pituitary. Therefore, when he operates on Sharik, he not only transplants the testes of a man into the dog's belly, he also replaces the dog's pituitary with a human one.[43] The second part of the operation—grafting the man's pituitary onto the dog's brain—represents an imaginative extrapolation of faddish ideas about the endocrine system's omnipotence. In the minds of Bulgakov's contemporaries, the power of the body's newly discovered chemical messengers (hormones) went far beyond matters of sexual prowess and rejuvenation. It appeared, as Eric Naiman has argued, that "the old belief in the 'sovereignty of the brain' had been displaced by new knowledge of hormones,

---

41   Bulgakov, *Heart of a Dog*, 104.

42   Freeman, Bloom, and McGuire, "A Brief History of Testosterone," 372.

43   Note that the first stage of the dog's operation is modeled after existing rejuvenation techniques that were in vogue at the time. The rage for rejuvenation therapy was based on the findings of the French physiologist Charles Eduoard Brown-Sequard, the Viennese surgeon Eugene Steinbach, and the Russian emigre (to France) Sergei Voronoff. Steinbach favored ligation of the vas deferens (tube tying); Brown-Sequard injected patients with a serum made from the seminal fluids of animals; and the Russian emigre Voronoff surgically grafted testicular tissue from monkeys into men. The latter procedure is close to the one depicted in *Heart of a Dog*. Although the surgical techniques pioneered by these men (and their many less scrupulous followers) were eventually discredited (for lack of long-term results), the early rejuvenation pioneers were operating on the sound principle that hormone levels decline as the organism ages, precipitating various signs of aging. To reverse aging, it seemed logical to replenish or replace the hormones.

the true 'builders of the living body.'"[44] Preobrazhenskii's "little experiment" is based on the premise that the endocrine system, controlled by the pituitary, determines the entire "human aspect."

The unprecedented operation goes beyond simple rejuvenation, which could be achieved by testicular tissue grafts alone.[45] Instead, Preobrazhenskii grafts onto the dog's brain the hormonal control tower that makes a human being look and act like a human. Indeed, in a matter of days the impact of the all-powerful chemical messengers is such that the dog acquires the appearance and the speech of a man. Bormental' exults at the discovery: "The [pituitary's] hormones may be described as the most important ones in the organism, they are the hormones of the human shape. ... Professor Preobrazhenskii, you are a Creator!"[46] Early on, the Professor arrives at a different understanding of the operation. Ten days after the operation, he falls ill when he grasps the import of what he has done. He understands that, although Sharikov has not yet shed the last of his canine propensities, the human secretions emanating from the pituitary have done their work: Sharikov no longer has a dog's heart, but a human one. In a few more weeks, the Professor predicts, the human hormones will have fully saturated the former dog's brain, at which point it will have lost all its former canine aspects (including even the propensity to chase cats). The pituitary hormones determine not just the human shape but also the human heart (soul). In this science fictional twist, Bulgakov took his lead from several articles in the popular press, which suggested that the discovery of hormones could replace the intangible religious conception of "soul."[47]

---

44 Naiman, *Sex in Public*, 143.

45 The 1920s saw the first heyday of the use of hormone replacement therapies for purposes of rejuvenation. See Kahn, "Recovering Lost Youth," and numerous recent articles that find instructive analogies between the history of rejuvenation surgery and the current wave of enthusiasm for hormone therapies: for example, Chandak Sengoopta, "Tales from the Vienna Labs: The Eugene Steinbach-Harry Benjamin Correspondence," *Bulletin of the New York Academy of Medicine*, no. 2 (2000): 2–7; B. P. Setchell, "The Testis and Tissue Transplantation: Historical Aspects," *Journal of Reproductive Immunology* 18, no. 1 (1990): 181–88.

46 Bulgakov, *Heart of a Dog*, 63.

47 Naiman, *Sex in Public*, 143. More than one contemporary commentator suggested that the discovery of the endocrine system obviated the need for a religious concept of the "soul." See, for example, Ts. Perel'muter, *Nauka i religiia o zhizni chelovecheskogo tela* [The science and religion of the human body] (n.p., 1927), and A. V. Nemilov, "Uznaem li my kogda-nibud' chto takoe 'dusha'?" [Will we ever know what the soul is?], *Chelovek i priroda* [Man and nature] no. 4 (1924). Naiman argues convincingly that this enthusiasm for endocrinology in the nonmedical press can be attributed in part to its status as a postrevolutionary scientific field. Furthermore, endocrinology was a science that could plausibly challenge

The problem is that Sharikov has obviously "inherited" the specific human heart of his "parent" Chugunkin. Preobrazhenskii realizes that he has only discovered the source of the "given human individual's" behavior, not the "human aspect in general."[48] Sharikov is simply Klim, resurrected. Bormental' suggests that had the dog received the pituitary of Spinoza, the outcome would have been different. This is true, but it does not satisfy Preobrazhenskii's eugenic goal, which is to improve humanity as a whole, not selectively enhance individual human beings.[49] The operation has demonstrated that a given individual can be transformed, but to what end? The transformation of a given individual into someone smarter, or younger, belongs in the Professor's mind to the trivial realm of rejuvenation. Preobrazhenskii sees no need to artificially produce a "highly advanced human," since any peasant woman can give birth to a Lomonosov, and nature regularly manages to produce geniuses by "stubbornly selecting them out of the mass of scum."[50] In Preobrazhenskii's view, the human race will not be improved by piecemeal operations transforming one individual at a time. Nor, as we have seen, will it be improved by coercive social measures that alter the environment.

Through this ambiguous portrayal of Preobrazhenskii, we see Bulgakov anticipating the subtle and inconclusive truths that are more fully unfurled in *The Master and Margarita*. In that book, the elegant and erudite Satan (Woland) looks at humanity and pronounces: "People are thoughtless, but, then again, sometimes mercy enters their hearts … they are ordinary people … on the whole, they remind me of their predecessors," while the gentle prophet Yeshua proclaims, seemingly against abundant evidence to the contrary, that all

---

religious explanations for the intangible aspects of human nature. In this way, the nascent field of endocrinology and the emerging field of genetics were alike: both had much to offer the scientific, secular Soviet regime, but the latter foundered on a politically motivated ideological campaign against "bourgeois biology" in the 1930s (Lysenkoism).

48 Bulgakov, *Heart of a Dog*, 104.
49 In this interpretation, Preobrazhenskii's position echoes that of Filipchenko (and most other Russian eugenicists). Filipchenko was adamantly opposed to the policy of selective sterilization practiced in the United States. Since there was no practical way to selectively breed for better people, and he considered it unethical to mandate sterilization, Filipchenko's eugenic platform remained largely theoretical. His 1925 article *Evgenetika v shkole* [Eugenics at school] advocates "eugenic" instruction in high schools, which he defines as simply a series of courses teaching the basics of human reproduction and the principles of Mendelian genetics. In other words, eugenics begins by inculcating a sound knowledge of biology and sex education.
50 Bulgakov, *Heart of a Dog*, 103.

people are good.[51] In *Heart of a Dog*, the mystery of the human heart remains inviolable—neither biological breeding nor cultural inheritance and social conditioning are a guarantee of its quality. Therefore, Preobrazhenskii is not a mad scientist trying to reverse the vector of human evolution, nor is he a eugenicist who thinks he can breed better people. He is a eugenicist in the image of Woland—half-demon, half-priest—who, in his extreme elitism seems to will evil (through his impatience with all forms of human weakness and with the schemes to improve them) but eternally works good (raises the bar of the arts and sciences, creates new frontiers of knowledge).[52]

In a recent essay, the cognitive scientist Steven Pinker notes that the reception of scientific ideas in any given society can be enhanced or distorted by the "moral coloring of science" prevailing in a culture.[53] He reminds us of the obvious: the reception of new scientific ideas is likely to be positive in a cultural era that champions the idea of rational progress and views scientists as heroes who vanquish disease, hunger, and hardship. In a cultural milieu wary of scientific hubris and skeptical about the motives of grant-grubbing researchers, however, new scientific ideas may provoke anxiety, skepticism, and resistance. Pinker proposes the following explanation for waves of cultural hostility toward science: "Our neural circuits for morality are overly receptive to the trappings of purity, naturalness, and custom, and they are too easily impressed by gravitas, indignation, conspicuous asceticism, and other advertisements of saintliness that may have scant correlation with actions that make people better off."[54] In other words, the "actions that make people better off"—in this context, sophisticated scientific research—are least tolerated by ideologies motivated by metaphors of simplicity and purity, and best tolerated in societies enamored of complexity and abundance. We can speculate that the construction of the scientist as a positive hero is accompanied by a moral climate that validates material abundance, human dominion within nature, futuristic expectations of a better and

---

51 Mikhail Bulgakov, *The Master and Margarita*, trans. Diana Lewis Burgin and Katherine Tiernan O'Connor (New York, 1996), 104.

52 Marxist philosophers and Bolshevik policymakers reached a different conclusion. By the early 1930s, the regime had firmly charted a course of official strict environmentalism. The Russian Eugenics Society was disbanded, the eugenics division of Kol'tsov's institute was abolished, chapters in both Soviet and translated western textbooks that treated the topic of human heredity were excised, and the word eugenics disappeared almost completely from Soviet discourse.

53 Steven Pinker, introduction, in Richard Dawkins and Tim Folger, eds., *The Best American Science and Nature Writing 2004* (Boston: Mariner Books, 2004), xix.

54 Ibid., xx.

more advanced stage of humanity. Fear of science and the construction of the "mad scientist" are accompanied, in this view, by a moral climate of asceticism, sexual as well as intellectual purity, and a backwards-looking utopian impulse that yearns for prelapsarian oneness with nature. Interestingly enough, the two "moral climates" proposed by Pinker were both present, and on a collision course, in the cultural moment that forms the backdrop of Bulgakov's novel.

On the one hand, the NEP era has been viewed positively as a time of liberal cultural policies and great intellectual diversity; Bulgakov's Moscow, in particular, has been portrayed as a scene of jazzy optimism with pockets of material opulence. On the other hand, NEP-era Russia was a time of unprecedented anxiety and uncertainty, as the constituents of a new social order (recently literate peasants, newly empowered workers, embattled "bourgeois" intellectuals) were suddenly called upon to (re)define the limits of their power and identity in a radically reconstituted society. In the rituals and rhetoric of the NEP culture Naiman has identified signs of a moral climate marked by asceticism, anxiety about excess, and a desire to reestablish ideological purity. We can conclude that in 1925, the jet stream of what had been a radically modernizing, forwardlooking utopian climate collided with another front—what Naiman has described as "revolutionary anorexia."[55] Both attitudes are represented in the portrayal of science, scientists, and society Bulgakov created in *Heart of a Dog*.

---

55 Naiman, *Sex in Public*, chapter 6.

Part Three

From Stalin to Sputnik and Beyond

Stalinism and the Genesis of Cosmonautics

MICHAEL G. SMITH

Smith, Michael G. "Stalinism and the Genesis of Cosmonautics."
In *Rockets and Revolution: A Cultural History of Early Spaceflight*,
by Michael G. Smith, 293–306. Lincoln: University
of Nebraska Press, 2014.

The Russian aesthetic of cosmic oneness, first refined by the Symbolist and Futurist poets and later adapted by the proletarian writers, survived into the Soviet 1930s in various ways. F. A. Tsander expressed it when he translated the Stalinist slogan "To catch and surpass" as meaning a leap forward to a truly communistic society in outer space, a place for "free labor" and "universal creativity." G. Arel'skii, the writer of space travel adventures, even called for a whole new poetry based on mathematics and physics. "Science is building its own cathedral of Reason," he wrote, for "our earth is but one among the infinite islands in the ocean of the universe." It was an insight demanding a whole new way of thinking and writing, "a new era of planetary history for humanity."[1] Aleksandr Prokof'ev's poetry reproduced the earlier Promethean values for a new Stalinist generation. A student from the *Proletkul't* circles in 1922, he still

---

1 The term is from F.A. Tsander, "Dogonim I peregonim," 26 October 1931, ARAN, f. 573, o. 1, d. 252, l. 1. G. Arel'skii, "O problemakh poezii buduschego" [Issues of a poetry for the future], *Vestnik znaniia* [Herald of knowledge] 2 (February 1930): 54–55.

celebrated the proletarian "We" of the revolution that "will be carried up to the heavens," predicting that communism would someday "dash off ships into flight"—and yes, even "to the stars."[2]

Official Communist ideology remained attuned to such imagery. *Pravda* valued Maiakovskii's poems for their cosmic "pathos" and "all-absorbing passion." The era of forced collectivization and industrialization was kind to the proletarian poets, their cosmist works reissued in new editions as forerunners of socialist realism. By definition this genre was all about the romanticism of heroic exploits, making miracles come true.[3] Here were the makings of an expressly Stalinist cosmism. Outer space, looking down on the planet, became one of its favorite frames of reference. "We have put socialism into practice," proclaimed one banner headline. "In place of Tsarist Russia heaves the great colossus of the USSR."[4] This extravagant globalism was a function of the very ideology of the Russian Revolution. It was built upon Marx's slogan "Workers of the World Unite." It was expressed in images of Lenin or of Bolshevik workers traversing the planet. It was screened cinematically in Dziga Vertov's film *One Sixth of the World* (1926), a visual celebration of the USSR's worldwide reach.[5] Propaganda posters featured Stalin's gigantic portrait fusing with Lenin's, like a new sun in the heavens illuminating the USSR. Stalin's own underground name, which blended the Russian *stal* (steel) with the name Lenin, was fortuitous too, allowing for a marriage between the images of the man of "steel" and the man of the "sun."[6]

Avant-garde artists retooled their techniques to the service of the Stalin regime. Konstantin Iuon repainted *New Planet* for the times, without the earlier fear and trembling of cosmic catastrophe, now with the "People" confidently at work, perhaps building a spacecraft or rebuilding their own planet, all against the background of cement mixers, searchlights, and stars. El Lissitzky's

---

2 Aleksandr Prokof'ev, *Sobranie sochinenii* [Collected works], 4 vols. (Moscow: Khudozhestvenania literaturia, 1965), 1:95, 107–8, 127–29, 188, 425.

3 A. Gurshstein, "Poet sotsializma" [The poet of socialism], *Pravda*, April 12, 1937, 4. See, e.g., M. P. Gerasimov, *Zariad* (Moscow: Tovarischestvo pisatelei, 1933). For context, see Boris Groys and Max Hollein, eds., *Dream Factory Communism* (Schiro-Frankfurt: Hatje Kantz, 2003), 107–15, 260–77.

4 Quoted from the magazine 30 *dnei* 5 (1931): 79–80; see also the front cover for 10–11 (1931): and *Krasnaia panorama* 39, September 23, 1927.

5 See these images and terms in *Komsomolskaia Pravda* [Comsomol truth]18, January 21, 1934, 3; and 2, January 1, 1934, 4. *Shestaia chast' mira* [A sixth part of the world], directed by Dziga Vertov (1926; Moscow: Sovkino).

6 Note the alignments of the signs of the zodiac and Lenin's portrait, along with Stalin's funeral oath for Lenin in 1924, in *Nauka i zhizn'* [Science and life] 1 (1936), front cover to page 3.

sculpture *Red Star*, made for the International Press Exhibit at Cologne (1928), showed a planetary system revolving around the new sun of proletarian values.[7] Kazimir Malevich offered the most towering of images: a study of Lenin as orbital "architecton," his arm pointed upward, reaching for space astride a series of skyscraper monuments and against the backdrop of Malevich's cosmic *Supremus No. 56*. Here was the ultimate parabola of the revolution—Lenin as rocket.

On the ground the Soviet Union now marked several natural frontiers for conquest: the "mobilization of the ether" through radio (*mobilizatsiia efira*); the "storming of the sky" (*shturm neba*) and "the "storming of the polar north" by airplane (*shturm severa*); the "storming of the earth's depths" by mines (*shturm nedr*); the "conquest of the stratosphere" via balloon or high-altitude plane (*zavoevanie stratosfery*); and even the "storming of the universe" by rocket (*shturm vselennoi*). Inspired by the first great "storming" of the Winter Palace in October 1917, these campaigns marked the vertical horizons of the Soviet state. As the poet Demian Bednyi wrote, "Our strengths, they're beyond measure / Heroes of the mines become heroes of the stratosphere." Or as one youth song put it:

> Komsomolists sing to the waters
> And they sing to the heavens
> Comrades suns and stars
> We'll become your masters.[8]

The rocket became a central image of pure mechanical prowess, Tsiolkovskii the herald of the conquest of the cosmos. Both suited the Stalinist preoccupation with reaching "ever higher" (*vsio vyshe*). Tsiolkovskii's rocket, together with Lenin and Stalin's revolutionary party, served the same generative purpose: moving human beings beyond Earth or moving historical events here upon it, against all odds. Astronautics, what the Soviets now began to identify more often as cosmonautics, became the science of the future, the realizable utopia of space travel.

---

7 See K. F. Iuon's painting *Liudi* (1930), in Ia. V. Apushkin, *Konstantin Fedorovich Iuon* (Moscow: Vsekhudozhnik, 1936), 78–79. El Lissitzky's sculpture (with the assistance of Georgii Krutikov) for the "Pressa" Exhibition at Cologne (1928) is in Sophie Lissitzky-Küppers, *El Lissitzky* (Greenwich: Graphic Society, 1968), plate 201.

8 Dem'ian Bednyi, "Stal'naia krepost'" [The steel fortress], *Pravda*, January 29 1937, 6; Leonid Ravich, "Vozdukhoflotskii marsh" [Air show], *Iunyi proletarii* 3 (February 1931): 15.

Rockets and Mass Politics

Within these various contexts, the Soviet state also promoted a broadbased campaign to educate the public in rocketry and space travel issues through the 1930s. Rocketry took center stage in the city spaces of Moscow: with lectures and exhibits at Gorkii Park, in the city planetarium, in the lobby of the Civil Air Fleet (*Aeroflot*), and at the headquarters of the Red Army. It found a special niche in the mass circulation press. This was no fleeting movement. A generation of children and teenagers was raised on the possibilities of rocketry and space travel, symbols of scientific-technological progress.

Some of the campaign's texts were naïve. The youth magazine *Knowledge Is Power* (*Znanie—sila*) devoted a whole issue to the rather far-fetched potential of Tsiolkovskii's dirigible rocket. The *Komsomol* offered rural children an uplifting cartoon about little Alesha, who dreamed of flying off to the moon in a "stratoplane-rocket."[9] Other texts were quite instructive, offering lessons on rocket physics, orbital mechanics, and basic astronomy. Iakov Perel'man's *Interplanetary Voyages* was published in its tenth edition by 1935, hailed as the "world's first" popular survey to deal with rockets and spaceflight. The state publishing house translated Max Valier's and Hermann Noordung's classics, inspiring young and old with the real possibilities of space stations.[10] It reprinted some of Tsiolkovskii's science fiction from before the revolution. In children's magazines he now became little "Kostia," the boy who came from nothing to become the "great Russian prodigy," the original "astronaut" (*zvezdoplavatel'*). He was the inventor of that marvelous machine, the rocket, closed on one end, open on the other, carrying its own propulsion by purely reactive force. Thanks to him, fourth graders learned, the USSR would become the first to "conquer the Moon."[11]

9 *Znanie—sila* [Knowledge is Power] 23–24 (December 1932). The cartoon about Alesha is in "Puteshestvie na lunu" [Journey to the moon], *Kolkhoznye rebiata* [Collective farm friends] 10 (1937): 36. See also A. Abramov, *Raketa* (Moscow: Molodaia gvardiia, 1931).

10 Ia. I. Perel'man, *Mezhplanetnye puteshestviia* [Interplanetary voyages] (Moscow: ONTI,1935). See *Komsomolskaia pravda* 81, April 5, 1934, 4; and 222, September 23, 1934, 4; M. Val'e, *Polet v mirovoe prostrantvo kak tekhnicheskaia vozmozhnost'* [Space flight as technology possibility], ed. V. P. Vetchinkin and translated by S. A. Shorygin (Moscow: ONTI, 1936); German Noordung, *Problema puteshestviia v mirovom prostranstve* [Issues of spaceflight], ed. and trans. B. M. Ginzburg (Moscow: ONTI, 1935).

11 K. E. Tsiolkovskii, *Na lune* [On the moon], ed. Ia. I. Perel'man (Moscow: ONTI, 1934); K. E. Tsiolkovskil, *Grezy o zemle i nebe* [Daydreams of Earth and Heavens], ed. Ia. I. Perel'man (Moscow: ONTI, 1935). Quoted from *Pioner* 21 (1932): 6–7; and 20 (1935): 10–12.

Children corresponded with "grandfather Tsiolkovskii," as they called him, building models of his various air and spacecraft. These groups included the All-Union Meetings of Young Aviation Designers, the Office of Young Inventors of the Society of Inventors, and the All-Union Children's Technical Stations, dedicated to cultivating technical and engineering skills. In late 1934 fifteen-year-old Mara Malkov organized a Laboratory for Reactive Propulsion in the Kharkov House of Young Pioneers (Ukraine), gathering a handful of his mates in the ninth and tenth grades. With great excitement they wrote Tsiolkovskii, asking for "all of Your books (absolutely all of them), and signed too." From their love of physics and model plane building, they now set out to build his rockets and even test Goddard's and Oberth's models, maybe even create a "museum exhibit on interplanetary communications." In all of these ways children became a priority audience for Tsiolkovskii's fantastic ideas. A widely reproduced photograph of the day depicted two youngsters at the old man's feet, in rapt attention, models in hand, listening to his kind wisdom.[12]

Tsiolkovskii's resurgent public fame and official recognition after 1930 were really more about the wider veneration for air power. "Man has conquered the elements" with his "metal bird," wrote the aviation publicist N. Bobrov, who was also one of Tsiolkovskii's first biographers. The regime recognized Tsiolkovskii as one of Russia's and the world's great aviation pioneers, worthy of inclusion in its "Big Life" biography series, inspirational stories for young readers.[13] His life was especially instructive because it perfectly paralleled the whole history of aviation. He was the first to conceive of an all-metal dirigible in 1892, three years before Count Zeppelin. He was the first to conceive of a functional airplane in 1894, nine years before the Wright brothers. He was the first to conceive of rocket power for spaceflight in 1903, nearly two decades before Goddard and Oberth. These historical and personal trajectories constituted Tsiolkovskii's "spirals to the sun." He would transform us, by airplane and dirigible and rocket, into points of light in the heavens.[14] For readers of the Young Communist League's newspapers, Tsiolkovskii's dirigible rocket flew

12 A. Volkov, "K. E. Tsiolkovskii i deti" [K. E. Tsiolkovsky and children], in Islent'ev, *K. E. Tsiolkovskii*, 223. Malkov's story is told in ARAN, r. 4, 0.14, d. 223, ll. 53–65. The photograph is in *Znanie—sila* 23–24 (1932): 6; and *Izobretenie* [Invention] 10 (1935): 5.

13 Nik. Bobrov, *Liudi-ptitsy* [Human birds] (Moscow: Osoaviakhim, 1930), 6–7; and N. N. Bobrov, *Bol'shaia zhizn': Tsiolkovskii* [A great life: Tsiolkovsky] (Moscow: Aviaavtoizdat, 1933).

14 Iu. Geko, "Spirali k solntsu" [Spirals toward the sun], *Priroda i liudi* [Nature and people] 2, January 30, 1931, 6–8.

highest among the great artifacts of aviation, in an ascending arc, just above the 1908 Wright *Flyer*. He had taught the "Soviet people" how to "fly farther than all, faster than all, higher than all."[15] And in one dramatic article, sponsored by the Soviet government and military, Tsiolkovskii confidently predicted nothing less than the evolutionary adaptation of the human race to "ethereal space"—our "migration" to the solar system's planets, asteroids, and moons; the "extraordinary propagation and perfection" of human beings as space colonists; even our retreat to another sun as our own began to fail.[16]

In 1932, in honor of his seventy-fifth birthday, the state awarded Tsiolkovskii the Order of the Red Banner of Labor in formal ceremonies in Moscow. He received a new home in Kaluga and a better pension. Scholarships were named in his honor; streets were renamed after him. A host of government agencies touted his achievements with meetings and discussions, telegrams and press releases. No matter that Tsiolkovskii was a thinker, an inventor of ideas more than things. In all of this his "sagacity and originality" had already matched and surpassed Western inventors. In a marriage of the personal and the national, his dreams for the "conquest of atmospheric and interplanetary space" became all-Soviet dreams.[17] He became the "patriarch of aviation and pioneer of astronautics," father of a whole "international planetary school" of rocketry pioneers. He represented the best of Soviet socialism, marking the "path to a future" of global and planetary peace, a utopia of which capitalism was capable of dreaming but incapable of achieving.[18]

Soviet propagandists also celebrated Tsiolkovskii as terrestrial and solar engineer, in league with several Soviet and American scholars who also counted Earth's energy by the measure of the sun (including astrophysicist Charles G. Abbot, director of the Smithsonian Institution and

15 See the cartoon drawing in *Komsomolskaia pravda* 197, August 24, 1934, 6. Ivanov, "Korifei tekhnicheskoi mysli" [Treasury of technological insights], *Komsomolskaia pravda* 218, September 19, 1940, 5.

16 Paraphrased from the thirteen "Steps in Reaction Development," in K. E. Tsiolkovskii, "Trudy o kosmicheskoi rakete" [Works on space rockets], in Dubenskii et al., *Reaktivnoe dvizhenie* [Reactive movement], 11–12. Tsiolkovskii revised these "steps" from an original sixteen-step plan that he had devised in 1926.

17 Ia. I. Perel'man, *Tsiolkovskii* (Leningrad: Gostekhizdat, 1932), 8–12, 69; I. Merkulov, "Tsiolkovskii," in *Bol'shaia Sovetskaia Entsiklopediia* [Great Soviet encyclopedia], 65 vols. (Moscow: OGIS, 1934), 60:734.

18 *dnei* 9 (1932): 53, 59; *lunyi proletarii* 10 (May 1933): 17; and *Nauka i zhizn' ll* [Science and life II] (1935): 54–55.

Robert Goddard's most dedicated patron). With them he appealed to the sun as the origin of universal life, worthy of veneration as the source of all energy and fuel resources.[19] He already knew that it would be the essential energy of interplanetary life and travel, powering the lush greenhouses of his space dirigibles. Solar mirrors might also be built and directed back on Earth, to power machines and cultivate deserts. The leading science fiction writer Aleksandr Beliaev praised his projects for the "reconstruction of the Earth" and the "reconsolidation of the globe," encasing its vulnerable parts in protective and productive glass membranes, all in preparation for the future settlement of space. Tsiolkovskii was that rare kind of pioneer who saw the planet from space, who measured it by an "astronomical scale," who counted life in "billions and billions." He was the first planetary man, filled with a "cosmic consciousness," a rare "love" and goodwill for our universal home. By way of his "cosmic rocket" he had written his name as a new shooting star in space.[20]

Tsiolkovskii's writings on dirigibles and rockets were also now published as "selected works." The first volume was dedicated to his long-suffering project to build an all-metal dirigible, a project again taken up by *Aeroflot* between 1932 and 1935, which worked on designs and models under his partial supervision. For the third and final time (as in 1894 and 1925) the all-metal dirigible was debated in Russia's military circles. Once again, nothing came of the idea—except publicity. Beliaev even wrote a story about it. Thus, Tsiolkovskii's all-metal dirigible only ever flew in fiction.[21] The second volume covered rocketry, now at the center of the RNII's mission, whose leadership sought out Tsiolkovskii's imprimatur, electing him as an honorary member of its Engineering Council and publishing several of his works. In his set of terminological standards for the new field of rocketry, G. E. Langemak assigned

19 B. P. Veinberg, *Solntse* (Moscow: ONTI, 1935); and Charles Abbot, *Solntse*, ed. Ia. I. Perel'man and translated by N. Ia. Bugoslavskii (Moscow: ONTI, 1936); K. E. Tsiolkovskii, *Budushchee zemli i chelovechestva* [The future of the earth and humanity] (Kaluga: Izd. avtora, 1928); and Tsiolkovskii, "Solntse i zavoevanie pustyn'" [The sun and the conquest of emptiness], *Vestnik znaniia* [Herald of knowledge] 5–6 (1933): 182–83.

20 Quoted from Aleksandr Beliaev, "Tsiolkovskii," *Iunyi proletarii* 31–32 (November 1932): 7–9; and Aleksandr Beliaev, "Pamiati velikogo uchenogo-izobretatelia" [Memories of a great scientist and inventor], *Iunyi proletarii* 23 (1935): 43–44.

21 K. B. Tsiolkovskii, *Izbrannye Trudy* [Selected works], vol. 1: *Tsel'nometallicheskii diri.zhabl'* [Metallic dirigibles], ed. Ia. A. Rapoport (Moscow: ONTI, 1934); A. Beliaev, "Vozdushnyi korabl'" [Airship], *Vokrug sveta* [Around the world], starting with nos. 10–12 (1934).

Tsiolkovskii's name to the famous rocket equation describing the relationship between the rocket's exhaust velocity and its mass ratio.[22]

Tsiolkovskii's reputation prospered through the 1930s, a mark of the regime's optimism. The Stalinist state encouraged its people to dream. Soviet adventures targeted younger audiences with "flights of fancy," in A. R. Palei's terms, joining real achievements in aviation with imaginative storytelling about space travel. Tsiolkovskii's rocket, or some prototype of it, figured into almost all of these stories. Palei's own novel *The Planet KIM* (1930), the story of how an enterprising commune of Young Communists (he called them Soviet "Robinson Crusoes") colonized an asteroid, also featured an authoritative preface by the astronomer K. L. Baev, one of the first publicists for Robert Goddard's rocket back in 1923. Once again, Baev confirmed the legitimacy of rocket science and the real possibilities of spaceflight. The certainty of calculus made it all so.[23] Aleksandr Beliaev was Tsiolkovskii's most dedicated publicist. In a series of novels and stories between 1933 and 1940, he cultivated Tsiolkovskii's dreams of space engineering via his "New Ark" (outfitted with the signature liquid buffers and solar greenhouse), a multistage "star cruiser" and "man-made comet." He made it "sail upon the waves of the ethereal ocean," a lovely and dazzling streak of golden exhaust upon the azure blue of the skies. It was a celebration of human mobility and genius and "happiness," the foundation for a new race of human beings to become "star dwellers."[24] Vladimir Vladko also took his readers to the nearby planets, speeding on such a human-made "comet," drawing an "intricate curve" through outer space. With mini-lectures on space engineering, chemistry, and biology along the way, Vladko treated readers to a series of Soviet firsts: the first All-Union Society for Interplanetary Communications, the first flights into outer space and to the moon, the first exploration of the prehistoric jungles and dinosaurs of Venus.[25]

---

22 See S. A. Shlykova, "K. E. Tsiolkovskii's Correspondence with the Jet Scientific-Research Institute," in *Soviet Rocketry*, ed. A. A. Blagonravov and translated by H. I. Needler (Jerusalem: Scientific Translations, 1966), 127–32.

23 A. R. Palei, "Nauchno-fantasticheskaia literatura" [Science fiction literature], *Literaturnaia ucheba* [Literary studies] 2 (1936): 119–27. A. R. Palei, *Planeta KIM* (Kharkov: Proletarii, 1930), a novel for teenage readers. KIM was an abbreviation for the *Kommunisticheskii Internatsional Molodezhi* (Communist Youth International).

24 See Aleksandr Beliaev, *Pryzhok v nichto* (Leningrad: OGIZ, 1933); and Beliaev, *Zvezda KETs* (Moscow: Detlit, 1940).

25 V. M. Vladko, *Argonavty vselennoi* [Argonauts of the universe] (Rostov-Don: Oblizdat, 1939). For another story that detailed Tsiolkovskii's and Tsander's rockets, see Iu. Lipilin, "Polet na Mars" [Flight to Mars], *Tekhnika—molodezhi* [Technology for youth] 12 (1940): 174–89.

These stories were not passing fads. At a number of local and national levels the government was committed to promoting science fiction and space fantasy. Note, for example, one radio contest for the best stories, drawings, and models on such topics as "The Arctic in 100 Years," "Aviation of the Future," and even "How to Fly to Mars." As the announcement stated, the Mars topic owed its inspiration to Tsiolkovskii's theories, bridging such diverse fields as astronomy, physics, engineering, and chemistry. Here was a perfect model for a middle school science fair, a way for children to ponder a future of spacecraft and space stations, rocket engines and solar energy. Aleksei Tolstoi's science fiction novel *Aelita* also enjoyed a new life into the 1930s, with both official approval and a genuine youth readership, now graced with illustrations of Tsiolkovskii's rocket headed toward a Lowellian Mars, studded with the infamous canals.[26]

Tsiolkovskii's own *Beyond the Earth* was not republished in the 1930s, but it found an even better venue as a feature film, *Cosmic Flight* (1936). Tsiolkovskii flew to space yet a second time, albeit still in science fiction. This time he flew not as the love-struck Los' but as the enterprising Soviet academician Pavel Ivanovich Sedykh, director of the "All-Union Institute for Interplanetary Communications," commander of a team of Soviet "astronauts": the Young Communist Marina and the Young Pioneer Andriusha, the "first" explorers on the moon. "Forward to the Cosmos," they proclaimed. The accent here was on the real, or rather on how only the USSR could really turn fantasies into realities, on a fact-based "flight of thought," as one commentator put it.[27] Tsiolkovskii served as scientific consultant to the film, collecting his thoughts and drawings in an album for the script. He offered sketches of the rocket (the *Stalin*), launch ramp, space suits, zero gravity environment, liquid acceleration barriers, and spacewalks; corrections about the look of the stars and sun and Earth from space; and strict advice on the mechanics and physics of spaceflight.[28]

---

26 From the pamphlet *Vzgliad v budushchee* [A look into the future] (Simferopol': Krymradiokomitet, 1941); Aleksei Tolstoi, *Aelita* (Moscow: Detlit, 1937), a juvenile edition with drawings by P. A. Aliakrinskii.

27 *Komsomolskaia pravda* 120, May 24, 1934, 6.

28 *Kosmicheskii reis*, directed by V. Zhuravlev (1935; Moscow: Moscow Film Studio). Several of the sketches are in K. E. Tsiolkovskii, *Works on Rocket Technology* (Washington, DC: NASA, 1965), 89, 236, 377–79, 382–83. The famous pilot M. M. Gromov also consulted on the look of the rocket cabin; the astronomer K. N. Shestovskii advised on the lunar landscape.

One of the last Soviet "silents," the film was a popular success, filled with captivating technology and comedic touches, including an "Earthrise" from the moon, some death-defying scenes, and the rescue of a cat. The crew even sent a Goddard-like signal flare back to prove their achievement: the bright letters *USSR*. When it premiered to Moscow's youngsters during the cold winter holidays of 1936, they broke into waves of cheers and laughter. The movie's launch ramp was especially emblematic of the Soviet future. Built at "Star City" (*Astrogorod*), it and the rocket dwarfed the magnificent city of Moscow itself, in the distance the planned "Palace of Soviets" and gigantic Lenin statue (to be larger than the Eiffel Tower and Empire State Building). Yet this ramp was not original. It was already a staple in European media and books, thanks largely to Max Valier, who first popularized it. Soviet graphic artists had even stolen Valier's ramp image and rocket flight in 1934—for a celebratory piece on flight into the stratosphere—Lenin's statue and the Moscow city center again conspicuously in the background.[29]

Tsiolkovskii's death on September 19, 1935, at "22 hours and 34 minutes," the beloved scientist reaching seventy-eight years of age, marked a peak in the Stalinist campaign for the cosmos. Kaluga honored him with a grand funeral. Fifteen thousand people attended, making their way along a cortege two kilometers long. Leaders of civil and military aviation gave speeches. An escadrille of airplanes from Moscow dropped leaflets about his life and lowered a wreath to his grave. His brain, weighing a full 1,350 grams, was turned over to the Moscow Institute of the Brain for safekeeping and study, not too far from Lenin's own. Tsiolkovskii's personality cult was on full display: the dreamer spurned by Tsarist authorities; the half-deaf genius struggling on alone; the enemy of gravity; the dirigible and rocket designer backed by rigorous mathematical proofs. It was a cult of stratospheric and space travel honoring the "all-metal interplanetary name of Tsiolkovskii." He was buried at Kaluga's outskirts. An obelisk, not yet a rocket, was mounted at his grave, amid birch and fir trees. Its inscription read, "Founder of the theory of reactive motion" and "Pioneer of the conquest of interplanetary space," along with Tsiolkovskii's own claim, from 1911, "Humanity will not remain forever on Earth."[30]

29 A. Garri and L. Kassil', *Potolok mira* [The roof of the world] (Moscow: Sovetskaia literatura, 1934), 12–121.

30 All of these images are based on my readings of *Izvestiia* and *Pravda* at the time of his death and on his biographies, with special attention to Lev Kassil', "'Zvezdoplavatel' i zemliaki" [Star-voyager and earthlings], in *K. E. Tsiolkovskii*, Islent'ev, 160–68. See also James T. Andrews, *Red Cosmos* (College Station: Texas A&M University Press, 2009), 86, 92–94.

During this campaign of mourning (and for years afterward) the media also gave wide coverage to the letters Stalin exchanged with Tsiolkovskii just before his death, with the strange effect, given their ages, of Stalin playing the role of "wise leader: the father," and Tsiolkovskii the adoring and appreciative citizen, the son. These letters became centerpieces of the Tsiolkovskii postmortem cult. In grandiloquent terms, he bequeathed his papers and legacies to the "Bolshevik party and Soviet power" so as to promote the further "progress of human culture." In their own professional correspondence to Stalin, the administrators of Soviet rocketry tapped into the hyperbole to justify more funding. I. T. Kleimenov, director of the RNII, warned that liquid fuel rocketry, the project closest to Tsiolkovskii's heart, should not die with him. A. K. Korneev, head of K B-7, wrote to Stalin that "the hour will soon come when our Bolshevik interplanetary ships will rise up to the unbounded vacuum of space."[31]

Stalin's own public persona also became a cult of "cosmic" force. In a wildly imaginary lecture from a future "School of Interplanetary Communications," the propagandist Karl Radek celebrated Stalin for the "daring of a great rebel" and the "cool calculation of a mathematician," a young man who was a "thirsty student of the algebra of revolution," images that recalled Stalin's early years at the Tiflis Geophysical Observatory.[32] One of the more infamous of appeals came from Osip Mandelshtam in his panegyric the "Ode to Stalin" (1937), which drew Stalin's profile as lines in the sky. He became the one "who has shifted the world's axis." He became a giant towering over mountains, a "Prometheus" bridging countries and continents. He became the great cultivator, sowing progress "like tomorrow out of yesterday—/ The furrows of a colossal plow reach to the sun."[33] After the hagiography of Richard Maurice Bucke and John Addington Symonds from the turn of the century, Mandelshtam turned Stalin into a modern-day Walt Whitman. A poem in *Pravda* made much the same point: "Between the heavens and the earth / He fills the whole world with his girth." Stalin became the quintessential "vertical" man, standing upon the mausoleum as the dead Lenin lay horizontal within it, at one point towering above

---

31 Kleimenov letter to Stalin, November 2, 1935, RGVA, f. 4, o. 14, d.1398, l. 54. See also Korneev's letters to Stalin, April 12, 1937, ARAN, r. 4, o. 14, d. 150, ll. 16–17; and June 15, 1937, RGVA, f. 4, o. 14, d. 1628, ll. 123–26.

32 Karl Radek, *Portraits and Pamphlets* (New York: McBride, 1935), 4, 12.

33 The translation and context is in Gregory Freidin, *A Coat of Many Colors* (Berkeley: University of California Press, 1987), 252–58.

Red Square, his portrait projected onto a tethered balloon, as if a new planet in the skies.[34]

These kinds of images help us better to understand H. G. Wells's second visit to the USSR in 1934. As a British celebrity with Soviet sympathies, he offered a reference point for the world, confirming just how dramatically the country had changed since his first visit with Lenin in the troubled year of 1920. He offered a "before and after" picture of Russia's long revolution. Wells arrived in Moscow by air, no longer the dilapidated site of one of his apocalyptic novels. Now he was flying into a "rigorous," vibrant city surrounded by a "patchwork of aerodromes" and many "hundreds of planes," to meet Josef Stalin, one of the great representatives of the "human future." True enough, as described in his "alternative" history, *The Shape of Things to Come* (1933), Wells saw both the United States and USSR as utopian civilizations in the making, each with a "major mass of human beings" ready to build the foundations of "an organized world-state."[35] Yet he favored Stalin and a "theory of world revolution" (one he shared with J. B. S. Haldane) meant to fulfill a "socialistic, cosmopolitan and creative" global government. Progress meant "abolishing distance"—by land and sea and air, among peoples and states, even between death and life. It meant mastering all life on the planet ("geogonic planning"); it meant reaching for outer space and immortality. William Winwood Reade's prophecies would come true: "This is the day, this is the hour of sunrise for united manhood. The Martyrdom of Man is at an end. From pole to pole now there remains no single human being upon the planet without a fair prospect of self-fulfillment, of health, interest and freedom."[36]

The film version of this fancy, *Things to Come* (1936), represented the future by a rocket, launched initially by Verne's cannon but piloted by courageous young people setting out to create a new civilization in outer space. It was a story line worthy of Stalinist socialist realism. Yet what might seem positively Fedorovian or Stalinist here was really at one with the very transformism at the heart of the Western experience. The aviation engineer

---

34 The quote is from "Rech' tov. Suleimana Stal'nogo" [Address of Comrade Suleiman Stalny], *Pravda* 99, February 19, 1936, 22. See the balloon on Stalin's seventieth birthday, in *Ogonek* 52, December 25, 1949, front cover. On Stalin and the "vertical," see Vladimir Paperny, *Architecture in the Age of Stalin* (New York: Cambridge University Press, 2002).

35 H. G. Wells, *Experiment in Autobiography* (New York: Macmillan, 1934), 685, 689–700.

36 H. G. Wells, *The Shape of Things to Come: The Ultimate Revolution*, ed. Patrick Parrinder (1933; repr., New York: Penguin, 2003), 393, 446, 508; J. B. S. Haldane, *Inequality of Man* (London: Chatto and Windus, 1932), 99, 266.

and science writer Waldemar Kaempffert perfectly summarized this futuristic vision as encompassing the cosmic: the reach for new sources of terrestrial and solar energy to power the industrial globe; the reach for longevity and even a kind of immortality through the new chemistry and biology; the reach for outer space and the planets by rocket. Thus, "the romances of yesterday," he wrote, become "the realities of today."[37]

---

37 *Things to Come,* directed by William Cameron Menzies (1936; London: Film Productions); Waldemar Kaempffert, *Science Today and Tomorrow* (New York: Viking, 1939), 246.

Klushantsev: Russia's Wizard of Fantastika

LYNN BARKER AND ROBERT SKOTAK;
Translations by Gregory Wain and Buck Shomo

Barker, Lynn and Robert Skotak. "Klushantsev: Russia's Wizard of Fantastika." *American Cinematographer* 75, no. 6 (1994): 76–83 and 75, no. 7 (1994): 77–82.

During a recent visit to Russia, Robert Skotak, Academy Award–winning visual effects director and head of 4-Ward Productions Inc., interviewed the pioneer Russian effects director Pavel Klushantsev.

When we think of Soviet or Russian cinema, we immediately recall tiers of swords raised against Teutonic invaders in officially sanctioned films like *Alexander Nevsky*; the slaughter of humanity on the Odessa steps and the birth of stylish, modern editing in *Battleship Potemkin*; the sheer size of Sergei Bondarchuk's *War and Peace*; the emotional sweetness of *Moscow Does Not Believe in Tears*; or the mesmerizing solemnity of Tarkovsky's *Andrei Rublev* and *Solaris*. Less clearly remembered is the modest list of Russia's visually compelling, special effects–laden films of the fantastic—or *fantastika*. A list of Russian films of fantasy, horror, or science fiction is a list of films resisted by government sponsors due to their very subject matter. It includes such titles as *Cosmic Journey* (1935), *Aelita* (1924), *Illya Muromets* (1960), *A Dream Comes True* (1963), *Andromeda Nebula* (1967), and *To the Stars by Hard Ways* (1982).

Road to the Stars (1957), a film that documents the history of space science and fictionally portrays a journey to the moon, and *Planet of Storms* (1962), a feature about the geological and biological dangers encountered by a group of cosmonauts on the planet Venus, are two exceptional specimens of Russian film *fantastika*. They were produced more than three decades ago under grueling conditions. Their creator, Pavel Vladimirovich Klushantsev, simultaneously bucked an uncooperative system and tackled the difficult subject of the visually "impossible."

Klushantsev is also no stranger to challenges of a technical nature. In the winter of 1956, the filmmaker found himself shooting scenes in a narrow bay on the Baltic Sea for the film *Road to the Stars*. With the wind whipping across the water, Klushantsev and his crew attempted to create a convincing shot of a spacecraft landing on the waves. The "spaceship" (a lightweight model built of thick waterproof fabric inflated with air) was suspended from cliffs on either side of the bay by a rope strung through ringlets on the craft's top. The crew's job was to slide the model down the rope to simulate the landing, a task that involved repeated adjustments amid the freezing water and wind. Incidents like this demonstrate the dedication and love of craft that typified the forty-five-year career of the Russian film pioneer.

Now in his 80s, Klushantsev has worked as cameraman, special-effects wizard, inventor, artist, animator, director, producer, and screenwriter on a wide variety of film shorts and on the impressive science-fiction feature *Planet of Storms* (1961). Like international film magicians George Melies, William Cameron Menzies, Ray Harryhausen, and George Pal, Klushantsev honed his abilities as a hands-on artist, mechanical expert and inventor and applied them to cinema, resulting in dramatic and often dazzling illusions.

With such a long history of achievements, why doesn't his name conjure memories of the effects-laden films he brought to life? Like many of his Russian filmmaking colleagues, Klushantsev fell victim to the Cold War. Most of his film shorts, especially impressive for their innovative design, photography, and special effects, were never shown in the US despite winning numerous international prizes. Footage from *Planet of Storms*, his sole feature, was purchased, edited, "Americanized" and inserted into several barely memorable "B" films. To add insult to injury, some of Klushantsev's inventive and ambitious effects techniques have been falsely credited to American filmmakers who developed similar methods or designs years later. Even so, this tenacious pioneer struggled and prevailed against the impossible odds of poverty and soul-crunching government control and censorship to produce a body of work that was, in his words, "founded on veracious fantasy … always to tell about the good and happy future of a wise, intelligent and friendly Humanity working for mutual good."

Klushantsev was born in Leningrad (then called Petrograd) in 1910. His father was a doctor; his mother, a housewife. "When I was seven years old, the Revolution took place. My father lost his job, and my mother took a job with very little pay; my childhood was spent in poverty. I was determined to become a mechanical engineer, and submitted an application to the Leningrad Technological Institute, but I was rejected. I came from the intelligentsia and [the Party] needed to create an engineer class from workers and peasantry. I enrolled in the Photo-Cinema-Technical Secondary School and finished in 1930 with a specialty as a cameraman."

The combination of his love of technical tinkering with newfound cinematographic skills enabled Klushantsev to gain a reputation as a problem solver: "Doing something that no one else was able to do allowed me to reach a stable position in cinematography, [but right away] my passion for innovation drew indignation from the authorities. I complicated their work. They resisted and created a great number of obstacles for me."

The accomplishments of Klushantsev and those of his colleagues become all the more impressive when placed in the context of these very obstacles. From the dawn of their film industry, Russian filmmakers ran into a labyrinth of technical, social and governmental barriers that proved almost insurmountable—barriers that epitomized and scarred the history of Russian film *fantastika*. From the time before Protozanov's silent classic *Aelita* (1924), through Andrei Tarkovsky's well-received *Solaris* (1972) and up to the present, years of social upheaval and struggle produced a core of remarkable film artisans. But through it all, the key strengths of Russian filmmakers—creativity and innovation—were frequently ignored or discouraged if the subject matter did not suit the needs of the "Center" (Moscow).

The story of pioneer Leo Kuleshov illustrates how early and how profoundly the problems of the Russian film industry had become entrenched. Inspired by the perseverance of his parents—his father was a starving artist, his mother a teacher—Kuleshov overcame the odds and directed his first picture, *The Project of Engineer Prite*, in 1917 at age 18. It was among the first Russian pictures to employ editing, close-ups and rapid, dynamic combinations of shots. His experiments during filming included the "Kuleshov Effect," the first attempt at editing various locations to make them appear as one. Yet *Engineer Prite* and subsequent films failed to win any governmental support. After the Revolution, Kuleshov took part in the organization of the First National Film School, but this too went unnoticed. Instead of being rewarded for his efforts, he found himself plagued by a lack of funds for even the most basic technical equipment. He also faced the constant ridicule of studio bosses who preferred Sergei Eisenstein's proletarian revolutionary epics to his more emotional, American-style melodramas.

With the onset of Stalinism (1934–53) came an even more severe form of censorship, as illustrated by the treatment of talented stop-motion animator Fyodor Krasni. During the filming of *Cosmic Journey*, Krasni's name, along with those of all the other crew members, was submitted to Stalin's office for official approval. An examination of the original script revealed that his name had been crossed out by Stalin's staff, who had added a notation dictating that he was to receive no credit on *Cosmic Journey* or any other film. Somehow, he had provoked the wrath of the Party and had been labeled a "fantasist" who should have turned his talents to "social realism." As a result, he became a "non-person."

Similar fates befell filmmakers Mikhail Koryukov (*The Heavens Call, Mysterious Island, A Dream Comes True*) and Alexander L. Ptushko (*The New Gulliver, The Stone Flower, Sadko, Illya Muromets*), who also struggled to retain artistic freedom against impossible odds. When Koryukov realized that science-fiction films, with their innate special visual requirements, would provide work for a multitude of special-effects artists, he and his colleagues wrote a letter urging an increase in fantastic film production. It was signed by many high-level officials, with the exception of Stalin himself. *Pravda* refused to publish the letter, but *Izvestia* did. In Koryukov's words, "The day after the letter was published, the chairman of our committee at the studio sent for me and asked, 'Who wrote this letter?' 'I did,' I said. Within 24 hours I had to leave Moscow." He was banished from his home and was never allowed to return. Ptushko, whose fantastic imagination lent itself best to fantasy tales of epic heroes, fell victim to the system in 1950, after Stalin issued an edict demanding that fewer films be made each year. Given no choice, Ptushko was assigned to finish a film that contained no fantasy elements at all—the pedestrian *Tri Vestrechi* (*The Encounters*), a jumbled, prosaic story of soldiers adapting to demobilization. Even his masterpiece, *Sadko* (1952), had to be compromised in order to become one of only five Stalin-approved films that year; Ptushko was forced to present a thinly veiled story about a Godlike leader who could control even the elements in order to aid the "poor, unhappy masses."

Additional problems for Russian filmmakers can be blamed on the Soviet film industry's restrictive, ponderous and divisive system. Klushantsev explained, "In the Soviet Union, cinematography was divided into four fields: artistic cinematography (with a plot and dramatic performances); animated and popular science cinema (educational films for schools and other training institutions); and films which report to the audience on the status of science and technology." Each specialty was assigned its own studios. "Occasionally, as an exception, artistic films were also made in the popular science studios, but that wasn't encouraged."

Klushantsev began and spent most of his career making popular science films. His smart solutions to mechanical and visual effects challenges moved him quickly from cameraman to director. In 1938, he organized a small workshop for special effects at Lennauchfilm (Lensciencefilm) Studio where he continued his "tinkering": "I often filmed from airplanes. In those days, airplanes had open cockpits and we had to work in the breeze, which necessitated designs for stronger cameras. I filmed underwater in 1938, before there were aqualungs or scuba divers. I built an apparatus including a diver's helmet [so] I could work hands-free."

During 1943, Klushantsev filmed military instructional films in the city of Novosibirsk, located in the center of Siberia. In the intervals between pictures, he experimented. "We still didn't have color film. We only knew how to use a primitive two-color method using red- and blue-sensitive films. The two negatives were printed on a positive film which was developed on both sides. It came out as a color positive, but the color transmission was poor." Klushantsev decided to take the process further on his own. "I adapted a camera for two reels of film. I put in an infrared film and used positive in exchange for the blue sensitive. I found a color representation of a flower in a book and filmed it with the two combined films. I printed a positive from each film and intensified the positives in the hut where I lived with my wife and daughter. Then I stuck the pieces together during editing. The producer was astonished." Everyone was amazed when he submitted his film to the Ministry. Suddenly, after the gray sequences, a flower in all of its beauty unexpectedly blazed onto the screen. Klushantsev, in a far-off Siberian hut, had produced "color film," which they didn't even have in Moscow!

After the war, Klushantsev produced his first film and began to explore special effects full time. The black and white film *Northern Lights* (1946) impressed superiors and paved the way for future efforts. Working with cameraman and colleague Anatolii Lavrent'yev, a long-time friend from technical school, Klushantsev set out to, in his words, "describe for the viewers the Northern Lights in all of their forms. A spotlight lit up a white paper 'sky' from below via a mirror on the floor using a sliding light at a very acute angle. Before falling on the paper, that light shined through two corrugated plates of glass that were moving towards each other, and so refracted into iridescent streams of light. Then it would pass by a cylinder with cotton balls stuck to it. The cotton balls cast shadows on the 'sky,' breaking up the rays of light. The cylinder turned and the contours of the radiance changed. All of this activity was accomplished with one electric motor, via a system of cords. There were pinpricks in the paper sky which had a tracing paper pattern behind it, backlit. Those were the stars. A frame with threads stretched across it slowly moved between the pattern and the 'sky.' When the threads covered the pinpricks, the stars twinkled."

Klushantsev's film *Meteors* (1948) was his first outing as sole screenwriter and won an award at the Venice Film Festival. Another instructional film, it dazzled audiences with its authentic-looking flying fireballs (spotlights sliding along a line) rocketing across a Russian winter sky. The film also introduced another technical experiment: "It was the first time 'Lavrent'yev and I utilized the 'luminostaged' method of shooting, which was later patented in his name. We had to show the solar system with the movement of the planets and orbital path of meteors. Animation wouldn't have worked here, since all of the action had to be of a floating nature and animation only worked for sharp, quick action." At the same time, the movement of the planets demanded a mechanism with turning axes, gliding orbits, et cetera. "We colored the celestial bodies with paint and illuminated them with ultraviolet light [blacklight]. On film it appears that we filmed only those celestial bodies, and all of the [unlit] mechanisms remain invisible."

By 1950, interest in space exploration was accelerating—a phenomenon due, in part, to classic films in the new genre such as George Pal's *Destination Moon*. While *Moon* played on American screens, Klushantsev was visualizing the creation of the galaxy for the popular science film *The Universe*. In it he combined the luminostaged method with stop-motion—the latter technique's first use in a color film. The apparatus he invented to track the movements of the heavenly bodies was so precise that "we set everything up, turned on the equipment, left to eat dinner and returned when the sequence was shot." Again, the cold disregard of his brilliance by some superiors was evident. "All of those mechanisms which I invented, drew, and ordered from factories no longer exist," Klushantsev said. "They were all thrown out as useless." Once again, however, the film won several international awards.

Klushantsev continued his exploration of scientific phenomena by making *The Secret of the Matter* in 1955. That film proved to be the launching pad for his newfound fascination with speculative fantasy. "At the end of the film, we wanted to talk about the perspectives that inexhaustible supplies of [atomic] energy open to man. I did that and, for the first time, became aware of all the fascination the future demonstrated." (It should be noted that "fantasy" in Russian space films was always "a scientifically grounded prognosis of the near future." This excluded the appearance of the implausible or threatening monsters from outer space so common in American films of the era. George Pal's *Conquest of Space* [1954] was a notable exception. Russian filmmakers strove to hold interest without relying on horror or shock.)

The Secret of the Matter featured an impressive ten-meter model of an atomic-powered ocean liner able to travel both on and under the ocean's surface. It was filmed in action on the Black Sea, but not without incident: "We used two ships," Klushantsev explained. "One towed the model, the other followed. Lavrent'yev and I sat with the camera on a beam which was mounted on the outer side of the ship's hull. We hung about half a meter from the water's surface. We submerged the model by releasing the air from the tanks that held it afloat, and raised it by inflating them. We were just getting out to open water when we saw a big wave. We turned back for shore. During the turn we started to roll over. Lavrent'yev and I had our heads dunked a meter and a half in the water. After half a minute, when the ship righted itself, we surfaced and managed to get a breath. We hung on and saved the camera—but lost the film."

On October 4, 1957, Sputnik was launched. It was the proverbial shot heard round the world, and ushered in the space race. The Soviet Union was first off the starting line; with the making of the internationally lauded *The Road to the Stars*, which included a realistic exploration of man's first orbital journey, Klushantsev's career was also about to get a rocket boost. As Klushantsev recalled, the ride had actually started three years before: "The writer-engineer Lyapunov had become interested in cosmonautics. He had met Konstantin Tsiolkovski, a pioneer of rocketry and space sciences. At that time, no one knew anything about Korolyev, the main construction engineer of Soviet space rockets. Work in that area was top secret. Lyapunov met one of Korolyev's closest companions, who helped him with theory, and he managed to write the book *The Thorny Path to the Stars*. After that, he was set afire with the dream of a film on the theme of the gradual expansion of man in space.

"By 1955, he had already written a screenplay in which he had set forth the theory of rocket technology and the possibilities it opened for humanity in the next decades. But not one wanted the screenplay! It was stupid to waste money on some unnecessary fantasy, they said. Several other producers also failed to back Lyapunov due to their fear of the technical difficulties involved in the production of such a film.

"Lyapunov found out about me and came to Leningrad. I clearly understood that the theme of his screenplay would give me the possibility to use the grandest scale of special effects, invention, and resourcefulness ever."

The film's "stellar abyss" was created by hanging a huge screen, made of wooden frames covered with a sheet of steel, from the ceiling of the stage. Small holes were punched in the steel and tiny incandescent lights were soldered into the holes. Their reddish tint was covered by a coat of blue lacquer. Lights of various strengths corresponded to the brilliance of different stars in familiar constellations, and various sections of the sky could be lit independently.

That was a simple problem to solve. Not so simple were rockets and weightlessness. "We had to simulate the take-off of a rocket with cosmonauts," Klushantsev noted. "No one knew how that rocket would look. No one knew what a launchpad would look like. We got in touch with the Leningrad Institute for Aviation Instrument Making. The dean gathered his most gifted senior students and gave them the task of projecting such concepts as the rockets, launch equipment, spacecraft, orbital stations and their interiors. Thus it wasn't just irresponsible fantasy, but a project founded in technology. The students got carried away and turned out a whole line of sketches. We selected the most effective and they became the basis for all of our models and set decorations."

Launching the model rockets required gadgetry on a huge scale: "We constructed a portable collapsable girder in the form of the Greek letter 'pi'—two poles and a crossbeam with a system of pulleys. The rocket hung from two thick steel threads. The lines were threaded through the pulleys, and around one of the poles hung a counterweight. Pyrotechnic cartridges were placed on the lower part of the rocket. With cartridges, the rocket weighed just a little bit more than the counterweight. That way it stood calmly vertical on the ground. The poles and crossbeam were out of the way of the camera. When the electric current ignited pyrocartridges, flames appeared under the rocket and it was shrouded in smoke. After a couple of seconds, it began to get lighter from the burning of the chemicals and the counterweights began to pull. The rocket tore off from the Earth, and, gaining speed, flew upward. When the weight hit the ground and the rocket hit the crossbeam, everything came to a halt. The method proved successful and we employed it in all of our space films."

Perhaps the most demanding challenge on *Road to the Stars* was creating the illusion of believable weightlessness. "The ordinary theatrical or circus methods of hanging in a girdle wouldn't do for us," Klushantsev notes. "That's good enough when the actor has to fly straight ahead in a line or in a circular fashion, not changing his position. We had to do slow floating with somersaults, turns, etc. In all of my space pictures we employed [several] methods of imitating weightlessness. The first method was the 'vertical shot.' The actor is dressed in a strong girdle and hangs from the ceiling via a thick steel rope, pulleys, and counterweights. The camera stays on the ground, the objective vertically above. The rope by which the actor hangs is hidden from the camera by his body."

To be effective, such a shot needs plenty of vertical clearance. Klushantsev and crew had to cut a hole in the stage floor to put their cameraman in the basement, again arousing the ire of the studio bosses. This method was used for shots in the spacecraft cabin and for shots depicting the building of an orbiting station in space. When Stanley Kubrick made *2001: A Space Odyssey* in 1968, he claimed to have been first to fly actor/astronauts on wires with the camera on the ground, shooting vertically while the actor's body covered the wires. But Pavel Klushantsev had actually used the technique years before.

Gaining camera mobility was another challenge, since Popular Science Film Studios were both ill-equipped and the poorest in the Soviet Union: "At that time, we didn't have any kind of camera crane. The carts [needed] for shots with action were handmade of wood on wooden rails." To give some of the space scenes a floating feeling, it was necessary to photograph the hanging actors using compound moves, which necessitated the construction of a complicated track system in the studio basement. "We made lengthwise tracks with a narrow cart on them," Klushantsev explains. "In a second cart on the 'crosswise' tracks, the cameraman was lying [stretched] out, with a scaffold holding the camera mounted over him. During the shots, I was with the camera, watching and moving in unison, skating lengthwise and crosswise."

For many shots, space-suited circus acrobats were used as stunt doubles. Klushantsev was particularly concerned when faulty equipment almost resulted in tragedy: "Once, during a shot of a cosmonaut hanging against the background of Orion, the double felt that the girdle was weakening on him and he began to slip downwards. Downwards meant [landing on] the camera, which would have smashed into the cameraman's face, killing him on the spot. Luckily, the quick reflexes of the acrobat snapped into action. With a sharp motion, he managed to flip over and grab a rope with his hand. We later found out that the straps of the girdle had rotted through and ripped off."

For other shots, the weightless effect was accomplished in another novel manner. "We manufactured a latticework 'barrel' four meters in diameter and six meters long out of wooden beams. We cleared out the workshop so that the barrel—which represented the cabin of the spacecraft—could roll back and forth across the floor. At the end of its path we made ramps so that it didn't smash into the walls but would roll up the ramp and roll back. We mounted set decorations—[as well as] all of the lighting equipment, the cameraman, and his camera—inside the barrel. [The cameraman] was in a special long box, fastened with straps, so that during the rolling of the barrel, he would be first right-side up, then upside-down. Two actors worked in the scene. One was firmly fastened to the roof in a chair solidly attached to the set. The other was able to freely walk or jump on the floor, walls or ceiling of the 'cabin.' The camera angle was always in the same position and the rotations weren't observed. Our cosmonaut freely crossed from the floor to the wall, then to the ceiling and walked about. For greater effect, the shot was overcranked and the action seemed even more slow and floating. In any case, it made the onlooker and the film workers feel perfectly nauseated."

While *Road to the Stars* was being edited in the autumn of 1957, Sputnik was launched. Officials demanded that this event be included in the film as a propaganda ploy. Footage was added and the film as released on November 7, 1957, in Leningrad, Moscow and Kiev. It eventually circled all five continents with great success and a portion of the project was shown to Americans as part of the CBS series *The 20th Century*, hosted by Walter Cronkite.

With this undeniable success, party officials finally understood that films about space travel and exploration could be very positive propaganda. What was discouraged in the past was suddenly given an official seal of approval. *Road to the Stars* also established Klushantsev as a "first class producer," allowing him to finally achieve his lifelong dream of "making artistic films, with storylines and actors—[moving] into 'big' cinematography, working in the fantasy genre with space themes."

He was at last in the position to make a film like *Planet of Storms*, which represented the biggest leap yet for Klushantsev; the project offered oppor-tunities to experiment with newer techniques to improve on illusions such as weightlessness. The "floating" segments in *Storms*, for example, didn't use stunt doubles. This time around, Klushantsev wanted to use well-known performers. "We prepared a special crane with a long narrow boom which had a rotating fork with hoops at the end," he recounted. "During the shots, we positioned both the actor and the crane so that the actor's body covered the equipment. He could be in a vertical, lying or sitting position."

Planet of Storms was not Klushantsev's first-choice project, however. Prior to starting the film, he'd developed a concept that he passionately believed in—a screenplay for a full-scale artistic film called *The Moonstone*. Unfortunately, the film never got off the launching pad. Klushantsev described the plot thusly: "In each of three developed countries—the U.S., U.S.S.R., and Germany— teams are secretly preparing for a flight to the moon. The countries find out about each other's work and agree to consolidate their priorities for [future] history. Whoever brings back [to the Earth] a 'piece of the moon'—a moonstone—will be considered the lunar pioneers. All three rockets are launched almost simultaneously. They land on the moon not far from each other. But all three have difficulties upon arrival. For each there is one solution: mutual aid. They bring back a moonstone found, taken and delivered by a mutual effort."

In *The Moonstone*, it was important to Klushantsev that everyone should finally stop dividing the world into antagonistic blocs, "that we should take each other's hand and jointly conquer the planets as a singular humanity." Unfortunately, his dream was not shared by high-level Party officials in Leningrad: "The opinion of the Party authorities was that we [shouldn't] cooperate with anyone in space affairs. [They felt that] our country was able to succeed without any help—[that] we could bring back a lunar rock all by ourselves."

Once again, the Cold War had stifled artistic freedom, and Klushantsev was forced to collaborate on a new screenplay that would meet Party standards. A year's work on *The Moonstone*, without pay, had been wasted.

Several drafts and arguments later, he and a new writer, famed author Alexander Kazantsev, agreed to abandon the moon for a trip to Venus, an idea that became *Planet of Storms*. Kazantsev's story ideas stemmed from a strong belief in a *Chariots of the Gods*–style theory that mankind had been visited by ancient astronauts. The more practical Klushantsev was not all that enthralled by the direction the story was taking (the plot centered around a group of stalwart cosmonauts who face a number of mechanical and natural disasters to discover ancient life on Venus), but by this point was ready to do anything to get the cameras rolling.

The script was approved and Klushantsev put his team together. His old friend Lavrent'yev again served as effects cameraman. Props and models, too extensive for the meager studio shops, were consigned to various factories that were expert at designing practical machinery; for example, an aviation factory constructed the realistic controls in the spacecraft cabin. Klushantsev had been inspired by the American film *On the Beach*, which featured a very believable submarine set. "I wanted to show a spacecraft with the same degree of realism as the submarine in this American movie," he said.

The "vyezdekhod"—an impressive flying car—was created by designers at an automobile factory and built in their workshop. (Interestingly, the craft bears some resemblance to the "landspeeder" which Luke Skywalker would pilot some sixteen years later in *Star Wars*.) "The flying car's motion was carried out very simply," elaborated Klushantsev. "A crane built especially for that purpose rode along rails. The car was sitting on the crane at a single point so that it could turn a complete circle. It was raised and lowered by the boom, and the body of the car hid the crane from the camera. For shots of the car over the sea, the vehicle was hung from a boom welded to the stern of a barge which was towed by a cutter."

As on *The Secret of Matter*, near-disasters at sea plagued this picture. At one point, the floating car and actors were nearly drowned by a huge wave. On another day, as the car was being towed over the sea to a beach location, the vehicle filled with water and sank to the bottom. It was recovered by divers and repaired, and filming continued.

"Robot John," and impressive automaton brought along on the Venus mission to aid his human cohorts, was designed collectively by all of the picture's artists, under Klushantsev's guidance and encouragement. The robot body was built by Aleksander Yakolevich Nadyezhin and a crew from the Design Kombinat at the Union of Artists of the USSR, a group ordinarily involved in the design and construction of props for museums, exhibitions, and store windows (the crew also assembled the spacecraft and other miniatures based on Nadyezhin's technical drawings). Inside Robot John was a man named Prudkovskii, a famous wrestling champion who could carry two men on his shoulders. He actually performs this feat in the film, during a scene in which the robot helps two cosmonauts cross a stream of molten lava.

Realistic undersea exploration shots were accomplished in the studio by a combination of techniques. "The floor was covered with a thick pile carpet that looked like moss," explained Klushantsev. "We spread out a heavy white aerosol fog [oil droplets sprayed out by a stream of liquid carbon dioxide]. It sank into the 'moss' and you couldn't see it until you set down your feet. Then it would lazily rise up, exactly like silt from the bottom of a reservoir under a diver's foot. A 'tub,' constructed of a steel welded frame glazed with thick windows, was hung over the actors. It was filled with water, ten centimeters deep. A spotlight, mounted above, shone down through the tub onto the actors. The water would splash and the light would refract into a streaming patch of light." This lightning trick, in combination with the fog, created the look of cloudy water. To complete the underwater illusion, a narrow aquarium with live fish was placed in front of the camera.

For other sequences, Klushantsev and his crew created a convincing volcanic eruption complete with smoke and "white-hot" lava. It was important that the lava should appear brighter than white light: "To create the effect [we used] an oily 'dough' with white chalk added. The pyrotechnicians mixed in an oil which quickly evaporated, giving [off] a white smoke. The surrounding hills were painted black with carbon soot. The cameraman compensated for the overall excessive darkness and gave the model a little more light than for normal exposure. [The white chalk 'dough,' now, in effect, overlit, glowed as if luminous.] The result [was] a 'searing' lava which you could dip your finger into!"

Various perspective combination shots were used to depict the spaceship "Sirius" on the surface of Venus. According to Klushantsev, "The whole ship at full height was built at roughly one-fifth scale. It stood about 50 meters from the camera. Its lower part, at true size, was palced at a distance of roughly 75 meters from the camera. The actors worked at the base of the ship in the far background."

One of the action sequences of the film featured a pterodactyl-type "bird" which attacks the cosmonauts as they explore the sea in their flying car. This was "an ordinary puppet, prepared for us by the artists of the Leningrad Puppet Theater under the supervision of dedicated puppet artist Valentina Vasil'yevna Malakhiyeva, who also managed the theater. The pterodactyl's wingspan measured roughly one meter. It hung from a steel pipe pushed through the backdrop. The pipe was hidden from camera by the bird's body. In case the bird tilted too strongly and revealed the pipe, we utilized a smokescreen in the background. Three puppeteers, including Malakhiyeva, ran the bird—one swinging the pipe, the second turning the head and the third flapping its wings."

Although *Planet of Storms* gained popular acclaim, Klushantsev wasn't satisfied. The screenplay never pleased him, and he thought the actors could have been better. Although the Party authorities in Moscow approved the film, the press was influenced by a screening for the Minister of Culture, an incident that fully illustrates the power and negative impact of official opinionmakers under a Communist regime: "Sitting in the theater and watching the film with [the Minister] were film workers and reporters who were waiting to find out the spirit their reviews should take—to praise it or to criticize it. When the picture ended and the room lights came on, the reporters surrounded [the Minister,] notebooks ready. 'What's your impression?' was their common question. She thought for a moment and said, more or less, 'In general, nothing. What I really didn't like was when the female cosmonaut cried. A Soviet woman cosmonaut shouldn't cry, even under such circumstances.' That immediately influenced the reporters and the press was cold."

A screening for the cosmonauts at Star City, however, resulted in high marks. they commented that it was exactly how they imagined a space expedition.

Planet of Storms was seen by approximately 20 million people in the first year and was sold to twenty-eight countries around the world, finding its greatest success among young children. It brought a large profit to the country, but marked the beginning and end of Klushantsev's "artistic" filmmaking. He considered the picture a labor of love; four years later, he returned to producing popular science films.

The next of these, *The Moon*, was produced in 1965 on a much lower budget than *Planet of Storms*. It successfully presented a colonized lunar surface with workers and families living in an elegant, multi-tiered lunar "city" designed by renowned science-fiction artist Yuri Shvets, with whom Klushantsev had collaborated years earlier on *The Universe*. Rocket trains, propelled by an enormous battery, traveled over the surface in horizontal tubes while a convincing, spider-legged lunar rover roamed the hills and craters. "*The Moon* won a gold medal for successful union of science and fantasy at a film festival in Trieste," Klushantsev recalled. "*Paris Match* sent a correspondent to question me about the rover. He was convinced that I had depicted some kind of government secret—that the rover already existed and that the Russians were already far ahead in the conquest of the moon. I explained to him that Shvets and I thought it up one night over tea. He didn't believe me."

The Klushantsev creative team faced an interesting challenge in filming a believable moon landing on the edge of a crater. "The duration of the sequence was two and a half minutes. Of course, with our budget we couldn't even dream about an enormous crane. And even if we'd had one, it could hardly have carried out a curved trajectory with a floating motion. Shvets and I decided to film with a camera lying on its side. That way, the camera's motion wouldn't have to be on a vertical plane. It could rise horizontally on rails in a cart. We built the [moonscape] set on its side. It was 16 meters high. We had to carry out the shot in slow-motion. We placed a specially prepared reduction gear in the camera, shooting roughly two frames per second. The vertical position of the moon's surface caused us to wait half a day [before] filming the crater Copernicus, to get the beams of light which occur during sunrise, when it is horizontal."

In the film *Mars* (1968), the first Earthling to set foot on the red planet landed on all fours—a space-suited dog got the honor. "We spent a long time training the dog and, in the end, it eagerly wore the spacesuit and easily ran around in it." *Mars* impressed a visiting American scientist who wanted to take a copy home to show authorities at NASA. He hoped to purchase a copy in Moscow, but everything became so complicated that he shrugged his shoulders and left without it.

Sadly, of all of Klushantsev's films, only reedited footage from *Planet of Storms* has received any extensive showing in the US. Integrated into lower grade sci-fi and fantasy films, some of the work of Klushantsev and fellow Russian filmmakers Koryukov and Ptushko has been "re-directed" by the likes of Curtis Harrington, Roger Corman, and a young Francis Coppola. *Planet of Storms* became *Voyage to the Prehistoric Planet*, directed by Harrington. Much of *Storms* remains intact, but the picture is marred by inferior dubbing and added sequences starring Faith Domergue and Basil Rathbone. A smaller amount of footage from *Storms* was used in *Voyage to the Planet of Prehistoric Women*, starring Mamie Van Doren and directed by Peter Bogdanovich.

Footage from Koryukov's *A Dream Comes True* (1963), a tale of Martian exploration with extraordinarily imaginative effects and design work by Koryukov and Yuri Shvets, was incorporated into *Queen of Blood* (1964), a sci-fi/horror flick directed by Curtis Harrington and starring a young John Saxon and Dennis Hopper.

Mikhail Koryukov's *The Heavens Call* (1959) and Ptushko's *Sadko* were given, by Corman, to USC film school grad Francis Coppola, who re-cut the movie and scripted in new English dialogue. *The Heavens Call* became *Battle Beyond the Sun*, and featured two Coppola-designed "sex monsters" battling it out on an asteroid. Whereas the cosmonauts in *Heavens* were seen gazing out at a beautiful statue, in *Battle* they are watching very thinly disguised phallic symbols fight to the death. *Sadko* was half-heartedly re-edited, atrociously dubbed, and released as *The Magic Voyage of Sinbad*. The names of actors and creators alike were, in the ultimate insult, Americanized: Ptushko, for example, became "Alfred Posco."

In 1970, however, Pavel Klushantsev enjoyed a measure of overdue respect when he was awarded an honorary title of Distinguished Artist of the Russian Soviet Federated Socialist Republic. He holds other orders and medals, but the most precious to him is a medal "for the defense of Leningrad," his birthplace. He retired in 1972 but continued to dabble in invention and write popular science children's books until 1988. Sadly, Klushantsev has not been able to spend his golden years in the comfort he richly deserves. He and his retired artist-animator wife life with his son, a computer specialist, and family in a tiny three-bedroom apartment in St. Petersburg, formerly Leningrad. At eighty-three, living on a meager pension, he must spend hours standing in line for food that costs thirty times its true value. Despite the hardships of the past and uncertainty of the present, his legacy and philosophy live on. "I was always in the position of Robinson Crusoe, dressed in hides and getting fire from rocks," he said. "It seems to me that all of our work speaks about the greater things that are important to people, like selflessness, courage, persistence, knowledge and desire. My coworkers and I earned less than our comrades who were making similar pictures. We made a huge sacrifice for the right to do interesting work. We read few books, almost never went to the theater, rarely got together with friends. We didn't sleep well because we were always risking our careers doing something for the first time. Even with all of that, people worked with me because they loved the cinema more than anything else in the world."

A Note from the Underground

The following is a letter written in May 1991, excerpted from Pavel Klushantsev's correspondence with co-author Robert Skotak. It chronicles the daunting conditions faced by the filmmaker and his fellow countrymen on a daily basis. Since then, conditions have actually worsened, perhaps as much as tenfold. Will the creative spirit, born of individuals like Klushantsev, weather the storm?

" ... Food products and industrial commodities, which are necessary for life, are catastrophically insufficient. It is necessary to search for these items, and if you find them, you have to stand in line for hours. But this is not all. The government raised the prices on all goods three times. The Mafia intercepts commodities until their goods enter the stores and then resells at a higher price, still a few times more than the normal price. My wife and I receive a pension of a total of 400 rubles a month. This is the equivalent of 10 dollars, for everything: the apartment, food, clothing, medical supplies and so forth. In your measure, this is below the poverty level. We, of course, do not exchange rubles for dollars; we buy everything in rubles ... our pension is only sufficient for the most modest food. We aren't starving. But nothing, except food, are we able to buy for ourselves. And this is a miserable existence requiring enormous strength in search and acquisition every day.

"It's necessary to stress the deficit of commodities and low wages which exist in a country run wild. [For ten years,] people ... have become exhausted from a difficult life, deprivation of religion, loss of conscience. They have forgotten the laws of morality, [and] they have become self-absorbed, robbing each other. There has been an incredible increase in crime, [and] a developing powerful Mafia, spreading in control—hence the terrible selfishness, mutual enmity without principles. Suffice it to say that calling for charitable help from Western countries—in the form of sending packages addressed to orphaned children and, most of all, poor people—is useless. Often the proceeds are incorrectly addressed, [and] packages are repeatedly stolen on all transports along the way.

"Of course it is offending. I worked in cinematography without stopping for 45 years. I have eight specialists, an operator, and a director in the highest categories; I have decorations and medals, [and] my pictures received awards at festivals, [as well as] medals and diplomas. And I have no possibility of carrying out the last years of my life in peace and comfort … "

Towards the Last Fairy Tale: On the Fairy-Tale Paradigm in the Strugatskys' Science Fiction, 1963–72

ISTVAN CSICSERY-RONAY JR.

Csicsery-Ronay Jr., Istvan. "Towards the Last Fairy Tale: On the Fairy-Tale Paradigm in the Strugatskys' Science Fiction, 1963–72." *Science Fiction Studies* 13, no. 1 (March 1986): 1–41.

> The history of revolutions, ... which politically spells out the innermost story of the modern age, could be told in parable form as the tale of an age—old treasure which, under the most varied circumstances, appears abruptly, unexpectedly, and disappears again, under different mysterious conditions, as though it were a fata morgana. There exist, indeed, many good reasons to believe that the treasure was never a reality but a mirage, that we deal here not with anything substantial but with an apparition, and the best of these reasons is that the treasure thus far has remained unnamed. Does something exist, not in outer space but in the world and the affairs of men on earth, which has not even a name? Unicorns and fairy queens seem to possess more reality than the lost treasure of the revolutions.

> Hannah Arendt

1. *Introductory Considerations.* If the genre terms *fairy tale* and *science fiction* were precisely descriptive, we would expect them to name antithetical genres: the fairy tale revolving around intentional-affective "magical thought"; SF determined by the implications of scientific rationalism. We know, however, that this is not the case. Most of what is classified as SF owes more to the

structure of the fairy tale than to any scientific ideas it purports to explore. One can decry this state of affairs as proof of the poverty of most SF writers' imaginations. Stanislaw Lem, in the essays of his published in English translation as *Microworlds*, has argued relentlessly that SF depends on atavistic sacred— mythopoeic paradigms that are wholly inadequate for the state of contemporary scientific knowledge.[1] Still, not only second-rate and commercially minded writers of SF have cast their tales in the fairy tale mold. Zamiatin[2] called Wells's scientific romances "urban fairy tales"—and he intended the phrase precisely and admiringly.

Some of the most interesting and intellectually sophisticated questions about the relationship of the two literary modes emerge from the work of Boris and Arkady Strugatsky, the leading scientific fantasists of the Soviet Union. Since the beginning of their career in the late '50s, the Strugatskys have explored in their SF the contradictory relationship between the utopianism implicit in the fairy tale and the critical rationalism implicit in science. In the following pages, I will sketch the course of this exploration, from its early "synthesis" in the technocratic utopianism of the early '60s, through the disillusionment and breakdown of the synthesis in the mid-60s, to its culmination in the Strugatskys' dark masterpiece, *Roadside Picnic*.[3]

My argument depends on certain definitions of the fairy tale and fairytale paradigm which should be clarified at the outset. By fairy-tale paradigm I mean a heuristic model of the pattern of relationships among narrative elements conceived to be characteristic of fairy tales by tale-telling cultures. These elements can be categorized thematically, syntactically, "morphologically," or by motif. Taken in isolation, they may be found in other, related genres; so that it is the total pattern of relationships that distinguishes the genres from each other. The paradigm is not a model of the basic elements common to all fairy tales. Particular tales will deviate from, or "deform," the model in certain respects, and often they will conflate aspects of the fairytale paradigm with those of

1   Stanislaw Lem, *Microworlds* (New York: 1985).

2   Yevgeny Zamyatin, *A Soviet Heretic: Essays by Yevgeny Zamyatin*, trans. and ed. Mirra Ginsburg (Chicago: University of Chicago Press, 1970), 261.

3   Following common SFS practices, I have resorted to abbreviated versions of the English titles of the Strugatsky tales I deal with once I have cited them in full. I should remark, however, that the rendering of those titles by their English translators does not always accord with the original Russian. Thus, the Strugatskys' title for *The Final Circle of Paradise* is equivalent to *Predatory Things of Our Time*; *Prisoners of Power* is *The Inhabited Island*; *Definitely Maybe* is *A Billion Years Before the End of the World*; and "Space Mowgli" is *The Kid*.

other genres; but the narrative significance of these deviations and conflations emerges from their relation to the paradigms.

Like many archaic genres, the fairy tale has pronounced formal regularities—it "wears its skeleton on the outside."[4] These formal regularities also invite certain thematic expectations. Together, these establish the conceptual "base" of the fairy tale upon which each historical variation plays its changes. Thus in the discussion that follows, I will refer to the contemporary "non-marvelous" genre of the socialist realist production novel as a form adhering to the fairy tale's paradigm, although the fairy-tale elements are present in it only in quite displaced form. Similarly, in tracing the development of the Strugatskys' SF, I will discuss the various ways in which they deform the fairy tale's elements, while adhering to its paradigmatic pattern "in the breach"—which then brings into relief the utopian thematics of the fairy tale, whose paradigm remains as a ghostly absence behind the "realistic" displacements.

As for "fairy tale," I use the term not in the strict sense of tales about elemental spirits, but as pragmatic shorthand for the type of tales included in Aarne's catalogue[5] as "magical tales" (Nos. 330–749) and discussed by Vladimir Propp, Honti, Nagy, Lüthi, and others.[6] Since I will be considering the Strugatskys' relationship to the fairy-tale paradigm, and not actual fairy tales from the ethnographic record, I will sometimes use the terms "fairy tale" and "fairy-tale paradigm" interchangeably.

For my purposes, the paradigmatic fairy tale is characterized by certain properties and absences, which are felt by listeners and tellers alike to be characteristic of "magical tales," in contradistinction to myths, on the one hand, and non-magical folktales, on the other. Some of these are:

(1) The mortal, human character of the hero, who is left to his own devices, regardless of his putative worldly position and class-power (as opposed to myth's markedly superhuman exalted hero);

(2) The everyday, "mundane" character of the narrative language which ties it to the mundane community (as opposed to the hieratic tone of myths appropriate for self-differentiating hierarchies);

---

4 János Honti, *Válogatott tanulmányok* [Selected articles] (Budapest: 1962), 51.

5 Antti Aarne, *The Types of the Folktale* (Helsinki: 1961).

6 Vladimir Propp, *The Morphology of the Folktale* (Austin: 1968); Honti, *Válogatott tanulmányok*; Olga Nagy, *Hősök csalókák ördögök* [Heroes, tricksters, devils] (Bucharest: 1974).

(3) The inevitability of the happy ending, which entails the fulfillment of some or all human desires and the expunging of evil (as opposed to the moira implied by myths);

(4) The non-transcendental character of the happy ending—i.e., the fulfillment of desire occurs in the world, not on a "higher," quasi-divine level of being;

(5) The mutual aid of magical-supernatural beings and the hero, linking the human and natural worlds (e.g., the hero is aided by the supernatural being as a reward for the hero's service to the supernatural being);

(6) A three-phase story, which progresses from a situation of lack (disequilibrium), through a conflict and collision between hero and villain(s) (mediation), to the annihilation of the lack (recuperation of equilibrium, with a positive gain, i.e., the prevention of a recurrence of the initial lack).[7]

2.1 *The Fairy-Tale Paradigm in Soviet Ideology.* The meaning a given oral or literary genre has for a culture can never be deduced merely by generalizing from its formal properties. The same form can be used, with minor differences in motivation, for quite contrary ideological purposes. What the fairy tale means for Russian culture should be approached historically, via the questions: Who uttered it, and for what purposes? Even so, the genre is not infinitely pliable. Its pronounced formal properties set limits on the fairy tale's message. Essentially, the fairy tale implies a certain set of general relations to its audience, which establishes a set of inherent themes. Whether it is used in the context of pagan, imperial, or Bolshevik ideology, whether it is told seriously or ironically, the fairy tale as a form cannot help but invoke certain attitudes and concepts, such as the wish for a utopia of benevolent power and universally reciprocated affection, a two-world universe divided between the everyday and the extraordinary, a cosmos governed by affective-intentional forces, etc. These attitudes may be judged and ridiculed in the telling, but first they must be called up.

---

7 Possibly, none of these characteristics is absolute. The Hungarian ethnographer Sándor Erdész has even speculated that a genre of "tragic fairy tale" exists in the Hungarian oral tradition (Sándor Erdész, *Ámy Lajos meséi* [The tales of Lajos Amy] [Budapest: 1968], 86). Nagy disputes this, attributing the tragic endings of some of Amy's tales to either his idiosyncratic modes of storytelling or generic conflation (Olga Nagy, *A táltos törvénye. Népmese és eztétikum* [The law of the shaman. Folktale and aesthetics] [Bucharest: 1978], 324n4).

The fairy tale has been a favorite narrative mode in Russian culture, and has been adapted to legitimize many regimes and social conditions. In the nineteenth century, many scholars and tale-tellers shared with their German counterparts the Romantic view that the fairy tale is the last preserve of archaic, "magical thought." It was held to reflect the *Volksgeist* in a world dominated by the systematizing and internationalizing forces of Enlightenment rationalism. According to this conception, the fairy tale is the "correction of the world"[8] representing a universe responsive to human desire versus myth's image of an impersonally "true" universal order.[9]

The fairy tale thus served as an antidote to both the symbolic systems of religion and the mechanistic world-descriptions of science.[10] Yet to the degree

---

8 Honti, *Válogatott*, 73–74; Nagy, *Hősök*, 19.

9 The conception that myth and fairy tale are modal opposites runs deep in the European critical tradition. Myth has been generally identified with narratives demonstrating notions of necessity, the power of moira over human aspirations. The fairy tale putatively affirms the opposite, the attainment of human desire through cooperation with nature after several de-mythicizing ordeals. Consequently, the fairy tale is often associated with oppressed peoples' resistance to the hieratic myths of legitimation of the dominant class. In Walter Benjamin's words, "The fairy tale tells us of the earliest arrangements that mankind made to shake off the nightmare which myth placed upon its chest" (Walter Benjamin, *Illuminations*, trans. Harry Zohn [New York: 1969], 102). Nagy emphasizes that the curse of the fairy tale is usually a cyclic, myth-like abolition of human time, which it is the tale hero's task to destroy in order to restore human time (*A táltos*, 127). This distinction was taken up in psychoanalytic criticism's distinction between the paradigmatic myth of Oedipus and the fairy tale's affirmation of the Pleasure Principle. A version of this underlies Bettelheim's definition of fairy tales as paradigms of psychological maturation, versus myth's representation of the ineluctable conflicts between "superego demands and id-motivated action, and with the self-preserving desires of the ego" (Bruno Bettelheim, *The Uses of Enchantment* [New York: 1977], 37.) For a dissenting view see: Claude Lévi-Strauss, *Structural Anthropology*, vol. 2, trans. Monique Layton (Chicago: Chicago University Press, 1976), 2:127–38.

10 The official philosophy of science of the USSR has been based on the conflation of at least four concepts: the principle of the primacy of matter; the objective reality of matter "existing and developing independent of the mind" (Lenin quoted in Loren R. Graham, *Science and Philosophy in the Soviet Union* [New York: 1971], 36); the existence of objective dialectical "laws" inhering in material nature; and the receptivity of scientific evolution to philosophical direction by the Party. None of these major points are in fact derived directly from Marx. The last concept, which was codified by the Stalinist idea that science is an aspect of the superstructure—analogous to Stalin's theory of language (see Arnold Buccholz, "The Role of the Scientific-Technological Revolution in Marxism-Leninism," *Studies in Soviet Thought* 20 [1979]: 148–49)—remained embedded in the 1961 Party Program even though that document acknowledges science as a productive force.

Only recently has the scientific establishment succeeded in freeing itself to some extent from these strictures, through the use of such methods of justification as scientometrics, the decidedly undialectical, "value-free" measurement of scientific successes, derived from

that Russian propagandists of "scientific" utopianism presented their views through the paradigm of the fairy tale, the tale was also used to create an image of science as the treasure chest of magical tools with which history's hero—the Russian nation, the proletariat, or Socialist Man—would create the promised utopia. This is one reason why the "scientific" nature of Marxism-Leninism constantly emphasized by Soviet ideologists has little relation either to scientific methodology or to a Marxist conception of the historical dialectic of science. Unlike the situation in the West, in the USSR scientific research has long been held to be in the service of the Baconian ideal of science, with the goal of utopian production and distribution of wealth in a classless society as the standard by which scientific work is said to be ultimately judged. Consequently, in Russia the fairy tale has been a far more important structure of intelligibility than empirical rationalism, and it has proved to be an invaluable tool for the formalization and dissemination of Soviet ideology.

The fairy-tale plot's main elements lend themselves to interpretation as symbolic representations of the main moments of the Marxian historical dialectic. In the first place, the ultimate task of the tale's hero is to mediate for humanity, acting as the agent of its transformation from powerlessness (domination by an alien power) to empowerment.[11] By struggling with and eventually defeating a villain, the fairy-tale hero destroys the force that initially disturbed the harmony of the human community. He does this by appropriating that force—i.e., using the power of the villain against the villain, and thereby "negating the negation." This parallels the liberatory violence of the agent of human history (in classical Marxism, the proletariat; but in Soviet SF, the scientific intelligentsia) against that fraction of the species that has broken with the whole of humanity in order to appropriate the human essence of others. The hero's victory establishes a new state of happiness transcending the conflict and alienation that had originally produced it.

Secondly, the fairy tale's villain generally gains its power by creating a "lack" with metaphysical significance, by stealing or hoarding the symbolic

---

the work of Derek De Solla Price (see Yaakov M. Rabkin, "Measuring Science in the USSR: Uses and Expectations," *Survey* 22 [1976]: 75–79.).

On the de-dialecticization of the Soviet philosophy of science, see: Alfred Schmidt, *The Concept of Nature in Marx*, trans. Ben Fowkes (London: 1971), 51–61; Graham, *Science and Philosophy*, 45–61; Herbert Marcuse, Soviet Marxism (New York: 1958), 136–59; and Buccholz, "The Role of … Revolution," 147–53.

11 Marie-Gabriel Wosien, *The Russian Folktale. Some Structural and Thematic Elements* (München: 1969), 104.

object of the heart's desire (the princess, the treasure, the golden apples, the shaman's magic horse, etc.), by terrorizing the land, or by forcing the hero to perform perilous tasks. This symbolism is easily adapted to the representation of class oppression, the alienation of work, and the destruction of communal bonds, all of which the socialist transformation is to overcome.

Thirdly, the hero's struggle with internal and external obstacles can become an image of the moral dialectic of the historical agents' selfrecognition as a class. The obstacles the hero faces are often alienated versions of the hero himself, such as false heroes, brothers, deceivers, not to mention the symmetrically opposed villain. Other obstacles are created by the hero's improper means, usually to acquire personal power that does not lead to the proper goal.

Fourthly, the hero's cooperation with magical donors implies that there is a tendency in nature allowing it to be co-opted to the human project of transforming nature into culture through the appropriation of natural forces. For Soviet ideology, this is an important point. The orthodox MarxistLeninist concepts of nature have been based on a reading of Engels's *Dialectics of Nature* and *Anti-Dühring* that objectifies the dialectic in physical nature.[12]

Finally, the happy ending, with its images of material abundance, leisure, and social concord, agrees with the utopian goals of revolutionary socialism.

A great deal of research has recently traced the folkloristic and specifically fairy-tale "morphology" of contemporary Soviet administration and official culture. Some scholars have discovered the fairy-tale paradigm even in Soviet legislation and in the training of international business negotiators.[13] In literary culture, the connection between socialist realism and the fairy tale is so close that Katerina Clark has proposed a "Master Plot" for the Soviet novel based on modifications of Vladimir Propp's wellknown master plot of the fairy tale defined in *The Morphology of the Folktale*.[14] The case of socialist realism demonstrates the extent to which the fairy-tale paradigm has been the privileged literary tool for propaganda. It is well known that the schema of socialist realism proposed by Zhdanov and Gorky was drawn from folkloristic models. When

---

12 Marcuse, *Soviet Marxism*, 143–45; Schmidt, *The Concept of Nature*, 52–61.
13 Michael Urban and John McClure, "The Folklore of State Socialism: Semiotics and the Study of the Socialist State," *Soviet Studies* 35 (1983): 471–86; Dean Grimes Farrer, "The Soviet Folktale as an Ideological Strategy in International Business Relations," *Studies in Soviet Thought* 13 (1973): 55–75; Felix Oinas, "The Political Uses and Themes of Folklore in the Soviet Union," *Journal of the Folklore Institute* 12 (1975): 157–75; and Frank J. Miller, "The Image of Stalin in Soviet Russian Folklore," *The Russian Review* 39 (1980): 5–67.
14 Katerina Clark, The Soviet Novel: History as Ritual (Chicago: 1981), 4–7.

socialist realism was first proclaimed as the official literary manner, at the First Writers Congress in 1934, Gorky demanded that writers should pattern their heroes on those of folklore.[15]

2.2 The Strugatskys and Technocratic Utopianism in the Early '60s. The Strugatskys began writing within the tradition of the socialist realist quasifairy-tale paradigm, which they adapted to represent the ideals of the generation of scientists and engineers whose leading position in Soviet culture had been validated by the success of the Soviet space program and the de-Stalinization of science. It is already clear in their early work that they intended their SF to "personalize" the future. Their goal was to rescue the vision of a socialist utopia from the monumental distance to which Stalin and the Stakhanovite cult of Socialist Man had placed it, and to return it to a human scale. The Strugatskys thus joined their SF to the general trend of the "humanization of Marxism" in the Eastern Europe of the '60s. Their model for this was space exploration, with its romantic associations with adventure and its heroic associations with the ethics of honest scientific method. In the era of space travel, the Strugatskys seemed to say, class struggle would end, the material and the social causes of scarcity would be defeated, and the earth would be united in a single utopian society, whose life would be given interest and meaning by its perpetual struggle with nature. The history of science would replace the history of class struggle. The conflicts that were to keep the dialectical movement of history alive were to be the ethical and cognitive problems faced by scientists and explorers as they encountered new worlds and new aspects of nature. There would still be choices, but they would no longer be between good and evil; instead, they would be between "the good and the better."[16] With the Strugatskys, science thus became the historical vehicle of a new fairy-tale paradigm, which was more realistically motivated than the old one (since the villains are never absolutely evil, nor are the happy endings

---

15 Ibid., 34; the implications of this prescription were made explicit when, in the famous campaign to immortalize Stalin in the '30s, some of the most highly regarded traditional storytellers and singers were brought to Moscow from the provinces to compose tales and ballads in which contemporary Soviet leaders were cast in the role of heroes (Ibid., 148). This was not solely because popular and folk forms facilitated the dissemination of Soviet ideology among the illiterate and semiliterate masses. The fairy tale, in its broadest sense (and thus including the heroic *bylina*), describes a world in which human will is capable of transforming hostile nature. It was clear to the Soviet cultural leaders that this worldview was more useful than any historical theorizing in attracting the populace to the tasks of crash modernization.

16 Darko Suvin, "Introduction to the Strugatskys' *Snail on the Slope*" (New York: 1980): 4. Sinyavski satirizes just this phrase on page 50 in: Abram Tertz [Sinyavski], *On Socialist Realism* (New York: 1960).

absolutely happy), but was identical in structure. This modification not only allowed the Strugatskys more artistic freedom to depict psychologically divided characters and ideologically ambiguous situations. It also gave them a powerful theme that expressed the hopes of the new Soviet technocracy in the late '50s—the multitude of scientists, engineers, and scientific students who were accorded new respect by the successes in outer space.

One cannot appreciate the importance of the Strugatskys' work without understanding the role of the Soviet scientific intelligentsia in the post-Stalin thaw. In the late '50s and early '60s, this intelligentsia was beginning to liberalize not only the actual practice of science, but also the role of the theory of science in the dominant philosophy of history. After a generation of rejection, new respect was granted under Khrushchev to the view that contemporary developments in science constituted a "second industrial revolution," the so-called Scientific-Technological Revolution (STR), and hence a radical transformation in the forces of production requiring adaptation in the ideological superstructure.[17] Propelled by the successes of the space-program, Khrushchev seemed willing to accept the challenge of acknowledging the idea of STR: namely, that Soviet society would have to commit itself to developing its scientific and technical resources in order to assure the final victory of Communism over Capitalism. Young members of the scientific elite, for whom the Strugatskys became literary spokesmen (indeed, of which they were members, since Boris Strugatsky was a computer scientist), believed this new ambition on the part of the regime and the Party promised them that they would be the primary architects of the new socialist utopia. It appeared that they had been empowered to take on the role of the revolutionary vanguard in a peaceful revolution.[18]

2.3 *The Case of Far Rainbow.* A good example of the Strugatskys' adaptation of the socialist-realist fairy-tale model is their novella *Far Rainbow*,[19] which was

---

17 Buccholz, "The Role of ... Revolution," 147–53.

18 There were abundant hints of this promise in the 1961 Party Program, which concludes with a vision of a peacefully attained, highly technological communist utopia: "When the Soviet people will enjoy the blessings of communism, new hundreds of millions of people on earth will say: 'We are for communism!' It is not through war with other countries, but by the example of a more perfect organization of society, by rapid progress in developing the productive forces, the creation of all conditions for the happiness and well-being of man, that the ideas of communism win the minds and hearts of the masses (John Triska, ed., *Soviet Communism. Programs and Rules* [San Francisco: 1962], 129.)

19 Arkady and Boris Strugatsky, *Far Rainbow*, trans. Antonina W. Bouis (New York: Macmillan, 1978).

published in 1963 and enjoyed great popular success throughout the '60s.[20] It tells the tale of a community of human scientists who have colonized an uninhabited, earthlike planet called Rainbow. The scientists perform experiments in the application of a new science, known as "zero-physics," which theoretically allows the instantaneous transmission of matter through space, a process they call "zero-transmission" or "zero-t." Rainbow is a lovely, paradisal world, where the scientists live with their families, where artists come from Earth to do their best work, where the children live in beautiful school colonies, and where the crops grow abundantly enough to secure the planet's autonomy from Earth under a purely formal civil administration. Scientists rule. It is utopia.

The idyll is disrupted by two forces, one internal, the other external. First, the internal order of the colony begins coming apart at the seams. A scarcity of portable nuclear reactors, known as ulmotrons, which are essential for the zero-physicists' work and must be imported from Earth, leads the scientists to tap and steal each other's supplies. The most intellectually developed human community verges on degeneration into a chaos of infantile selfishness. But far more disruptive is the strange phenomenon known as the Black Wave. After each zero-t experiment, an enormous wave of plasma rises at the planet's poles and moves towards the equator. Usually, these waves can be dissipated by specially designed "energy-gulping" machines. But at the start of *Rainbow*, a particularly energy-exhausting experiment produces a wave of unprecedented size. The gulpers are unable to halt its advance, the wave destroys the crops and steadily approaches the colony's capital, situated on the equator.

At the capital, only one small spaceship is available to evacuate the inhabitants. Because it can accommodate only a very few, panic ensues. The spaceship's wise pilot, Gorbovsky, who has just landed that day with a shipment of ulmotrons, takes command and issues the order that only the children and their teachers may be evacuated. The physicists must remain on the planet, and perish, and so must their records, with the exception of a set of "warning notes" about the Wave. Gorbovsky and his crew join the doomed colonists to

---

20 A poll of its readers taken by the Soviet journal *Fantastika* in 1967 showed the enormous popularity of the Strugatskys' work in general, as well as of the early *Far Rainbow* in particular. The results (cited in Alan Myers, "Some Developments in Soviet SF since 1966," *Foundation* 19 [1980]: 46–47) were as follows: (1) *Hard to Be a God*, A. and B. Strugatsky; (2) *Monday Begins on Saturday*, A. and B. Strugatsky; (3) *The Martian Chronicles*, Ray Bradbury; (4) *Solaris*, Stanislaw Lem; (5) *The Invincible*, Stanislaw Lem; (6) *Far Rainbow*, A. and B. Strugatsky; (7) *Stories*, Robert Sheckley; (8) *I, Robot*, Isaac Asimov; (9) *Return from the Stars*, Stanislaw Lem; (10) *Predatory Things of Our Time* [*Paradise*], A. and B. Strugatsky; (11) *Andromeda*, Ivan Yefremov.

make room for the children, one of whose teachers is an ex-starpilot competent to fly the ship to safety. After the ship departs, the colonists feel overwhelming relief. They accept their fate with joyous bravado as the two waves converge over them.

Rainbow contains interesting elements of a critique which may have seemed audacious at the time the novella was first published. It can easily be read as an allegory about nuclear testing, a matter that was very much under public discussion in the early '60s. The zero-physicists and their obsession with their new science are analogues of the scientists of the Manhattan Project; the zero-t experiments correspond to atmospheric nuclear tests; and the black wave is a not very displaced image of fallout. Rainbow itself is a fantastic version of the Soviet "Science Cities," the enormous artificial cities that Khrushchev had built for concentrating large numbers of scientists and technicians to facilitate the centralization of scientific work. The comic scramble for the ulmotrons satirizes the perpetual shortage of equipment that plagues even the most "autonomous" scientific projects in the USSR.

The point of the satire is not clear, however. The scale of the black wave catastrophe, the depiction of the scientists as problematic characters, and the fact that some of those with Russian names are at least complicitous in allowing the catastrophe to occur (Malyaev, Rob Sklyarov) are significant departures from the the bland nationalistic orthodoxy of most Soviet SF. The zero-physicists—who live, after all, in a classless society—destroy all the life of a surrogate Earth in their attempts to master nature. On the one hand, the authors imply that science's desire to serve humanity can easily lead to world-destroying projects. On the other hand, there is moral heroism ready to save humanity from science. Gorbovsky drops into this confusion literally from the sky. Against the claim made by Lamondois, the project director, that the most valuable thing on Rainbow is the zero-physicists' work, Gorbovsky retorts: "our most valuable asset is our future ... the children."[21] With Gorbovsky acting as a model, the adults on Rainbow agree to the rescue of their children without regrets. He restores their self-respect by inspiring them to accept their sacrifice courageously. Thus, a *homo ex machina* solves a sticky problem that he had no share in causing. In the same way, there are no regrets for the destruction of Rainbow, which perishes without tragic, or even pathetic, significance. In the end, the catastrophe appears to be less a humanly induced cataclysm than a natural one.

---

21 A. and B. Strugatsky, *Rainbow*, 8:109.

This easy surrender of Rainbow muddles the fiction's critical point. None of the characters is rooted in the planet, and consequently it has no significant human history. It is only a "physicist's planet,"[22] intended to be expendable by its authors as well as its colonists. Nor do the Strugatskys differentiate clearly in the tale between the critique of scientific hubris and the idealization of scientific courage. Nothing in the tale opposes the shift in emphasis from the scientists' obsession with their world-destroying project to an upbeat, bittersweet tale of moral heroics and right values preserved. The zero-physicists' redemption seems to come much too easily.

Darko Suvin's interpretation of Rainbow as "a clear parable for the price of historical knowledge and progress"[23] may indeed be what the Strugatskys intended. But the tale can also be read as a fairly classical parable of the dangers of overstepping human limits and thereby imperiling the whole species. Yet if the tale is a warning about real science, it is directed more to schoolchildren than to adults. It affirms a world in which positive values must win out, even if at great cost to the past. (Consider Gorbovsky's comparison of his queasiness before announcing his decision to evacuate only the children—a decision that involves his own death—to "something like those last moments before a final exam.")[24] The confusion created by the artificial resolution required by the juvenileadventure fiction mode in which the story is told leaves the moral far from clear. Moreover, the threat to humanity and the earth posed by a science alienated from the values that spawned it is not allayed in Rainbow by the scientific community itself.

2.4 Far Rainbow as a "Humanized" Production Novel. This ambivalence is the perhaps inevitable result of an experiment in infusing the idealized form of the socialist-realist fairy tale with innovative critical elements. With a few—but, as we shall see, significant—deviations, Rainbow's action can be decomposed precisely into the moves of Clark's Master Plot of the orthodox socialist realist production novel.

The production novel had been the privileged form of fiction under Stalin. It generally told the tale of an energetic positive hero (or, more rarely, a heroine) who arrives at a development project bogged down by bureaucratic inertia or sabotage. In a realistically motivated version of the classical fairy tale, the hero's

---

22 Ibid., 5:65.
23 Suvin, "Introduction," 6.
24 *Rainbow*, 8:103.

task is to restore the will to produce and to build socialism that the villainous enemies of the Revolution have sapped. The hero then undergoes trials and temptations, receives the help of a donor-like authority figure in touch with the laws of history and nature, and combats the villains. In the end, the hero succeeds in restoring revolutionary energy, will, and discipline.

This genre satisfied several important ideological needs at once. Because of its simplicity and invariant form, it easily absorbed popular literary elements and created the effect of "epic wholeness" appropriate for mythicizing official Soviet ideology.[25] By the same token, it eschewed the complications of psychological motivation and the complex relationships among milieu, character, and narrative form that were the trademark of Western modernism and its referent, the alienated consciousness of bourgeois social relations. The "Master Plot," or archetype, of the socialist realist production novel as Clark describes it is simpler than Propp's master plot of the fairy tale, and it lacks explicitly magical elements. Still, the production novel's structure of narrative action is identical to that of the fairy tale. The tasks are more realistically, even prosaically, motivated. So are the villains and the donors. But the prescription that the production novel end with the completion of the task, embodying the victory of Soviet civilization, shows that the historical wish-fulfillment of the happy ending is more important than any other epic element.

Clark divides the action of the production novel (typified by Gladkov's *Cement* [1926]) into several phases, each of which has its appropriate moves. In the first phase, the Prologue or "separation," the hero arrives in, or returns to, the microcosm in which he must effect his eventual heroic mediation. Then, in the phase of "setting up the task," the hero sees that all is not well in the microcosm—specifically, the tasks of production are not being fulfilled. The hero then designs a scheme for the righting of the wrongs. Next, according to Clark,[26] "when the hero presents his plan to the local bureaucrats, they say it is too 'utopian'—that it would be impossible to fulfill it in terms both of technical feasibility and available manpower and supplies." The third phase, the "transition" or period of trials, begins when the obstacles appear to the hero's plan. These Clark divides into two categories: prosaic and dramatic/heroic, or mythic. The prosaic include problems with supplies, manpower, and equipment; bureaucratic corruption or slackness; worker apathy and discontent. The dramatic/heroic include such things as natural disasters, enemy invasions, class enemies,

---

25 Clark, *The Soviet Novel*, 9–10.
26 Ibid., 257.

counterrevolutionary terrorists, struggles with an antagonistic bureaucracy, etc. The hero may also face problems in his love life or in controlling his emotions. The final moment of the transition is the hero's journey to the "center" or to Moscow to seek help from more authoritative people than are available in the microcosm. The fourth phase is the Climax, when the fulfillment of the task is threatened. At first, the hero's task appears unrealizable, usually when one of his dramatic/heroic obstacles seems to threaten its completion. In the course of the encounter with this obstacle, an actual, near, or symbolic death occurs. Also in this phase, the hero may have moments of grave self-doubt. A fifth phase, of "incorporation," follows the climax. Here the hero has a talk with his mentor, who gives him the strength to carry on. In the last move, the Finale, or "celebration of incorporation," the task is completed, usually marked by a ceremony of celebration. The love plot is resolved; a funeral is held for the tragic victims killed during the climax; and the hero "transcends his selfish impulses and acquires an extrapersonal identity."[27] Finally, "in a speech marking the completion of the task, or in some intangible form, such as the birth of a child, the theme of regeneration and of the glorious time that awaits future generations is introduced as a thematic counterpoint to sacrifice and death."[28]

Through ritualized literary elements, the production novel represents certain Marxist–Leninist axioms, assimilated to Stalinist Russian nationalism. It depicts the highest values of the Soviet orthodoxy: work, in the form of communal industrial production (in opposition to individualism and the selfish practice of power); commitment to the building of socialism and the struggle against reaction; and acquiescence to the power of the central authorities. The first two of these values are consonant with humanistic Marxism, and the Strugatskys freely adopted those characteristics of the production novel that represented them. The third value, however, was difficult to harmonize with the first two. Especially during the de-Stalinization period and in the cultural struggles of the early '60s, the young intellectuals blamed the failure to create a true socialist society on their elders' blind acquiescence to the Party's and Stalin's despotism. The Strugatskys used the socialist realist paradigm for the new values of this period by adapting the first two values to the themes of scientific exploration. In their work, the exploration of the cosmos and the establishment of contact among intelligent life-forms replace the goal of Soviet industrialization and the conquest of hostile nature for use by socialist

27 Ibid., 259.
28 Ibid., 260.

society. The building of socialism is projected into the dialectic of the human future—that is, the adventure of humanity after the revolution. The question of authority—perhaps the fundamental problem of Soviet ideology—the Strugatskys tried to solve by constructing ideally "human" heroes, able to combine deep sympathy for the human species with great scientific understanding.

Rainbow is a far more genial and complex work than the tendentious Stalinist novel. One could argue that it deviates quite strongly from the fairy-tale paradigm, since most of its protagonists die at the end, leaving the chilly bionic immortal, Camill, alone on a wasted planet. *Rainbow* has perhaps more affinities with the ballad than the fairy tale—the narrative, in fact, closes with the zero-pilots singing a "Ballad of Far Rainbow" as they prepare to die. But if it is a ballad, it has been "rotated through" the fairy-tale form. The characters celebrate their "happy deaths," as if their sacrifice and courage were the heart's desire they had been seeking all along; only Camill is unhappy, for he cannot join them in death and thereby match Gorbovksy's model of humanism. *Rainbow* clearly attempts to go beyond the naïveté of the orthodox socialist realist form with this reversal of expectations. It might also be read as a compromise between the orthodox form and the anti-fairytale inversion of socialist realist conventions. The latter, exemplified by Dudintsev's influential *Not by Bread Alone* (1957), retains the elements of the classical production novels, but inverted: the hero is ultimately destroyed by the enchanted world of bureaucracy and despotism. In *Rainbow*, the Strugatskys seem to offer an alternative both to the bankruptcy of Stalinist *partijnost'* (party-consciousness) and the pessimism of the anti-Stalinist novel: a tragic sociohistorical problem with a happy ending. It is nonetheless constructed from same structural elements as the socialist realist production novel, and its action naturally falls into the conventional parts described by Clark.

The novella's two foci of action, Gorbovsky and the Rainbow colonists, each develop according to the archetypal pattern, dovetailing throughout the narrative. Gorbovsky's sequence of actions has few surprises. Nostalgic for some earthy communality, from which his many years as a starpilot have separated him, he arrives on Rainbow (which is also a "return" of sorts, since he is visiting an old friend, and because Rainbow is so reminiscent of Earth) in the middle of a "production crisis"; he "sets up the task" of creating order among the scientists, and ultimately of rescuing the children; in a "transition" phase, he confronts "prosaic" obstacles created by the zero-physicists' anarchy, and the overriding "dramatic/heroic" obstacle of the Black Wave; he is rather ideally free of fears and doubts in the "climax," although he does exhibit some anxiety about his decision to evacuate only the children; he is "incorporated" into the colonists' community by choosing to stay on Rainbow with them, and he joins them in their "celebration" at the tale's conclusion. For their part, the zero-physicists also begin "separated" from the basic problems of the human species; they, too, must set up the task of dealing with the Black Wave, and with their own shortcomings (Patrick's intellectualism, Sklyarov's emotionalism, Rob and Tanya's lovers' quarrel, the panic and cowardice of some of the colonists); once they accept Gorbovsky's decision, they are reincorporated as a community, as well as with the rest of the human species, to whom they now send their heirs; finally, they indulge in a celebration of their recovered moral goodness.

Rainbow's most significant departure from the master plot is the absence of the hero's journey to the "center" to seek help from authoritative people. It is the mark of Gorbovsky's and Rainbow's "autonomy" (a matter very dear both to the colonial administration and the planet's agronomists in the tale) that the heroic decisions must be made in place, on Rainbow. The moral authority-figure in the Strugatskys' novella is willing to come into the endangered community and make the ultimate sacrifice for it. Gorbovsky thus represents the Generation of the '60s' ideal reversal of Stalinist monumentalization and hierarchical distantiation.

By the same token, there are no "pure" villains in the book. Because class struggle no longer occupies humanity's energies, the scientists' flaws can only harm them and their own offspring. Nor is nature a hostile force, as it is in so many of the '30s' novels of conquering the Arctic or the desert. The Black Wave is simply Rainbow's natural response to the zero-t experiments. It is interesting that, in a reversal of the Stalinist "setting up the task," in which the positive hero drives the workers to attain ideal goals against the defeatists' and saboteurs' advice, in *Rainbow* it is the positive hero who informs the zero-physicists that their plan is impossible because of material limits (i.e., the size of the spaceship). And the most important material limits are placed on zero-transference by Rainbow's nature. These are significant reversals of the socialist realist topos, embodying another of the Strugatskys' main themes: that honest science confronts real, even if temporary, material limits to development and cognition that require serious moral-ethical reflection, unlike the Stalinist-Lysenkoite delusion of Soviet omnipotence.

Rainbow is a naïve work in the Strugatskys' oeuvre. It still demonstrates the epic wholeness that was held to be one of the virtues of socialist realism. It purports to be an image of a dynamic utopia: a good society that continues to grow through its conflicts with nature and human nature, thereby solving the problem of how to imagine a utopia that is still a part of the dialectical process. To depict qualitative change without sacrificing the image of wholeness, the Strugatskys had to abstract the action of their tale from the recognizable, concrete historical problems of the present—excepting the "safe" issue of atmospheric nuclear testing. They present a resolution on the margins of the world, which has ambiguous implications for the actual society of the present. The destruction that brings forth the new (or rather, the renewed) sense of human species-consciousness in *Rainbow* happens so far from the earth that there is no reason to fear that it might have any effect on actual earthly reality. The zero-t cataclysm is like nuclear disaster, but it is also quite different. At the very least, a nuclear world-destruction might still be avoided, perhaps by following the good example of the zero-physicists of the future. Hence the novella's dizzying double-focus: the concrete scene of destruction in *Rainbow* remains alien, but the abstract moral consciousness of the fallible-heroic colonists is the familiar ideal morality of utopian virtue that is to be practiced here and now.

3.1 The Fiction of the '60s: The Degeneration of the Wish. After *Rainbow*, the Strugatskys gradually abandoned the juvenile adventure mode of socialist realism, with its abstract utopianism and virtuous foregone conclusions. Their works began instead to emphasize the obstacles in the way of achieving utopia. In the works before 1964, not only was the victory of the socialist revolution and the institution of a terrestrial utopia assumed, but the whole cosmos was conceived as a scene where the only problems facing humanity are the struggles with nature and contacts with other species. With *Hard to Be a God* (1964),[29] a new theme entered their fiction: the degeneration of the utopian wish, the possibility that humanity may not be able to achieve its utopia because of its incapacity to wish for its own good.

With *God and The Final Circle of Paradise* (1965),[30] the Strugatskys brought their settings and situations closer to familiar earthly social settings ... and to ethical-psychological dilemmas posed by complex social situations. Although the setting of *God* is another planet, it is populated by human beings who differ from the earth's only in certain aspects of their history; *Paradise* occurs on Earth, in an imaginary Country of the Fools which mimics Western consumer society. With these more concrete settings, the Strugatskys also

---

29 A. and B. Strugatsky, *Hard to be A God*, trans. Wendayne Ackerman, by arrangement with Forrest J. Ackerman (New York: Seabury, 1973).

30 A. and B. Strugatsky, *The Final Circle of Paradise*, trans. Leonid Renen (New York: DAW, 1976).

began to pay more attention to the problems encountered by their scientific adventurers and less to the uplifting heroic solutions.

The Strugatskys' new interest in the problems retarding the utopian resolution necessarily led to a change in their attitude to the fairy-tale paradigm. In the fairy tale, the problems—i.e., the obstacles the hero meets and his ways of dealing with them—are subordinated to the overriding movement toward a happy ending. It is this inexorable movement toward happiness that gives the fairy tale its moral value in the eyes of its partisans. For the utopian philosopher Ernst Bloch, this is what makes the fairy tale an example of *Vor-Schein*, or anticipatory illusion, which he believed inspires human communities to persevere in the struggle for utopia. For the English fantasist J. R. R. Tolkien, the inevitable "eu-catastrophe" endows the fairy tale and its modem counterpart, fantasy, with the power of regenerative estrangement and the capacity to create an image of confidence in life and the universe when there is no "reason" for it.[31] And it is this sudden, extra-systemic grace that makes the fairy-tale world an image of the possible co-operation of nature and "the liberated man," as opposed to the "fatedness" of human beings depicted by "the nightmare of myth."[32]

Unlike simple wish-fulfillment, the fairy tale represents the life of the wish in strict form: from the recognition of a lack in "reality" and the methods of satisfying it, complete with the aid of donors from outside the human social world, to its fulfillment. Because the wish of the fairy tale is fulfilled a priori, the whole tale is an image of the synthesis of thought and action, desire and reality. The happy ending guarantees not only a feeling of joy and consolation at the end of the tale. Because the positive resolution is necessary for the tale to be what it is, it also determines that each one of the hero's thoughts and deeds, each move in the tale as we follow it, be defined by its value for reaching the goal. Not just any trick or tool will work for the hero; the supernatural helper must be summoned only in certain situations and only in certain ways, and the helper's aid can often only be obtained by helping the helper first. Unlike myth, in which the rules of human conduct are dictated by supernal authorities without much regard for human desire, the correct course of action in the fairy tale is determined by the humanly desired, social end. One might say that the affective–ethical happiness of the end radiates back into the action, encouraging appropriate good conduct in the hero through its influence. In the words

---

31 Bloch and Tolkien, quoted in Jack Zipes, *Breaking the Magical Spell. Radical Theories of Folk and Fairy Tales* (London: 1979), 132–44.

32 Benjamin, *Illuminations*, 102.

of one of the Strugatskys' protagonists, the novelist Banev of *The Ugly Swans* (1967), "the future extends its feelers into the present,"[33] making the future manifest as a point from which the actions and thoughts of the present will be judged. As the hero overcomes obstacles with the help of this influence from the future, he gains in "spirit," the power derived from happiness. Whenever a character in a fairy tale transgresses the rules, and acts in the interest not of the communal end but for personal gain, he or she loses correspondingly in spirit.

As long as they were writing fantasies of post-revolutionary utopian human beings encountering the "external" problems created by nature, the Strugatskys' stories simply assumed that their characters had sufficient spirit to overcome those obstacles. But as their emphasis shifted from the heroic resolutions to the obstacles created by, and within, the human protagonists themselves in their relations with one another and their own psyches, "spirit" itself—its nature and origin in social life—becomes the main problem. Like tale heroes themselves, the Strugatskys seem to have breezed through the early ordeals of representation, only to come upon an unexpectedly new and unnerving obstacle: the dispiriting influence of the "actually existing" alienation of humanity from nature and other human beings … and from the happy ending of human history. We can put the Strugatskys' somber turn in this way: their protagonists gradually begin to think that the obstacles to the happy ending are so ingrained in the human condition that they may not be able to overcome them and still remain human. Consequently, the heroic task—for the protagonists, their authors, and their audience, equally—is to retain the drive for utopia despite its inconceivability in an alienated world.[34]

The theme becomes the classic modernist theme of disillusionment, conceived as the degeneration of the wish—the problems created when the great dialectical fairy tale's hero, Humanity, loses its ability to recognize what it really lacks. Hence *Paradise*'s epigraph from Saint-Exupéry: "There is but one problem—the only one in the world—to restore to men a spiritual content, spiritual concerns."[35] With the degeneration of the wish, the dialectical fusion of theory and practice splits, too. Once the inevitability of the fairy-tale ending is cast into doubt, none of the principals can be sure that the informing wish, and the actions taken to fulfill it, are the right ones. Thought and action become

---

33 A. and B. Strugatsky, *The Ugly Swans*, trans. Alice and Alexander Nakhimovsky (New York: Macmillan, 1979), 2:23–24.

34 Frederic Jameson, "Progress versus Utopia; or, Can We Imagine the Future?" *SFS* 9 (1982): 157.

35 Antoine de St Exupery, *A Sense of Life* (London: Funk and Wagnall, 1965), 1:5.

uncertain, and incapable of bestowing power. The futuristic humanity which the Strugatskys envision after 1964 can no longer think critically. It sinks into apathy and conformity, content with personal satisfactions, while militarism, bureaucracy, and consumerism transform the utopian wish into its parody: the dreary dystopia of war, irrational rationalization, and physical comfort deadening to the intellect. The despiritualized humans of the future lose the power to imagine any good beyond their own personal gain, and thus lose the power to wish for the species' happiness.

3.2 *Breaking Up the Fairy-Tale Paradigm*. The Strugatskys developed a formal correlative for this alienation of theory and practice resulting from the degeneration of the power to wish for the future, by shaking apart the epic wholeness of the fairy tale's form into its parts. These, deprived of the unifying strong force of the happy ending, are separated from one another into distinct narrative "zones."

Each fairy tale is constructed of three fundamental narrative phases, which can be broken down further into associated functions, as in Propp's archetype of the fairy tale. In the initial phase, the lack dominates. This phase depicts an estranged version of the real social world of the reader, whose norms are those of the familiar human universe. The concrete lack it suffers indicates that it is dominated by an extraordinary force. Often, this force imposes on it a cyclically repeated pattern which it is the hero's task to break. The second, mediate phase is the scene of the hero's obstacles. This is the world of enchantment, the "other world," where the laws of nature are different from the human world's. Here the hero acquires the aid of the supernatural beings and engages the villain that has caused the lack in combat. The happy ending, the recuperative phase, is the least concrete of the phases, since it is rarely a locus in its own right. It corresponds to the final synthesis. It restores the lost value to the social world, but with an enormous gain over the initial phase. The happy ending embodies an ontological transformation, a humanly achieved redemption of communal life from alienation.[36] The hero liberates the social world from its earlier condition of being, its helplessness versus the enthralling evil. With this new freedom, the human world and the supernatural world coexist in harmony, won through mutual aid and shared effort. These three phases occur in two complementary loci of the fairy tale; many tales explicitly speak of them as two halves of the same universe. The hero's task is to mediate—to establish a human

---

36 Pierre Maranda and Elli Köngäs, *Structural Models in Folklore and Transformational Essays* (The Hague: 1971), 16.

link between them, and to dissolve the supernatural domination, the magic spell of myth.

The fairy tale is an "unreflective" form. The affective, cognitive, and instrumental interests it represents through its functions are embedded in the structure and not named as such. Even so, individual storytellers usually do provide motivations for the action of their tales. Motivations, or the reasons why things happen in the tale, are the most changeable aspects of the fairytale narrative— so much so that Formalist and Structuralist scholars of the fairy tale deny that it is a defining element.[37] Yet motivations are the propositions with which the tellers reinforce the connection between the tale and the shared culture of the teller and audience. They mark the teller's interpretations of and commentary on the tale, his or her theoretical understanding of the "raw material," which is traditionally viewed as an object with an existence independent of any one telling or any one teller, and thus often requiring interpretation in the teller's cultural context. These theoretical interpretations have counterparts within the tale's action, in the formulaic rules of conduct and address, which the would-be hero must adhere to or face failure and destruction. Such formulaic norms and cautions indicate that the hero must possess or acquire a consciousness of the logic and the ethics of the magical world in order to fulfill his task. They may be vestiges of incantation or ritual speech; in any case, they imply that correct thought is inseparable from correct action. A protagonist acting with bad motives (however the teller may describe them) will necessarily violate the magical norms, and will necessarily fail to achieve the goal. The reverse is equally true. In this sense, the happy ending hypostatizes right thinking and right action as a single state of affective goodness.

The motivations, or rationalizations, of the tale may refer to any of the main spheres of human interest implicit in the tale: the affective bonds and desires of social life associated with the lack, the instrumental rationality associated with the magical tools, and the cognition associated with the protagonists' "education" and understanding of the magical and social worlds.

---

37 Propp's attitude towards motivation is clearly inspired by the Formalist view of the tale as an objective conceptual object. Motivations "belong to the most inconstant and unstable elements of the tale" (Propp, *Morphology*, 75). Arguably, this excludes the very thing that gives a tale communal "life." In my remarks, I have accepted Nagy's view (*A táltos*, 323n54) that Propp's notion that "the verbal motivation is an alien element of the tale" can be traced back to the sketchiness of the archival material with which Propp worked. Lévi-Strauss's strategy (143) is to include motivations among the terms and functions that are ordered "hyper-structurally" by myths.

But the fairy tale teller does not usually make these interests available for reflection and commentary as conceptual objects, a process that might feed back to and affect the form of the narrative. Hence Bakhtin's notion that the forms whose conventional generic structures create the sense of epic wholeness are inappropriate for the novel, which must have a searching form appropriate for its searching content.[38] The fairy tale implies as a generic a priori an indivisible unity of the affective, cognitive, and instrumental aspects of human life. In each step of his career towards the happy ending, the hero embodies their unity, which he realizes for the world at the tale's conclusion. The only alternative to this is the total breakdown of the whole. The misuse of tools, the abuse of affectional relations, and the faulty understanding of the norms involved in the task all lead to failure. It is an either/or condition. In the socialist realist production novel, this unity could be maintained because of the inflexible imperatives of Stalinist ideology: right affection is always embodied in courageous commitment and fidelity to the Party and the people; right instrumentality is always embodied in the completion of the technical project that will build socialism and the nation; and right cognition is always made manifest in *partijnost'*—all of which are aspects of a single Marxist–Leninist utopian completeness.

Beginning with *God*, the Strugatskys broke up the fairy tale's dialectical unity of qualities, which they had emulated in their early works like *Rainbow*, into three separate symbolic "zones" of action that are structurally closely intertwined, but which are held apart by the lack of a unifying resolution provided by the inexorable utopian happy ending. One of these "zones" is the scene of the tale's social reality, the equivalent of the "lack-world." Usually, this image of the real social world of the reader is altered and defamiliarized by social and technological innovations; but it is essentially an allegorical displacement of reality. The second narrative zone is a quasi-"magic circle" where the usual laws of the reality—the norms of the first zone—do not apply and whose principles are inscrutable to the characters. As a result, in this zone the characters are forced to act "in the dark." This is the chronotope of the *novum*, which in the Strugatskys always appears as an actual alien space, usually a "hole," or a fringe, of the real world. These zones function as rationalized versions of the fairy tale's magical realm. The third of the Strugatskys' narrative zones is appropriately "outside" the narrative action, since it represents the alienation of theory. These are zones of reflection which appear in the novels as episodes in which two

---

38 Clark, *The Soviet Novel*, 38.

or more of the characters debate the theoretical implications of the problems raised by the nova of the quasi-magical realms and their implications for the ethical and cognitive life of humanity.

The Strugatskys' fiction of the '60s and early '70s is marked by the gradual inversion of the values the authors assign to each of these narrative zones. In the earlier works—such as *God* and *Paradise*—the zone of displaced social reality is populated by a perverse humanity: the benighted Arkanar of *God*, apparently doomed to deviate from the known course of sociohistorical evolution, and the Country of the Fools of *Paradise*, which appears to have called a halt to its spiritual development in order to luxuriate in material abundance. The magical zone in these novels is represented by the classless, utopian society of the rest of terrestrial humanity, which enjoys the power of advanced moral consciousness. The quasi-medieval Arkanarian rebels view the woods where they observe the helicopters of, and receive money from, the agents of the Institute of Experimental History as an enchanted forest. In *Paradise*, this rationalization of the magical zone is much stronger: the utopian Earth from which the Security Council's agents enter the Country of the Fools is never shown directly. Only Zhilin's responses to the materialistic apathy of the Fools informs us that the rest of humanity has a higher consciousness. Ostensibly, the future utopian society has extraordinary powers. In *God*, these are explicitly confused with fairytale magic—and the defamiliarized versions of contemporary social reality (i.e., Arkanar as the Stalinist USSR; the Country of the Fools as the consumption-intoxicated West) must treat them as a historical *novum*. Because of the enormity of the social, psychological, and spiritual problems besetting these versions of ourselves, the happy ending embodied by the utopian agents cannot practice its encouraging, inspiriting power.

Even more troubling than the present's resistance to what should be its inevitable future—a perversion equivalent to the beguiling of the fairy-tale hero by evil forces—are the implications this has for the future. The dialectical unity of the fairy tale falls to pieces if one stage resists the movement of the whole. Just as *Rainbow*, for all its formal and thematic unity, impresses us as ambivalent because the colonists win their moral victory without recognizing that they have destroyed a surrogate Earth, so *God* and *Paradise* cast doubt on the utopian future. Rumata/Anton's ethical questions about whether to intervene in Arkanarian affairs or not are decided ultimately by accepting the authority of the Institute. Why does Rumata remain so troubled? There appears to be no material-historical reason to fear the developments in Arkanar, since the victory of the revolution is known to be inevitable,[39] even if it is delayed by the peculiar historical conditions there. More importantly, the earthly utopia is so much more powerful and technologically advanced that there can be no reason for it to fear anything that Arkanar does. That would be as absurd as if the gods of Olympus were to fear the history of mortals. But Rumata/Anton's dilemma has more than an ideal, spiritual content; since, in the materialist-realist universe of the tale's discourse, the characters are all human, they are all involved in the same human historical process. Rumata's confusion comes from understanding that either the utopia is infallible in its own right—for instance, the agents are really godlike—or they are just as subject to the unknowns of human history as the Arkanarians. Either they cannot be touched by evil, or they are obligated to fight it. (Perhaps the major flaw of the novel is the imbalance of power between Earth and Arkanar, leading one to question what Arkanar can offer the "Dons" from the Institute comparable to Gorbovsky's opportunity to die his happy death.) The historical subtext of the novel shows the dilemma in glaring clarity: either the historical deviation of Stalinist tyranny is "beneath" the utopian concerns of the future-oriented culture of the '60s—the humanistic Marxism of the European New Left and the reform-minded intelligentsia—and hence need not be irritated into new life, or it is a historical threat to the future that requires ethical engagement in the present.

In the same vein, Zhilin's conclusions in *Paradise*—that few of the council members of his utopian society will understand that the affluenceaddiction of the Fools is not the work of a malevolent conspiracy, but the result of poor choices and poor thought on a mass scale—reflect poorly on his superiors. The initial plot device, the secret investigation of the Country of the Fools, establishes at the outset that the Security Council is more suspicious than enlightened. Zhilin has little hope that the Fools can be educated to take a humanistic perspective—yet he does not feel that they are any less human than himself. Since he has gone among the Fools to help prevent the spread of goods-addiction to his own society, his whole mission raises serious questions about the insecurity of his utopian home—and about the authors' commitment to the inevitability of the approach of utopia. The often-discussed abstractness of *Paradise*[40] may be a result of this vagueness about the status of the would-be donor: for instance, the Security Council and the utopian society it works for.

---

39 *God*, 6:138.
40 Darko Suvin, "Criticism of the Strugatsky Brothers' Work," *Canadian-American Slavic Studies* 6, no. 2 (1972): 300.

By placing the power of the donor in question, the Strugatskys also dissolved the fairy-tale form without constructing an alternative.

The inevitability of the protagonists' right action is guaranteed in the fairy tale by the ending's "reverse influence." This inevitability evaporates when the obstacle resists solutions. It is significant that in these works the Strugatskys published in 1964 and '65, the main characters occupy the position of the magical donors. The position of the hero is occupied by the deviant society. If the agents of the utopian future cannot inspire the present to work for its own future, the tale (and history) becomes mired in the middle.

The Strugatskys' narratives always attempt to mediate this problem by presenting theoretical debates and cogitations in prominent parts of the action. Characteristically, the parties to these meditations (always including the central protagonist) elaborate fundamental ethical positions until it becomes clear that the questions they involve are intellectually undecidable, thanks to the limits of humanity's knowledge of the world. These debates settle nothing except that it is impossible to come to an intellectualconceptual understanding of the social-historical problems. Thus, they repeat the dilemmas of the action in the process of interpreting it.

These bouts of thought, which correspond to the fairy tale's motivations and magical norms, were favorite devices of the Strugatskys even before *God*. They are essential devices in socialist realism as well, although there they are transparently "decideable." But as the Strugatskys' work evolves—beginning with Rumata's dialogue with Budach at the end of *God* on what one should ask of a god—the debates become increasingly complex and painful, as if to illustrate over and over again the '60s' cliché that "truth is complex."[41] Just as the significance of the novels' action becomes muddled, despite the Strugatskys' brilliant and vivid narratives, the debates cast doubt on the ability of thought to comprehend its own historical conditions and problems. The fairy tale's structure is clearly evident in these works, but it too is "in the dark," groping for a way to discover its own inevitability.

3.3 *The Inverted Fairy Tale.* Beginning in 1966, with Kandid's tale in *The Snail on the Slope*,[42] the relationship of the narrative zones changes in the Strugatskys' fiction. Their work begins to show the influence of writers whose main theme is the hero's struggle with insurmountable obstacles: Kafka (whose work appeared

41 *God*, 8:196–98.
42 A. and B. Strugatsky, *The Snail on the Slope*, trans. Alan Meyers (New York: Macmillan, 1980).

for the first time—briefly—in a Russian edition in 1964), Hemingway, Orwell, Lem, Kobo Abe. The Strugatskys seem to have found themselves less and less able to assume, not to say depict, a utopian future based on idealistic projections from the present. Rather than moving away from despotism, the Brezhnev-Kosygin regime had filled the power vacuum of the deposed personality cult with reinforced bureaucratic philistinism. Public support for reform was absent, except among certain segments of the intelligentsia. The mere idea that the present might produce a scientifically adventurous and morally good society seemed the stuff of ideological fantasy. The closest the Strugatskys ever came to its depiction is the magical Research Institute of Thaumaturgy and Spellcraft in *Monday Begins on Saturday* (1966)—tellingly, a fantastic farce in which the utopian beings are magi with benevolent supernatural powers.[43]

In Kandid's tale, the relationship between the magical and real zones reverses itself. The displaced present is represented by the aboriginal villagers of the great Forest. According to Suvin,[44] these simple natives represent the nonintellectual masses who are deprived of their history and information about the radical changes that they are made to suffer in their world. Subjected to various forms of what appears to be telepathic mental manipulation, they are incapable of reflecting on their past, and seem doomed to repeat their customs and thoughts incessantly. Even so, they demonstrate human compassion, by healing the pilot Kandid after his helicopter crash and absorbing him into their social structure. The world of the *novum* is represented by the "Splendid Maidens," parthenogenic, telepathic Amazons who are apparently the products of a drastic evolutionary transformation. These "Maidens" gradually assimilate the native women of the Forest, usually by forcible abduction. Meanwhile, they subject the Forest to inscrutable and cruel engineering projects that radically alter the Forest's topography and climate. Possessing a new mental power to control organic matter and even to create new forms of life, the Maidens have no compassion for the old order of the analytical, male-dominated bureaucracy, which they are bent on destroying.

Kandid's strange tale cannot be boiled down to a univocal culturalhistorical referent. In one sense, Kandid represents the intelligentsia, which, finding itself in an unintelligible Forest of social life, must choose between solidarity with the unreflective and stupefied masses or serving an immensely powerful new

---

43 A. and B. Strugatsky, *Monday Begins on Saturday*, trans. Leonid Rene (New York: DAW, 1977).
44 "Introduction," 16.

order hostile to the intelligentsia.[45] Kandid feels the choice is already made for him: for the Maidens he can only be a tool, at best, while for the villagers he can be a protector. The historical process may favor the Maidens, but the ethical demands of compassion and solidarity require him to protect his villagers. The most significant change from the earlier works is that the zone of the displaced present society is the world of muddle-headed, helpless villagers; and the *novum*, far from being the utopian future congruent with classical humanistic visions, belongs to the cold, inhuman Maidens, whose grandiose projects and brutal tactics evoke comparisons with Stalin's experiments in crash industrialization and mass collectivization.

The theory-zone in Kandid's tale is also new and strange. Like the natives, Kandid finds it difficult to maintain a train of thought from one moment to the next. Only in the concluding pages does he understand his situation clearly ... and there is no assurance that he will maintain that clarity of thought. Parallel to his journey to escape the Forest and return to the Directorate is his journey to understand the mysterious forces transforming the Forest and his place in that alien world. The process of interpretation is extremely difficult. The villagers are unintelligible because they cannot remember the past in a rational pattern. The Maidens are inscrutable because their minds are apparently so different from the human that they are functionally "aliens." Kandid's own mind is also numbed by the Maidens' mental jamming. Consequently, the debates and dialogues are barely coherent attempts to find a common ground of thought. Kandid makes his decision at the end of the tale to stay with the villagers— at least until he can escape the Forest—not on the basis of clear authoritative imperatives like the rule of nonintervention in God. Lacking clear information, Kandid discovers he must choose on the basis of his own human understanding of right action, even if he is an evolutionary atavism.

In Kandid's tale, the fairy tale's happy ending is replaced by resistance to the ending. The historical happy end appears to be reserved for the new evolutionary prodigies, for whom the human villagers are merely pesky obstacles. For Kandid, and for the humanity he feels obliged to defend, the obstacle is the scene of life—a happy end for the human species is almost too much even to imagine. And as the happy ending is thus "alienated" by being bestowed on the alien Maidens, the qualitative dimensions of the fairy tale are also deprived of their coherence and separated from one another. Although he is a scientist, Kandid is deprived of cognition. He has no way to process the information he

---

45 Ibid., 12.

acquires. He makes his choice to protect his villagers on the basis of affection for the community that nurtured him. On the other side, the Maidens' world does seem whole: their affective bonds among one another are extremely strong; their instrumentality is enormously powerful and made in the feminine image (or at least in the Strugatskys' conception of archetypal feminine qualities); and their scientific cognition is clearly "other," and more powerful, than the Directorate's science of "dead things."[46] It is whole ... but wholly unintelligible to humanity.

In two of the later fictions, *The Ugly Swans* and Pepper's half of *Snail* (1968), this inversion of values becomes even more marked. Pepper's tale is pure muddle: every significant term shifts its meaning, as if resisting all obligations to be a dependable representation. The displaced present is the Kafkaesque Forest Study and Exploitation Authority, "The Directorate," a maze of bureaucratic absurdities just as inscrutable as the bizarre natural phenomena of the Forest it is supposed to study. In Pepper's tale, the Directorate is an image of contemporary scientific work, simultaneously too rigidly anthropocentric to respect the mysteries of the material world and too bureaucratic to make any headway in controlling it for human use. Neither Pepper's actions (which essentially go around in circles) nor the Carollian dialogues he participates in (which he can never comprehend, even though he is a professional linguist) can escape from the inertia of the Directorate. His questioning of the Directorate is eventually resolved when he discovers that he has been made Director, and finds he has been placed on the "administrative vector" which is "the basis of all else" and "has its base in the depths of time."[47]

In *Swans*, the reversal is complete. The zone of the displaced present is a wretched provincial town, where the exiled novelist Victor Banev and his circle of convivial drunks waste their lives in the Big Brother-like regime of "Mr President." The zone of the *novum* is the leprosarium, where the "slimies," evolutionary prodigies similar to, but considerably more sympathetic than, the Amazons of *Snail*, are collected to do scientific research for Mr President's military-industrial complex. These slimies are the "ugly swans" of the title—making explicit the fairy-tale origin of the book. In the tale itself, the motif of the Pied Piper crops up several times to motivate the slimies' apocalyptic transformation of history; they take all of the town's children with them into the evidently paradisal future of their own creation, liberating them from their unworthy parents. In *Swans*, the evolutionary prodigies are redemptive, not destructive. They save

---

46 *Snail*, 8:185.
47 Ibid., 10:230.

the future generations of humanity even while they destroy the irreversibly corrupt present. The novel's protagonist, Banev, like Kandid, "understands nothing" except the importance of decency and the need to wish for utopia.[48] Banev is one of the few adults assimilated to the winners of historical evolution. But the new world is probably not for him. The slimies act as donors who magically liberate the human children. In the end, however, *Swans* is weaker than Kandid's tale, for the slimies' gift of liberation comes without any significant human participation. The liberated children are not questing heroes; they are creatures of the slimies' education. In our terms, then, the point of the novel is that the utopian transformation—even if it is a glorious one—is alien and inconceivable. It may not be benevolent to humanity as humanity knows itself. Banev has such strongly divided loyalties—both to the weakness of human beings and to the strength of the slimies—that he remains an outsider in both worlds, with no power to create a world which he would willingly be "inside of."

4.1 Roadside Picnic. The themes and techniques of the Strugatskys' fiction I have been discussing culminate in *Roadside Picnic*, one of the most significant works of recent SF.[49] It is a fable of the despair of the '60s' intelligentsia facing the complete destruction of the reform movement, which was betrayed—as the fable has it—not so much by the Brezhnev regime, as by the moral-spiritual conditions which made that regime possible: the inertia of the masses in a world undergoing a convergence that is a bitter parody of the one Sakharov had hoped for in his memorandum of 1968. This is the convergence of Eastern and Western ennui, the fruit of global acquiescence to purely material satisfactions and the abdication of all higher moral purposes—the victory of "realism" over utopian idealism.

The novella tells of the aftermath of a "Visitation" by mysterious extraterrestrials to the imaginary Canadian town of Harmont (along with four other unidentified spots on the globe), where they stayed for a few hours invisible to human beings. Their arrival was attended by several nonfatal cataclysms. When they departed, they left behind a sharply circumscribed area filled with mysterious, and often dangerous, objects and phenomena, and named the "Zone." As the world gradually quarantines the Zone and its incomprehensible reality, the "treasures" of the Visitation are leaked from it and used to create commodities

---

48 Swans, 10:187.
49 A. and B. Strugatsky, *Roadside Picnic*, trans. Antonina W. Bouis (New York: Pocket Books, 1978).

and weapons. The backbone of the story is the ambiguous Pilgrim's Progress of Red Schuhart, an uneducated but fiercely proud and loyal "stalker," who smuggles forbidden objects out of the Zone to sell to underworld fences. Red returns grudgingly to the perilous Zone again and again to support his family, and to escape from the dreary, apathetic life of the social world to the intensity of the Zone. In a desperate attempt to find a miraculous way to reverse the degenerative mutation of his only child (which is an effect of the Visitation), Red ultimately goes on a murderous quest to the heart of the Zone, searching for a Golden Ball that the superstitious stalkers claim will grant one's dearest wishes. When he reaches the Ball, he is forced to think for the first time in his life about his place in the world and the way the world should be. In the end, he can only utter a wishprayer to the powers he believes lie behind the Ball: "HAPPINESS FOR EVERYBODY, FREE, AND NO ONE WILL GO AWAY UNSATISFIED!"[50]

Picnic is the Strugatskys' most polyvalent and ambiguous work, but its narrative strategy is quite lucid. The tale systematically dislodges each element of the fairy-tale paradigm from its conventional whole and inverts it. Each moment and function of the tale is alienated from its conventional issue, and as a result the whole fairy-tale form is inverted.

In one of the best commentaries on *Picnic*, Stanislaw Lem contends that the realistic elements of the tale, which make it an admirable "experiment in the philosophy of history," are gradually devoured by elements of the "black fairy tale."[51]

There is no question that among the Strugatskys' works, *Picnic* is the most obviously bound to the fairy tale's universe of discourse, and this relationship is not concealed. Fairy-tale motifs appear explicitly in the narrative itself, almost always in "black" versions. The stalkers are given to identifying the Zone with "Pandora's box"[52] and the mysterious artifacts as the treasure of the *1001 Nights* brought by the Visitor-genie.[53] The Zone is "the hole into the future,"[54] a place without time,[55] the path to the other world: "The further into the Zone, the nearer to Heaven," say the stalkers, only half ironically.[56] These fantastic

---

50 Ibid., 4:153.
51 Lem, *Microworlds*, 275.
52 *Roadside Picnic*, 2:90.
53 Ibid., 1:35.
54 Ibid., 1:37.
55 Ibid., 1:30.
56 Ibid., 1:17.

identifications are easily rationalized in the realistic manner of the tale, for the uneducated stalkers are notoriously superstitious. But there are also episodes that support these identifications without irony. Red's foray into the Zone with the Institute for Extraterrestrial Cultures' research scientist, Kirill Panov, at *Picnic*'s outset is a version of *Hansel and Gretel*. As a sort of zero-degree scientist, Red determines a safe course and the location of a deadly "graviconcentrate" by tossing metal nuts and bolts ahead of the expedition's car. Their vehicle then follows the path laid out on the return trip to the Institute. The Zone itself is depicted as a rationalized version of an enchanted region, where the grass is a black bramble and shadows extend in the wrong direction.[57] Inside it is the "treasure"—a rare artifact left by the Visitors—in a sinister garage, "guarded" by monsters: in this case, a pool of "witches' jelly" and the mysterious silvery web that causes Kirill's death. The opening foray is repeated in even more overtly fantastic form in Red's climactic quest in chapter 4.

In the novella's design, the deployment of the chapters imitates—still in an inverted, "black" manner—the formal construction of the tale of the three wishes. Each of the three chapters of Red's tale is built around an implicit or explicit wish, each of which boomerangs, leading to a profound loss (thus inverting the fairy tale's conventional ultimate gain). The action of the first chapter begins when Red wishes to dispell Kirill's depression about his inability to understand the Visitors' technology. Red offers to bring Kirill "back to life" by leading him to an extremely rare artifact, known to the stalkers as a "full empty." The tactic works for a short while: "Kirill came back to life before my eyes."[58] Once in the Zone, however, Kirill proves to be too clumsy and confident in his institutional insulation to see the dangers of the garage; and Red is too accustomed to working alone to think of protecting Kirill at every step. Kirill accidentally entangles himself in a web of which he never even takes cognizance. Thus, Red's wish to revive Kirill leads instead to Kirill's death.

The second chapter's theme is Red's wish to provide his wife and mutant child with a stable middle-class life. After the Institute begins to use robots for exploring the Zone, Red is unable to survive on his lab assistant's pay. He turns to stalking again, but he insists on maintaining some independence from the criminal gangs that smuggle objects out of the Zone to sell to governments and the private laboratories. This wish for independence and dignity also boomerangs when he is betrayed to the police by a former accomplice. To

57   Ibid., 1:19, 26.
58   Ibid., 1:9.

support his family while he is in prison, Red agrees to sell a jar of "witches' jelly"—which even the Institute's research scientists are forbidden to study—to a gang supplying the military-industrial complex.

The concluding chapter centers on Red's desperate wish to find a miracle that will return his daughter to human form. This wish gradually transforms itself into the utopian prayer that closes *Picnic*, leaving the outcome suspended in the reader's imagination.

Only by discounting the drastic ambiguity of *Picnic*'s ending can one maintain that it is simply a "black" fairy tale. For no fairy tale, not even a parody of one, can support an ambiguous ending. Instead, *Picnic*'s movement through the "black" universe of the inverted fairy tale to an open ending restores the fairy tale's utopian form as a trace, if only in the possibility that Red's utopian wish might be fulfilled. If Lem were right, if *Picnic* were a bitter satire of the fairy tale's naïveté, then the narrative would assume, at least implicitly, a moral superiority to the form on which it otherwise depends "parasitically." This superiority would be based on "realism," the satirist's knowledge of the way things "really" are. But far from devaluing the ideal form (i.e., the tale of the successful wish for the heart's desire), *Picnic* attacks the "reality" corrupting the heart so that it no longer can wish for its own happiness. This structural irony is in the romantic tradition: there is no appropriate form for human desire other than the fairy tale, but the fairy tale is impossible in the age of science, space travel, and Visitations by extraterrestrial travellers. Consequently, each of the conventional elements of the fairy tale is grotesque—caught midway in a Manichaean universe, between the archetypal form of desire and the "graviconcentrates" of valueless realism. *Picnic* thus demands to be read not as an inverted fairy tale, but as an ambivalent or "meta" fairy tale—demanding that its readers move with it through a reality emptied of freedom to a radical and self-conscious restatement of the uncertainty necessary if the utopian hope is to be conceived at all.

Taken together, these considerations show *Picnic*'s originality and richness, and the enormity of the distance the Strugatskys traveled between *Rainbow* and *Picnic* without ever abandoning the fairy-tale paradigm completely. Had the Strugatskys consciously set out to subvert each element of *Rainbow*, they could not have done so more thoroughly than they in fact did in *Picnic*. For example, *Rainbow* takes place on a distant planet voluntarily inhabited by a population that willingly accepts the hegemony of the zerophysicists. The heroism of the protagonists of *Rainbow* would have been impossible on a less abstract, lyrical world. So many more of the victims of the Black Wave would have been innocent of zero-physics that the scientists' sins against them would have been unmanageably great. Moreover, the children's rescue required an Earth they could be sent to, a home base with which the zero-physicists could reestablish connections that they had broken in their impatience to break through the limits of Nature. In a sense, *Rainbow*'s action occurs so high up in the ideological superstructure that it does not even threaten the base of species existence. The important thing—as Gorbovsky informs us—is to save the sense of the future, by saving the children. The link between the Black Wave and zero-science is unambiguously direct—which allows the tale to depict a closed moral circle of sin-retribution-release.

In *Picnic*, by contrast, the action is not only earthly, it is *earthbound*. The Visitation—which the novella's scientific *raisonneur*, the Nobel laureate Pilman, calls the greatest event in human history—does not interest the masses in the least. The scientists of the Institute, for their part, are the opposites of the zero-physicists. Far from having a new theory of space-time that might humanize the cosmos, and a planet to expend on testing it, the Institute's xenologists are flummoxed by the Visitation which has intervened in their world. They have "systems of equations, but no way to interpret them."[59] In a sense, the Visitation deprives the Institute's researchers of what theory they previously had. They can do no more than pragmatically fit various artifacts into the everyday life of the consumer society; they have no idea how to penetrate into the essence of the objects, since they do not know the first principles necessary to test them. While *Rainbow*'s zero-physicists work out their superior science detached from the problems and inertia of social history, the characters of *Picnic* live in the dreary middle of existence, unable to see out of their own world even after they have been given sure signs that other worlds exist.

The heroes, too, contrast sharply. Gorbovsky comes from the sky without earthly social obligations and with a mind unclouded by doubt. He assesses the situation clearly, recognizes what must be done, provides the proper tool for doing it, and deduces the correct sentiments from the Rainbow colonists. Red, on the other hand, lives in a perpetual muddle, exerting all of his prodigious energies in a losing struggle to make ends meet for himself and his family and to maintain his dignity and personal autonomy in a corrupt world. His life is a depressing search for the tools, the clear thinking, and the right wish that will solve these problems. In *Picnic*, it is the Alien that comes from the sky, not the *homo ex machina*. There is no other home to escape to.

---

59 Ibid., 3:109.

The most poignant inversion—and in the Strugatskys' symbol system, the most significant—has to do with the fate of the children. The zerophysicists' children are saved in the nick of time; the scientists realize that the future of the species takes precedence over all other considerations. *Picnic*'s difference from *Rainbow* could not be made sharper. Red's child is born with animal eyes and "covered with a silky golden fleece";[60] her parents affectionately name her "Monkey." Although at first she is bright and garrulous, she gradually devolves literally into a beast, unable to recognize her parents or to speak a human language. At the other pole, the evil gang leader Buzzard Burbridge's stunning daughter, Dina—whom Burbridge claims was one of the wishes the Golden Ball fulfilled for him—is so callous and hateful that Red considers her "a plastic fake, a dummy."[61] Where the human protagonists of *Rainbow* accept the need for sacrifice and their own historical responsibility to protect their descendants, in *Picnic* it is *bellum omnia contra omnes*—and "every man for himself, only God takes care of everybody."[62]

4.2 The Alienation of the Paradigmatic Elements. To account for the tale's artistic strategies and its intellectual force, we must study the way in which the Strugatskys develop their system for breaking up the epic wholeness of the socialist realist fairy-tale paradigm. The subversion is already evident in the fragmentation of the narrative into five sections (including the short introductory interview with Pilman). This technique departs from the unity of action and the free-indirect narrative focus on a central character that was the Strugatskys' typical technique after *Rainbow*. Three of the sections are phases in Red's dark quest. The other two center on Pilman. The fragmentation is not drastic. The breaks between periods of Red's life are appropriate for depicting its increasing desperation as it grows from the faint utopian hopefulness in chapter 1 to the murderous drive of the conclusion.

The separation of Pilman's discussion with Noonan (about the nature and effect of the Visitation) from Red's story in chapter 3 also departs from the Strugatskys' usual practice of making the "theory zone" an important moment in the plot of the central protagonist, usually occurring at a moment when he must articulate the various interpretations of the events in which he is taking part. The discussions are necessary to show that the hero has at least understood

---

60 Ibid., 2:66.
61 Ibid., 4:127.
62 Ibid., 2:85.

some of the affective-ethical implications of the *novum*'s intervention in reality, even when the situation can never be fully understood cognitively. Red, who alone in *Picnic* might be in a position to fulfill the hero's mediating function, does not participate in the conversation with Pilman. He does not learn, as the reader does, the various scientific hypotheses about the Visitation. Nor does he hear Pilman's own jocoserious hypothesis, the one privileged by the title.

The distance between Pilman and Red is very great. They never meet—again a departure from the Strugatskys' usual technique of bringing all the main characters face to face. They have, in a sense, nothing to say to each other. The Zone has left theoretical reason, represented by Pilman, impotent and baseless, while human affections, represented by Red, are driven more and more intensely by the need to find a justification in the world. The penultimate chapter (Pilman's talk with Noonan) and the final chapter (Red's final quest) are two versions of the same problem, in which Red and Pilman are mired in different ways. Noonan realizes that the scientists are especially afraid of going down "into the pit":

> They're afraid, too, he thought ... The highbrows are also scared. And that's the way it should be. They should be more afraid than all us regular folks put together. We don't understand a thing, and they understand how much they don't. They look into the bottomless pit and know that it's inevitable, they must go down into it. Their hearts catch, but they must go down, and descend they do, but how, and what will they find at the bottom, and most important, will they be able to climb out?[63]

Red, for his part, cannot wait for science to determine whether it will ever understand the Visitation. He drives on into the Zone—"the hole into the future"—unable and unwilling to think about his actions until he reaches his goal, the Golden Ball.

The alienation of the tale's structural elements from one another creates a fairy-tale form in which the central elements are left so ambiguous that they are functionally mysterious. *Picnic* deforms the paradigmatic form of the fairy tale, so that the protagonists and the reader do not know for certain what the lack is, who the donors are, and what must be done with their magical gifts. Its ending is so far from happy that is not even the opposite—it is simply "off the page."

---

63 Ibid., 3:115.

The alienation of the paradigmatic elements embodies the alienation of the qualities of "the whole life" from one another. There are actually three separate stories in *Picnic*. Each seems to proceed oblivious to the others' existence, each representing the fate of one of the dominant human interests when it is alienated from the others. Red's story represents the fate of purely affectional existence; Pilman's, of purely cognitive existence; and the Visitation, of the purely technical. The ideal social and individual life requires the interdependence of all three of these qualities, each of which is impotent or destructive when left on its own. Red's utterance of the utopian prayer-wish at the end of the novel constitutes a moment when these three qualities come together for the first time.

4.3 *Pilman: The Alienation of Cognition.* In the Strugatskys' work, the theoretical discussions in which motivations for the fantastic phenomena are proposed always involve the application of dialectical rationality to problems that until then have been conceived superstitiously or monologically. The data they are meant to rationalize are almost always too strange to be adequately explained. Still, in the Strugatskys' cosmos the effort to think dialectically is clearly necessary to sustain humanity's desire for freedom and its adaptability to the *nova* it may encounter. The burden of thinking dialectically in *Picnic* is carried by Pilman alone—and this narrative tactic casts doubts on the vitality of dialectical thought in Harmont's lack-world. In their other works, the Strugatskys' central protagonists are usually scientists who often double as romantic explorers or secret agents. (The exceptions are the linguist Pepper of *Snail* and the writer Banev of *Swans*—and scientific theorizing plays a very slight role in those works.) *Picnic* is unique among the Strugatskys' major works in that the scientific theorizing is extremely important for the action, but the central figure is a completely uneducated man.

Pilman's discussion with Noonan about the Visitors has a prominent place in the book, and Pilman's list of the hypotheses that have arisen to explain the Visitation is a tour de force. Because of this, and because the Strugatskys' other works assign philosophical dialogues a central place, some commentators view Pilman as equal to Red Schuhart in dramatic importance. But Pilman must be seen in context, in relation not only to Red, but to the only other scientist in the tale, Kirill Panov.

Kirill, made careless by his enthusiasm for creating the conditions for utopia, runs straight into the dangers of Zone. Pilman avoids the Zone's danger altogether. He knows he can offer no testable hypotheses. The Roadside Picnic theory is not, as he makes clear to Noonan, a scientific idea at all, since it is based on an obviously anthropomorphic moral analogy. He knows that none of the scientists studying the Zone can be considered natural scientists any longer, since xenology—the study of alien intelligence and civilizations—is a spurious science, based entirely on anthropocentric identifications.[64] Since the Visitors were intentional beings, rather than natural phenomena, their behavior cannot be understood without understanding their motives and minds. Humanity can know only that the Visitation happened and that humanity has responded to it by ignoring it, going on with its business as usual. Pilman is not superior morally because he maintains a cool, ironic distance from the business of the Zone. As he tells Noonan, there is a chance that the dissemination of the Zone's artifacts may be disastrous for the whole world; but he is not in a position to do anything about that. His skeptical open-endedness does not take him any further towards restoring spirit to the world than Kirill's utopian enthusiasm—or even Red's desperation.

Pilman thus represents the irremediable alienation of cognition and theory from the active, irresponsible life of the post-Visitation world. He contemplates with equal serenity the idea that human reason is an evolving reflex, which, when it is fully developed, may make humanity inflexible and vulnerable to all dialectical changes of quality in the cosmos,[65] and the highly unscientific sentiment that humanity's greatness lies in its ability to survive all of its attainments.[66] Pilman seems to be equally prepared for new knowledge gleaned from the Visitation and passive survival of the effects of the Visitation's objects entering human society. Pilman is a scientist with no science to do. His business is with surviving the Visitation. He is a scientist who has of necessity become an experimental metaphysician.

Compared with Red, Pilman is a talking head. He is attractive precisely because his complex observations are purely intellectual, and he is not mired in the mud of life. But in *Picnic* the mud of life is augmented by the Zone's objects until it becomes the equivalent of *Rainbow*'s black wave, threatening to inundate everything else. Pilman is no more in the position to be a moral authority than the "Wavists" of *Rainbow*, who coolly observed the behavior of black waves while ineffectually opposing the zero-t experiments. Red's conversion at the end of the tale comments on this. When he is transformed by his despair,

---

64 Ibid., 3:105.
65 Ibid., 3:106.
66 Ibid., 3:108.

he is changed, not into a Pilman-like skeptic, but into the desirer of the heart's desire, the discoverer of the principle of hope.

4.4 The Visitation: The Alienation of Instrumentality. The central mystery of *Picnic* is the identity of the Visitors. It is tempting to accept at face value Pilman's assessment that the Visitors cannot be known if they do not choose to show themselves, and to leave the question of their identity suspended. But how one interprets the ending of *Picnic* cannot be separated from how one interprets the Visitors. I believe that the usual interpretations of the ending (i.e., that Red's final prayer-wish is a sign of his defeat) have been influenced by a too-easy bracketing of the Visitors.

It is indisputable that the Visitors are similar to human beings. Lem has pointed out that the stalkers need no tools to break down the Zone's objects— proof that the objects are on a human scale.[67] Pilman rigorously holds, nonetheless, that we cannot know anything about the Visitors from these traces alone, since we cannot escape importing our anthropocentric projections into every hypothesis. But as readers we are not limited to the same facts as Pilman. We know that the fictive facts, and the hypotheses that the fictional characters concoct to explain them, are not real responses to events in the history of science, but analogies. We treat the quasi-hypotheses and quasi-data as significant because of their metaphorical

character and the pattern that the authors used for generating them. We expect that that pattern of analogy will be relevant to the writer's social and psychological concerns, rather than mere formal imitations of the history of science. So we must go beyond Pilman and examine whether the Visitors might be more familiar to us as readers of metaphorical SF than they are to Pilman as a skeptical and conservative scientist. Anthropocentric projection is not something a reader of SF can avoid; it is the basis for making sense of the fiction.

In the fairy tale, the lack/curse is dissolved by the hero with the help of the donor's magical tools. The association of the Zone's objects with magical devices (Pandora's box, Aladdin's lamp, and the wish-fulfilling pearl) invites us to place the Visitors in the position of the fairy tale's supernatural donor. As usual in *Picnic*, this fairy-tale motif is ironically inverted: the curse on the lack-world, rather than being removed, is augmented by the ironic superabundance of potentially mediating magical "gifts." The Visitors have left behind artifacts that clearly might teach humanity a great deal about the universe. Some of

---

67 Lem, *Microworlds*, 265.

them stimulate life-processes; others seem to create inexhaustible supplies of energy; still others may function according to as yet unimagined conceptions of space-time. Kirill hopes that the objects will behave in an appropriately fairy-tale/utopian way: that understanding the new science of the artifacts will give humanity rational control over nature by abolishing scarcity, which he evidently assumes is the root cause of human oppression. But in the fairy tale's cosmos, the donor's gift can never be "accidental" or in damaged condition (as Lem speculates the Visitation's objects may be[68]). Even when the donor is invisible or disguised, its "donation" is always an intentional gift or reward, establishing a link between worlds.

The donor's gifts are the guarantees of reciprocity. They prove the intentional-moral connection of the social lack-world and the enchanted world, between human desire and the forces of nature. But only traces of the Visitors exist, in the magic tools, and these come without operating instructions. Because they are objects without subjects, they have no intentional value. They are deprived of any signs that might give humanity an idea of their purpose and moral charge in a cultural system—even if only in the alien culture of the Visitors. That knowledge might at least create a cultural cusp, an overlapping zone for elaborating similarities of socio-technical and cultural behavior. But "gifts" deprived of purpose are only signs of otherness. There is no way to use them for transforming human consciousness—or even to know whether or not they are destructive "Satanic temptations," as the counter-stalker Gutalin believes.[69] In *Picnic*, the element of address and encounter—the words exchanged between magical beings and the hero that establish the connection of the human with the cosmos—is completely lacking. The Visitors evidently desired no encounter, no contact; and in this they are apparently doubles of humanity. Neither side is interested in the other. Indeed, whatever the Visitors may be, they are similar enough to humanity to emphasize their otherness. By not making themselves known to the conscious beings on the earth who are inferentially so much like them, the Visitors have actually refused contact.

Because there is no new structure of values to accompany the Visitation's objects, nothing prevents them from being absorbed by the structure already in place. That assimilation is inevitable . . . and perversely appropriate. Their traces fit naturally into the web of instrumental reason, commodity production, and exchange that dominates the lack-world. In the modern world that Red resents

---

68 Ibid., 326.
69 *Roadside Picnic*, 1:39.

so deeply, it is precisely the desire to use science and technology to create a greater human subject—for instance, a species consciousness overcoming alienation—that is lacking. Like the silvery web that kills Kirill, the Harmont lack-world is a web of objects no longer controlled by human subjects.

Red alone resists this enchantment, until the very end. Until then he considers the Zone's artifacts only as means for creating affective happiness: the "full empty" is for "reviving" Kirill, the swag is for supporting his family, the "witches' jelly" for tiding them over while he is in jail. But by the end, the man who formerly would save the life even of his worst enemy is willing to kill an innocent young man to reach the Golden Ball. This can be interpreted as Red's capitulation to the hopelessness of the world, his enchantment.[70] But we can also read it as the recognition on Red's part that there are no "pure spirits," especially in a world dominated by objects. Indeed, Red's need to make his wish to the Golden Ball is the ultimate expression of the need to compel the tools to serve the deepest human desires, "the wishes that, if they're not granted, it's all over for you."[71]

One reason why the Visitors are absent is that the Visitation itself is an image of the scientific-technological explosion, a process that has increasingly come to seem "subjectless"—an impersonal, indifferent, objective evolution blindly operating according to its own runaway feedback, autonomous of the human desires that created its conditions. The dangers the extraterrestrial artifacts pose to human society are clearly the same as those posed by the irrational military and commercial use of contemporary terrestrial technology. The demoralization they augment is the demoralization of contemporary societies. Pilman's Roadside Picnic theory thus refers not so much to the landing of extraterrestrials as to the way humanity in the contemporary world uses its own technology—as if it, too, were an alien species that might wish at some future time to fly from a blasted zone of its own making. The Visitation is the catastrophic intervention of humanity's own image of the future into the present: it is "what we will be like." The Enlightenment's dream of humanity evolving into a fully rational species becomes a grotesque parody in the aftermath of the Visitation. Humanity is, instead, in danger of becoming a fully *rationalized* species. Pilman at one point wonders whether its reason may not ultimately become a destructive trait in the long run of the species' evolution.[72]

---

70 Simonetta Salvestroni, "The Ambiguous Miracle in Three Novels by the Strugatsky Brothers," *SFS* 11 (1984): 30.

71 4:132.

72 3:106.

In Harmont, as in contemporary civilization increasingly alienated by the technology on which it depends, rationality becomes a grotesquely external- ized object capable of dominating and enervating its own subject.

Read in this way, *Picnic* demonstrates the Strugatskys' complete disillu- sionment with the technocratic utopianism of the *Rainbow* period, and with it the hopes the Soviet scientific intelligentsia entertained about the power of the STR to transform Soviet society. In fact, the Brezhnev regime, fearing the revolutionary effect of science on social theory (demonstrated unam- biguously by the central place the theory of the STR occupied in the Czech program of "humanizing socialism,"[73] repudiated the technocratic theories of socialist development and returned to the traditional authoritarian position that the political system is to guide the development of science.[74] In terms of the Strugatskys' thematics, this means that the technology of the modern age develops "on its own," out of human theoretical control, since neither capital- ism nor the Soviet state will guide it in the best interests of the species.

In other words, the identity of the Visitors is left a mystery primarily because they are not only like us, they are us: they are our image of our own future. The Strugatskys have used the theme of the "return of the future" in many of their works. In the last tale of the 1967 edition of *Noon: 22nd Century*,[75] "What You Will Be Like," Gorbovsky relates to his fellow starpilots how he was once visited in space by one of our descendants, who fixed his ship for him and explained his presence as a gesture of gratitude and confidence-building directed to the past from its own future.[76] The same idea is implicit in *God*, although in a darker tone: the narrative wishes to leave us in no doubt that Arkanar will ultimately reach the classless utopian state enjoyed by the ter- restrial agents of the Institute of Experimental History. Hence, the presence of the agents on Arkanar should be enough to build morale. In *Monday*, the idea appears whimsically. The young magi of the Institute of Thaumaturgy and Spellcraft speculate that there exist "countermovers," beings who travel back in time from the future. They explain the Tungus meteor crater as the result of the landing of one of the countermoving spaceships.[77] The main protagonist of

---

73 See Buccholz, "The Role of ... Revolution," 159.
74 See Linda Lubrano Greenberg, "Soviet Science Policy and the Scientific Establishment," *Survey* 17 (1971): 62.
75 A. and B. Strugatsky, *Noon: 22nd Century*, trans. Patrick L. McGuire (New York: Collier- Macmillan, 1978).
76 Ibid., 318.
77 *Monday*, 206.

Swans, Banev, is explicit: in a table speech to his drunken cohorts, he ironically exhorts them to help "prevent the future from extending its feelers into the present."[78] Later, he calls the village's children "phantoms from the future."[79] The "return of the future" is so constant a motif in the Strugatskys' fiction that one can argue that it is the underlying premise of their work. They write SF to create images of the future which "return" to influence behavior in the present, by creating a model with which to place the present in perspective. When it is a positive image, it accords with both utopia and the fairy tale—exaggerating the best qualities of humanity in the present and encouraging people to continue to struggle for happiness. But when the mediation is blocked, the future returns as an image of the present stripped of "spirit." And that is what the Visitors are.

The landing, with its blasted Zone and its quasi-psychopathological effects,[80] corresponds to the shock of the STR, of which we are the unconscious

---

78 *Swans*, 2: 23–24.

79 Ibid., 5:77.

80 In the period between 1964 and 1972, but especially after 1966 with *Snail*, the Strugatskys often depict deformations of reality made to resemble the deranged perception of schizophrenic thought. Their protagonists stand in a gulf separating two hostile worlds, each of which is defined by the alien and hostile structure of its space. In *Snail*, for example, Pepper is trapped in the Directorate's Kafkaesque world of labyrinthine space, while Kandid is trapped in the grotesque fluidity of the Forest. The Strugatskys generally identify the real with what Lukács called "the unbridgeable 'maleficent space' of the present" extending between subject and object in the reified perceptual universe of capitalism (in Joseph Gabel, *False Consciousness* [New York: 1975], 149). In this reified reality, no significant and permanent change in relations is possible without the intervention of a *novum*. This intervention usually has the characteristics of what is classically known as *Weltuntergangserlebnis* [WUE] (or "world catastrophe syndrome") familiar among schizophrenics (Ibid., 288–96). The WUE is always experienced as a heteronomic disruption of a reified world. It can be either catastrophic or redemptive, the complete destruction of the individual's perceived world or the eruption of value into a valueless world. The main point is that it is always heteronomic, and thus analogous to the *novum*. The Strugatskys' protagonists often feel they are involved in a general WUE, and try their best to link it to a dialectical causal chain. Kandid experiences the Forest as a limitless, ever-changing entity that cannot be structured as a totality. The Amazon-like Maidens exert their superior force through a "fluidification" of reality: by controlling oozing saps, fogs, and atmospheric humidity; by the flooding and swamping of villages, ostensibly to create environments for a "mermaid world"; and by reproducing parthenogenically in steaming amniotic lakes. The theme of the dissolution of the reified real through catastrophic fluidity appears also in Swans, where the "slimies'" first significant act is to produce an incessant rain that ends only after their apocalyptic victory.

As with schizophrenics, the disruption of the overstable space is usually identified with "aliens"—beings with magical/superior powers with which they are able to save the trapped subject or, more often, to exert invisible, hostile influences. This projection of magical essences onto human beings—which Gabel (119–36) argues underlies racist

precisely in the utterance of the wish. In Red, the valuegiving subject contracts into one desperate, uneducated man holding an object that combines the most advanced extraterrestrial artifact with the most primal human wish-fulfilling tool. It is absolutely spare, since it is the only object left with any meaning, and absolutely full, since it glows with the hope of the whole human species. It is the true "full empty." The suspended conclusion also implies that the question of whether the transformation of social reality into a utopian tale can be realized is not articulable. Left alone with Red's wish, the reader must also participate in Red's exit into the ball, out of the narrative and into personal commitment or moral death. The authors leave the responsibility for the resolution with the reader, to whom Red's *de profundis* is, in the last analysis, addressed.

4.6 The Last Fairy Tale. This reading of *Picnic* differs from most others because it accepts the possibility that Red's wish could come true in the world of the tale, and that this possibility accords completely with the ambiguous manner in which *Picnic* is constructed. Critics as different as Salvestroni and Lem agree that Red's wish is likely to fail. Lem holds that the Golden Ball is the subject of "a naïve belief, one of those popular legends which rose up in the wake of the visit."[87] Salvestroni is sure that the "grace" Red desires "more likely than not will not come."[88] For my part, I believe that the internal evidence of the tale directs the reader to suspend judgment about whether Red's wish-prayer will come true, and by the same token, to entertain the fairy-tale structure of motivations far more seriously than as a mere "naïve belief." The open-endedness of *Picnic* is radical precisely because it requires the reader to entertain possibilities "off the page" of a world as different from the one depicted in *Picnic*'s Harmont as the apocalyptic utopia that concludes *Swans* is.

Lem recognizes that the fairy-tale elements are important for *Picnic*, but he takes them to be inconsistent with the "thought-experiment in the domain of the 'experimental philosophy of history'" that he considers the most valuable quality of the tale.[89] The Golden Ball must not grant wishes as long as the tale is a realistic thought-experiment. If it can grant wishes, the tale has jumped the track into arbitrary fantasy. Lem also believes that "the Strugatskys by no means desired" the novella's similarity to the fairy tale. I gather Lem bases a good deal of his interpretation on correspondence with the Strugatsky brothers, who have

---

87 *Microworlds*, 275.
88 "Ambiguous Miracle," 301.
89 *Microworlds*, 260.

apparently agreed with him on many points (see *Microworlds*, 276; and "The Profession … ," 49).[90] But I believe I have shown that the fairy-tale manner of *Picnic* cannot be considered unintentional in any serious sense. There are too many motifs and structural allusions to the fairy tale, and too few unambiguously realistic moments in the narrative, to justify an exclusively naturalistic interpretation. It is not the sudden introduction of fairy-tale motifs that jars the reader in chapter 4, but the foregrounding of elements that had been in the background in the preceding chapters. And if we view the Visitors not merely as a new version of "alien monsters," but as a symbolic projection of humanity's own alienated technological evolution, the apparent conflict between the "impartial" SF mode and the partisan fairy-tale mode dissolves.

Picnic can be read as a generic criticism of the kind of SF that takes science to be all there is. In the first place, Red is placed in a position that makes science impossible. He is not only uneducated and superstitious, he is also unprotected by the social prestige of institutional science or the laws of bourgeois society. He lives his life in the underworld: the underworld of social life; the Zone, a clear symbolic displacement of Hell; and the psychic underworld of depression, disillusionment, crime, and finally murder. Viewing these aspects together, Red's journey corresponds to the hero's journey through the alienated world, in search of the lost treasure. Pilman's ideas are pure angelisms here. They cannot affect Red, since they do not create value. Red's path—and *Picnic* as a whole—leads to the heart of despair. The only hope remaining is that one can get through despair to the other side. Whether such a transformation can take place the tale leaves in suspense. But whatever the outcome, the fate of the whole fictional world—Red, Monkey, Harmont, the earth—have fused in Red's wish, focusing on the last possibility for reintegration.

The narrative is not only the "vehicle" for this symbolic quest for the happy ending; it, too, is fused into the suspended resolution. Just as Red abandons all hope in reality and his ability to isolate himself from the corruption of Harmont, the narrative gradually casts away more and more of the realistic structure of intelligibility, and its pretense of value-neutrality. Just as Red has had to wander from the initial utopianism represented by Kirill through a labyrinth to the wish that embodies everything Kirill had desired, the narrative also wanders from the initial expedition into the Zone, with its many fairy-tale motifs, through a world of aimless hypotheses and unintelligible reality-effects, to recapture the

---

90 See *Microworlds*, 276; and Stanislaw Lem, "The Profession of Science Fiction: XV: Answers to a Questionnaire," *Foundation* 15 (1979): 49.

fairy tale's value-centeredness. The Strugatskys in *Picnic* inverted the elements of the fairy-tale paradigm in order to pose the possibility of their sublation—the negation of their negation—to a new level of hope in happiness represented by the happy ending. Of course, the tale's conclusion only allows the possibility. A less ambiguous ending would be intolerably trivial. The task of the narrative's journey has been to create the conditions under which the happy ending might be entertained again in a world that has made the conditions for its emergence almost impossible.

When we view *Picnic* in this light, it is clear that the fairy-tale structure, far from being an error, is the dominant subtext of the narrative. The Strugatskys tie the outcome of the tale to one's ability and desire to hope for the happy ending. That is the sine qua non of liberation from the species' subjection to its own creations; without that first desire, the tale of the species has nowhere to go.

5. *After Roadside Picnic.* With *Picnic*, the Strugatsky brothers appear to have exhausted the possibilities that the deformed fairy-tale paradigm offered them. In the early '70s, the critical debate in the USSR surrounding the Strugatskys' "pessimistic" SF was at times uncomfortable for them, sometimes involving highly placed official critics. It was apparently resolved in favor of a semiofficial compromise. In Suvin's opinion, the Strugatskys recognized that this "coexistence" of the older, orthodox, neo-Stalinist mode of SF and their own social-philosophical and critical SF had "fairly clear bounds," and that the Strugatskys "have for the time being recognized such boundaries and are keeping within them."[91]

Even before the publication of *Picnic*, the Strugatskys had returned to the detective/secret agent/adventure romance mode of the *Noon* tales, *God*, and *Paradise*, with *Prisoners of Power*[92] and "Space Mowgli,"[93] both first published in 1971. In those tales, the estrangement of reality is held within strict limits. Their worlds are, for the most part, extraterrestrial, humanoid, and fully rationalized, and the earthly human protagonists again take on the role of problematic donors from a utopian, classless society. In "Space Mowgli," we even see a resurrected Gorbovsky.

91 "Criticism," 304–5.
92 A. and B. Strugatsky, *Prisoners of Power,* trans. Helen Saltz Jacobson (New York: Collier-Macmillan, 1978).
93 A. and B. Strugatsky, *Escape Attempt* [A volume including "The Kid from Hell," "Space Mowgli," and "Escape Attempt"], trans. Roger Degaris (New York: Macmillan, 1982).

Since *Picnic*, the Strugatskys have published relatively few works. The most important of these are *Definitely Maybe* (1976)[94] and *The Beetle in the Anthill* (1980).[95] The former belongs in a class of its own with regard to its generic paradigm, combining elements of the open-ended detective story with a satirical fantasy. *The Beetle* is a reprise of many of the Strugatskys' themes of the '60s. It is primarily a detective tale whose protagonist—the secret agent of *Prisoners of Power*, Maxim Kammerer—searches for the agent Abalkin, who, although ostensibly completely human, had originally emerged from an egg left by the mysterious, cosmos-traveling Wanderers. Whether Abalkin is a superhuman "time-bomb" set by the Wanderers or whether he is a potentially beneficent superman, no one knows—least of all Abalkin himself, who is a generous, sensitive man suddenly discovering his own mystery. In the end, he is destroyed "just in case," leaving Maxim with oppressive doubts about the ethical courage of his species. Many of the elements of *Picnic*'s deformed fairy tale flicker in *Beetle*. The title itself evokes Pilman's conception of humanity in the Zone as the insects swarming over an abandoned picnic site. But these elements are completely submerged by the foregrounded detective plot and Maxim's ceaseless cogitations. The Strugatskys' brilliant gift for depicting enchanted alien worlds appears for only a moment in *Beetle*, in Abalkin's memories of the blasted planet Hope, whose children are beguiled away by the unseen Wanderers through mysterious gateways, in a dark variant of *Swans'* Pied-Piper motif. Until the Strugatskys bring us more new worlds, we cannot be sure that their latest works represent the end of their critical SF or a new phase of it.

---

94 A. and B. Strugatsky, *Definitely Maybe*, trans. Antonina W. Bouis (New York: Macmillan, 1978).

95 A. and B. Strugatsky, *The Beetle in the Anthill*, trans. Antonina W. Bouis (New York: Macmillan, 1980).

Tarkovsky, Solaris, and Stalker

STEPHEN DALTON

Dalton, Stephen. "Andrei Tarkovsky, Solaris and Stalker: The Making of Two Inner-Space Odysseys." The BFI. December 31, 2014. http://www. bfi.org.uk/features/tarkovsky/. Accessed February 27, 2017.

Andrei Tarkovsky was not a fan of science fiction. When pressed on the subject, the grand master of Soviet Russian cinema dismissed the SF genre for its "comic book" trappings and vulgar commercialism. The son of a poet, Tarkovsky was an uncompromising visionary who dreamed of making films that combined the devotional majesty of medieval icon painting, the symphonic beauty of Bach and the moral weight of Dostoevsky. Even so, Tarkovsky still happened to make two of the most revered and visually ravishing SF epics in the modern cinematic canon. Bookending the 1970s, *Solaris* and *Stalker* are epic inner-space odysseys with more in common than just the same director. Both were based on cult novels. Both share key cast and crew members. And both are cryptic cautionary fables about men who boldly go to the outer limits of human knowledge, where they encounter alien entities that can read their minds and grant their deepest desires. So be careful what you wish for.

A deeply religious man who believed great art should have a higher spiritual purpose, Tarkovsky was an exacting perfectionist not given to humour or humility. His signature style was ponderous, verbose, and literary. But he turned to science fiction almost as career salvation, to get himself out of a fix with the Soviet film authorities. *Solaris* came about after his previous feature *Andrei Rublev* had been denied a domestic release, while his next submitted script was deemed too bourgeois and personal by the doctrinaire ideologues of Goskino, the USSR State Committee for Cinematography. That screenplay was shelved, later to resurface as *Mirror*.

Instead, Tarkovsky proposed a film version of Polish author Stanislaw Lem's philosophical 1961 SF novel *Solaris*, reasoning that a futuristic thriller set on board a remote space station would prove populist enough even for the censorious commissars of Soviet cinema. He was right. A small-screen adaptation had already aired on Russian television, which also helped his pitch. Endorsed by Lem, the director and Fridrikh Gorenshtein completed their first script in 1969, shifting two-thirds of the action to Earth. But the changes angered both Lem and the Mosfilm studio committee, so Tarkovsky produced a second draft more faithful to the novel. The project received official approval from Goskino in the summer of 1970. Lem's compact novel begins with psychologist Kris Kelvin arriving on a space station floating close to the surface of Solaris, a planet covered by a vast sentient ocean with the disturbing power to read human minds and reproduce perfect copies of their deepest memories, like a giant 3-D printer with the godlike ability to replicate life itself. Sent to assess whether the station should be closed down, Kelvin is thrown into emotional turmoil when confronted with a doppelganger of his ex-wife Hari, who committed suicide years before.

Tarkovsky's film diverges from Lem's space-set yarn with a long preamble set on Earth. Played by the brawny, soulfully brooding Lithuanian actor Donatas Banionis, Kelvin is introduced in an idyllic country landscape as he bids farewell to his parents at their lakeside dacha. These languid close-up shots of water and nature are pure Tarkovsky, recurring like musical motifs through his body of work. At the dacha, Kelvin also consults with Berton (Vladislav Dvorzhetsky), a discredited astronaut who once witnessed disturbing hallucinations on the surface of Solaris. The retired spaceman later sends further cryptic warnings via videolink from his car as it speeds through an ultra-modern city, which is nameless but clearly shot in Tokyo. Like *Blade Runner* a decade later, *Solaris* takes contemporary Japan as a template for the high-tech urban future. Switching between color and monochrome, this long and largely wordless sequence is set to Eduard Artemyev's ominous electronic score. This again is classic Tarkovksy: hypnotic vistas unfolding at real-time speed in lengthy, unbroken shots.

Arriving on board the shabby and battered space station, Kelvin finds the surviving human crew to be obstructive and erratic. But his own coolly rational self-belief is soon shaken when Solaris sends him an uncanny double of his late wife Hari (Natalya Bondarchuk). Kelvin initially manages to eject the phantom from the space station, but Solaris keeps conjuring up further copies, exacerbating his long-buried guilt over her suicide. Given a second chance, he tries to save Hari, but the tragedy repeats itself over and over. At this point, the story spills over from scientific puzzle into psychological horror movie. "True horror is in having to watch someone you love destroy herself," writes author and critic Philip Lopate in his liner notes to Criterion's deluxe 2011 DVD release, stressing the thematic parallels between *Solaris* and Hitchcock's *Vertigo*: "the inability of the male to protect the female, the multiple disguises or resurrections of the loved one, the inevitability of repeating past mistakes."

Adding an extra frisson of autobiography, Tarkovsky initially planned to cast his ex-wife Irma Rausch as Hari. He then changed his mind, signing Swedish star Bibi Andersson, former muse to his directing idol Ingmar Bergman. But finally he settled on Bondarchuk, the young Russian beauty who had first introduced him to Lem's novel. Hari's death scenes gained extra resonance in 2010 when Bondarchuk revealed she had an affair with Tarkovsky during the shoot, and attempted to kill herself after they split in 1972. One of the sly ironies of *Solaris* is that the human visitors come to study Solaris, but the planet ends up studying *them*. Dense with scientific speculation, Lem's novel is essentially about the impossibility of communicating with any alien life forms that mankind might find in deep space. But the film is a much more personal story about guilt, shame and the search for some divine pattern at work in the cosmos. As usual with Tarkovksy, the story takes on an explicitly religious dimension.

Lem disliked Tarkovsky's interpretation, accusing him of making *Crime and Punishment* in space. But there is crossover between book and film. A scathing speech by one of the station's crew appears in both: "We don't want to conquer the cosmos, we want to extend the boundaries of Earth to the cosmos. We are only seeking Man. We don't want other worlds, we want mirrors." While the novel ends on an ambivalent note, the film has one of the most haunting final twists in SF cinema. Crushed by guilt and grief over Hari, Kelvin returns to his parents in the idyllic country house seen in the opening scenes—but this comforting illusion is just a giant replica created by the planet-sized brain of Solaris. It looks like home, but Kelvin can never go home again. "The characters in *Solaris* were dogged by disappointments, and the way out we offered them was illusory enough," Tarkovsky later wrote in his cinematic memoir *Sculpting in Time*. "It lay in dreams, in the opportunity to recognise their own roots—those roots which forever link man to the Earth which bore him. But even those links had become unreal for them."

Predictably, the first cut of *Solaris* provoked the Soviet censors, who ordered Tarkovsky to remove all references to God and Christianity. The director stood his ground, only conceding to minor edits. He was rewarded with his first international breakthrough hit, winning the Grand Jury Prize in Cannes and earning a cult following in the west. At home in Russia, the film stayed on limited release for fifteen years, selling more than 10 million tickets. Moscow's propaganda machine hailed *Solaris* as a superior Soviet riposte to *2001: A Space Odyssey*. Tarkovksy was certainly scornful of Stanley Kubrick's psychedelic SF epic, calling it "a lifeless schema with only pretensions to truth," devoid of depth or human emotion.

"For some reason, in all the science-fiction films I've seen, the filmmakers force the viewer to examine the details of the material structure of the future," Tarkovsky told Russian film journalist Naum Abramov in 1970. "More than that, sometimes, like Kubrick, they call their own films premonitions. It's unbelievable! Let alone that *2001: A Space Odyssey* is phoney on many points even for specialists. For a true work of art, the fake must be eliminated." Such fighting talk was partly standard Cold War rhetoric, of course, and partly the egomania that drives most great film directors. On reflection, Lopate claims in his Criterion essay, the rival cosmic visions of Kubrick and Tarkovsky actually have much in common. "Hindsight allows us to observe that the two masterworks are more cousins than opposites," he writes. "Both set up their narratives in a leisurely, languid manner, spending considerable time tracking around the space sets; both employ a widescreen mise-en-scène approach that draws on superior art direction; and both generate an air of mystery that invites countless explanations." But nothing dates faster than yesterday's vision of the future, of course, and Tarkovsky's space opera has not aged as gracefully as Kubrick's. The garish interior of the Solaris space station, designed by Mikhail Romadin, now looks alarmingly like an Austin Powers bachelor pad. The churning ocean beneath—made with acetone, aluminium powder and dyes—also radiates a threadbare Hammer Horror cheapness. Ironically, Tarkovsky's earlier films still feel more timeless and contemporary than *Solaris*, perhaps because the director treated the futuristic setting like a superfluous detail.

"Unfortunately the science fiction element in *Solaris* was nonetheless too prominent and became a distraction," Tarkovsky wrote in *Sculpting in Time*. "The rockets and space stations —required by Lem's novel—were interesting to construct; but it seems to me now that the idea of the film would have stood out more vividly and boldly had we managed to dispense with these things altogether." Later in the decade, Tarkovsky would return to his dream of a philosophical SF epic that transcended genre entirely. His final domestic feature before exiling himself to western Europe was *Stalker*, freely adapted from the 1971 novel *Roadside Picnic* by the brothers Arkady and Boris Strugatsky, a dark satire which had been heavily censored by the Soviet authorities.

The book takes place in a fictionalised western country around one of six special Zones left behind after extraterrestrials briefly visited Earth en route to another galaxy. Inside the Zones, potentially deadly disruptions in the normal cosmic rules occur, confronting brave visitors with their true selves and granting their deepest wishes. There is a great disturbance in The Force. Initially working with the Strugatskys, Tarkovsky penned his first screenplay for *Stalker* in 1976. Stripping away much of the SF elements, he replaced the alien backstory with a more opaque astronomical explanation for the paranormal Zones. The plot revolves around a single journey led by a professional Zone infiltrator—the stalker of the title—and his two soul-weary companions, Writer and Professor. Tarkovksy cast the angular, intense Alexander Kaidanovsky as Stalker, plus *Solaris* veterans Anatoly Solonitsyn and Nikolai Grinko as his fellow travellers. *Stalker* would become the most tortuous and troubled production of Tarkovsky's career, a drawn-out ordeal which may even have hastened his early death. Initial locations were scouted in Tajikistan, but a powerful earthquake made that shoot impossible. Further searches in Uzbekistan, Turkmenistan, Azerbaijan, Georgia, Ukraine, and Crimea proved fruitless. Tarkovsky eventually found new locations in the Baltic state of Estonia: a dilapidated ship repair yard, a crumbling hydroelectric station, an abandoned oil processing plant and other postindustrial ruins around the capital Tallinn. Shooting exteriors in Estonia during spring and summer of 1977, Tarkovsky and his cinematographer Georgy Rerberg used a new Kodak 5247 stock supplied by Berlin-based producer Sergio Gambarov. But on return to Moscow, they found the processed footage was an unwatchable shade of dark green. Months of work had been ruined by technical error or, as the director suspected, sabotage.

"Tarkovsky was certain the film was swapped," the film's sound designer Vladimir Sharun told Moscow newspaper *Komsomolskaya Pravda* in 2001. "This newer Kodak which Gambarov sent specifically for *Stalker* was stolen and in some way or another ended up in the hands of a certain very well-known Soviet film director who was Tarkovsky's adversary. And they gave Andrei a regular Kodak except that nobody knew about this and that's why they processed it differently. Tarkovsky considered it a result of scheming by his enemies. But I think it was just the usual Russian sloppiness." This disaster was the final straw for Rerberg, who walked off the film, never to return. With his state-funded budget in jeopardy, a devastated Tarkovsky was initially reluctant to continue. A minor heart attack in April 1978 seemed to confirm his superstitious fears that the project was cursed. But he recovered and eventually came up with a smart solution, persuading the film board to finance a new, longer, two-part version of the script. Thus, *Stalker* evolved from dystopian road movie to somber spiritual quest.

Filming resumed in Tallinn in June 1978, with Alexander Knyazhinsky behind the camera. But there was further on-set friction when a freak summer snowfall delayed the shoot. According to Sharun, cast and crew filled the long, empty days in their run-down suburban hotel with epic binge-drinking sessions. Some even got wasted on cheap cologne mixed with sugar. A furious Tarkovsky ended up sacking several crew members, branding them "drunks," "cretins," and "childish degenerates." He even fired his art director Shavkat Abdusalamov for the glorious offense of "behaving like a bastard."

Finally completed in 1979, *Stalker* stands up today as probably Tarkovsky's most beloved, enigmatic, and endlessly absorbing film. It remains a strikingly beautiful and uncanny viewing experience, containing some of the director's most experimental innovations. The soundtrack is more avant-garde *musique concrete* than music, with clanking mechanical ambient noises woven into Artemyev's minimalist electronic score. The blighted landscape outside the Zone is mostly filmed in gorgeous sepia-tinted monochrome, while inside bursts with lush greens and warm brown earthtones. Nobody makes dank, rusting, postindustrial decay look quite as pornographically seductive as Tarkovsky. The film is also layered with echoes that spoke directly to Cold War audiences thirty-five years ago, and still resonate today. Kaidnovsky's gaunt, shaven-headed Stalker instantly invokes familiar imagery of the emaciated inmates of the Soviet Union's Gulag prison camps. Indeed, the character is an ex-convict who embodies the bitter irony that real freedom lies *behind* the barbed wire of the Zone, not within his country's rulebound borders: "for me, it's prison everywhere," he says. Anybody living behind the Iron Curtain would have felt the biting subtext.

But Tarkovsky always resisted the "wild conjectures" of viewers looking for deeper metaphorical and political meanings in *Stalker*. "People often ask me what the Zone is, and what it symbolises," the director wrote in *Sculpting in Time*. "The Zone doesn't symbolise anything, any more than anything else does in my films; the zone is a zone, it's life, and as he makes his way across it man may break down or he may come through." After a thriller-like first half, the film moves into more ruminative mood in its final hour. Deep inside the Zone, Stalker and his bickering fellow travelers suddenly get cold feet as they approach the mystical Room where our deepest wishes allegedly come true. While Writer agonizes about his mediocre and shameful occupation, Professor contemplates destroying the miraculous Room with a nuclear bomb to prevent it falling into the wrong hands. Stalker merely berates his companions for their cowardice and uncertainty: "you're not even capable of thinking in abstractions."

This feels like Tarkovsky preaching directly to his audience: the artist as messianic seeker of truth, berating the so-called experts for their spiritual short-comings. "The Stalker seems to be weak, but essentially it is he who is invincible because of his faith and his will to serve others," Tarkovsky explains in *Sculpting in Time*. "Ultimately artists work at their professions not for the sake of telling someone about something, but as an assertion of their will to serve people." These religious undertones surface again during the closing scene, in which Stalker returns to his long-suffering family. His wife (Alisa Freindlich) gives a resigned monologue direct to camera about how she has devoted herself to her single-minded husband, despite the pain and disappointment she knew it would bring. In the cryptic final shot, the couple's sickly daughter (Natasha Abramova) moves three glasses across the table using psychic powers. After Stalker's fruitless magical mystery tour inside the Zone, it seems the real miracle has been waiting at home all along.

This bewitching twist was sparked by Tarkovsky's interest in Ninel Sergeyevna Kulagina, a superstar psychic famed in Soviet Russia for her telekinetic powers. "Tarkovsky believed in miracles, no question," Vladimir Sharun told *Komsomolskaya Pravda*. "He firmly believed in the existence of flying saucers and he even claimed he saw one near his home in Myasnoe, in the Ryazan province. Tarkovsky wouldn't allow any doubts in the existence of extraterrestrials. Incidentally, it all harmoniously combined with his faith in God. He knew the Gospels of St. Matthew and St. Luke practically by heart and could quote whole paragraphs." Inevitably, *Stalker* caused the obligatory tensions with Moscow's cinema Tsars. Goskino advised Tarkovsky to make the film faster and more dynamic. With defiant wit, he replied that it should be "slower and duller at the start so that the viewers who walked into the wrong theater have time to leave before the main action starts." Winning the Ecumenical Jury Prize in Cannes, *Stalker* sold 4.3 million tickets in the Soviet Union and became an evergreen cult movie in the west, where critics hailed it as a Cold War political allegory, and even a Russian cousin of Francis Ford Coppola's *Apocalypse Now*.

Tarkovsky shot his final two features as an exile in the west. He left the Soviet Union behind, and never returned to science fiction. But he did express an unlikely admiration for James Cameron's *The Terminator*, claiming "its vision of the future and the relation between man and its destiny is pushing the frontier of cinema as an art." In December 1986, Tarkovsky died of lung cancer in Paris. He was just 54. The same illness had already killed his favourite leading man, *Solaris* and *Stalker* co-star Anatoli Solonitsyn, and would later also claim his wife and directing assistant Larisa Tarkovskaya. Sound designer Vladimir Sharun believes all three were victims of the deadly *Stalker* shoot in Tallinn, just downstream from a toxic chemical plant. After the collapse of the USSR, a fanciful conspiracy theory emerged that the former KGB boss Viktor Chebrikov engineered Tarkovsky's death as punishment for his increasingly anti-Soviet views, but this remains pure speculation.

However negative his views on science fiction, Tarkovsky enriched and elevated the genre, inspiring others to follow suit. Steven Soderbergh directed a slick but dramatically inert remake of *Solaris* in 2002, starring George Clooney as Kelvin. Christopher Nolan's 2014 blockbuster *Interstellar* includes a veiled homage, when Matthew McConaughey's astronaut hero returns from the cosmic void to find his wooden farmhouse home recreated on a space station high above Earth. Other recent films including *Contact, Sunshine, Another Earth, Gravity* and *Arrival* all share some DNA with Tarkovsky's cerebral, metaphysical SF classic. The film has also inspired stage plays, musical compositions and visual artworks like Dmitry Morozov's *Solaris* project, a bowl of green liquid gloop that responds to human brainwaves.

The ravishing ruin porn of *Stalker* left its own deep cultural legacy. Its powerful disaster-zone aesthetic helped spawn an entire subgenre of dystopian future-shock thrillers, from Lars von Trier's *The Element of Crime* to David Fincher's *Alien 3* to John Hillcoat's *The Road*. Von Trier later dedicated his high-art horror movie *Antichrist* to Tarkovsky. With hindsight, some commentators later hailed *Stalker* as a cinematic prophecy of the 1986 Chernobyl meltdown and the collapse of the Soviet Union generally. Launched in 2007, the Ukrainian postapocalyptic computer game *S.T.A.L.K.E.R.* picks up the Chernobyl theme, overlaying it with key elements from Tarkovsky's film. The enduring cult of *Stalker* seems to renew itself for each generation. As recently as 2012, the film was remade as *Zone* by Finnish director Esa Luttinen, satirized by the late Russian auteur Alexey Balabanov in his darkly surreal comedy *Me Too*, and lovingly deconstructed by British author Geoff Dyer in his playful 2013 memoir *Zona*. "The Zone is a place of uncompromised and unblemished value," Dyer writes. "One of the few territories left—possibly the only one—where the rights to *Top Gear* have not been sold."

Andrei Tarkovsky's immersive inner-space odysseys are equal parts pretentious and transcendent, maddeningly slow and spellbindingly beautiful. But like any Old Master leaning over his canvas, Tarkovsky understood that any mission to unlock the miracles of the heavens above begins with a search for intelligent life on Earth.

RESOURCES:

1) Philip Lopate essay from the Criterion DVD of Solaris:
   http://www.criterion.com/current/posts/239-solaris-inner-space
2) Some visual art inspired by Solaris:
   http://www.bjarre.org/works/solaris.html
3) A mind-reading art installation named after Solaris:
   http://www.wired.com/2014/10/a-mind-reading-mirror-that-reflects-your-emotions-inspired-by-solaris/
4) Footage of the famous Russian psychic who inspired the last scene of Stalker:
   http://www.youtube.com/watch?v=xGy_wgWvge0
5) Last scene of Stalker:
   http://www.youtube.com/watch?v=dNiVFCWMrqI

Part Four

Futures at the End of Utopia

Viktor Pelevin and Literary Postmodernism in Soviet Russia

ELANA GOMEL

Gomel, Elana. "Viktor Pelevin and Literary Postmodernism in Soviet Russia." *Narrative* 21, no. 3 (2013): 309–21.

Back to the USSR?

Postmodernism rose to prominence on the ruins of utopia, the utopia in question being the Soviet one. Of course, the disintegration of the USSR occurred later than the formation of postmodernism as a cultural dominant (variously dated to the '60s, the '70s, or even the early '80s). But there is no doubt that disillusionment with the Soviet experiment contributed to what Fredric Jameson called the "incapacity to imagine Utopia" as a significant feature of Western postmodernism.[1] In his 1994 book, *The Seeds of Time*, Jameson laments "what has vanished from the postmodern scene," which is the distinct "Second World culture" whose distance from "commodity fetishism" made it into a viable alternative to global capitalism.[2] According to him, with the collapse of the Soviet Union, this alternative has been foreclosed and postmodernism now reigns supreme over the increasingly homogenous cultural landscape. From this point of view, Russian postmodernism is a Western

---

1 Fredric Jameson, *Archaeologies of the Future: The Desire Called Utopia and Other Science Fictions* (London: Verso, 2005), 293.
2 Fredric Jameson, *The Seeds of Time* (New York: Columbia Univ. Press, 1994), xvi–xvii.

import, an imposition of the "cultural logic of global capitalism" upon the erstwhile socialist country.

It is true that the rise of postmodernism in Russia coincided with the end of Communism. In the spring of 1991 a conference on postmodernism took place in the Literary Institute in St. Petersburg and after that, with Soviet censorship removed, the trend became the cultural dominant almost overnight. Acknowledging this coincidence, Russian literary scholar Mikhail Epstein has an explanation for it that is radically at odds with Jameson's. He argues that rather than being a Western alternative to the "Second World culture," postmodernism is a direct continuation of it[3]: "I believe that the similarity between postmodernism and Communism is not accidental; the two represent two phases of the same ideological and aesthetic project in Russia."[4]

This striking claim implies that Russian postmodernism, despite superficial similarity to its Western counterpart, is in fact an expression of a different social, political, and cultural dynamic. Perhaps the homogenizing capacity of global capitalism has been exaggerated; perhaps the "cultural logic" of post-Soviet Russia depends as much on the unresolved issues of its national history and identity as it does on the more familiar processes of market economy and technological development. If indeed utopian disillusionment has been foundational to postmodernism, the country whose attempt to build a utopia resulted in a national catastrophe has experienced this disillusionment in a different way than those watching from the outside.

In this paper, I will argue that what Foucault calls "the epistemological figures" of Soviet civilization[5] are central to Russian postmodernism.[6] The carryover of these figures into a different sociocultural reality is a symptom of historical trauma, or rather, the trauma of the reentrance into history.

Russia underwent a series of violent upheavals throughout the twentieth century, but for the duration of the USSR, these upheavals were subsumed into the teleological master narrative of building a utopia. The collapse of the Soviet system was, as Russian scholar Vladimir Loskutov argues, "not only our return

---

3 Unless otherwise indicated, all the translations from the Russian are mine.

4 M. N. Epstein, *Postmodern v russkoi literature* [Postmodernism in Russian Literature] (Moscow: Vysshaya shkola, 2005), 68.

5 I will refer to the seventy-three years of the existence of the Soviet Union not as a historical "mistake" of an oppressive tyranny but as a cultural and social entity with its own distinct articulations of such basic concepts as humanity, nature, time, space, and so on. Perhaps the best way to describe this period is by using Foucault's concept of the episteme.

6 Michel Foucault, *The Order of Things: An Archeology of the Human Sciences*, trans. A. M. Sheridan Smith (New York: Random House, 1974), x.

to history but our acquisition of history."[7] The sensibility that has resulted from this "return to history" is different from the timelessness and anomie of Western postmodernism; it is characterized by a need to process the lessons of the failed utopia and to integrate them into a new national narrative. It is not the "inability to imagine utopia" but rather the ability to remember it too well that has shaped Russian postmodernism.

Despite its capitalist economy, Russia is still living in a particular kind of "post," which is not reducible to the general malaise of postmodernity: "A strange aspect of the post-Soviet situation in Russia and other former republics of the USSR is that, almost two decades after the disintegration of the old state, they still remain and identify themselves as post-Soviet."[8] What Jameson calls "the rudiments and nascent forms of a new socialist culture" did not disappear overnight simply because the political structure changed.[9] These forms have persisted in Russian postmodernism as ghosts of an undead utopian narrative haunting new stories and histories. But it is precisely their presence that makes Russian postmodernism, in contradistinction to its Western counterpart, uniquely sensitive to the problematic of time and history.

The collapse of what Susan Buck-Morss called the "dreamworlds" of utopia "shattered an entire conception of the world on both sides" of the Iron Curtain.[10] But if in the West it has created what Jameson describes as "a society bereft of all historicity,"[11] in postcommunist Russia it has resulted in a society obsessed with regaining history and time. Epstein's argument that (Western) postmodernism and Soviet Communism were in some sense alike hinges on their timelessness: according to him, in the last decades of the USSR, time "lost its linearity and became locked in the cycle of repetition ... the future has been brought into the present."[12] And with the end of this "eternal present," Russia found itself back in a history it did not recognize. It is not surprising, then, that despite many similarities, Russian literary postmodernism is both structurally and thematically different from its Western counterpart. It is the postmodernism of historicity, exploring the many postmodern spaces in search of lost time.

7 Vladimir Loskutov, *Postsovetskii totalitarism* [Post-Soviet Totalitarianism] (Ekaterinburg: Uralskaya akademiya gosudarstvennoi sluzhby, 2006), 18.
8 Boris Kagarlitsky, *Back in the USSR* (London: Seagull Books, 2009), 1.
9 Jameson, *Seeds*, 77.
10 Susan Buck-Morss, *Dreamworld and Catastrophe: The Passing of Mass Utopia in East and West* (Cambridge, MA: MIT Press, 2000), x.
11 Jameson, *Postmodernism*, 18.
12 Epstein, 88–89.

Vitaly Chernetsky cogently argues that there is no single planetary postmodernism but rather a cluster of related phenomena, which express, in different ways, "the waning of the utopian impulse."[13] In the postcommunist world, the failure of utopia has become part of (mis)remembered history, whose exploration serves to foreground the issues of national identity, totalitarian violence, and social cohesion. It is a *temporal* postmodernism, as opposed to the spatial postmodernism of the West. Rather than suffering from amnesia, the Russian literary avant-garde seems to be in the grips of a post-traumatic stress disorder.

In this essay, I will focus on the writer universally recognized as one of the chief practitioners of postmodernism in Russia today: Viktor Pelevin. Pelevin's work has been called "the most essentially 'postmodern' of contemporary Russian prose."[14] The author of *Omon Ra* (1993), *Chapayev and Void* (1996), *The Sacred Book of the Werewolf* (2005), and most recently *S.N.U.F.F.* (2011), in addition to a number of short stories and novellas, Pelevin, through his edgy use of science fiction, cyberpunk, metafiction, pastiche, and playful self-referentiality, has been categorized alongside Italo Calvino, William Gibson, Haruki Murakami, and other internationally known postmodern writers. At the same time, his writing cannot be understood outside the context of the traumatic memory of the Soviet period: "While chronologically most of Pelevin's writing falls in the post-Soviet era, his thematic concerns signal the determination by the late-Soviet cultural condition as the key aspect of his work."[15] Since I cannot do justice to the entirety of Pelevin's complex and challenging work here, I will analyze in detail several representative texts as epitomizing both structural and thematic features of post-Soviet postmodernism. This analysis will engage three axes of postmodernism: space, simulacrum, and subjectivity.

Space and/or Time

In Pelevin's 1993 novella "Zheltaya strela" ("The Yellow Arrow"), the protagonist Andrei lives on an infinite train endlessly going across an Eastern-European-style terrain. The passengers believe that "there is nothing but the

---

13 Vitaly Chernetsky, *Mapping Postcommunist Cultures: Russia and Ukraine in the Context of Globalization* (Montreal: McGill University Press, 2007), 10.

14 Sally Dalton-Brown, "Ludic Nonchalance or Ludicrous Despair? Viktor Pelevin and Russian Postmodernist Prose," *Slavonic and East European Review* 75, no. 2 (1997): 216.

15 Chernetsky, *Mapping Postcommunist Cultures*, 107.

train" despite the evidence of the insipid landscapes going by.[16] Life on the train is shabby, ugly, and crowded, ending with the window-burial as dead bodies, along with assorted rubbish, are tossed outside. Andrei attempts to solve the ontological mystery of his world by contemplating gnostic ideas of multiple demiurges, peering into the "afterlife" through his car's windows, and eventually deciding he wants to "get off the train alive," which he accomplishes at the end as the train unaccountably stops.[17]

Impossible spaces are a staple of postmodernism; at first sight, "The Yellow Arrow" seems to belong with such texts as J. G. Ballard's "Report on an Unidentified Space Station" (1982) and Adam Robert's *On* (2001), both crafting fictional worlds with non-Newtonian topologies.[18] Brian McHale describes such worlds as "designed ... for the purpose of exploring ontological propositions."[19] Jameson sees these "ontological propositions" as symptoms of the underlying spatiality of the postmodern episteme: "we now inhabit the synchronic rather than diachronic ... and it is at least empirically arguable that our daily life, our psychic experiences, our cultural languages are today dominated by the categories of space rather than categories of time."[20] But "The Yellow Arrow" differs from its Western counterparts in two significant respects. First, structurally: its synchrony turns out to be a diachrony in disguise. And second, generically: it is as much a historically specific figural allegory as it is a postmodern fabulation.

Postmodern chronotopes register "a shift in sensibilities from a predominantly temporal and historiographic imagination to one much more concerned with the spatial and the geographic."[21] "The Yellow Arrow," however, registers a shift in the opposite direction. Andrei achieves an insight into the nature of his world when he begins to perceive the train's movement in space as movement in time. A mysterious letter he receives before the train stops tells him that formerly people believed that the train was moving forward into the future.[22]

---

16 Victor Pelevin, *Works in Two Volumes; Vol. 2. Buben verkhnego mira* [The Gong of the Upper World] (Moscow: Terra, 1996), 251.

17 Ibid., 261.

18 "The Report ..." depicts an infinitely large space within a small station; Roberts' novel takes place on an infinite vertical surface.

19 Brian McHale, *Postmodernist Fiction* (New York: Routledge, 1987), 43.

20 Jameson, *Postmodernism*, 16.

21 Paul Smethurst, *The Postmodern Chronotope: Reading Time and Space in Contemporary Fiction* (Amsterdam: Rodopi, 2000), 15.

22 Pelevin, *Works*, 283.

But the letter reveals that "the past is the locomotive that pulls the future / . . . You are facing backward / Seeing only that which has vanished."[23]

The train is an iconic image of Soviet culture, harking back to the glorified history of the civil war. In the famous song *"Nash parovoz vpered letit"* ("Our Locomotive is Flying Forward") the train's destination is the commune of the future.[24] Pelevin's train has no destination. Aimless wandering in space becomes a figure for the contingent unfolding of history that refuses to conform to the teleology of utopia. Instead of the future pulling history inexorably toward its final stop, it is the past that pushes the train ahead into the open-ended future. It is only when Andrei realizes that the ride is going nowhere that he is able to get off.

However, the conditions on the train are not simply an ironic recycling of Soviet clichés. They are much more historically specific. The train is undergoing its own privatization, with hustlers busy selling an overstock of toilet paper with Saddam Hussein's pictures on it, while an avant-garde artist is taking advantage of new freedom to paint Budweiser cans with mock-nationalistic images. As opposed to Western postmodernism's deployment of impossible spatial topologies where the inner logic of such a space is pushed to its logical extreme, in "The Yellow Arrow" the logic is constantly undercut by references to countries (India, Britain, China) and events (the First Gulf War) that are impossible to squeeze into the train chronotope.

Chernetsky calls the novella a "partial allegory for the late/post Soviet condition," stressing the historical continuity between the 1980s and 1990s.[25] This aspect of the novella is more than just a continuation of the strong Soviet tradition of censorship-evading allegory; it also contributes to its thematic concern with time rather than space. The allegory of "The Yellow Arrow" relates to a series of historically specific events; thus it can be classified as figural, in contradistinction to personification allegory, which embodies an abstract moral lesson.[26] The distinction between figural and personification allegory is not absolute: it is arguable, for example, that George Orwell's *Animal Farm* is both, since it attacks what Orwell called "the Soviet myth" both by encoding the actual events of Stalin's rise to power and by critiquing the hypocrisy of Soviet

---

23 Ibid., 284.
24 The song was written in 1918 (lyrics by B. Skorbin, music by P. Zubakov) and was popular throughout the Soviet period.
25 Pelevin, *Works*, 110.
26 Quilligan, Maureen. *The Language of Allegory: Defining the Genre* (Ithaca, NY: Cornell University Press, 1979), 115.

ideology.[27] Still, figural allegory is clearly the more historically grounded of the two simply by virtue of its accessing of a specific narrative of actual events.

The figural aspect of "The Yellow Arrow" opens up its claustrophobic self-enclosed space to the events that its readers were undergoing at the time of the novella's publication, emphasizing the provisional, unfinished, open-ended nature of both the text and its referent. Paul de Man argued that allegory always involves temporality because of the necessity of relating its signs to preceding signs or narratives. In Pelevin's novella the disjunction between the inner logic of the train's impossible space and its allegorical relation to the present-day events urges the reader to engage with the text on an immediate political level, while mocking the Soviet-style reification of such an engagement.

A similar interaction between allegorical temporality and postmodern spatiality occurs in Pelevin's novella "Zatvornik and shestipalyi" ("Hermit and Six-Fingers") (1991). The novella depicts a grotesque world bounded by a wall, with many suns and sporadic darkness, infested by night predators and presided over by cruel and incomprehensible gods. The two title characters, Hermit and Six-Fingers, exiled from the society of their fellows, embark on a sort of philosophical odyssey, trying to understand the nature of their world, while debating life, death, poetry, and solitude. It becomes clear, eventually, that the two are chickens living on a run-down collective poultry farm.

Echoes of *Animal Farm* are unmistakable, and so are influences of the famous Russian moralist Ivan Krylov (1769–1844), whose animal fables were familiar to every Soviet schoolchild. But Pelevin's novella eschews the simple one-to-one correspondence of a fable by creating an eerily compelling fictional world. The reader is initially unaware that the two characters are chickens; the allegory slowly penetrates this world rather than imposing the need for a figurative interpretation from the beginning. The unfamiliar space through which the two chickens travel on their way to freedom creates the "cognitive estrangement" proper to SF.[28] But the cognitive and the political are brought together, as the mystery of Hermit's and Six-Fingers' claustrophobic world becomes the mystery of the dead-end Soviet society:

"What can be done in life?" asked Hermit.
"What what? Why are you asking stupid questions? Everyone runs to the food trough. This is the law of life."

---

27 Quoted in Gary Johnson, *The Vitality of Allegory: Figural Narrative in Modern and Contemporary Fiction* (Columbus: The Ohio State University Press, 2012), 18.
28 For a definition of cognitive estrangement, see Suvin.

"I see. So why is there anything?"

"What anything?"

"The universe, the sky, the earth, the suns. Everything."

"Why? This is how the world is."[29]

The novella ends with Hermit and Six-Fingers learning to fly and escaping the "giant ugly gray building" of the farm as they rise above it.[30] This ending is not simply a paean to the new freedom, still unsullied by the realities of post-Soviet chaos and poverty. It is also an abandonment of the spatial chronotope in favor of another dimension that offers individual choice beyond the fatalistic "this is how the world is." The vertical ascent of the two rebels shifts their (and the reader's) perspective, so that the all-encompassing world of blood-splattered gods and manifold suns is cut down to its proper size of a chicken coop. This shift aligns the verticality of the flight with the temporal axis of history. The chickens' escape from their Animal Farm is an escape from a utopia-gone-sour into the dangers and uncertainties of history.

In Western postmodernism, temporality often falls apart into a heap of simulacra, "a vast collection of images."[31] In Pelevin, the striking images of an infinite train and chicken-coop universe reference the senescent utopia, while the temporality of change and escape is generated by the flaws and incongruities, which link his fictional worlds to the Russian history-in-the-making.

Chernetsky argues that Pelevin's spaces can be best understood via the Foucauldian concept of heterotopia. Elaborated in Foucault's 1967 essay "Of Other Spaces," heterotopia is a subversive flaw in what Henri Lefebvre called the "spatial practices" of society:

> There are also, probably in every culture, in every civilization, real places—places that do exist and that are formed in the very founding of society—which are something like counter-sites, a kind of effectively enacted utopia in which the real sites, all the other real sites that can be found within the culture, are simultaneously represented, contested, and inverted. Places of this kind are outside of all places, even though it may be possible to indicate their location in reality. Because these places are absolutely different from all the sites that they reflect and speak about,

---

29 Pelevin, *Works*, 165.

30 Ibid., 194.

31 Jameson, *Postmodernism*, 15.

> I shall call them, by way of contrast to utopias, heterotopias. (Foucault, "Of Other")

Heterotopias for Foucault include such decidedly non-utopian locales as jails, madhouses, and even cemeteries. The important thing, in his view, is not the actual disposition of a heterotopic site but rather its relation to the dominant spatial practice. In his reading of Pelevin's heterotopias, Chernetsky emphasizes their "foregrounding of … plurality, the crucial emphasis on otherness."[32] But Foucault himself situates his discussion of heterotopias in the familiar by now diagnosis of the essential spatiality of the postmodern episteme: "The present epoch will perhaps be above all the epoch of space. We are in the epoch of simultaneity: we are in the epoch of juxtaposition, the epoch of the near and far, of the side-by-side, of the dispersed" ("Of Other"). Time, however, has not disappeared but rather has become apprehended through its projection onto space. The fact that history is no longer conceived as a linear narrative of progress makes it possible to represent temporality through the structure of multidimensional space. Pelevin's impossible spaces in their "foregrounding of plurality" represent the inversion of the monolithic space of the Soviet master narrative: a heterotopia to its utopia.

The Soviet Matrix

Jean Baudrillard's notion of the simulacrum is central to the articulations of postmodern aesthetics. Baudrillard conceives of the simulacrum as copy without origin, which erases the distinction between reality and representation. The simulacrum is perhaps the most popular aspect of postmodernism, instantly graspable by anybody with access to the Internet. Starring in a multitude of Hollywood blockbusters, from *The Matrix* and *The Thirteenth Floor* to *Inception*, the concept has spawned an entire universe of video and role-playing games.

The simulacrum, in Jameson's interpretation, has a symptomatic relation with postmodernism's loss of historicity. It becomes a consolation prize for our inability to construct a coherent narrative of the past: "we are condemned to seek History by way of our own pop images and simulacra of that history, which itself remains forever out of reach."[33] In the USSR, however,

---

32 Chernetsky, *Mapping Postcommunist Cultures*, 89.
33 Jameson, *Postmodernism*, 25.

the situation was reversed: History, in the sense of a Marxist master narrative, was not only instantly accessible but altogether inescapable; it was rather history—images, memories, and records of actual events—that was out of reach. In the post-Soviet period, the epistemology of simulacra becomes a way to access individual experience, previously buried under the weight of the collective master-narrative.

Pelevin's novel *Omon Ra* (1992) is narrated in the first person by Omon Krivomazov, whose unusual first name is given to him by his perpetually drunken policeman father, who dreams of his son joining the Party, becoming a policeman, and having a happy life by owning a small plot of land. Omon's dreams, however, go in a different direction: he is enchanted by a cardboard model of a USSR spaceship he encounters in the Young Pioneer camp and decides to become an astronaut. Accepted to the Meres'ev Flying School, named after the World War II hero who lost his legs but returned to serve on the frontline, Omon eventually discovers that the entire Soviet space program is a succession of falsifications, a state-sponsored fake of science, exploration, and even physical reality. Pressured into a one-way trip to the moon, which is supposed to simulate an unmanned rover landing, Omon accepts his death in the service of the propaganda machine—only to end up in an underground tunnel in Moscow, jolted by commuters and boarding a metro train. There is no space program, no heroic self-sacrifice, and perhaps not even a Moon.

Superficial similarity to such Western texts of simulacra as J. G. Ballard's "Thirteen to Centaurus" (1965) or *The Matrix* obscures the originality of *Omon Ra*. It is both a postmodern questioning of epistemology and a pointed satire of Soviet propaganda's propensity for falsification, evasion, and outright lies. The late-Soviet reality was a giant simulacrum of itself, in which, as everybody knew, statistics, media coverage of current events, and history books were entirely unreliable. But Pelevin's critique of this ideological mirage comes from an unexpected direction. Instead of appealing to the modernist notions of universal truth or reality, he situates resistance to the totalitarian simulacrum in the individual capacity for self-creation.

Omon is perfectly aware of the fact that Soviet "reality" is a sort of collective solipsism and yet this realization in no way impairs his willingness to die in the service of the fake space project. He recounts a grotesque story of a father-and-son team who, dressed as bears, exposed themselves to the bullets of foreign diplomats taken to a model hunt. The son is wounded by Kissinger and bleeds to death; the father becomes an instructor in a course on heroism taught to the space cadets. Omon's reaction to the story is a renewed commitment to his mission:

> I suddenly understood anew the long-familiar and stale words: "In life there is always a place for heroism." ... It was not Romantic nonsense but rather a clear and accurate statement of the fact that our Soviet life is not the last court of appeal for reality but something like its forecourt. ... [In a moment of crisis] ... there opens a door leading to heroism, not outside but inside, in the very depth of the soul.[34]

In other words, the ideological simulacrum enables the individual experience of transcendental self-sacrifice, and thus it is immaterial whether it corresponds to external reality or not.

The novel revisits the famous debate between O'Brien and Winston Smith in Orwell's *1984*, in which O'Brien appears as a sort of totalitarian postmodernist, arguing that objective reality is created by the dominant discourse. Smith casts about for an epistemological terra firma to ground his counter-argument and eventually finds it in what he calls "human nature," which he links to the body's experience of pleasure and pain. But the final word is O'Brien's, since his torture of Smith demonstrates how the body can become a blank slate of ideological manipulation and how pain can be used to shape perception. Smith is forced to see that two plus two equals five and ends up loving Big Brother.

Similarly, Omon's O'Brien, Colonel Urchagin, situates the fight between Communism and capitalism in the "pure soul" of the heroic Soviet subject: "One pure and honest soul is enough for our country to win the space race; one such soul is enough for the red banner of triumphant socialism to be planted upon the far-away Moon. At least for a moment such a soul is necessary because this is where this banner will be raised. ... "[35] Both O'Brien and Urchagin agree that the social reality is a collective simulacrum that is sustained by the dedication and faith of ordinary people. The real race between East and West is over the colonization of the inner, rather than outer, space.

Nor does the body provide any ontological grounding for reality. In the Meres'ev Flying School the cadets' feet are amputated to imitate the titular hero and yet this atrocious initiation is accepted as unquestioningly as the institutionalized Soviet diet of tasteless soup, chicken-and-rice, and compote,

---

34 Viktor Pelevin, *Omon Ra* (Moscow: Vagrius, 2001), 69.
35 Ibid., 158.

periodically mentioned in the novel. Everyday discomfort, physical pain, and even death can be overcome by, and even subsumed into, the collective simulacrum.

Chernetsky reads the ending of *Omon Ra* as a representation of "the experience of the breakdown of deception and self-deception ... [and] subversion of the totalitarian mindset."[36] But this breakdown is not predicated on the discovery of the external truth, resistant to the manipulation of power. Rather, Omon's escape from the totalitarian narrative of utopian heroism hinges on his acceptance of alternative narratives as equally valid and/or satisfying. He exits the Soviet Matrix into a virtual reality of his own making.

Remembering his childhood conversations with a mystically inclined babysitter, Omon decides to "choose" his own god and finds in the falcon-headed Ammon-Ra[37] a template for his inner self, "the protagonist of my inner adventures."[38] One opposes the totalitarian simulacrum by creating one's own. Resistance lies not in reality but in more and better illusions. Omon's friend Mit'ka is executed after he reveals, under hypnosis, multiple "past lives," which range from ancient Mesopotamia to Nazi Germany. But they also include Ivan Efremov's iconic Soviet utopia *The Andromeda Nebula*, whose fictional narrative is seamlessly incorporated into Mit'ka's "recollections." The danger to the totalitarian Matrix is not the truth but rather the DIY formation of individual simulacra. The ending of the novel has Omon contemplating the "red line" of the Moscow Metro, considering where to go.[39] Choice rather than revelation is the escape hatch from the virtual prison.

The Inner Republic of Inner Mongolia

Pelevin's most famous novel is *Chapaev i Pustota* (1996). Even translating the title poses an ontological conundrum, which only intensifies as the action unfolds—if indeed it does.[40] *Pustota* means "void" in Russian, but it is also the name of the narrator/protagonist who alternates between two realities: that of the post-revolutionary Russia, in which he is the commissar of the legendary civil war hero Vasily Chapaev, and that of 1990s post-Soviet Russia, in which he

---

36 Ibid., 110.
37 Pilots and spacemen were routinely compared to "falcons" in the USSR.
38 Pelevin, *Omon Ra*, 76.
39 Ibid., 161.
40 The novel was translated (by Andrew Bromfield) as *Buddha's Little Finger* (New York: New Directions, 2000), which seems entirely unrelated to the Russian title but in fact is quite relevant.

is an inmate of a psychiatric hospital being treated for a "split false personality disorder."[41] The structure of the novel imitates the famous paradox of a man-dreaming-of-being-a-butterfly-dreaming-of-being-a-man (which is explicitly referenced at one point) and eventually dissolves into a dizzying welter of philosophical speculations, Buddhist references, intertextual allusions, and in-jokes. Alexander Genis describes it as taking place on "the boundary between different worlds"; and indeed, the reader never knows whether either of the two textual worlds is "real" and by the end of the novel, stupefied with lectures on Aristotle, Plato, Buddha, and Jung, no longer cares.[42]

This is exactly the point of the novel. It confronts one of the Soviet icons—Chapaev, the hero of the eponymous 1934 movie and the butt of endless Soviet jokes, ranging from the subversive to the obscene. By repositioning the civil-war myth in the context of Buddhist speculations on the void as the foundation of the illusory reality, *Chapaev i Pustota* enacts its own theme: the dissolution of all the verities of Soviet civilization in the acid of the historical trauma of its sudden end. And primary among these verities is the concept of the unified subject. Not only does Petr Pustota randomly transition between his distinct selves but so do his fellow inmates in the psychiatric hospital: the gay man named Maria who is in love with Arnold Schwarzenegger; the "new Russian" Volodin; and the suicidal intellectual Serdyuk. Moreover, Pustota mysteriously has inner access to their experiences, so that the plethora of partial, overlapping, and split selves extends across the narrative space—and this is not counting Chapaev himself, who vacillates between a mystical guru and a drunken slob. The novel dramatizes the collision and confusion not just of different worlds but of different selves that are careening at random across the sociohistorical spacetime of a fallen utopia.

The "schizophrenic" dispersal of the subject is another defining feature of postmodernism. Jameson describes it as "the waning of affect," in which the modernist "alienation of the subject is displaced by the latter's fragmentation."[43] Baudrillard links this fragmentation with the precession of simulacra, while Foucault in *The Order of Things* celebrates the "death of Man." The enforced humanism of the Soviet episteme has quickly given way to posthumanism,

41 Viktor Pelevin, *Chapaev i Pustota* (Moscow: Vagrius, 1996), 20.

42 Alexander Genis, "Borders and Metamorphoses: Viktor Pelevin in the Context of Post-Soviet Literature," in *Russian Postmodernism: New Perspectives on Post-Soviet Culture*, ed. by Mikhail Epstein, Alexander Genis, and Sobodanka Vladiv-Glover (New York: Berghahn Books, 1999), 212–24.

43 Jameson, *Postmodernism*, 12–14.

which celebrates the "intensities" of the dispersed subject rather than the heroic self-abnegation of the unified one. It turns out that once the ideological exoskeleton has been removed, the Soviet New Man is even more likely to fall apart into a collection of random self-narratives than his Western counterpart, rather like Mit'ka of *Omon Ra* with his fictional past lives.

But paradoxically, the disintegrating postmodern subject of *Chapaev i Pustota* turns out to be as collectively significant as the steely New Man of the original Chapaev movie. Instead of retreat into private experience, the fragmentation of subjectivity figures modalities of national trauma. Jameson links the end of the subject to "the waning of the great high modernist thematic of time and temporality."[44] In Pelevin's novel, it is a sudden rush of time into the empty spaces of fallen utopia that breaks the subject apart.

The two "lives" of Petr Pustota are located at the two crucial points in Russia's recent history: the Revolution and its failure. In a conversation with his psychiatrist, he tells Pustota that his "split false personality disorder" is a symptom of post-Soviet Russia's ambivalent relation with its own history, in which it is trying to repudiate the past and yet remains welded to it: "I've thought a lot why some people are capable of starting a new life—let's call them New Russians … while others are stuck in non-existent relationships with shadows of the extinguished world."[45] This question leads to a long philosophical discussion that references, inter alia, the ideas of the Silver Age regarding Russia's mystical choice between East and West, the nineteenth-century radical Chernyshevsky, and differing perceptions of time in Asian and European cultures. The final diagnosis of Pustota's condition is that he refuses to accept progress and change, thus remaining stuck, just like the country itself, in the unusable past. Pustota counters that "change" is the handiwork of scoundrels looking out for mere chance; and indeed, his encounters with the revolutionary intelligentsia and proletarian warriors tend to support this claim: the former are mostly decadent drug addicts, the latter—drunken brutes. If history is the choice between violence and greed, Pustota's eventual embrace of his own void of subjectivity is quite understandable. By achieving a sort of pseudo-Nirvana, in which time, space, and subjectivity are revealed as unstable and provisional constructs, he steps off the wheel of history, finding refuge in "[his] precious Inner Mongolia."[46]

---

44 Ibid., 16.
45 Pelevin, *Chapaev i Pustota*, 47.
46 Ibid., 398.

Inner Mongolia is precisely the space where the disintegration of the subject meets the chaos of history. It is both an actual region of China on the border with Russia and a state of being, in which the time-hopping that has bedeviled Pustota is subsumed into peaceful timelessness, and the split personality is healed by renunciation of the self. The fact that Chapaev, of all people, acts a guide to this mystical retreat is a hilarious, yet bitter, spoof of the elasticity with which Soviet cultural icons were pressed into the service of the current ideological needs. The Chapaev of the Soviet legend, based on the adulatory movie, which was based on the equally false biographical novel by Dmitri Furmanov (who is a minor character in Pelevin), is as much an empty simulacrum as the Chapaev of Pelevin's novel who wields "Buddha's little finger" instead of his customary machine gun.

The narrative framing of the novel reinforces the connection between the travails of the subject and the chaos of history. Even though Pustota's narrative itself gives no ontological priority to either the 1920s or the 1990s, his manuscript is introduced by the "Chairman of the Buddhist Front of Complete and Final Liberation," who claims it was in fact written in the "first half of the 1920s" in the actual Inner Mongolia.[47] This is not so much to tip the scales of dream and reality as to remind the reader that no matter how absurd, the dance of ideological simulacra has political consequences. The senselessness of history is directly proportional to its atrociousness. Or as Chapaev sagely points out, "this world is so constituted that we have to answer all questions in the midst of a house fire."[48]

Ending the Ending

In *Archaeologies of the Future*, Jameson argues that utopia reunites experience and history as "existential time is taken up into a historical time which is also paradoxically the end of time, the end of history."[49] Postmodernism, growing like mold on the corpse of utopia, is characterized by the irresolvable schism between the two, in which spatiality, simulacrum, and split subjectivity function as symptoms of our traumatized inability to imagine "the end of time."

In Mikhail Epstein's analysis of the similarities between Soviet Communism and postmodernism, both are seen as refusals of history. The teleology that

---

47 Ibid., 7.
48 Ibid., 352.
49 Jameson, *Archaeologies*, 7.

Jameson sees as necessary for our experience of temporality is, in Epstein's view, inimical to it. Thus, he classifies both postmodernism and Communism as reifications of the utopian impulse which deny the open-endedness of the future in favor of the eternal present. Soviet Communism is "the plenitude of the present time … desire to become our own 'descendants' and live in that present which was imagined as the future."[50] Similarly, postmodernism is the utopia of post-history; it exists in the eternal present because there can be no future in a world devoid of time.

Despite their ideological differences, these two diagnoses of postmodernism are rather similar in that both imply that utopia is irreconcilable with contingent, unpredictable, non-teleological temporality—with history as opposed to History, in Jameson's terminology. The end of the USSR marks the failure of one attempt to tame the contingency of time. The rise of the postmodern episteme dominated by the apocalyptic discourses of the "end of history," "end of Man," and "end of reality" may be another such attempt. But despite its economic and political hardships, the fate of post-Soviet Russia demonstrates that history will not be stopped. Epstein argues that in contemporary Russia, "history has 'thawed out' after decades of frost."[51] Paradoxically, this return to history facilitates the rebirth of the utopian impulse not as desire for "the end of time" but as search for a radically different future.

Viktor Pelevin's post-Soviet postmodernism may be seen as one of the ways Russian culture tries to come to terms with its disastrous past and forge a new artistic language for its uncertain future. Neither an imitation nor a repudiation of Western postmodernism, Pelevin's oeuvre represents a bold attempt to expand and modify such postmodern artistic tropes as space, simulacrum, and fragmented subjectivity to respond to Russia's unique national needs. As such, it is a true Second World innovation: not as a glimpse of utopia but rather as a reminder of history.

---

50 M. N. Epstein, *Postmodern v russkoi literature* [Postmodernism in Russian Literature] (Moscow: Vysshaya shkola, 2005), 88.
51 Ibid., 467.

The Forces of Kinship: Timur Bekmambetov's *Night Watch* Cinematic Trilogy

VLAD STRUKOV

Strukov, Vlad. "The Forces of Kinship: Timur Bekmambetov's *Night Watch* Cinematic Trilogy," in *Cinepaternity: Fathers and Sons in Soviet and Post-Soviet Film*, ed. Helena Goscilo and Yana Hashamova (Bloomington: Indiana University Press, 2010), 191–216.

In Timur Bekmambetov's *Night Watch* and *Day Watch* the father and son are divided by their loyalties to the opposing forces of Light and Darkness, and each of them finds this separation excruciatingly painful. The director chooses the realm of the family, with a special focus on parent–child relations, to explore the social phenomenon of authority. He constructs a myth that accounts for Russia's contemporary social structure, a myth that serves as a source of morality and generally as the origin of civilization. Prompted by the structure of the films, I analyze the father–son relationship as a set of cultural oppositions and choices that culminate in the concept of the secret workings of fate. The underlying structure of the myth illuminates Bekmambetov's assertion that, unless the Oedipus complex is resolved, a person's identity is incomplete, and therefore a sociocultural transition is not possible. My discussion addresses the issue of familial and social disengagement propagated by the films, and authority as a guarantee of father–son and, ultimately, national unity.

The Figure of Oedipus and the Workings of Fate

Night Watch [*Nochnoi Dozor* 2004] and *Day Watch* [*Dnevnoi Dozor* 2005][1] are the first two installments in a planned sci-fi/fantasy/horror/vampire trilogy

---

1 *Dnevnoi dozor* [*Day Watch*]. Dir. Timur Bekmambetov. Pervyi kanal, Kinokompaniia Tabbak, Bazelevs-Prodakshn, 2005; *Nochnoi Dozor* [Night Watch]. Dir. Timur Bekmambetov.

based on a series of hugely popular fantasy novels by Sergei Luk'ianenko. Though *Night Watch* and *Day Watch* develop the same narrative, the former lays the foundation for the second part of the series. The events of the films relate to three major time periods: 2004, 1992, and the distant past. From the first film, we learn that there is a new type of social order, whereby "Others" [*inye*], who possess supernatural powers, live among normal humans. The Others fall into two groups—the Dark ones, who gain their power by feeding on the blood of humans, and the Light ones, who are supposed to protect people from their Dark opponents. Although being one of the Others is biologically predetermined, a human being can be "initiated" and become a vampire if she or he falls prey to another vampire. The division into Light and Dark Others results from an ancient conflict brought about by a curse imposed on a virgin who once lived in Byzantium. The conflict culminated in the Middle Ages, when the armies of Light and Dark forces, under the leaders Geser (Vladimir Men'shov) and Zavulon (Viktor Verzhbitskii), respectively, met in battle on an ancient arched bridge. When it became clear that the Dark and Light forces possessed equal powers and the clash was doomed to finish in mutual extermination, Geser halted the fight; the forces of Light and Dark signed a truce to end the devastating battle. Since then the forces of Light govern the days, and the nights belong to their Dark opponents, and each side establishes a Watch to ensure peace.

Bekmambetov domesticates the members of the Day and Night Watch: in modern Moscow, the former roam the night as vampires, and the latter operate under the cover of Moscow's electric utility repair crew [*Gorsvet*]. The director also transplants the metaphysical conflict of good and evil into the private realm of the family and the individual, whereby a person's experience is also a paradigm of destiny. Bekmambetov connects the two spheres, the private and the public, the real and the fantastic, the actual and the allegorical, through the myth of Oedipus as dramatized in Sophocles' tragedy *Oedipus Rex*.[2] The events of the myth become a defining element of the films' thematics and stylistics, as well as an engine for the father–son dynamic.

The first film's prologue is staged in a manner recalling the visit of Laius, the ruler of Thebes, to an oracle who tells him that his son will supplant him. With the agreement of Laius's wife, Jocasta, the baby is left on a mountain to

---

Pervyi kanal, Kinokompaniia Tabbak, Bazelevs-Prodakshn, 2004; leading producers: Aleksei Kublitskii and Varvara Avdiushko; producers: Anatolii Maksimov and Konstantin Ernst; screenplay: Sergei Luk'ianenko and Timur Bekmambetov; photography: Sergei Trofimov; and music: Iurii Poteenko.

2 The exact date of production is unknown, possibly around 425 BC.

be eaten by wild animals. In *Night Watch*, in 1992 Moscow, Anton (Konstantin Khabenskii) seeks help from a sorceress, Dar'ia (Rimma Markova), in order to regain his unfaithful wife, Irina (Mariia Mironova), only to learn that his wife carries another man's child—information that subsequently proves inaccurate. The comparison with the myth reveals the nature and the dynamic of the conflict: Anton's suspicions of Irina's infidelity and his desire to avenge his wife prompt him to ask the sorceress to terminate Irina's pregnancy. Bekmambetov shows the origin of the conflict in the destruction of the family rather than in the conspiracy of the husband and wife to maintain their power.

Anton's first encounter with his son, Egor (Dmitrii Martynov), occurs twelve years later on a train on the Moscow metro. Having drunk some pig blood in order to catch a vampire, Larissa (Anna Dubrovskaia), who attacks innocent victims in Moscow, Anton is lured to his son, but luckily a cursed woman, Svetlana (Mariia Poroshina), distracts him from engaging in a vampiric act. The scene relates to the part of the Greek myth in which Oedipus, on his way to Thebes, meets an old man—Laius—who is rude and aggressive, and therefore falls victim to Oedipus's uncontrollable fury. The association with the myth defines the scene on the Moscow metro as that of attempted murder and identifies Anton's symbolic function no longer as that of Laius (the victim of filicide) but rather as that of Oedipus (the perpetrator of filicide). Indeed, both Anton and Oedipus find it hard to control their instincts (the latter is blinded by his rage, the former is under the influence of the intoxicating drink); both act aggressively toward a member of their blood family because they are unaware of their true identity and believe they are dealing with complete strangers. Thus, the switch in Anton's symbolic function (Laius → Oedipus) suggests that *Night/Day Watch* presents a case of a *reversed* Oedipus complex, to be analyzed later in the chapter.

The viewer is not confused by the transformation of Anton's role thanks to a temporal discontinuity: via non-diegetic means, Bekmambetov uses a title to signal that twelve years elapse between Anton's visit to the sorceress and his first encounter with Egor. From the point of view of diegesis, the director allows twelve minutes before the characters' first meeting. To achieve his purpose, Bekmambetov borrows the principle of a temporal gap from *Oedipus Rex*. Sophocles uses the delay of twelve years to signify his hero's maturation and his inauguration as the King of Thebes and Jocasta's husband, thus focusing on the figure of Oedipus and his self-discovery.[3] In *Night Watch*, the time

---

3 Sophocles, *Antigone, Oedipus, Electra*, trans. H.D.F Kitto, ed. Edith Hall (New York: Oxford University Press, 1994), 49–51.

discontinuity enables the director to shift some of the myth's events to the plane of the contemporary and thus to signal his interest in constructing the myth in the present rather than uncovering the events of the past. In other words, Bekmambetov sees the original father–son conflict as unfolding in its actuality and defining the future rather than the current situation. Bekmambetov underscores his point by allowing virtually zero historical distance between the time of the making of *Night Watch* and the events the film presents: although the events of the myth relate to the mythical past, *Night Watch* constructs the mythical present as the story unfolds. The director enhances the simultaneity of historical processes of the real and universal qualities of the magical worlds by appropriating motifs and narrative tools from the ancient myth. For example, the future of the child (Oedipus; Egor) is defined not only by his parents' ambitions but also by the interference of other subjects—or, metaphorically speaking, by fate. Shepherds take pity on the baby and, instead of leaving it to die, present the boy to the childless King of Corinth, Polybus, who brings him up as his own, giving him the name "Oedipus."[4] Similarly, the Night Watch intervenes and prevents the murder of the unborn child in the process of being aborted by the sorceress. Bekmambetov interprets this interference as a point of entry into the magical world ruled by fate rather than reason. Anton therefore begins to function as a mediator between the seen and the unseen, between the real and the imaginary, and between good and evil.

Another important parallelism[5] between the myth and the film is their use of oracles and messengers as tools that propel the narrative. In the myth,

---

4 Ibid., 54–57; Here I analyze only the most striking similarities. Secondary themes and details of representation are not necessarily void of interest. For example, the name of Oedipus—swollen foot—suggests his unbridled sexuality (erect penis) and tracks its origin to his brutal parents. In the play his name and the actual foot deformity are used as *evidence* in support of his origin. In *Night Watch*, the director has to provide convincing *evidence* for Anton as well: when the Night Watch intervenes, they file a report against Dar'ia that is later used against Anton to convince Egor of his father's murderous intentions. Ironically, the Night Watch appears in disguise—as a lioness and a bear (i.e., as wild animals that may have eaten Oedipus); and so forth.

5 Another example of parallelism between the film and the myth is the portrayal of the real mother and her function in the narrative. Jocasta is shown as a knowing mother: from the moment of her conspiracy with her husband till the final scene when, having momentarily realized that Oedipus is her son, she rushes out and later hangs herself by the hair, Jocasta is presented as an agent of her own destiny. In Night Watch, the director saves Egor's mother, Irina, from the ordeals of guilty motherhood: she abandons her flat and the film's narrative altogether just before the father, Anton, arrives. His arrival precedes the crucial scene of recognition that changes the course of father–son relations: Anton notices a photograph of Irina and Egor and realizes that Egor is his son.

Oedipus learns from the oracle of Apollo that he will kill his father and marry his mother. In *Night Watch,* in 2004 Moscow, AntonOedipus receives his second prophecy in the form of a telephone call. An unidentified caller commands Anton to capture Larissa, who is pursuing Egor. The analogy between the two texts reveals that Larissa and Egor form a male/female relation whose bond is suggested by the anticipated vampiric intercourse; Anton therefore functions as their symbolic child whose purpose is to prevent their congress. Another important instance of comparison is between the scene in the myth in which the Corinthian messenger arrives to tell Oedipus that Polybus is dead and that he was Oedipus's adoptive father, and thus Oedipus is the murderer of Laius,[6] and the scene in *Night Watch,* in which Anton accesses secret files on Night Watch's intranet to learn that his own clan categorizes and uses him as a murderer. The correlation demonstrates Anton's own role in discovering the truth about himself and his past: like Oedipus, he becomes a tool of his own fate as he brings his investigation to a conclusion to proclaim himself guilty of his murderous attempts.

Bekmambetov utilizes the matrix of the myth in order to concatenate the otherwise disjunctive structure of the film. With the help of implicit allusions, he rebuilds a complete chronology of events and renders the ancient myth's thematics. For example, Bekmambetov retains the metaphor of the road where the father and the son meet for the first time, to convey the workings of fate as well as to suggest that his characters' search for identity is not accomplished. Both Anton and Egor are nomads whose space has not yet been determined. Like Oedipus, who may not remain in Corinth and is twice exiled from Thebes, they remain on the road, or in the Gloom[7]—the in between space of individual and cultural identification—thus maintaining their free status. In *Night Watch,* with the help of digital imagery, Bekmambetov demonstrates what is known as Oedipus "road rage," a sudden attack of anger when he "sees red" and is unable to control his temper. The director allows Anton's vampiric gaze to penetrate Egor's skin; the father sees—and so does the viewer—the pulsation of blood in the arteries in the son's head. The image of Egor's circulation system is accessible to Anton and the viewer only, and not to Anton's fellow train

---

6   Sophocles, 92.
7   Gloom offers the experience of synesthesia and the paradoxes of perception with the fallacy of sense and speech. Bekmambetov demonstrates the overdetermination of false sensory perception, and verbal error set off the special nature of a knowledge that can be spoken only through the distorting mechanisms of language, the processes of condensation, displacement, splitting, and doubling that Freud studies intensively in his *Interpretation of Dreams.*

passengers. Thus, the viewer is invited to participate in the scene and in Anton's—male—gaze. This means that the events of the first film are presented from Anton's point of view, and the director wishes his audiences to associate with the figure of the father in the father–son conflict, a perspective that is doomed to be reversed in the second installment of the trilogy.

Another example of how the Greek myth influences the visual paradigm of the film is the scene of the liberation of Ol'ga (Galina Tiunina). Geser presents Anton with a stuffed owl; in his kitchen Anton accidentally guesses the spell and releases Ol'ga from the body of the bird in which she has been trapped for sixty years. The scene, of course, relates to the story of the Sphinx, a hybrid creature with the body of a lioness, the head of a woman, and wings, and a monster who terrorizes Thebes.[8] In the film the scene is visually orchestrated in the manner reminiscent of the two most famous Greek representations of Oedipus solving the riddle of the Sphinx. The owl is poised on a kitchen table facing Anton; as he pronounces the spell, the owl transforms into a woman; she asks Anton to turn away and continues to occupy her pedestal until the metamorphosis is complete. In *Night Watch* Ol'ga accompanies Anton, and together they form a symbolic parental relation with Egor as their child. In the scene of recognition, when Anton identifies Egor as his son, they all come together in a typically domestic setting with Anton watching television and Ol'ga sewing up Egor's shirt and chatting with the boy.

The myth's notion of contamination (Thebes succumbs to a vile plague, which kills children and animals, and is caused by pollution or by the sin of the unpunished murder) is rendered in the film thanks to the character of Svetlana. Her mother has a fatal renal disease and requires a kidney transplant but categorically refuses Svetlana's offer of her kidney, prompting her daughter to a moral assessment of her motivations. Kidneys remove waste products and excess fluids from the body via the urine, thereby maintaining a critical balance of salt, potassium, and acid; symbolically a kidney is an organ of purification, and a kidney problem suggests contamination or aberration. Svetlana's motive is thus impure, and, having realized it, she puts a curse on herself. Her curse is so powerful that it threatens to destroy the city of Moscow.[9] Svetlana's masked

---

8 Sophocles, 50–52.

9 In the process of visualization the curse takes the form of a funnel—in Russian, *voronka*—which is a Freudian symbol relating to female desire and concepts of maternity. The funnel is made of crows—in Russian, *vorona*—whereby the crow symbolizes an evil omen. Thus, in construction of visual paradigms, Bekmambetov utilizes the method of free associations. In psychoanalysis, this method is used to undermine authority. Therefore, if Anton is a model

wish for her mother's death inverts Anton's explicit desire for the elimination of his son. As Svetlana and Anton eventually form a couple, Bekmambetov accentuates the connection between contamination and incomprehension, or guilt and fate (Anton, like Oedipus, is completely unaware of the nature of his own deeds). Anton's blindness[10] is rendered with the help of digital imagery that transforms his eyes into those of a vampire. In addition, he constantly wears dark glasses that obstruct his vision (i.e., blinded vision versus blinded language); and, finally, he wanders in the Gloom, or permanent darkness, which ultimately suggests impurity, ignorance, and displacement. The characters of *Night Watch* strive to overcome contamination by embracing either their parental (Anton) or filial (Svetlana) duty. Unlike in the myth, in the film the crime per se never occurs, since on three occasions Anton has the opportunity to murder his child, but, luckily, each time he fails to do so. Thus, the film's emphasis falls on the motivation and morality rather than the consequences, whereas ancient Greeks perceived Oedipus guilty of his father's death, since, in accordance with their law, the act itself rather than the motive defined a crime.

Like Sophocles' play, *Night Watch* demonstrates that a man's character is his fate, for it is in fulfilling his personal characteristics—his relentless pursuit of knowledge, his perseverance and confidence in himself, and his proneness to anger—that Oedipus meets his destiny, unwittingly realizing the prophecies.[11] *Night Watch* invokes the concept of fate and fatalistic visions of experience that are shown to create, guide, reward, and afflict the characters. Picturing fatal forces, the film, like the myth, introduces the entire concept of divinity, or superhuman personalities who control the rules and the events of our lives according to their own principles, which generally remain unintelligible. These are not only the figures of Geser and Zavulon (substitute fathers—empowered men who issue orders) but also of Anton, Svetlana, and Egor, a divine family. Critically, in the film's most poignant scene, which should be identified as a rite of passage,[12] Egor enters the pantheon of "the chosen

---

of self-divided, sublimating authority who is unable to properly emulate himself, then the director undermines his authority as the hero of civilization.

10   In the myth, having learned the whole truth, Oedipus rushes to Jocasta but finds her dead, so he takes the brooches from her dress and uses them to gouge his eyes. He thus attacks the eyes that are known for seeing through reality's confusion to the truth. Later he administers his own punishment: he exiles himself.

11   Sophocles, 96–99.

12   Anton participates in Egor's entry into the symbolic realm: the father spills his blood to save his son who has lost consciousness. In this way the director visualizes the *blood* relation between these two characters.

ones" in the presence of his blood father and Ol'ga, who, just like Svetlana, functions as Egor's substitute mother.[13] Ol'ga accounts for Egor's otherness as follows: "An 'Other' has superhuman abilities because throughout his life he has met superhuman challenges and he has had to put forth superhuman efforts." This—as with many other scenes in the films—is perceived as an imaginative act, as it permits characters and subsequently the viewer to understand the situation and establish a relationship with the controlling forces of existence. Such a relationship takes the form of communal practice, since Egor enters the Symbolic order at the same time that he joins his clan. In the fatalistic universe, a character who confronts fate becomes a hero; in *Night Watch,* the conflict is personalized, as the father and son challenge each other, and it may not be resolved—as it is not resolved in *Day Watch*—until a secession of power is established. The role of the hero in a Greek tragedy is to explore the roots of his society's beliefs; here the hero questions the clan's policies. Egor freely articulates what his father only suspects, that is, the arbitrariness of the divide between the Dark and Light forces. In *Night Watch* Egor, unlike Anton, is shown to be able to make decisions in response to a crisis and to step forward and take risks in the face of fate. It is this personal quality of will and determination that separates Oedipus from the chorus in *Oedipus Rex,* and Egor from Anton in *Night Watch,* as the chorus and Anton both acknowledge their timidity, bewilderment, or anxiety in the face of the crisis.[14] Thus, in *Night Watch,* Anton is portrayed as a follower who subsequently will require his son to become the leader.

The Family and the Construction of the Ego

In Freudian interpretation and in Bekmambetov's appropriation, the Oedipus complex is the decisive crisis from which arises, by virtue of the mechanism of identification, each individual's structure as a personal ego. The films explore the ways in which unconscious desire is limited, organized, and structured through the activities of the social world. The myth is used to symbolize how the unconscious is socialized. The Oedipus complex describes the triangular configuration constituted by the child, the child's natural object (mother), and

---

13 To clarify, Irina, Ol'ga, and Svetlana are three mother figures similar to the female triad of the Oedipus complex: the woman he assumes to be his "real" mother, Merope; the unknown mother of his fears, with whom he is fated to commit incest; and Jocasta.

14 Sophocles, 55–65.

the bearer of the law (father).[15] Therefore, it is the prime site for observing the operation of internalizing and identification (or "taking in" that which is outside, and here, the regulations on sexuality imposed by the father or, more generally, by the social order) and making it central to the psyche.[16]

The narrative structure of *Night Watch* utilizes a temporal discontinuity to account for Egor's present age—twelve years old—which undoubtedly suggests that he occupies the fifth stage of psychosexual development (six–twelve years).[17] According to Freud, the latency stage has its origins in the resolution of the Oedipus complex and the start of the child's identification with the same-sex parent (Egor → Anton).[18] However, because of Anton's absence, Egor's solution of the Oedipus complex has been delayed and has therefore resulted in problems such as adjusting to a group (Egor is never shown in the company of his peers; instead, as the final scene of Satan's banquet demonstrates, he chooses to associate with a more mature club, the Day Watch); phobias (Egor's initial fear of vampires later turns into his uninhibited exploitation of his vampiric inclinations); and other juvenile delinquencies. He requires his father's intervention to progress to his final—genital—stage of development. When Anton fails him, Egor chooses Zavulon as his father figure and achieves maturity. The difference between the roles of Anton and Zavulon is visually marked: in the final scene of *Night Watch*, when Anton and Zavulon clash in a brutal fight on top of an apartment block, Anton defends himself with an electrical light pole (i.e., he needs to appropriate his phallus from outside), whereas Zavulon extracts his spinal cord and turns it into a magic sword (i.e., he produces and governs his own weapon).

Although Egor chooses Zavulon as his mentor, he inherits his blood father's relentless pursuit of knowledge, which, in Freudian terms, is defined as the epistemological drive. The origin of the drive lies in the curiosity of the child confronted by the enigma of sexuality or, as presented in the films, by the enigma of the Day/Night Watch opposition, whereby the first is conveyed as a form of vampirism, in itself a form of sexuality. It is possible to claim that Egor's vampirism is, in fact, a sublimated sexual drive (*Day Watch* shows that

---

15 Sigmund Freud, *Totem and Taboo*, trans. James Strachey (New York: W.W. Norton, 1952), 18–75.

16 Sigmund Freud, Introductory Lectures on Psychoanalysis, trans. W. J. H. Sprott (London: Hogarth, 1957), 26–38.

17 Ibid., 113–17.

18 Ibid.

the victims of his bloodsucking are women),[19] or a movement from the luring relationship with his father to a new Symbolic order, by means of his phobia and its transformations. When in the final scene of *Night Watch* Egor chooses the Dark side, his father appears in his life as the figure that interferes with the satisfaction that the child is trying to obtain, and thus it is not surprising that the son denies his biological father as well as the law of civilization that the father introduces.[20] To Egor, the Day Watch constitutes the pleasure principle (ironically manifested in the realm of the everyday as a lavish lifestyle).[21] Anton, and with him the Night Watch, opposes it with the reality principle that carries the burden of the imperatives of culture.

In *Totem and Taboo* Freud tried to give the Oedipus complex a historical foundation and constructed a myth: one day the sons killed the primal father and ate him, and there followed a new social organization founded on guilt.[22] Likewise, Bekmambetov constructs a creational myth that involves the Dark and Light forces invisible to the human eye but accountable for the existing social and cultural organization. Bekmambetov, like Freud, mythologizes fictional events to reveal the hidden truth of the language, as words may mean the opposite of what they say. The truth that language conveys shifts from what is said and what is known to the unspeakable—the taboo or the truce. In Freudian terms, the contents of the unconscious, which are contained in the oracle, can no longer be suppressed and break forth into the light. To Oedipus-Anton, truth comes only through struggle and with painful reluctance.[23]

Since Anton's own Oedipus complex has not yet been resolved (his blood father is never portrayed or even mentioned in the films), he needs his son to undo his own past to determine the present. Oedipus first must suppress all the embodiments of the empirical father that gave him a false certainty, for only through the murder and the recognition of it can he experience the father not as a mere absence but as a presence that marks him forever. This explains Anton's persistent desire to eliminate Egor. His first attempt is disguised as a sorceress's act: he is frustrated because his wife has rebuffed him and he wants

---

19 The women Egor assaults include Svetlana (i.e., his adoptive mother). Thus Bekmambetov reveals the dynamics of the Oedipus complex as Egor desires his mother and achieves his purpose symbolically through an act of vampirism.

20 In Lacan's view, the father introduces the principle of law, particularly the law of the language system. When this law breaks down or of it has never been acquired, as in Egor's case, then the subject may suffer from psychosis.

21 Freud, *Lectures*, 120–21.

22 1–17.

23 Freud, *Lectures*, 87.

revenge. He acts on the grounds of false knowledge, as he is made to believe that the child is not his. In other words, the male child's desire for the mother is contradicted by paternal authority backed by the father's real and imagined power to harm him, which Freud conceptualizes as the boy's fear of the threat of castration.

Anton's second encounter with the son takes place on the Moscow metro while Anton is still unaware that Egor is his son. Now the murder is disguised as an act of vampirism, which suggests an incestuous intercourse but also "common blood"—that of filiation. In a later scene Anton, still unaware of Egor's identity, enters his flat and thus performs a symbolic penetration. Prior to this encounter, Egor is enveloped in the fantasy of a narcissistic link to the mother. Anton's intrusion transfers Egor from his dyadic state—he is never shown in a domestic setting again—into the triadic structure in which he needs to obey the demands and regulations of reality. The boy's development is based on the assumed dichotomy between the father and mother whereby the former symbolizes reality and maturity, and the latter, fantasy and narcissism.

Finally, in the scene on top of the building, where the murder is disguised as a fight between Anton and Zavulon, and Anton—this time perfectly aware of Egor's identity—acts on the basis of fabricated knowledge, Bekmambetov reveals some deeply internalized "aggressivity."[24] It is derived from both the boy's hostility toward the father and his fantasy that the father is murderously hostile to him. The latter is illustrated in a straightforward manner: Anton threatens to kill his son with a knife. According to Freud, this threat not only forces the repression of sexual desire but institutes a new structure within the mind, the superego, the source of an unconscious but continuing scrutiny of a person's wishes.[25] In *Night Watch* this shift takes place in a new way: Egor never conforms to his biological father's authority;[26] on the contrary, he takes the side of the Dark force and chooses Zavulon as his authority figure. Egor thus undermines the authority of his blood father, and identification with the real father never occurs. If, according to Freud, the father embodies the constraining force of society, then Egor rejects one set of laws (Night Watch) in favor of another (Day Watch).[27]

---

24 Jacques Lacan, *Ecrits: A Selection*, trans. Alan Sheridan with a foreword by Malcolm Bowie (New York: Routledge, 2001), 9.
25 Freud, *Lectures*, 141.
26 Ironically, his name suggests "ego" as a manifestation of his fixed identity.
27 Freud, *Lectures*, 87.

From Anton's perspective, the construction of the ego follows the pattern of (1) unrecognizability of the father; (2) transgression of the father; and (3) fabrication of the Father (described above as false knowledge, lack of knowledge, and fabricated knowledge). This pattern reaffirms Lacan's idea that the Oedipus complex is a portal into a different order of experience, the Symbolic order of language and culture, which, as the "Law of the Father," structures all interactions, even the early, extraordinary intimate ones between mother and infant.[28] For the same reason that Freud saw the Oedipal father as defining reality for the child (by placing a limit on narcissistic fantasy), Lacan claims that these structures derive from the "No" of the father because they depend on the recognition that complete possession of the other, complete wholeness, is impossible and that something exists outside the mother-infant bond.[29]

While Anton undergoes a linear development, the films themselves are structured as a symbolic loop in terms of time, space, and progression. At the end of the second film, in 2004, Anton returns to Dar'ia's apartment and on the wall writes "No" with "the chalk of fate," thus negating his previous act (agreement to exterminate his unborn child). In other words, he subjugates himself to the "law" and resolves his own Oedipus complex. Bekmambetov demonstrates Anton's advancement by allowing him to return to the past and relive the events of the day back in 1992: on his way to Dar'ia's apartment he meets Svetlana, and the film encourages viewers to assume that he follows her and never reaches the sorceress's apartment. In *The Seminar*, Book XI, Lacan writes: "The real is that which always comes back to the same place."[30] Indeed, Anton returns and embraces the Real. The Real should not be understood in the Freudian sense, which distinguishes the world external to the human mind from one's own imaginings. Rather, in Lacan's terms, the Real is the endless daunting power that supersedes the power of the Symbolic.[31] While *Night Watch* strives to convince the viewer of the presence of transcendental powers within the mundane, the ending of *Day Watch* disavows those powers. The confrontation between Geser and Zavulon is reduced to a chess game, and the great magicians are portrayed as typical Russian retirees enjoying their afternoon in a park.

---

28 Lacan, *Écrits*, 139–46.
29 Ibid., 152–53.
30 Jacques Lacan, *The Seminars*, trans. Dennis Porter, ed. Jacques-Alain Miller (New York: W. W. Norton, 1992), 49.
31 Ibid.

The Dialectics of Parenthood

According to Freud, paternity becomes identified through death.[32] The films present maternity as empirically verifiable (in fact, the status of Egor's mother or of Galina Rogova [Irina Yakovleva], the murdered vampire, is never questioned), whereas paternity constitutes uncertainty, fiction, or speculation. Fatherhood always remains an abstract notion or a shadow, as when Anton literally turns into a ghost when he enters Egor's apartment through the Gloom. Eventually the narrative reverses Freud's observation, for the father returns in material form but loses his abstract authority. In other words, the films rely on the mythology of parenthood, whereby, according to Freud's notions of the taboo that regulates the circulation of women in a tribe, the father is dismembered to be re/membered in the abstract.[33] Indeed, the father looms far larger in death, for by virtue of no longer being bodily accessible, he has become ubiquitous, institutionalized in the law that the son attempts to transcend. With this celebration of cerebration, *Night/Day Watch* presents the familiar landscape of the matter/mind dualism, with its networks of gendered alliances: form/substance, body/soul, nature/culture, and private/public.

Duality is the main structural component of the films. Characters are divided regarding their psyche, social affiliation, and moral stance. The divide also cuts across families by the types of parenthood already aggregated in the myth of Oedipus, and categorizes family members regardless of their gender, class, and other social categories. Egor is constantly torn between two models of paternity, incarnated in Anton and Zavulon—that is, between his biological father and his adoptive/substitute father,[34] who tries to replace the missing father and compensate for the deficiencies in the child's education. Further, the two major father figures in the films—Geser and Zavulon—function as spiritual fathers/mentors for Anton and Egor, respectively. Inevitably the child (Egor) is fascinated with his teacher (Zavulon) and convinces himself that the mentor loves him in return, yet as a son he fails to realize that the object of his affections is not his mentor but, rather, his own biological father (Anton).

---

32 Freud, *Totem and Taboo*, 3–6.

33 Ibid., 1–18.

34 *Day Watch* also explores the paradigm of the substitute mother. Alisa performs this function with regard to Kostia, the young vampire. She not only is his object of desire but is also a maternal figure. To achieve her goal, Alisa undergoes symbolic castration (she chops off one of her fingers) and thus is able to embrace his youth.

In fact, Egor is attracted to Anton (in *Night Watch,* in the scene in Egor's apartment, where Anton appears as trustworthy, strong, and affectionate) until he discovers Anton's real identity and past actions. The father's sudden return therefore marks the separation between father and son.

The Anton/Egor dual dynamic slots into a broad series of child/parent conflicts. While Anton makes an arduous effort to regain his son, the father (Valerii Zolotukhin) of Kostia (Aleksei Chadov) becomes obsessively protective over his child, trying to ensure that Kostia does not indulge his thirst for blood. The fears of Zolotukhin's character spring from guilt, since he initiated his son into vampirism during the boy's childhood—that is, he interrupted his normal progression toward identity formation. In contrast to Anton, Kostia's father is portrayed as a loving parent, tender and caring, who, in the absence of the mother, fulfills the maternal functions; for example, he does his son's laundry. In keeping with the films' scrambling of gender roles, he actualizes his parental instinct through traditional paradigms of femininity.

Secondary characters are also organized in child/parent groupings: Svetlana and her mother; Svetlana's neighbor and his mother; Galina's daughter and mother; Dar'ia and her daughter, and so forth. In these groupings, characters struggle to maintain uneasy relationships: Svetlana's mother is fatally ill; the neighbor's mother dies under the influence of an evil spell; Galina is murdered; Dar'ia daughter, Mashen'ka, is permanently trapped in the body of a rubber spider-like doll. Other—predominantly male—characters, such as Semion, Ignat, and Tolik, have neither children nor permanent partners. In short, the personae in the fictional universe of *Night/ Day Watch* are either unable to form a traditional nuclear family or are engaged in unstable or inadequate relationships.

The secondary characters and the conflicts they introduce into the narrative illuminate the condition of the main character. In *Night Watch* the character of Anton displays the tragedy of an individual: he fails in his relationship with Egor as well as in the prospect of (re)marriage. After his wife's departure and his unsuccessful contract with Dar'ia, Anton abstains from relationships with women in self-imposed penitence. He drops out of his social milieu, begins to drink, and learns how to be aloof and disdainful. His search for his own identity (he is dubious about his involvement with the Night Watch) is also a search for the concept of a father's role and thus is symptomatic of the impending split between the social order of Soviet and post-Soviet Russia. His desire for change inevitably carries within it the anticipation of failure and loss.

The Curse of the Vampire

Anton validates his parenthood not only through attempted filicide but also through symbolically incestuous assault. In *Night Watch,* having drunk blood in order to adopt temporarily the identity of a vampire, Anton is lured to drink his son's blood. The scene conjures up disquieting notions of an indissoluble union—a kind of marriage between human and vampire—as well as a symbolic incestuous union between parent and child.[35] On the Moscow underground an old lady, oblivious of Anton's state, calls him by the common Russian blasphemy that literally means "bloodsucker" [*krovopiets*]. Thus, on one level, *Night/Day Watch* exploits the classic interpretation of possession by ingestion, whereby the vampire's lust for blood is more than a reflection of the human or animal appetite for food and drink. On another level, "bloodsucking" is a metaphor for human parasitism and exploitation in general. Finally, in Freudian terms, Anton's vampiric inclination represents the return of the masculine repressed.[36] Sexual repression means that the human characters must be presented as celibate: Anton abstains from sex for twelve years (as does Svetlana, who—before she learns that she is an Other—is unable to enter a sexual relationship despite her strong sexual desire).

The films are full of the imagery of blood, which denotes not only violence and aggression but also filial relations. As *Night Watch* opens, Anton consumes a mixture of his own blood and alcohol, prepared by the sorceress in order to exterminate his child. *Day Watch* concludes with a banquet scene, in which, while Egor contends with Svetlana, Dar'ia feeds Anton with *vinaigrette,* a popular Russian vegetable dish whose ingredients include beetroot; it looks like a salad made of human flesh. In both instances, Anton consumes what symbolically should be interpreted as the body of his son, and thus the films evoke a creational myth of Kronos, chief of the Greek gods in the first generation, who, when told that one of his children will supplant him, devours them one by one. The use of the Greek myth in the films encodes resignation to the passing of time (Kronos—chronology), the overtaking of age by the young, and the necessarily step-like character of the genealogical ladder through time.

Thanks to Anton's vampiric experience he warms to his son, because he is able to understand his son's drive emotionally as he builds his sympathetic

---

35 For vampires, blood is the equivalent of semen.

36 Freud, *Lectures,* 92; The fear of the vampire, or, rather, the fear of becoming a vampire stems from a combination of love, hate, and guilt, which, according to Freud, results from a child's incestuous love for the mother and hatred for the father (*Totem and Taboo,* 1–18).

identification with Egor. The other identificatory experience that brings Anton closer to his son results from his psyche's entry into a female body: in *Day Watch*, in an act of supernatural invasion of a human personality, Geser exchanges the bodies of Anton and Ol'ga in order to hide him from persecution by the Day Watch, who accuse Anton of murdering the vampire Galina Rogova. As Anton embraces the symbolic female, he is able to carry out his nurturing and protecting instinct. Growing increasingly concerned with his son's life, he is ready to sacrifice his professional standing and ultimately his own life for the sake of Egor's well-being. Anton risks everything when he breaks into the storeroom where the Night Watch keeps material evidence of the Day Watch's nasty deeds and steals the hat Egor lost at the crime scene when caught sucking a victim's blood. Thus, Anton is presented as a self-sacrificing father; however, he remains a criminal because he has broken the laws of parenthood and the policies of the Night Watch.

The crimes of the father allow Bekmambetov to render the idea of the child's victimization. For that purpose, the director constructs an image of a sympathetic vampire, an unwilling victim of circumstances/fate and a complex mix of rage, retaliation, and redemption. The vampire body of Alisa, Kostia's inamorata (Zhanna Friske, ex diva of the Russian pop group *Blestiashchie*), is filled with melodramatic significance. She is forced to wear the ring of Zavulon (the head of her clan), which suggests her sexual and emotional subjugation to him. The possession of the ring signifies lost innocence and victimhood. Kostia's refusal to drink human blood is also a sign of sacrifice, which, in melodramatic terms, is crucial to the establishment of virtue. The signs of virtue are made visible (in a Freudian gesture, Alisa cuts off her finger) and powerful (Alisa's acts initiate the destruction of Moscow) to render the idea of the struggle for children's innocence to be acknowledged and their virtue to be recognized. The Alisa-Kostia-Zavulon dynamic strives to assert the cultural aspect of the Oedipus complex—namely, that civilization develops at the expense of sexual instincts—by showing how Alisa's sexual drive almost annihilates the civilization it has built.

Bekmambetov utilizes sets of father–son relations—Kostia-Zavulon, Egor-Anton—to call the viewer's attention to the idea that children are victims of their parents' actions. Galina Rogova's daughter loses her mother and remains in her grandmother's care. Egor is victimized in a number of ways: he is used as bait by the Night Watch; he falls prey to Andrei and his girlfriend; he is the "prize" to be won in Geser and Zavulon's games of power; and he experiences direct threats on his life, pain (high blood pressure and nose bleeding caused by the vampire's lure, and loss of consciousness upon entering the Gloom), fear, and moral pressure when he is forced to choose between the Light and Dark forces. In the first film his vulnerability is shown through nearnakedness—in trunks at the swimming pool, shirtless at home. Though the most powerful Other, he is portrayed as defenseless, disoriented, and perplexed.

Another child character for whom the director creates empathy is Kostia, who, like Egor, is victimized by his blood father. A victim of fatal circumstances (his father "initiated" him into vampirism when he was a child), Kostia experiences a guilt that equates with original sin—that is, the sin of the father rather than the sin of the child. Kostia symbolizes the moral conscience that Zavulon, the head of his group, lacks. Alienated from his clan and unable to connect with Alisa because she is controlled by Zavulon, according to the affirmation-denial dynamic, Kostia rises up against the parent—not his loving father but the tyrannical father figure of Zavulon. Consequently it is not his blood parent but rather an adoptive father who performs his sacrificial murder in order to retain his control over the female member of the clan (Alisa). The scene of Kostia's death is orchestrated in an extremely dramatic manner and thus evokes the passions of Greek tragedy and the aura of metaphysical crisis. When Zavulon is in the banqueting room of the Kosmos hotel celebrating Egor's birthday, Kostia bursts in clutching a bone (a phallic symbol), with which he threatens to kill the leader of Day Watch. Zavulon, by his magic, makes the bone rise in the air; he holds Kostia, and together they dance a macabre tango. The bone drops between them; Zavulon presses Kostia fiercely to him, and the bone pierces Kostia's body, killing him. Zavulon continues to hold Kostia in his devilish embrace, moves out of the room by breaking the window, and keeps on moving in the air. Hovering high above the ground Zavulon finally releases Kostia's corpse. Kostia's death sequence does not finish here: released by Zavulon, Kostia's body is supposed to fall on the ground, but the camera shows that only his hat reaches the snow.

Thus, Zavulon manifests his power over his adoptive son through the latter's corporeal, symbolic, and metaphysical deaths. The metaphysical pathos of the scene lies in its inversion of Jesus Christ's temptations of signs: "Then the devil took Him into the holy city and had him stand on the pinnacle of the temple, and said to Him, 'If you are the Son of God, throw yourself down.'"[37] Satan attempts to force Christ to prove God's power through command and might rather than through suffering and pain.

Kostia's story is the prime example of how, in *Night/Day Watch*, both parental and filial figures experience guilt and are symbolically punished or sacrificed.

---

37 Matthew 4:5–6.

Their execution takes the form of murder or disappearance. The example of the latter is the destiny of Kostia's father. In *Day Watch* he begins to show signs of an uneasy conscience about having introduced his own son to vampirism, and he collaborates with Zavulon in the hope that the latter will mollify his demands on Kostia. He agrees to murder the vampire, Galina Rogova, so that Zavulon can accuse Anton of the homicide and violation of the truce. At the end of *Day Watch* their conspiracy is revealed, and Kostia's father is eliminated, removed from the narrative by the Great Inquisitors. The figure of Kostia's father demonstrates how guilt transforms into moral corruption and degradation, signaled in the film by the character's profession of butcher as he frequently appears among dismembered animal carcasses. By eliminating both Kostia and his father, Bekmambetov shows that the whole family is contaminated by impurity, symbolically represented as vampirism: the bloodline transmits not only vitality but also defilement.

Patriarchy and History

In *Night/Day Watch* the sense of history is created by the depiction of three clearly demarcated generations[38] the older adults—Geser, Semion, Ol'ga,[39] Zavulon, Dar'ia, and Kostia's father; the younger—Anton, Svetlana, Alisa, Kostia, and Galina; and children—Egor and Galina's daughter. The films accentuate the generations' biological, psychological, and social differences. The older generation appears knowing, seasoned, and emotionally stable; indirect references are made to the tragedies and painful experiences the older adults endured in their social and private lives, and overcame. This is particularly true regarding the Night Watch: for example, Geser and Ol'ga wear Soviet World War II military uniforms in a photograph shown in *Day Watch*; in *Night Watch* Semion recalls how he suffered shell shock after stepping on a mine in 1941. In contemporary Moscow, the actions of their generation are concerted and decisive; the characters represent responsibility and capacity for sacrifice. For instance, in *Day Watch*, Semion dies in a car crash but, in the process, saves his team. Most important, they never question the truce. Powerful figures of

---

38 To reiterate, in the fictional world of *Night/Day Watch*, the bloodline exists only between Anton and Egor—between the perestroika and post-Soviet generation—thus signifying a break from the Soviet culture that is eventually bridged by Anton's symbolic association with his adoptive father, Geser.

39 Ol'ga appears quite young for her generation, because she spent sixty years as an owl and, apparently, this slowed down the aging process.

complete authority for their groups, they have earned that authority through previous experience and knowledge of life.

The older generation of the Night Watch noticeably differs from the younger one in relation to new technologies brought about by the modern age. Semion is an extremely skillful driver of his old-fashioned yellow truck, but he does not know how to use computers. Geser rarely comes in direct contact with new technologies; he is a representative of an old school of Soviet managers who relies on orally reproduced instructions and commands. So Egor finds understanding outside the Night Watch: he turns to Zavulon because he is the most technically savvy person of the older generation: in the first film, for example, he plays a computer game[40]—a skill that appeals to Egor's generation, enabling them to speak a common language.

The characters' generational membership overlaps with their historical associations. Geser and Zavulon, as well as other characters in their age group, are "Soviet people" in the sense that they have lived for most of their lives under the communist regime. Egor—born in 1992—symbolizes the post-Soviet generation, and Anton's contemporaries belong to the transitional generation of perestroika. They are portrayed as nonconformists—Others—who question the truce and its implications—that is, the old social order and the laws governing it. For example, Alisa overthrows Zavulon's power; Kostia argues with his father about the evils of vampirism. However, these characters representing "transition" remain unsuccessful or only partly successful challengers: Alisa escapes Zavulon's bonds but fails to keep Kostia, who dies because of his father; Anton manages to strike a favorable moral balance but is incapable of reestablishing parental relations with his son. Anton commits treason not only against his father's generation but also against his own son. It is apparent that Bekmambetov disparages the perestroika generation; at the same time, he redeems it, however, by entrusting its representatives with the magical "chalk of fate" and subsequently granting them a chance to rewrite/reconcile with the past and determine the future.

CONCLUSION

Anton's return to the past, which defies historical/chronological progression, is possible and accountable because the notion of reversible transformation

---

40 The computer game shows a fight between two avatars who resemble Anton and Zavulon. The game precedes the actual fight, and thus Bekmambetov introduces the idea of predestination and reveals Zavulon's desire to kill Anton.

governs the narrative and symbolism of the two films. The plot of *Night/Day Watch* is based on retributive tactics that Dark and Light forces adopt against each other, whereby vengeance is paralleled by a strong sense of equality and justice. Alisa attempts to take revenge on the murderer of her best friend, Galina; Larissa retaliates against the Night Watch for misleading and unfairly inculpating her; Egor carries out a harsh reprisal against his father, and so forth. Equally vampirism is used as a narrative device that blurs the edges of the landscape (through digital imagery), characterization, moral dispositions, and mood shifts so as to enhance the interplay of the real and the fantastic that produces mystery, hesitancy, and doubt. Moreover, characters constantly change into animals and birds (Ol'ga → an owl, Dar'ia → a frog, Il'ia → a bear, etc.); Ol'ga and Anton exchange bodies; Zavulon's spinal column turns into a sword; Egor's destructive yo-yo flies back; and so on. Finally, computer-generated imagery suggests plasticity of matter and the possibility of infinite modifications. This narrative mode and cinematic style present the generational conflict and father–son confrontation not as irreparable but instead as reversible, not as fixed but fluid, not as one dominated by predestination but rather by the logic and pragmatics of the day

The dual conflict of the film, and thus the seemingly stable structure of the narrative, is undermined by the triangular—and therefore unstable—paradigms of characterization and imagery, which swirl around the Freudian concepts of the id, ego, and superego, as well as Lacan's Symbolic, Imaginary, and Real. The triad is rich in symbolism (for example, the three roads: hell-purgatory-paradise), and it overrides the dichotomy of the Night versus Day Watch by introducing a new element (for example, the films' social structure the Night Watch versus the Day Watch is destabilized by the presence of people who do not belong to either group). Moreover, the characters function in three historical periods and in three types of space: place = presence, nonplace = absence, and the Gloom. The spatial triad may alternatively be interpreted as the underground, the surface, and the space above ground because these places are where Anton's attempts at killing Egor take place: on the metro, in the apartment, and on the roof of the house. The films also present three different generations, three forms of existence (life, death, and being in a body of another subject). The poetics of both films challenges their philosophy of the ancient divide and the truce, and incorporates transformation and change to signify progression from one generation to another. Thus *Night/Day Watch* presents a two-fold conflict: one involving Anton's relationship with women, particularly his ex-wife and Svetlana, the other involving his son Egor. Alternatively, the conflict may be viewed as a combination of Oedipal triads: in *Night Watch* the son rejects his father because the former has already established a stable relationship with his mother; in *Day Watch* Egor rejects Svetlana as his surrogate mother and desires to bring Anton into the realm of his own family.

The films focus on male maturation, which they connect with vampirism, while generally presenting monstrosity as a male attribute. The initiation of the vampire is symbolic of sexual initiation: for example, Egor begins to drink human blood at the age of twelve, namely, at puberty; Andrei (Il'ia Lagutenko, the leader of an extremely popular musical band, *Mummii Trol'*) seduces Larissa and substitutes a vampiric bond for their sexual relationship; and Kostia's father first initiated his wife into vampirism and, upon her death, turned to his son, transforming his sexuality into vampiric desire. The film series represents a male tragedy, for *Night Watch* stresses Anton's flaws as father, and *Day Watch* shows his incapacity as husband. The tragedy is grounded in the notion of error that overwhelms a man: Anton finds himself in the world of tragic appearance that contains and conditions his—and generally—the human condition from the beginning, including a man's nature and aims, and his role as husband, father, and member of a social group (the Night Watch). The conflict between child and parent assumes the form of a power struggle: in *Night Watch* Anton and Egor clash over the validity of the past; in *Day Watch* the control over time shifts into the future, as Egor and Svetlana contend for the love of father/lover, respectively. On the metaphysical level, the collision between Egor and Svetlana, the most powerful magicians ever born, results from the eternal conflict of Dark and Light forces, with Anton as their mediator: he is a communicator between the past and the present; between male and female; and between the Soviet and post-Soviet generations. Thus, the director shows how the radical political and social changes of the 1990s undermined parental authority, especially that of the father. The crisis of the father systematically coincides with the crisis of masculinity. The director enables his protagonist to overcome both these crises in the realm of the fantastic through the process of identification based on the Oedipus complex.

Thus, the films are simultaneously concerned with verification (Anton is paranoid about establishing his paternity, which creates a sense of historical perspective) and veracity (Geser consistently provides an alternative account of historical events). Both notions signify cultural systems that aim to mediate the world by introducing meaning. The films teach us that causality—father–son affiliation—is just another form of historical representation; history itself depends on conventions of narrative, language, and ideology,[41] which are presented as a divide between those who are able to stand aside from the conventional account of the past—Others—and those who are not. Bekmambetov presents a link between the two through the figure of Anton and his relations with his son, whose personal conflict also constitutes a generational conflict. The latter takes the form of a continuous battle between the Dark and Light forces, to which Bekmambetov gives a Freudian slant and Oedipal structure. The director demonstrates an unholy combination of filicide and cannibalism/ vampirism as a divine patriarchal prerogative. Accordingly, the films emphasize the role of paternity and the importance of the son as heir and perpetuator of the lineage. *Night/Day Watch* raises the questions of biological determinism and cultural potency: the films portray Anton as an impotent father, as someone incapable of fathering children and maintaining parental relations with them daily. In broad terms, the historical period of the 1990s is under the influence of Anton's generation and is defined as that of enervation, incapacity, and affliction. When Anton meets Svetlana in 2004 (*Day Watch*), after twelve years of sexual abstinence, his sexual desire normalizes, enabling reclamation of paternal potency. Eventually he reestablishes his parental authority (on the personal level) and reconstructs the social and cosmic order by maintaining the balance instituted by the truce. The latter signals the possibility of historical and cultural reconciliation and a national unity that charts the symbolic progression from paternity to patronage. To reiterate, this advancement becomes possible because Anton reconnects with the Soviet past through the figure of his adoptive father, Geser, and simultaneously establishes a link with the post-Soviet generation through his blood child, Egor, and, by so doing, determines the nation's future.

---

41 In her *A Poetics of Postmodernism: History, Theory, Fiction* (New York: Routledge, 1988), Linda Hutcheon writes, "Historiographic metafiction ... refuses the view that only history has a truth claim, both by questioning the ground of the claim in historiography and by asserting that both history and fiction are discourses, human constructs, signifying systems, and both derive their claim to truth from that identity" (93).

The Antiutopia Factory: The Dystopian Discourse in Russian Literature in the Mid-2000s

ALEKSANDR CHANTSEV

Chantsev, Aleksandr. "The Antiuopia Factory: The Dystopian Discourse in Russian Literature in the Mid-2000s." *Russian Studies in Literature* 45, no. 2 (2009): 6–41.

What is demanded ... is the explicit, conscious, and consciously self-justifying attempt to devalue the uppermost values, to depose them as highest values. At the same time, this implies a decision to take seriously the intermediate state that the devaluation of the highest values produces, by simultaneously fixing on our earthly world as the only reality, and a decision *to be* in that decision as a historical one. Nihilism is now no longer a historical process that we as observers merely have before us, outside ourselves, or even behind us; nihilism reveals itself as the history of our era, which imposes its own effective limits on the age, and by which we are claimed.

—Martin Heidegger, *Nietzsche and the Void* [Nitsshe i pustota]¹

[P]olitical activities, of all those in public life the most efficient and the most visible, are the final product of others more intimate, more

---

1 M. Khaidegger [Martin Heidegger], "Evropeiskii nigilizm," in Khaidegger, *Nitsshe i pustota*, uncredited translation into Russian (Moscow: Algoritm/Eksmo, 2006), n.p. [Quotation from Heidegger's *Nietzsche*, vol. 4: *Nihilism*, trans. Frank A. Capuzzi (San Francisco: Harper and Row, 1982), 48. Emphasis in the English original. Page references for later citations from this edition are given below in square brackets. —Trans.]

impalpable. Hence, political indocility would not be so grave did it not proceed from a deeper, more decisive intellectual indocility.

—José Ortega y Gasset, *The Revolt of the Masses*[1]

Due to the deterioration of the political climate and the transformation of political consciousness in this country's literature ("high" literature, "mainstream" literature, and "trash" literature simultaneously) some rather strange processes have recently begun. In the 1990s and the early 2000s, mainstream literature in Russia was basically trying to erase various historical traumas (beginning with the 1917 Revolution and the Civil War [1918–21], extending through the reconceptualization of World War II, and ending with the Gulag and the disintegration of the USSR) and stressing apocalyptic ideas (Pavel Krusanov's *Bite of an Angel* [Ukus angela] and Vladimir Sorokin's *Ice* [Led]). Now a slew of fictional works has arisen, literally before our eyes, in which the imagination explores the near political future.

Books that, to one degree or another, follow this trend—whose novelistic form originated with Dmitrii Bykov's *The Evacuator* [Evakuator]—include Sergei Dorenko's *2008*, Ol'ga Slavnikova's *2017*, Bykov's *ZhD*, *The Hostage* [Zalozhnik] by Aleksandr Smolenskii and Eduard Krasnianskii, and Vladimir Sorokin's *Day of the Oprichnik* [Den' oprichnika].[2] All these books, qualitatively diverse as they may be, have captured the public's attention, won literary awards,[3] received critical attention,[4] and been eagerly discussed in the press.

---

1 Kh. Ortega-i-Gasset [José Ortega y Gasset], *Vosstanie mass*, trans. A.M. Geleskul and S.L. Vorob'ev (Moscow, 1991). [Quotation from José Ortega y Gasset, *The Revolt of the Masses* (New York: W. W. Norton, 1932, 1960), 67. —Trans.]

2 Dmitrii Bykov, *Evakuator* (Moscow: Vagrius, 2005); Sergei Dorenko, *2008* (Moscow: Ad Marginem, 2005); Ol'ga Slavnikova, *2017* (Moscow: Vagrius, 2006); Bykov, *ZhD* (Moscow: Vagrius, 2006); Aleksandr Smolenskii and Eduard Krasnianskii, *Zalozhnik (Operatsiia "Memorandum")* (Moscow: Vagrius, 2006); Vladimir Sorokin, *Den' oprichnika* (Moscow: Zakharov, 2006). See also the recently released *Rublevka Fortified District* [Ukrepraion "Rublevka"] (Moscow: Vagrius, 2006). Our selection holds to the chronological principle overall, while sometimes sacrificing chronology to thematic consistency, especially since the chosen titles were published only a few months apart.

3 Notably Slavnikova's novel, which was a Great Book [Bol'shaia kniga] finalist, won the 2006 Russian Booker and the Student Booker for 2006, and was picked by *Knizhnoe obozrenie* as the best book-length prose published in Russia for 2006.

4 Liza Novikova, commenting on Bykov's *ZhD* and Sorokin's *Day of the Oprichnik*, was the first to juxtapose these two works in terms of their evident thematic kinship ("two satirical treatises, two verdicts passed on our reality"). See L. Novikova, "Knigi za nedeliu" [Books of

That would probably not have happened had they dealt only with calculatedly ripped-from-the-headlines, sure-bet scandals (although they all, in one way or another, touch on the "2008 problem"—whether or not Putin would step down from the presidency and who would be selected as his successor), this epidemic spread of "election campaign" motifs in literature is proof of how timely and, at the same time, how painful the topic of the country's near future is to the public mind.

Furthermore, the exploration of identical problems by authors on opposite sides of the literary and social field (Smolenskii, the former banker and oligarch, and Bykov, the writer and journalist sounding off with his antiliberal slogans; Slavnikova, the representative of "pure" literature, and Minaev, the "glitzy" writer/businessman) should be perceived as highly indicative: these books appeared in 2006 and 2007, in a veritable avalanche. The witty forecast of a critic summing up the previous year and predicting the next—"we may also expect the market to be flooded with novels that in one way or another 'anticipate' the parliamentary and presidential elections. The spate of antiutopias and political treatises that swept over fiction in this country during 2006 will not ebb in the coming year"[5]—was borne out, if only by the fact that Sergei Minaev's novel, much touted as a potential bestseller (Minaev's previous production, the novel *Soulless* [Dukhless] really had been a bestseller in 2006), was given the telling title *Media sapiens: A Tale of a Third Term* [Media sapiens. Povest' o tret'em sroke].[6] Due to this "descent" of the dystopian discourse into mass literature, we may say that Alvin Toffler's famous call to build "utopia factories" has been successfully realized, except that this country has characteristically switched negative for positive, with the result that what has actually gone up, right before our eyes, is an "antiutopia factory."[7]

In pondering why this set of problems is so socially timely, the following questions must be answered. Why have futurological prognoses geared to the imminent supplanted the erasure of historical traumas in literature? Why has the topic of abstract apocalypse in works published in the 1990s and early in this century been replaced by concrete though downright pessimistic

the week], *Kommersant''*, no. 155 (3486) (August 23, 2006), available at www.kommersant.ru/doc .html?DocID=699575 [all URLs accessed December 2008—Ed.].

5 A. Miroshkin, "Strategiia schast'ia" [Strategies of happiness], *Knizhnoe obozrenie* [Book review] no. 1 (2007): 4.

6 Sergei Minaev, *Media sapiens. Povest' o tret'em sroke* (Moscow: AST, 2007).

7 Minaev's opus won the 2006 "SNAFU" [Polnyi abzats], *Knizhnoe obozrenie*'s "anti-prize" for the worst book of the year, and that award was well earned.

forecasts? How is literature generally trying to handle the current situation, in which public policy is going away and the political is being transformed and sublimated in contemporary Russia?

These questions are directly linked to the genre definition of the works under examination here. The most accurate way to define these sociopolitical phantasms, one supposes, would be as dystopias, but as a far from classical type of dystopia.[8] The first thing that leaps out at us is that these works, while maintaining the form of dystopian forewarning and orientation toward the future, actually deal with the present: "fantasy is a means of mentally rationalizing the very principles of social organization in the form of a hypothetical war, enmity, competition. ... Following the powerful lead of certain cultural groups, it presents as a mode of intellectual control over the problems of social change and the pace and direction of the social dynamic, and as a conditional aesthetic reaction to the problems arising therein."[9] The element of satire inherent in dystopias is present and even exaggerated in certain writers (Sergei Dorenko's rendition of our heads of state is likely to elicit a squeamish disgust even in those who have never counted themselves among their admirers), but something key is missing. Not one of these books offers an even remotely recognizable plan for a *positive* future; the plan found, exceptionally, in Slavnikova's *2017* is in fact a reprise of the distant past (the 1917 Revolution). This brings the works under examination here into close juxtaposition with the Aleksandr Garros and Aleksei Evdokimov collection of stories *Juche* [Chuchkhe], whose action is set in the near future but also encompasses the events of several past years (the Yukos debacle, for example), while its fierce polemical critique and its denial of the present comes without so much as a hint that Garros and Evdokimov have a program of their own for positive development in the country.[10]

As we can see, in examining Slavnikova's novel, in which a "revolution in masquerade" erupts in 2017, replaying the revolution of a century earlier, it may be said that we are dealing with a denial of history: "In history, this process [the revival by force of great events from the past—A. C.] is called

---

8 Since the interpretation of such terms as "ectopia," "practopia," "cacotopia," and "contratopia" has yet to be settled, we shall employ the possibly less nuanced but more distinct "utopia/dystopia" dichotomy.

9 B. Dubin, *Slovo—pis'mo—literatura: ocherki po sotsiologii sovremennoi kul'tury* [Word, writing, literature: Essays on the sociology of modern culture] (Moscow: Novoe literaturnoe obozrenie, 2001), 27.

10 Aleksandr Garros and Aleksei Evdokimov, eds., *Chuchkhe* (Moscow: Vagrius, 2006). For further detail, see A. Chantsev, "Vita nova gadkikh lebedei," *Novoe literaturnoe obozrenie*, no. 82 (2006): 423–30.

restoration: it is a process of the denial of history and the antievolutionist revival of earlier models."[11] The denial of history is projected into the future, thereby spilling over into a negation of that future: consequently, these books cannot possibly be regarded as works of futurology.

Utopian literature—and dystopian literature, too, by and large—appears when society becomes certain that the current situation can survive the long haul and is manifestly apt only to deteriorate in the future, while the individual is beset by a sense of alienation from any involvement in history. In that sense, the novels we examine here are nothing but a natural documentation of frustrated resentment and society's predominant confusion in the present political situation, and their popularity is evidently associated with the way in which they satisfy the need of Russia's readership for utopian catastrophilia. The emotional coloration of that need brings with it more than a whiff of scandal, being akin to a fascination for the tabloids' description of sundry gory events. None of these authors goes beyond the transmission of that catastrophilia. Without even attempting to propose their own plans for the future, they substitute instead a critique of the present, extrapolating the current situation into the future and adopting what is in essence an escapist stance. These works thus undoubtedly take on the formal features of the dystopian genre, but that does not make them pure dystopias, because a real dystopia—in its implicit, maximally coded, or apophatic form—entails at least the hint of a "brighter future," of *how things should be*.[12]

These authors are wholly invested in producing a caustic treatise (Bykov in *ZhD*, Prokhanov in *The Motorship "Joseph Brodsky"* [Teplokhod Iosif Brodskii], and Dorenko in *2008*), have a fine touch in describing various technologies, both "physical" (the fantastically cyberpunk gadgets described in Sorokin's novella) and "political" (technologies to shape public opinion and manage

---

11 Zh. Bodriiiar [Jean Baudrillard], *Obshchestvo potrebleniia* [Consumer society] (Moscow: Respublika/Kul'turnaia revoliutsiia, 2006), 132. [Quotation from an uncredited translation of Baudrillard's *The Consumer Society: Myths and Structures* (Thousand Oaks, CA: Sage, 1998), 99. Page references for the following citations from this edition are given below, in square brackets. —Trans.]

12 "Some will explain the emphasis on social interaction and politics in contemporary Russian literature as showing that Russia is healing, is concentrating, is Acquiring Ideas." Thus Sergei Shargunov, political figure and writer, comments on works by Sergei Dorenko, Aleksandr Prokhanov, and Zakhar Prilepin ("Dom mod uveshan flagami" [Fashion house decorated with flags], *Ex Libris NG*, July 20, 2006, http://exlibris.ng.ru/subject/2006-07-20///1_house.html). But in our view, it can equally well be proof of the opposite, of a situation so burdensome and so explosive that one has a constant desire to discuss it.

people in Smolenskii and Krasianskii), for the analysis of all sorts of tendencies in contemporary society but not for generating new meanings that might serve to unify a divided society.[13] Thus, Slavnikova documents society's need for that unification, the need to search for points of contact with the Other, which ultimately leads to the avoidance of the Other: "All the same, this resembled neither a popular revolt nor a military putsch. Moscow was reminiscent of a huge railroad station packed with troops and refugees, *where all were searching for their own kind.*"[14] Of course, one has to ask whether the described society itself has a vested interest in producing—or is generally ready to produce—the political and ideological ideas that will unify it. But we permit ourselves not to answer that question, contenting ourselves with pointing out that the mass production of such works is becoming an increasingly important factor in public life—and noting another property of these antiutopian works, their isolationist nature.

Indicative here are Bykov's *ZhD* (where Russia is the only country lacking stocks of the magical fuel phlogiston, which leads it to drop out of the world community) and Sorokin's *Day of the Oprichnik* (where Russia, separated from Europe by a high partition resembling the Berlin Wall, "goes its own way," living a life that is a stylized "reprise" of our medieval past). Both seem to have generally concluded that Russia has definitively and irretrievably pulled away from the whole world, has forfeited in principle (or is being obliged to forfeit) the potential for cultural/political interaction with other countries, is doomed, and has been buried under the burden of its own problems and unresolved tensions.[15] These "futurologist" writers care only about how the country's death

---

13 Aleksandr Prokhanov, *Teplokhod Iosif Brodskii* [Motorship Joseph Brodsky] (Ekaterinburg: Ul'tra.Kul'tura, 2006).
14 Slavnikova, *2017*, 549 [emphasis added —A. C.].
15 Even Hardt and Negri, leaders of the antisystem militants and authors of the sensational treatise *Empire* are willing to concede: "We should not get caught up here in the tired debates about globalization and nation-states as if the two were necessarily incompatible. Our argument instead is that national ideologues, functionaries, and administrators increasingly find that in order to pursue their strategic objectives they cannot act and think strictly in national terms without consideration of the rest of the globe" (M. Khardt [Michael Hardt], A. Negri [Antonio Negri], *Mnozhestvo: voina i demokratiia v epokhu imperii*, translation from the English ed. V. L. Inozemtsev [Moscow: Kul'turnaia revoliutsiia, 2006], 84). [Quotation from Hardt and Negri's *Multitude: War and Democracy in the Age of Empire* (New York: Penguin, 2004), 60. —Trans.] This assertion is all the more important given that the position of Russia's political elite is—to put it mildly—contradictory. For all the current leadership's isolationist pronouncements, it has extraordinarily powerful links with Western financial and economic entities. On this, see a recent interview given by Mikhail Sergeevich

throes look, how long they will persist, and who or what will deliver the coup de grâce.

Returning now to the genre definition of the tendency we are analyzing, all of the above permits us to define these works as political satire (sometimes verging on lampoon, as in Dorenko and Prokhanov), which—unusually for satire—is adorned with fatalistic sentiments. Even those properties, though, give us no grounds for defining these works as "pure" dystopia: mockery of an untoward situation in society is part of that situation, is implanted on a simulative level into the situational matrix and reproduces itself there, as, for example, in Slavnikova's novel, where not only does a century-old revolution repeat but every new president resembles the one who went before. (Incidentally, on the subject of that matrix: if one concurs with the conclusions drawn by Michael Hardt and Antonio Negri and with Jean Baudrillard's durable prophecies, some fairly innocuous protest movements such as the Greens or the Alterglobalists are a necessity to the management systems of states and/or transnational corporations, in that they allow young and potentially dangerous members of such systems to "blow off steam.")

Yet the sweeping emotive impetus of the individual books does give us grounds to surmise that many authors would be unlikely to agree with that definition, inasmuch as a dystopia is what they patently intended to create. In that case, an adjustment of the definition would be in order: these novels are satire that believes itself to be an antiutopia. But one more not exactly encouraging fact must also be acknowledged. The refusal to offer a positive version of the future signals two things: it automatically eliminates introspection of any kind, which in extreme cases implies agreement with a situation that the author finds outrageous, and it results in a simple statement of that situation's junctures and tendencies.

Following these preliminary observations, we now proceed to examine the political, ideological, and moral conceptions that are documented in these works and show how those conceptions have been aesthetically "processed."

The Bloody Annexation of Land by Land

We would like to begin our analysis with a book that was not mentioned earlier to avoid confusing the reader, since Aleksei Ivanov's *Heart of the Uplands*

Gorbachev, "Shpionskie voiny: zhivoi sezon" [Spy wars: Current season], *Novaia gazeta*, July 23, 2007.

[Serdtse parmy], a solid historical novel about the annexation of the land of Perm by the principality of Moscow, is conspicuously lacking the features of a futuristic satire or a treatise on the 2008 presidential elections.[16] In our view, however, its metaphorical documentation of contemporary political tendencies, oriented toward the near future, is self-evident.

The forces motivating Ivanov's novel are the idea of building a strong state, rigidly managed from the center, and completely annihilating both local and individual autonomy from the ubiquitous will of the state, both of which find direct parallels in the image of "Putin's Russia." So, for instance, the campaign against the independence of unruly republics such as Chechnya that was initiated by the present Moscow center, the presidential appointment of governors and his own representatives in the federal districts, and the destruction of politically influential commercial forces (Yukos again) repeat almost verbatim the fifteenth-century situation as described by Ivanov, when overly freedom-loving lands that in olden days had deemed themselves independent of the center were brought into subjection by Prince Ivan III of Moscow [1462–1505].

Ivanov stated in an interview that the archetype of Moscow's confrontation with the outlying regions is eternal and "100 percent" analogous to the present day, but his intentions and evaluations are perhaps less important than his general documentation of certain processes and some of the minutiae thereof. (Being a Perm patriot and having depicted its original historical legacy in other works, in *Heart of the Uplands* Ivanov distinctly sympathizes with the war waged by Mikhail of Perm but acknowledges the historical logic that dictated the need to centralize Rus.)

The process whereby the lands of the Urals were subjected to the "beneficent yoke of the state" was thus a bloody one ("land is annexed to land by blood").[17] It is accompanied by the enforced religious conversion of the local population: "you are to accept Christ for the sake of the future, so that the folk of Perm may be preserved amid the Russian people forever, that they shall not be stamped out by the Muscovites. For the sake of your salvation, do you understand?"[18] For Perm, annexation by Moscow was tantamount to actual

---

16 Aleksei Ivanov, *Serdtse parmy* [Heart of Parma]. The first (abridged) version was published in Moscow in 2003. Here we quote from the full-length version (St. Petersburg: Azbuka-klassika, 2006).

17 Ibid., 211. [The quotation about the "beneficent yoke of the state" comes from Eugene Zamiatin, *We*, trans. Mirra Ginsburg (New York: Bantam, 1972), 35. —Trans.]

18 Ibid., 478. Ivanov was not the first in the newer literature to articulate the motif of the aggressive expansion of the state and the subjection of previously independent regions: suffice it

salvation (from Tatars attacking from the southeast) but at the same time to a loss of identity (the rejection of pagan local customs is symbolized by the protagonist's abandonment by his wife, a pagan priestess, after the acceptance of Russian annexation). At a higher level of generalization, this loss of identity can be read as the end of history for the people of Perm as a separate entity—the replacement of their personal, original history and their involvement in the shaping of history, with the impersonal will of the state. The impersonality of the sovereign's will is underscored by the contrast between the vivid, charismatic people of Perm and the arid Moscow boyars headed by Grand Prince Ivan Vasil'evich (Ivan III). The images of the commanders in his entourage who were commissioned to subjugate Perm come back to us as we analyze the caricature of Putin in Sergei Dorenko's novel, which describes the president as a passive and universally indifferent potentate:

> Prince Fedor the Motley was not born cruel. ... He spilled blood, a great deal of blood, and sometimes innocent blood, but found no pleasure in it. It had to be done. ... The Motley got everything he wanted in life. But having received everything, he suddenly realized to his surprise that he did not need all that much. He was not enticed by wealth, fame, honor, the love of beautiful women. He was no longer enticed by anything at all. He was like an arrow in flight that had penetrated all obstacles but lacked the strength to fly farther. He was a little comforted by the thought of power, but how much more power could there be?[19]

It should also be noted that *Heart of the Uplands* is the only novel of its type in which, although no theory of the future is presented, there is a certain inherent "moral imperative," which stands counter to state coercion: the assertion of the artless idea that the lot of a person who must "live out his own human destiny"[20] is even so contingent on a change of ruler, on wars, and the like, since "in the human being all the same there always remains something ineradicably human, and that humanity cannot be sold or repudiated and perhaps can only be killed together with life itself."[21]

---

to recall *Bite of an Angel*, by the "Petersburg fundamentalist" Krusanov, which describes with manifest sympathy and some gusto operations both in the Caucasus and "internationally" by the troops of a fictitious Russia/Byzantium, couched in the traditions of "alternative history."

19 Ivanov, *Serdtse parmy*, 294–95.
20 Ibid., 210.
21 Ibid., 474.

The Next Have Arrived

Dmitrii Bykov's novel *The Evacuator* weaves together two fairly simple elements of myth. First, there is "love in wartime"—the affair of the Muscovite Katia and her coworker Igor', who seeks to engage her in a game that "only two can play" (telling her that he is an extraterrestrial) and comes up with a detailed plan for journeying with her to his "home planet."[22] All this takes place during a rising wave of terror perpetrated by Chechen separatists, which ultimately causes Russia's state institutions to collapse. The book's "extraterrestrial" component is presented as an intentional, parabolic abstraction, but the meaning of that parable is not completely clear. (If we don't count the rather hackneyed claim that private happiness is the antithesis of social cataclysm, we can interpret this love story as an attempt to achieve personal freedom by means of pointedly private phantasmic speech.)[23] Second, there is an "apocalypse now"just as the Yandex search engine advertises that "everything will be found," so in Bykov, everything that physically can be blown up will be blown up, from Moscow retail centers to provincial nuclear power plants.

It is worth examining the second, "apocalyptic" component of *The Evacuator*, especially since the traditional interpretation of war as chaos and destruction has recently become almost a rarity against the backdrop of a resuscitated modernist understanding of war as an element in a successfully functioning system: "We know that the system has traditionally and power-fully drawn on the aid of *war* to survive and to revive. Today the mechanisms and functions of war have been integrated into the economic system and the mechanics of daily life" (Jean Baudrillard).[24] It is of war and the "mechan-ics of daily life" (and love as the most vivid manifestation of life) that Bykov writes. War as the most graphic expression of catastrophe and general discord is present in other works on the topic of interest to us here. So, for instance, Sorokin's novel refers to a "time of troubles," while the Caucasus is fenced off behind a wall like that which separates Russia from Europe; a civil war begins in Slavnikova's novel, and Dorenko's *2008* ends with the simultaneous threat of

---

22 Bykov evidently used his own 1996 narrative poem "The Military Coup" [Voennyi perevo-rot] in the plot of *Evacuator* [www.plib.ru/library/book/2396.html].

23 Compare with "narrative as the embodiment of self-awareness also emerges in Zamiatin's novel through the procedure adopted to 'deprogram' the hero, freeing him from the control of language that belongs to no one and of omnipresent domination (a path that would later be trodden by Orwell's protagonist)" (Dubin, *Slovo—pis'mo—literatura*, 36).

24 Bodriiiar, *Obshchestvo potrebleniia*, 80.

a catastrophic act of terrorism and of civil strife, after which the authorities in Russia call in American troops to bring the situation under control.

The conceptually detached depiction of similar inklings is graphically demonstrated in a text that has no direct bearing on our topic, *The Pins* [Bulavki], an intentionally absurdist and introverted play by Aleksandr Anashevich whose two female leads suffer recurrent bouts of panic: "Soon this city, too, will be splitting at the seams and writhing in pain. It will be destroyed. They will all die." The women discuss the "war," "civil strife," and "looting" that can be escaped only by fleeing "to Cheliabinsk or Vorkuta."[25] Here, too, and even more so than in *The Evacuator*, the sense of an abstract "apocalypse now" is of far greater importance than the concretization of the threat.

If Bykov's novel is set in the future, that future is close at hand; most likely its time frame coincides with the time of publication, which was 2005 (in fact, one character says that "two more years have creaked by" since 2003).[26] *The Evacuator* describes Russian society as being in a state of total crisis, pervasive erosion, and panic. There are constant explosions in Moscow, as cafes, retail centers, and whole districts (Sviblovo) are blown up. As in Dorenko's novel, Bykov's terrorists capture a nuclear power plant, although we cannot know for sure if they end by blowing it up: "People in the city are saying that a nuclear power plant has been blown up." "Sukhinichi?" "Uh-huh. But then, other people are saying that it hasn't been blown up, just captured. The radio's keeping quiet; they're not saying anything."[27]

Things are blowing up due to accident or terrorism over an ever-expanding area: there are explosions in other Russian cities, "it has already started" in the United States,[28] and things are amiss in Europe, too ("panic on the roads of Germany and France").[29]

In the absence of reliable information and as the catastrophe escalates, the government gradually falls apart: the subway is closed, the center is cordoned off, telephone service is down, and there are no newspapers (the "glossy magazines held on longer than the rest, and that was logical in a way, because in a moribund country everything is back-to-front, the laws are turned inside out,

25 A. Anashevich, "Bulavki: p'esa dlia chteniia *Aleksandora Anashevicha*" [Safety-pins: A play for reading *Aleksandor Anashevich*], *Kriticheskaia massa* [Critical Mass] no. 1 (2006), available at http://magazines.russ.ru/km/2006/1/aa5.html.

26 Bykov, *Evakuator*, 172.

27 Ibid., 190.

28 Ibid., 89.

29 Ibid., 196.

and what is most viable is what no one needs"), and it is forbidden to leave the country.[30] The alarmist catastrophilia—a topic that Bykov pursued further in his next book, ZhD—is constantly exacerbated, which is, in and of itself, a property common to ages of crisis. In his analysis of Nietzsche's worldview, Friedrich Georg Jünger demonstrated the development of its pathological aspects, in a description that is exceedingly apposite to the social symptoms we are analyzing here: "All at once, everything around seems poisoned. Everything looks as though a large, unseen corpse had poisoned the air. Fear, hatred, mistrust begin to grow more rapidly. The question of trust is posed time and again; those responsible, guilty, are sought. Responsibility is handed from person to person, around and around. ... Accusations grow harsher: new procedures and methods are cultivated. They serve to intensify and augment suspicion. ... Naked cruelty emerges."[31]

Yet, for all the manifest relish with which the narrator recounts the explosions, the death throes of the state, and the rest of the eschatological nightmare (there cannot be, as a matter of principle, any question of empathy for the potential victims: the characters only regale one another with emotional accounts of the latest explosions, considering them if not actually justified then at least a zero option in the current situation), it is more important to examine the causes and consequences of what is happening.

The explosions carry with them, not overtly but implicitly, the "Chechen spoor": ordinary people are convinced that Chechens did it; Shamil Basaev [prominent Chechen terrorist—Trans.] posts a promise on his Internet site to "blow up all of Moscow"; Chechens are harassed on the streets; individuals from the Caucasus are expelled from Moscow; eastern cafes are wrecked; and the street markets are closed.[32] Even though one of the book's characters, a Chechen girl rescued by the heroes from the street and taken aboard the

---

30 Ibid., 56.
31 F.G. Iunger [Friedrich Georg Jünger], Nitsshe, trans. from the German by A. V. Mikhailovskii (Moscow: Praksis, 2001), 168 [retranslated from the Russian —Trans.].
32 The Russian government nearly enacted these last two xenophobic details in 2006, when, after security force "raids" inspired and sanctioned by the authorities (a consequence of the political conflict with Georgia in October 2006) on Georgian restaurants and casinos, those establishments were (temporarily) closed and traders from the Caucasus and Central Asia were all but physically ejected from the street markets pursuant to a new law on the use of foreign workers in branches of the municipal economy. Admittedly legal workarounds were soon found, but only after the market stalls had been left with no one to man them. For further detail, see, for example, http://news.bbc.co.uk/hi/russian/russia/newsid_6346000/6346415.stm.

spaceship, turns out to be a terrorist wearing a suicide belt (because what other kinds of Chechens are there?), no one really believes in that "spoor": "He blew it up himself. What do the Chechens have to do with it? What, then—did they find any hexogen there? ... It's a war. Yeah, right—a friggin' war. But who's the war against? To have a war, you at least have to see the enemy," says an uneducated soldier who might have been expected to blame the Chechens for everything.[33] "The terrorist acts were tolerated because a might could be sensed behind them that was not to be trifled with. With each new explosion, people blamed the authorities with increasing certainty and were ever more willing to sympathize with their adversaries," Katia argues (alluding to the numerous reports in the media here and abroad on "traces of provocation" in the spectacular acts of terrorism committed in the late 1990s and early 2000s).[34] "It's a sign of the times. Evil without a reason, perpetrated by a monster, by a purposeless force. Radical Islam is absolutely beside the point. It will become a victim, too, only not just now. What I'm telling you is that these and those are on level ground and they've annihilated each other. And the next have arrived," Igor' the "extraterrestrial" explains to her.[35] The novel ends with Caucasians and Russians fleeing Moscow together.

It is highly characteristic that Katia denies any Chechen involvement in the explosions ("well yes, but they're not evil, even though they are murderers and all the rest of it. ... Well, what I mean is they're *other*"),[36] while Igor' talks about the "next." Thus, the enemy turns out to be absolutely undefined—which is, to say the least, strange and implausible, since the explosions and other calamities have been going on for a while. Even allowing for censorship and the media's problems in getting the story out, it is impossible to imagine a situation in which a series of large-scale terrorist acts would happen without anyone claiming responsibility or being found out. Bykov, one imagines, needs this artistic implausibility so that he can allocate the role of enemy to a completely unknown, undefined, almost natural force—to the maximally abstract Other.

The narrator attempts to fill the place of that Other with the Russian state, its people, or some systemic crisis long in the making and fraught with general dissolution: "for the state, in preaching disintegration, doubles its strength, by sanctifying with its authority something long desired. Disintegration was revealed to be the secret dream of almost the entire populace, because there

---

33 Bykov, *Evakuator*, 115.
34 Ibid., 57.
35 Ibid., 264.
36 Ibid., 85 (emphasis added—A. C.).

had long been no good reason to create and nothing to create with, plus creation would, in essence, cost the creators more than it was worth. Perhaps they bore the burgeoning terror so submissively because they had from the beginning been convinced deep down that what was happening was well deserved, that such developments were natural."[37] (Bykov was to revisit this idea in ZhD.) The Evacuator is, furthermore, filled with stubbornly hypnotic repetitions of passages claiming that the state is causing the explosions or that things are blowing up for no apparent reason.

But the state's involvement in the explosions remains on the borderline of rumor, which is symbolic since, first, it refers us to the Soviet past (in Slavnikova's novel, too, where rumor is the main source of information, or, as Boris Dubin has put it, "in revolutionary-era Russia the echo of a detonation in society called forth waves of rumor, witticisms, and jokes, accompanied by negative projections, by 'black shadows'—denunciations and information leaks"). Second, "'news' would, understandably enough, relate only to the socially different, the culturally bizarre, the alien" (Dubin again). Third, rumor flourishes in a society that no longer has any universally acknowledged values ("rumor ... functions only in the kind of world which the sacred ... has vanished").[38] This last description relates to totalitarian society and is familiar to us from [George] Orwell's 1984: "The rocket bombs crashed oftener than ever, and sometimes in the far distance there were enormous explosions which no one could explain and about which there were wild rumors."[39] Orwell's novel also offers the insight—which Bykov was to reiterate many years later—that, looking behind those explosions, one would find not enemy stratagems but the operations of state itself, with the aim of keeping its citizens constantly under threat of war: "The war, therefore, if we judge it by the standards of previous wars, is merely an imposture. It is like the battles between certain ruminant animals whose horns are set at such an angle that they are incapable of hurting one another. But though it is unreal it is not meaningless. It eats up the surplus of consumable goods, and it helps to preserve the special mental atmosphere that a hierarchical society needs. War, it will be seen, is now a purely internal affair. ... The war is waged by each ruling group against its own subjects."[40]

37 Ibid., 57.
38 Dubin, Slovo—pis'mo—literatura, 72–73.
39 Dzh. Oruell [George Orwell], 1984, in Oruell, 1984. Skotnyi dvor, trans. D. Ivanov and V. Nedoshivina (Perm: Kapik, 1992), 114. [This quotation and the one below are from the online version of 1984 at http://gutenberg.net.au/ebooks01/0100021.txt. —Trans.]
40 Ibid., 148.

Bykov would return to the plot device of a phantom war in *ZhD*, where the "contractual" nature of civil war would become common knowledge.

In creating this profoundly pessimistic picture of a doomed society that is perishing more from rumor than from terrorism, Bykov produces a lively portrait of decline, chaos, and social stagnation. Yet he not only fails to hint at a way out of this situation but does not even commit himself to defining the source of the threat or naming the enemy. Instead, he replaces that enemy with the maximally schematic image of the Other, which is also based on rumors that the characters just happen to hear.

The Tragic Anticipation of the Abominable

Sergei Dorenko's artistically clueless novel *2008* was, one imagines, noticed only because of the "media-friendly" figure of the author himself—a former "television hit man" and prominent player in a sensational trial, now a commentator for Ekho Moskvy, the radio station. Dorenko's idea of publishing a treatise/novel meshes perfectly with the contemporary Russian politician's general inclination to use literature as a way of making news and as a way of supplementing his glamorous image as a man of the world.[41] It also sits well with the scandalous content of this novel-length lampoon, which takes aim at almost all the politicians currently in office (who, unlike in Prokhanov's and Smolenskii and Krasnianskii's novels, are not hidden even under transparent pseudonyms) and at the sitting president (the book is dedicated "To the memory of Vladimir Putin").[42]

In the novel, Putin has become an "impromptu Taoist," preoccupied with acquiring ancient Chinese wisdom. He has left his entourage on its own to resolve the "third-term problem," while Chechens capture a nuclear power plant and plan to blow it up when the wind is coming from the appropriate direction for a nuclear cloud to put an end to Moscow. This episode, incidentally, has a

41 See, for example, *Trupy Bol'shogo teatra* [The Bolshoi theater's corpses] by LDPR [Liberal-Democratic Party of Russia] deputy Aleksei Mitrofanov and Aleksandr Sorokin (about the alleged love affair between the ballerina Anastasiia Volochkova and former Prime Minister Mikhail Kas'ianov) (Moscow: Eksmo, 2006).

42 This novel thereby validates a quality that is, sad to say, frequently inherent in our domestic opposition, as Rozanov noted some time ago—the tendency to attack the individual in power rather than the system as a whole. "Revolution in Russia altogether boils down to a plot of one type or another, yet when did a plot ever have power against a state but not against an individual?" (V. Rozanov, *Opavshie list'ia* [Fallen leaves] [Moscow: Sovremennik, 1992], 333).

direct analogy in the capture of an oil refinery in Iuliia Latynina's novel *Jahannum* [Dzhakhannam] and the threat posed to the nearby city if holding tanks containing chemical reagents are exploded when the wind is right, and it betrays a particular social phobia that seems to have taken root here in recent years.[43]

The plotline of terrorism and political cataclysms begins toward the end of the book, since Dorenko's efforts up to that point seem to have gone into creating the most freakish possible image of the president. Putin throws tantrums in front of his bodyguards, takes a mistress at Berezovsky's place in the country, orders ants about in a Chinese shack, and so on. The cartoonishness of this image, teetering on the verge of vulgarity, is also no accident. So, as Lev Gudkov has written, Russia's power structure, being traditionally alienated from the man in the street, may either be idealized or "become a target of abuse, of indignation, when it is perceived to be no more than a purely de facto administrator." In the latter case, the "slow processes of destatization take on the forms of new, desacralized (for example, televised) notions of power as something malformed, feeble, buffoonish, and mundane."[44] It is in this tenor of a televisable parody that Dorenko structures his "critique" of those in authority, and of the president in particular. His novel emphasizes how weak and anemic the president is, how lifeless (he needs to study Taoism to acquire immortality, while the "Merlins at the Kremlin court" have been ordered to study it, too, stopping barely short of being instructed to create a Putin clone): "he had the face of a cyborg missing its batteries."[45] Like the images of the Moscow boyars in Ivanov's *Heart of the Uplands*, this grotesque portrait symbolizes the impersonality of power, its soullessness, lifelessness, and vacuity (the discussions of Chinese philosophy and the trip to China to visit a spiritual advisor revolve around the concept of Tao, which is identified with the Great Emptiness).[46]

As in Bykov's novel, the terrorists (the "reports" make no bones about their being Chechens) capture the Obninsk nuclear power plant (which is a real installation, unlike Bykov's nonexistent Sukhinichi plant). Panic ensues: roads are closed, people flee Moscow, documents are burned at the Lubianka, food is given away,

---

43   Iu. Latynina, *Dzhakhannam, ili Do vstrechi v Adu* [Jahannam, or until we meet in hell] (Moscow: Eksmo, 2005).

44   L. Gudkov, *Negativnaia identichnost'* (Moscow: Novoe literaturnoe obozrenie and VTsIOM-A, 2004), 103.

45   Dorenko, *2008*, 18.

46   President Putin's meeting with masters of the Chinese martial arts had an unexpected sequel in March 2007, when the real Vladimir Vladimirovich Putin, whose enjoyment of Oriental martial arts is well known, welcomed Shaolin monks to the Kremlin and reminisced about his visit to their monastery (www.newsru.com/religy/27mar2007/shao.html).

and so on. Yet the panic is mostly in officialdom (bureaucrats run for their lives, the president's family is sent to London, etc.), whereas ordinary people stay calm. "No one had any good reason to be breaking store windows. ... Shorthanded as they were, they organized the distribution of everything that was left. They coped without the police. ... People went, for example, to work, where no one was particularly expecting workers to show up and there were no bosses. ... Flag-waving films were broadcast. They decided that themselves and went ahead and broadcast them." "The tragic anticipation of the abominable was creating order, an unhysterical, quiet, taciturn order."[47] As in Bykov's novel, the "simple people" may run from the approaching peril but do not go catatonic like the powers that be, which points less to the people's courage than to the artificiality of these authors' constructs, where, in creating images of terrorist acts and panic, they render them abstract, leave them dangling, as it were, in the air, as just another way to badmouth those in command. Neither Bykov nor Dorenko feels any need to construct a positive program, to show the causes of the crisis or conceptualize them artistically; they are far more engaged by the journalistic discourse.

But in Dorenko's novel, after vats filled with ammonia are blown up at Ostankino, Moscow is almost abandoned and the Chechen terrorists storm the Kremlin but are beaten off by National Bolsheviks under the command of Limonov, who have decided, "in all the commotion," to make a revolution. The novel ends with Limonov capturing the Kremlin (and appointing the no longer imprisoned Khodorkovsky his "minister of the economy"), Bush sending his marines to Russia, and the insurgents getting ready to blow up the power plant, while Putin is locked away and forgotten in an underground bunker.

The use to which Dorenko puts the figure of Eduard Limonov in his novel is emblematic. A Limonovite uprising also features in *San'kia*, a brutally "realistic" novel by the National Bolshevik Zakhar Prilepin[48] that almost channels Gorky's *Mother* [Mat'] and ends with the "SS" (the Creative Union, *Soiuz sozidaiushchikh*, the name of a party led by a man with the surname Kostenko)[49] capturing thirty-nine municipal administrative offices across Russia and barricading themselves there against the police and the troops of the Ministry of Internal Affairs. The catastrophic thrust of Prilepin's novel—which does, it is true, also have a salient political component (since Prilepin actively positions himself as a follower of Limonov, posting on the National Bolshevik site, voicing his solidarity with the

---

47 Dorenko, *2008*, 221.
48 Zakhar Prilepin, *San'kia* (Moscow: Ad Marginem, 2006).
49 We remind the reader that Limonov's real surname is Savenko.

ideals of that "party" in interviews, etc.)—lessens any distance between this book and those examined earlier: "there is no motherland";[50] the "nasty, dishonorable, and incompetent state that slaughters the weak and bestows freedom on the vile and vulgar"[51] is founded on nothing but centralized power, "not a common God, not faith in the future, not common hopes, not common despair—nothing, not a single thing to hold it together!"[52] This book also contains alarmist motifs similar to those in the Bykov and Dorenko novels: "I'm still waiting for you all to run out here to the country, all you city folk; the time is coming fast. Nothing's burning out there yet, in the city? It'll be burning soon enough," the protagonist's uncle, a country dweller, says to him.[53]

As a complement to this novel, we could mention *Russia, a Third-Class Car* [Rossiia: obshchii vagon], a novella by the young poet Natal'ia Kliuchareva (a Debut Prize finalist in 2002).[54] We have active Limonovites here, too, on the periphery and dire warnings such as "there is no Russia" and "Mother Russia is vanishing," and the hero "has no fear at all" of Chechens, while President Putin is presented in extremely negative terms, embodying the vacuity of power and resembling Lieutenant Kijé. He is described as a "cardboard creature," a "little figure in a grey jacket," a "manikin," and a "grouch." This novella's distinguishing feature is certainly not that at the end a revolution begins, the center of Moscow is barricaded off, and the Duma is seized by the townsfolk but that the revolution is powered here not by young Limonov supporters but by pensioners deprived of their benefits.[55] Yet the finale harbors a hint that the people's successful uprising is only something that the hero, Nikita, sees in his dying delirium.

In the aggregate, these works manifest a supposedly mass (pensioners, police, and army in Kliuchareva; students and soldiers in Prilepin) discontent with the current regime. Once again we have to state that the crux of the uprising's portrayal is not a positive program of change nor even the political coloration of the grievances (which are almost identically expressed, although their content is likely to differ when articulated by Sergei Dorenko, an anti-Western populist and member of the Communist Party of the Russian Federation, the National

---

50 Prilepin, *San'kia*, 72.
51 Ibid., 114.
52 Ibid., 267.
53 Ibid., 319.
54 See N. Kliuchareva, "Rossiia: obshchii vagon" [Russia: The bandwagon], *Novyi mir* [New world] no. 1 (2006), (http://magazines.russ.ru/novyi_mi/2006/1/kl2.html).
55 While Kliuchareva was writing her novella, Russian pensioners were demonstrating against the "monetization" of their benefits.

Bolshevik Prilepin, and the near-anarchist Kliuchareva) but the airing of grievances for their own sake, which is nothing new in Russian culture and was categorized, to serve a different purpose, long ago by Semen Frank: the "faith of that age
must not be defined as faith in political freedom nor even as faith in socialism, but
by its internal content may be defined only as faith in revolution, in the overthrow
of the existing order. The difference between parties was certainly not expressed
by a qualitative difference in worldview but mostly by a difference in the intensity of hatred for what then existed and a repulsion from it—by a qualitative difference in the degree of revolutionary radicalism."[56] The comparison of today's
Umsturzsituation[57] with the days of the 1917 Revolution cannot but cause alarm,
because the "nihilist morality," which is the "basic and most profound feature of
the Russian intellectual's spiritual physiognomy" and consists in the "rejection of
objective values," is inherent in most of the works being analyzed here.[58]

Power Delightful and Alluring

Sorokin's *Day of the Oprichnik*, which surprised many by its deliberate simplicity and its renunciation of most of the stylistic and conceptual experiments that
had previously been intrinsic to Sorokin, is even so not only a logical sequel to
his recent *Ice* trilogy but also the beginning of a new stage in his oeuvre.[59]

One day in the life of Andrei Danilovich Komiaga, a distinguished
oprichnik, lays bare all the metamorphoses undergone by the Russia "of the
Domostroi."* After the Red Time of Troubles, the White Time of Troubles,

---

56 S. Frank, "Krushenie kumirov" [The fall of the giants], in *Sochineniia*, Frank (Moscow:
Pravda, 1990), 118.

57 This term from Heidegger is usually translated from German as "revolutionary situation" or
"tipping point."

58 S. Frank, "Etika nigilizma" [Ethics of nihilism], in *Sochineniia*, Frank, 87.

59 That this novella may have a sequel of its own is confirmed by a recently published story
that Sorokin defines as yet another "fantasy on a Russian theme," featuring "'candy cane'
(cocaine), Chinese computer games, and boyars: Sorokin, "Sakharnyi Kreml'," *Nedelia.
Prilozhenie k gazete "Izvestia"* [The week: Supplement to the newspaper 'News,'" January 9,
2007, www.izvestia.ru/reading/article3099980/.

* In 1565, Tsar Ivan IV the Terrible divided his realm into two unequal parts. He turned one
of these over to the boyars and retained the second, the *oprichnina*, under his direct control.
There he set up a private army of *oprichniki* (sing. *oprichnik*), who terrorized the rest of the
country until Ivan dissolved the oprichnina in 1572. The *Domostroi* is a book of instruction
on household management written in about the same period. The "Russia of the *Domostroi*"
implies a conservative, old-fashioned culture. Maliuta Skuratov, mentioned below, is probably the best-known oprichnik.—Ed.

and the Gray Time of Troubles, Komiaga tells us, Russia has experienced Rebirth and Transfiguration. The country is walled off from Europe and the Caucasus and maintains friendly relations only with China. All production is concentrated in China (as in the world of Bykov's *ZhD*), only officials who can converse in Chinese keep their jobs, and China imposes its will on the United States and the rest of the world in a manner somewhat reminiscent of the image of the mighty Orduss in the "Eurasian symphony" *There Are No Bad People* [Plokhikh liudei net] by Holm van Zaichik. But, in step with Lev Gudkov's apt observation that the "present Russian great-power nationalism is by nature not aggressively proselytic but a nostalgic, quasi-traditionalist variant of isolation-ism,"[60] the Russia described in the "new dystopias" never wages a foreign war (the war in Bykov's *ZhD* is a civil war), which distinguishes the present situation from that described in the literature of the recent past—in Krusanov's *Bite of an Angel* (2000), where Russia not only fights aggressively against other countries but even seems ready to destroy the entire world. Russia's might in Sorokin's novel is reinforced by its technical progress. Curiously, Sorokin alone among these authors (except Slavnikova), employs science-fiction motifs and even cyberpunk technical innovations in his dystopia: robot-driven vehicles barrel at unprecedented speeds along bilevel roads, food service is performed only by robots, long-distance communication is effected by means of holograms, there is a full electronic dossier on every one of Russia's citizens, and so on.[61]

The isolationist tendencies that characterize all the novels we are examining here reach their apogee in Sorokin's novel (in *ZhD*, contradictory as Bykov's position may be, that isolationism is evaluated more negatively than not, as the reason why the nation has been brought to its knees, whereas in Sorokin's satire, Russia's utter isolation serves it well).[62] After monarchist

---

60 Gudkov, *Negativnaia identichnost'*, 166.
61 The excellent quality of roads in the technocratic Russia of the future—as, it must be sup-posed, the antithesis of this country's traditional woes (its idiots and its roads)—is to be found in many Russian-language utopias and antiutopias including Aleksandr Chaianov's *Journey of My Brother Alexei to the Land of the Peasant Utopia* [Puteshestvie moego brata Alekseia v stranu krest'ianskoi utopii] (1920), Iakov Okunev's *World to Come* [Griadushchii mir] (1923), and Vasilii Aksenov's *The Island of Crimea* [Ostrov Krym] (1979) (the latter does contain some good roads, although they are not in the union but in indepen-dent, White Guard-ruled Crimea). By contrast, *Moscow 2042* [Moscow 2042], Vladimir Voinovich's highly venomous antiutopia, shows a Soviet Union of the future with almost no decent roads, not even in downtown Moscow: the "asphalt was cracking here and rearing up there, and in some places was altogether gone."
62 So, for instance, the inhabitants of the imaginary khanate of Khazar (which evidently stands for Israel [the historical Khazar khanate adopted Judaism as its state religion—Ed.]) are

forces come to power, the Russians "voluntarily" burn their passports on Red Square (though anyone who lived in the Soviet Union will be well aware how "voluntary" that action really was); their only sustenance is turnips and kvass; instead of borrowing from other languages, they use a pseudo-Russian argot (in which a Mercedes becomes a "brood mare"); and they flaunt their enthusiasm for a return to their "primordial"—more accurately, their stylizedly medieval—identity. In Aleksandr Chaianov's peasant republic in the Russia of 1984 (!!!), incidentally, we encounter the same effusive blossoming of a folklorically Russian propriety as in Sorokin: "Little boys blew, as they had in the good old days, into clay whistles shaped like roosters, just as they did in the reign of Tsar Ivan Vasil'evich and in Novgorod the Great. Double-row accordions struck up a brisk polka. In short, everything was fine and dandy."[63] It is a complex judgment call as to whether Sorokin (or Tatyana Tolstaya in *The Slynx* [Kys']) used this 1920 novella as a pattern, but the similarities and their evaluation of what they are describing are certainly symptomatic of our time.

In portraying the rebirth of national patriotism, Sorokin is most likely only extrapolating into the future and carrying to the point of satirical grotesquerie current state trends with evident causes:[64] "the collapse of reformist illusions and expectations must unavoidably result in a return to some variety of the ideology of a 'cohesive whole.' ... The only possible surrogate for a society as a cohesive whole is the fiction of the 'people' in that society's past. In other words, the acknowledgment of the civil society's untenability led to an organically conservative utopia of the 'national past,' a utopia of a great power with a unique mission in the world" (Lev Gudkov).[65] The rebirth of Rus in *Day of the Oprichnik* is guaranteed by society's increasing religiosity (Komiaga prays fervently every morning).[66] This would be an apposite place to recall both literary

---

portrayed in Bykov's novel with such undisguised vexation that the reader is probably supposed to welcome Russia's isolation from that particular state.

63 A. Chaianov, "Puteshestvie moego brata Alekseia v stranu krest'ianskoi utopii" [Journey of my brother Alexei to the peasant utopia,' in *Vecher v 2217 godu. Utopiia i antiutopiia XX veka* [Evening in the Year 2217. Twentieth-century utopias and anti-utopias] (Moscow: Progress, 1990), 197.

64 "There is no rationale behind interpreting Sorokin's book as a fantasy of Russia's future, a warning, or a prediction. The idea of that future is superficially positioned and, when extracted from the text, seems banal and trite. ... But as a satire, Sorokin's book is exceedingly engaging—a playful, integral, properly proportioned, well-made text" (A. Latynina, "Skazki o Rossii," *Novyi mir* no. 2 (2007), available at http://magazines.russ.ru/novyi_mi/2007/2/la15.htm).

65 Gudkov, *Negativnaia identichnost'*, 661–62.

66 For the motif of religious renewal in this country (and of civil unrest and war), see also A. Starobinets, *Ubezhishche 3/9* (St. Petersburg: Limbus, 2006), 386–87.

analogies (the mandatory Christianization of lands annexed to the principality of Moscow, as described in Ivanov's novel) and real "prototypes" (Russian politicians' invocation of Orthodoxy as a new ideology).[67] The tourist-trap medievalist "Russian spirit" that rules in the novel is also seemingly modeled on the most recent changes made to the architecture of Moscow.[68] Another feature expressed in this novel is the larger role of the security services in contemporary political life. The revived oprichnina is becoming the most important force in society: the oprichniki who have the tsar's ear censor the arts, supervise economic activity, and have been commissioned by their own superiors and by the monarch himself to seek out "enemies within" ("scribblers and fomenters of unrest"), while the monument to Dzerzhinskii on Lubianka Square (whose restoration Soviet revanchists are urging as I write) has been replaced by one to Maliuta Skuratov. Censorship rules the land, intellectuals are flogged in front of the old university building on Manège Square, and dissidents air their views in television programs beamed in from abroad.

The reinforcement of the agencies—and, more broadly, of the tendencies—of repression is an extremely characteristic detail, demonstrating to us, despite assurances from the narrator (who has, by the way, a "vested interest"), the latent weakness of the state and the internal contradictions within it (or why would it need such powerful "agencies"?).

Increased xenophobia and anti-Semitism are also part of the picture. Although pogroms are a thing of the past, and Komiaga stipulates "just to be safe" that there is toleration toward Jews, a sovereign decree "On Orthodox

---

67 While this article was being written, lively discussions were ongoing on the acceptability of making the study of the fundamentals of Orthodoxy mandatory in schools. See, for example, "Politika RPTs: konsolidatsiia ili razval strany?" [The politics of RPTs: Consolidation or devolution of the country?] This letter, signed by ten members of the Russian Academy of Sciences, opposed the clericalization of secondary schools in Russia (and references a number of antecedent documents on the same issue): *Kentavr. Naucho-populiarnoe prilozhenie k "Novoi gazete"* [Centaur: Popular science supplement to the new paper] no. 3 (2007): 1–2 (*Novaia Gazeta*, July 23–25, 2007).

68 Compare with "meaning that the layout of Stoleshnikov Alley will now highlight in plain view a three-story-high piece of *khokhloma* [the style of lacquer painting found on bowls and cups—Ed.]" (K. Metelitsa, "Patsan—skazal—patsan sdelal. Novyi vitok novo-russkogo stilia: kto by mog podumat'" [The boy said, the boy did: New turn in the new Russian style: Who would have guessed?] *Nezavisimaia gazeta*, February 8, 2007: www.ng.ru/style/2007-02-08/12_pacany.html); and "currently enjoying another heyday, the 'Luzhkov style' [named for Yuri Luzhkov, mayor of Moscow—Trans.] ... is, on the strength of its central element's specific features, coming to look more and more like classic Stalinist architecture" (G. Rezvin, "Moscow na tretii srok" [Moscow Third Time], *Kommersant'*, August 23, 2002).

Names" has been passed whereby "all citizens of Russia not baptized in the Orthodox faith must not be given Orthodox names but, rather, names that correspond to their nationality,"[69] which in and of itself is reminiscent of a further detail from the Soviet past: the Soviet newspapers' wholesale revelation, during the campaign against "rootless cosmopolitans" in the late 1940s, of pseudonyms adopted by Jews, and, at the extreme, of the sleeve or lapel patches issued to various ethnic and social groups in the territories occupied by Nazi Germany. The reversion to ancient tradition also turns out, on closer inspection, to be a grotesque development of present-day tendencies. Researchers have noted that in Soviet times (to which, as many analysts surmise, the power structure is now inclined to revert as to an ideal exemplar) were seen certain traits manifestly inherited from medieval Russia (for example, the system of preferential allocations and deliveries of foodstuffs to the "elect" recalls the feudal "feeding" [kormlenie] system).[70]

Also symptomatic is the image of the tsar, who has gathered all power to himself. That power, Komiaga muses, is as "delightful and alluring as the lap of a virgin goldwork embroiderer."[71] So, for instance, the sovereign makes only virtual appearances, in the form of a screenless video projection. The description of one such transmission is characteristic: "the Sovereign says nothing. From the ceiling he surveys us with his alert, gray-blue gaze. We grow calm. Silence again hangs in the air."[72] What is important in this instance is not only the association with the sitting president (who has gray eyes) and the sacred connotations of power (the tsar delivers his message from above and from thin air, as does the Holy Spirit from heaven) but also the localization of his image in silence and emptiness.

---

69 Sorokin, Den' oprichnika, 164.
70 On this subject, see Tamara Kondrat'eva, "Sovremennoe gosudarstvo kak vlast' po 'Domostroiu'?" [Modern government as patriarchical power?], Novoe literaturnoe obozrenie [New literary review] no. 81 (2006) (http://magazines.russ.ru/nlo/2006/81/ku5.html). To support her idea of the "nonlinear" flow of historical time and the combination of traditions from diverse historical periods within the framework of a single age, Kondrat'eva cites examples of medieval practices being followed in Soviet times (a system analogous to kormlenie [in which officials lived off the regions where they served—Ed.]; an archaic lexicon employing terms such as "sedition" [kramola], "minion" [prispeshnik], "turncoat" [dvurushnik]; etc.). Sorokin's Komiaga, incidentally, places a high value on the symbolic honors shown to him, which involve breakfast with the tsarevna, dinner with the chief oprichnik, and a seat close to the latter at table.
71 Sorokin, Den' oprichnika, 9–10.
72 Ibid., 182.

Emptiness is the essence of this "dystopian" nonexistent Russia. A famous prophetess answers Komiaga's question as to what will happen to Russia in the spirit of the Oracle in *The Matrix*—"Nothing will happen"—thus crystallizing a doubt that is far from new: "perhaps Russia is as much a mirage as everything else that surrounds us? In our spiritual emptiness, we cannot find a convincing refutation of that nightmarish fantasy" (Semen Frank).[73] That emptiness is, most naturally, able to subsist only on officially sanctioned violence, on power ("while the oprichnina lives, so Russia shall live").[74]

The Conservation of Life and a "Revolution in Masquerade"

In Slavnikova's *2017*, probably the most complex and multileveled work presented here, the romance between a gem cutter named Krylov and the mysterious Tat'iana, who proves to be the terrible Mistress of the Copper Mountain, plays out against a backdrop of statewide cataclysms that begin in the Urals during the celebration of the October Revolution centennial and are accompanied by mythological excursuses associated with Uralic (or, in Slavnikova's novel, "Rifeic") folklore.

What jumps out at us from this novel rife with literary references is the interplay with the aforementioned Ivanov's *Heart of the Uplands* and *The Rebellion's Gold* [Zoloto bunta].[75] What unites the works of these two authors may be tentatively defined as a geographically localized mythology. In their descriptions of the pagan Ugro-Finnic culture in all its manifestations, Ivanov's *Uplands* and *2017*—with its Mistress of the Mountain alias the Stone Maiden (who calls distinctly to mind the priestess of Ivanov's novel), Poloz the Great Snake (corresponding to Ivanov's dragon that lives under the earth), the Deer with Silver Hooves, shamans, spirits of the earth, icy flame, and so on—do indeed have a great deal in common.[76] These novels, for instance, not only

---

73 Frank, "Krushenie kumirov," 166.
74 Sorokin, *Den' oprichnika*, 223.
75 Most of the allusions appear to be to Bulgakov's *The Master and Margarita*: the main characters roam the city streets like Bulgakov's lovers, Krylov is pursued by a paunchy sleuth who resembles Behemoth in his "human" form and whom Krylov tracks unsuccessfully all over the city as Ivan does Woland and his entourage, etc.
76 In Slavnikova's book, the two main characters sail the mouth of the Chusovaia, in an evident interplay with the Ivanov oeuvre: the location of the river and the motif of sailing down it are also present in Ivanov's novels *The Rebellion's Gold* and *The Geographer Drank Away His Globe* [Geograf globus propil], while the history of the riparian towns and villages supplies the theme of his regional travelogue *Message: The Chusovaia* (St. Petersburg: Azbuka-klassika, 2007).

contain comparable characters—"gem smugglers" [*khitniki*] in Slavnikova and "rock diggers" [*skal'niki*] in Ivanov (although "gem smugglers," but of the eighteenth century rather than the twenty-first, are also described in *The Rebellion's Gold*); they are also similar in essence, since the characters in both stories appreciate the risks they must run, have a sense of their elect status, and, most important, are sensitive to the "call of the earth." *2017* also makes much of the topic of local separatism: "unslumbering Moscow" installs a "bureaucratic elite" in the "capital of Rifei Territory."[77] The ancient myths revive as the country's internal crisis intensifies, taking on the role of an alternative to current reality, and "chthonic" folk beliefs begin to emerge from beneath the yoke of the coercive order imposed by the state.

Slavnikova's description of what our state will be like in the near future contains traits—the restoration of the past (both medieval and Soviet) and cyberpunk futurology—that patently relate *2017* to *Day of the Oprichnik*. But Slavnikova's emphasis on such motifs is weaker than Sorokin's; rather, she provides them as cursory mentions or intimations that create a complex and multileveled futurological canvas. In the world inhabited by Slavnikova's characters, laser keys are used to open vehicles; mobile telephones with videolink capabilities and books with holographic jackets are all the rage; the wealthy heroine, whose name is Tamara, has an African maid, which attests to the spread of globalization, and so on. There is an explanation for such a small number of innovations: the surge of technical novelties along the lines of "cellular video links, bioplastics, ultrathin monitors, holographic video, and the first chips being used in medicine, in cosmetics, even in laundry detergent" seems to have been artificially stalled around 2010, because in a world of ultrahigh tech, as Tamara says, "out of eight billion Homo sapiens, seven and a half are of no use for anything."[78] The novel also presents the isolationist rebirth of the medieval "Russian spirit": in a restaurant, the business-woman Tamara is seated at one of the good tables, "under a stylized portrait of the president of the Russian Federation, which showed the head of the Russian state as an epic hero riding a frightfully shaggy steed and holding a sword the size of a board from a sturdy fence" and is treated to four different kinds of kvass.[79] Another part of the deal is the revival of the worst elements of the Soviet past, transformed here into Grand Guignol; Lenin's mummy has been removed from his mausoleum and taken "on

---

77 Slavnikova, *2017*, 72.
78 Ibid., 212.
79 Ibid., 197.

tour" around the country;[80] and "on the threshold of the October Revolution centennial" there is a "television broadcast about the restoration of destroyed monuments and a new and improved Dzerzhinsky."[81]** Schools are "reviving the traditions of Soviet pedagogy."[82] The simple people are stocking up on stew in jars that "bring to mind antipersonnel mines";[83] they live in "Khrushchev specials" [Soviet-style apartments —Ed.] and gather in the kitchen to chat. Tamara, while trying to run her business, runs into bureaucratic obstacles that are in the worst of Soviet traditions.[84] The picture painted by Slavnikova is all the more contradictory and variegated inasmuch as it combines the Russian/Soviet in everyday culture with the European/American: $600 bills are trendy now, while movie theaters are showing the latest Hollywood blockbusters and serving popcorn. In Slavnikova's book (as in Sorokin's novel), the immediate present is subjected to a simulative (and never-ending) reiteration in the future, as eloquently demonstrated by the image of a "president who in appearance resembles less his direct predecessor than the great Putin, who was now serving candidates as an ideal exemplar."[85] The position of mayor is filled by an "identical copy, followed by another, which had people telling each other that a certain politician of happy memory and his successor and the present father of the Rifeians whose person adorned hundreds of building sides and frontages in the run-up to the festivities

---

80 Which is, however, also reminiscent of the secularized version of an ecclesiastical practice that has become widespread in Russia during the last decade: the transfer of particularly venerated relics from one church to another.

81 Slavnikova, *2017*, 212. We remind the reader that in Sorokin's novel, Dzerzhinsky's place on Lubianka Square went instead to "Maliuta" Skuratov.

** Felix Dzherzhinsky headed the first Soviet political police, known as the Cheka from its acronym in Russian. His statue stood outside the headquarters of the political police until enthusiastic crowds tore it down after the collapse of the Soviet Union. The Putin years saw growing public support for restoring the statue to its original place.—Ed.

82 Ibid., 170.

83 Ibid., 380.

84 As a plot detail, the preservation of Soviet reality (a source of simultaneous horror and nostalgia) is nothing new. In Andrei Volos's *The Mascaw Mecca* [Maskavskaia Mekka] (Moscow: ZebraE/Eksmo and Dekont+, 2003), a place by the name of the Gummunist Territory has seceded from Russia. Furthermore, this novel, which may be regarded as one of the earliest modern antiutopias, externalizes the fear of the "neighbors to the East," since Moscow has become a predominantly Muslim city. But the phobias that Volos's novel articulates with restraint and reservations are taken to the extreme in Elena Chudinova's anti-Western novel, *The Mosque of Notre Dame de Paris* [Mechet' Parizhskoi bogomateri] (Moscow: Iauza, Eksmo, and Lenta-plius, 2005). For further detail on this book, see, for example, O. Chernoritskaia, "Prokliatie vysokikh idei" [Curse of high ideas], http://zhurnal.lib.ru/c/chernorickaja_o_l/ctud.shtml.

85 Slavnikova, *2017*, 372.

were one and the same person. And that … presented no technical problem whatsoever."[86] The Russia of *2017*, pervaded as it is beyond all measure by the cults of the dead and of reduplication, is evidently about to fulfill the prediction of Sorokin's prophetess that "nothing will happen."

All these details ultimately produce a discrete and complex picture whose chief components are an extreme historical pessimism, a gloomy, stifling atmosphere, and the characters' eschatologically escapist self-images. So, when Tania tells Krylov at the outset that she could fly with him to the moon,[87] and he replies that there is no air there, she responds, in ringing tones, "How sure are you that we're breathing air right now?"[88] Shortly thereafter she will speak of the individual's strategic irrelevancy to the process wherein history is molded and about human defenselessness, her opinion being that history is created by only impersonal official forces and no effort will ever come to anything: "no one can protect anyone. What good will you be against three? And what about five?"[89]

The metaphor of airlessness is key to the description of the historical *atmosphere*:

> Some fifteen years ago, it began: it was as if the air itself had been all used up, so that everyone with any money dashed off to purchase containers filled with Alpine or Antarctic concentrate. … What happened then was what the more cutting-edge glossies called a format shift. Krylov remembered the avalanche of words on that subject, the whole rivers of silken magazine pages and floating on them … the multicolored portraits of opinion leaders. The conservation of life affected to be an unprecedented onset of novelty. Everyone suddenly felt like the hero of a novel, which is to say a character in an invented reality; everyone became eager to speak out, without the slightest responsibility for anything that was being said. Krylov had not forgotten himself and Tamara … being jostled about in mob scenes that were called either political exercises or art projects— which were, essentially, one and the same thing. All the politicians were putting themselves out there as art projects. … What next? Everyone must have had some sense of the world's mendacity. … What took shape was a

---

86 Ibid., 239.
87 Even the plot device of a secret romance with meetings in "safe houses" while civil strife rages all around is close to that described in Bykov's *Evacuator* (whose heroine ends by agreeing to fly away with her beloved "to his planet") and refers back to Bulgakov's *The Master and Margarita*.
88 Slavnikova, *2017*, 25.
89 Ibid., 39.

new culture with an inner unity—the culture of a copy with no original, regulated by thousands of restrictions.[90]

This excerpt (which closes with a direct reference to Baudrillard's theory of simulacra) includes all the properties of changes foretold for the imminent future; they are reactionary, gradually imposed on society (the characters are even vague as to how it all began and where it went from there), ludic and simulative in nature, and fundamentally derivative. In such a situation, "simple" people react by taking flight, one at a time, into private life, as do Krylov and Tania, and then, when that proves to be no salvation, into an artificially constructed lair. Krylov hides away from everyone in an apartment that he has lucked into, that he tells no one about, and that he "had no intention of allowing anyone into" (not even the police or a plumber), so that he, "sitting in his small silence, like Ikhtiandr in a barrel, ... could rejoice in his fragmentary deafness."[91]

After the world described in the novel has lost the fundamental humanist mind-set, historical time is the next to go: "both days and nights became astonishingly transparent, all the everyday mechanisms of oblivion were breaking down, and everything that happened, happened today."[92] In this situation, society's only way out, and one that is almost natural for society to take, is a root-and-branch demolition of reality—a revolution, that is. But as it later transpires, even revolution is futile.

During the citywide celebration of the centennial of the October coup of 1917, which is structured in the traditions of Soviet authoritarianism (a portrait of the mayor is "stretched across half the façade"), city folk masquerading as Red Army soldiers and White Guards start shooting at each other, and there is a monstrously powerful bomb blast, the riot control troops are sent in, and the square is cordoned off. Krylov's prediction—"there'll be screw-ups like that all across the country. Everywhere, on account of it being a round date, people will be cramming pointed military caps onto their heads and struggling into White Guard epaulets, and everywhere it will end up going too far"—proves correct.[93] The situation wherein the celebration of a revolution's anniversary

---

90 Ibid., 238–39.
91 Ibid., 226. Since it was not Ikhtiandr [the eponymous "amphibian man" from Aleksandr Beliaev's novel *Chelovek-amfibiia*—Trans.] but Prince Gvidon from Pushkin's story ["The Tale of Tsar-Saltan"—Trans.] who was ensconced in a barrel, Slavnikova's metaphor may be seen as a simultaneous allusion to two famous works.
92 Slavnikova, *2017*, 389.
93 Ibid., 335.

morphs into a real revolution is, incidentally, not particularly uncommon, if you think back to Andrei Platonov's hero, who "dreamed of the Revolution as a parade." The very theme of conflict persisting from the time of the Civil War evidently harks back to Aksenov's *Island of Crimea* (in both books, people perish in the course of "solemnities"—the celebration of the Revolution centennial in Slavnikova's and the welcome arranged for the Soviet troops by the Crimeans in Aksenov's). Meanwhile, there is also a "revolution for the fun of it" in *The Peacemakers* [Mirotvortsy], a novel by Boris Fal'kov, who lives in Germany, in which Pervomaisk celebrates the anniversary of its liberation from the Germans and those festivities segue into a populist uprising and the secession of a city district.[94] After this novel was already on sale, furthermore, a sort of micromodel of a "revolution in masquerade" came about in Budapest during the government crisis in October 2006, when Hungarian right-wing oppositionists commandeered a T-34 (a Soviet tank that is associated in Hungary with the suppression of the anticommunist uprising of 1956) from a museum and used it as a battering ram against the police.[95]

The "revolution in masquerade" that is proclaimed by the authorities in Rifei Territory (which is, apparently, a stand-in for the writer's home town of Ekaterinburg) is communicated to other parts of Russia, with clashes between "Reds" and "Whites" in Perm, Astrakhan, Krasnoiarsk, Irkutsk, and along the Angara River.[96] "In Petersburg, revolutionary sailors seized a branch of the naval museum, namely the cruiser *Aurora*, and tried to use its forecastle gun to shoot up the dank Winter Palace," but the fusillade is a big flop because welding torches had long ago rendered all the *Aurora*'s weapons inoperative, so that "it all came down to nothing more than a great iron din and the delivery of the hooligans to the nearest police station."[97] Even so, the "victims of those costumed clashes were numbered in the hundreds, and not only in official estimates."[98] The government resigns, the president is officially hospitalized (although rumor has him under house arrest), power is transferred to a provisional presidential council (as seen on television, a

94 See B. Fal'kov, *Mirotvortsy: provintsial'naia khronika vremeni Imperii* [Worldmakers: A provincial chronicle of the imperial era] (St. Petersburg: Letnii sad, 2006).

95 See the Lenta.ru site for October 24, 2006 (http://lenta.ru/news/2006/10/24/tank/). [See www.abc.net.au/news/newsitems/200610/s1771780.htm for a contemporary English-language news report. —Trans.]

96 Slavnikova, *2017*, 371.

97 Ibid., 373–74.

98 Ibid., 374.

serried row of strained-looking people, many of them old—the very image of the regrettably renowned State Emergency Committee).*** The "Virus of History" and the "Epidemic of History" spread to Moscow, too, where the streets are full of "citizen parades" while "in an alley, adolescents in the blue pointed caps once worn by Soviet kindergartners and leather jackets festooned with a chain mail of scarlet Soviet pins took running kicks at mush-mouthed foreign cars and upended them."[99] This is a graphic parallel to the Limonov supporters in Dorenko, Prilepin, and Kliuchareva, who are young people "uniformed" in leather who also employ Soviet emblems (the hammer and sickle on a "party" banner).

The causes and features of that revolution are extremely interesting, even as described by the characters in the book, who ought to have been active participants in it but are actually its passive targets. It bears no resemblance to the real revolution that they had imagined: "it was partly the revolution of a century ago acted out as bloody mysteries; and partly, sad to say, it was criminality run rampant; and partly it was secretive political strategists playing fast and loose with the public at large, their intent being to brew up a new leader in one of their cauldrons."[100] This roster is reminiscent of the heroine of Kliuchareva's novella, whose inability to understand the causes and mechanisms of current events is expressed with youthful directness: "Dammit all, though, nobody gets this revolution. What's going on? Where do we go? What do we do? ... It turns out that nothing needs to be done. Hang with your buddies, jump and run, and it'll still go on doing its thing anyway, like you weren't even there. We never pictured the revolution like this. We thought we'd matter a whole lot."[101] As Tamara remarks, "right here and right now there are no properly packaged forces able to give a voice to this situation. ... So forms from a century ago will be used, as the closest fit. Even if they're fake, bogus. History will react to them. The conflict itself will identify the masqueraders as participants in the conflict. The conflict has existed all along, ever since the 1990s, but it's still short the get-ups—the revolutionary greatcoats, the riding breeches, the leathers. The conflict has nothing presentable to wear."[102]

*** The State Emergency Committee was the locus of an attempt to restore communism in August 1991. —Ed.

99 Ibid., 538–89.

100 Ibid., 390.

101 Kliuchareva, "Rossiia: obshchii vagon."

102 Slavnikova, *2017*, 335.

This confirms not only the derivative nature of any revolution in contemporary Russia but also the country's lack of a pronounced political opposition, which is here replaced by a covert conflict within society itself that has yet to find an outlet, that is directed at society itself, and that not even revolution can resolve.

The Collapse of a Country in its Death Agony

The Hostage (Operation Memorandum) [Zalozhnik (Operatsiia "Memorandum")], a novel by the ex-banker Aleksandr Smolenskii and the journalist Eduard Krasnianskii that gained notice on the strength of a massive publicity campaign mounted by its publishers and professed to cover some sensationalist political ground, continues in the tradition of works on high society and low politics that also includes Dorenko's book.[103] The real point of convergence between Dorenko's *2008* and *The Hostage* is an artistic laxity that verges on bad taste. Besides being full of ridiculous misprints,[104] *clichés* (all the Italians are passionate, all the French are gourmets), and dutiful embellishments ("searing emotions"[105] and a "delicious tremor"[106]), the third-person narrative is constantly reaching for the "glossy-magazine" style in its descriptions of high-society receptions, the depravity of the powers that be, true masculine friendship, the solidarity among present and former members of the security services in the spirit of "once in, never out," and so on. The book is set in the 2002–6 timeframe and revolves around a mysterious memorandum purportedly signed by Boris Yeltsin (Uralov in the novel) before leaving the presidency that regulated what his successor could and could not do. Although bearing a total of fifteen signatures—of the former and current presidents, various oligarchs (Boris Berezovsky lurks here under the even more transparent pseudonym of Elenskii, an allusion to Platon Elenin, the main protagonist of Pavel Lungin's

103 Some newspapers printed excerpts from this novel not among the book reviews but in the political section. See A. Gamov, "Zagovor protiv prezidenta" [A conspiracy against the president], *Komsomol'skaia pravda*, March 14, 2006 (www.kp.ru/daily/23672/50813/). An excerpt from the book with commentary by the political strategist Gleb Ivanovskii was placed simultaneously under the headings "Politics" and "The Bookshelf."
104 "assy upravleniia" [presumably *osi upravleniia* ("drive shafts")—Trans.]: Smolenskii and Krasnianskii, *Zalozhnik*, 478.
105 Ibid., 574.
106 Ibid., 575.

film *The Oligarch* [Oligarkh]),[107] and leading politicians—the secret memo also has an appendix known to only five individuals, which places on record that Putin (in the novel simply the "president") has agreed to step down after two terms, ceding his place to Uralov's daughter or someone else put forward by the first president's family. Troubled by the president's policy and worried that he might cling to power even after his second term, the five "signatories" want to publicize the memorandum, thus precipitating a public scandal and thwarting any referendum on a third term. The plot then follows the search for copies of the memorandum, the security services' efforts to prevent its being found, and sundry other political machinations.

Overall, this book displays as profound a historical pessimism and as negative an image of present-day Russia as the other works in our selection. Both in the center and in outlying areas, corruption flourishes, there are murders for hire, potentates both major and minor squander money and are physically incapable of running the country as it should be run ("Who in this country can do the job? Can anyone at all here do the job?"), and so on.[108] The authors' invective is so generalized and so rhetorical that it might as well have been borrowed from either a left-wing or a right-wing columnist (since both exist in present-day Russia). They do not recommend themselves by their originality and are of value primarily as a statement of social fears enunciated in the same rumor-driven style as in Bykov's *Evacuator*: all the decent people in St. Petersburg allegedly "died in the blockade";[109] "everybody" is emigrating;[110] the tyrannical security services, which defy comparison even with "Stalinist times,"[111] "trample almost all the democratic principles" one after another;[112] *à la Evacuator* (again), "tragedy follows on tragedy."[113] In step with the newspaper rhetoric, the state of Russia today is likened to that of a terminal patient: "all

---

107 *The Hostage* is in general highly reminiscent of other books about the disgraced oligarch [Boris] Berezovsky and "antipopulist plots" hatched by the country's highest leadership, written by Iulii Dubov, another big businessman, long before the opus we are analyzing here. *The Lion's Share* [Bol'shaia paika] (Moscow: Vagrius, 2000) deals with the face-off between business and power; and *The Lesser Evil* [Men'shee zlo] (Moscow: Kolibri, 2005) implicates the Federal Security Service in a plot to blow up buildings during the presidential campaign of V. V. Putin (F. F. Rogov in the novel).

108 Smolenskii and Krasnianskii, *Zalozhnik*, 40.

109 Ibid., 236.

110 Ibid., 299.

111 Ibid., 408.

112 The list of what has been trampled goes on for two whole pages (Ibid., 407–8).

113 Ibid., 411.

the increasingly decrepit vessels and organs that kept it [the regime—A. C.] alive were solidly plugged by problems both large and small that would never again, under any circumstances, be able to work their way to the surface. Then the collapse would begin. As it does in a patient at his last, hopeless gasp due to the helplessness of the doctor in a hospital at its last, hopeless gasp due to its own helplessness in a town at its last, hopeless gasp due to its own helplessness in a state at its last, hopeless gasp due to its own helplessness."[114] The oligarch Dukhon sums up the situation: "The country is circling the bowl."[115] Invective as banal as this has not been news since Chaadaev first proclaimed it: "The spiritual principle, invariably subordinate to the secular, has never found a foothold at the summit of society: historical law, tradition, have never been exclusively dominant here; life has never arranged itself invariably here; finally, there has never been so much as a trace of a moral hierarchy here."[116]

These lamentations, couched as newspaper columnists' commonplaces from the days of perestroika, provide the backdrop for intimations of more significant tendencies. There is, for instance, a suggestion of that old topic: the disappearance of the country and total emptiness. When one of the characters waxes indignant—"but for normal people, and there are quite a few of those in this country, to be completely disoriented?"—his conversation partner chimes in, declaring that he himself felt as if he, too, was "in a vacuum."[117] The country is falling back "into the past," in a manner fully realized in Sorokin's novel.[118] As another of the characters says, "All that is needed for evil to triumph is … for people of sound mind—people like you and I, for example—to do nothing. I beg you to ponder at your leisure if there are many of them standing alongside the president."[119]

The Smolenskii/Krasnianskii novel differs conspicuously from most of the works analyzed above in that its Russian president is an entirely positive figure, even though most of the characters believe him guilty of violating

---

114 Ibid., 296.
115 Ibid., 427.
116 P. Chaadaev, "Apologiia sumasshedshego" [A madman's apology], in Chaadaev, *Polnoe sobranie sochinenii i izbrannye pis'ma* [Collected works and selected letters], vol. 1 (Moscow: Nauka, 1991), 531. [This is a literal translation from the Russian, since the available published English translation diverges too greatly from the Russian text. —Trans.] Also compare with "A Show" [Predstavlenie] by Iosif Brodskii [Joseph Brodsky]: "'They've bungled up the country' / 'Lend me ten rubles 'til pay-day.'"
117 Smolenskii and Krasnianskii, *Zalozhnik*, 221.
118 Ibid., 427.
119 Ibid., 226.

democratic freedoms and of causing all the country's other woes. That is why the main protagonists are pursuing their schemes to prevent him from being reelected to a third term. That is the issue, but what the president himself wants is never discussed in this novel. The authors develop the same antiquated, vintage 1915 ("Nicholas II—good, Rasputin—bad"), if not earlier, motif of bad advisers: "Poor president, if he has such a presumptuous entourage and such lamebrained advisers."[120] As in Dorenko's book, the president is accused only of a certain passivity (which, to digress, is very odd, since most of Vladimir Putin's critics fault him for "tightening the screws" and "taking the country back to the Soviet Union"—for being politically active, that is, which is not at all compatible with personal apathy). "Whatever happened to the forcefulness, the toughness, the character that people in Russia liked so much at the beginning?" one of the president's subordinates wonders during a conversation with him.[121] Shown to be a loving and caring father (unlike in Dorenko's *2008*, where Putin is seen as a despotic husband), the president is almost timid in his dealings even with his daughters (one of whom, for a reason never made entirely clear in the novel, absconds with the memorandum text): "'forgive me,' he murmured dejectedly."[122] This passive president is endangered by the schemes of the powerful "signatories"; and even the security forces that are protecting him are doing so at their own risk, keeping their boss in the dark about what they are doing. In chapter 28, the president is sitting in an armchair that dwarfs him and "would have swamped even someone as gigantic as the Olympic wrestler Karelin."[123] That detail underscores how diminutive the president is and how drawn to the vanishing point, which is entirely characteristic for the ruler of a county in which even members of the power elite and its economic counterpart are "in a vacuum."

Colonel Vasin Has Gone AWOL

Since a detailed analysis of Dmitrii Bykov's highly controversial (declared by the cover blurb to be the "least politically correct book of the new millennium"), voluminous, and ambitious "narrative poem" *ZhD* (of his several decodings of the title, which include *Zhivago*, *Doctor*, the author prefers *Zhivye dushi* [Live souls])—which, as Bykov himself acknowledges, sublimates all the ideas in

---

120 Ibid., 234.
121 Ibid., 211.
122 Ibid., 564.
123 Ibid., 210.

his oeuvre and contains features of mythological magical realism, "lieutenant" (military) prose, and above all a political treatise—would bear no direct relationship to the theme of this article; we only trace how motifs of interest to us are realized in its plot.[124]

In the Russia of the future (although the exact time is not defined, the zeitgeist is distinctly reminiscent of our day) a permanent and probably contractual war is being waged between the "Khazars" (Jews, Westernizers, and liberals) and the "Varangians" (Russian nationalists), which is ultimately resolved by an apocalyptic miracle that is evidently supposed to attest to the eternal character of that conflict.[125] The novel's characters journey through a country debilitated by war, devastation, and economic adversities, along its endless fronts and behind the lines, where things are relatively peaceful. The reader is probably expected to reach a conclusion resembling that of Boris Grebenshchikov's famous song (the very song, as the novel's heroine assures us, that was responsible for starting the mechanism of historical dissolution in 1990): "And we have nowhere to run. / This land was ours, / Until we got caught in the struggle. / She'll die if she's nobody's. / Time to give this land back to ourselves."****

The main emotion engendered by this book is something that Bykov himself, in the foreword, calls the sensation of being homeless in one's own country. It is to demonstrate that sensation that themes previously encountered in *The Evacuator* are visibly reinforced in this "narrative poem." The figure of the enemy in the endless war again remains undefined (the numerous adages trotted out by the authors may even lead one to conclude that the Varangians and the Khazars are essentially one and the same), although the military operations being conducted are compellingly reminiscent of the Civil War (the "main part of its history came about within rather than without, and its main conflicts were, once again, internal") and are manifestly masochistic.[126]

---

124 See my review "V ogne polemicheskoi voiny" [In the fire of a polemical war] (August 23, 2006) at www.booknik.ru/reviews/fiction/?id=11188/.

125 An interpretation of the "national question" that contrasts with Bykov's is found in Vladimir Voinovich's antiutopia *Moscow 2042*, in which the opponents of the totalitarian, non-Soviet society of the twenty-first century are called Simites, after their leader Sim Simych Karnavalov, but these Simites preach nationalist/monarchist ideas à la Solzhenitsyn, whom Voinovich is parodying here.

**** This quotation is taken from an uncredited English translation of "The Train on Fire" (Poezd v ogne), an antiwar song by Grebenshchikov, available at http://aix1.uottawa.ca/~jdclayt/Overheads/rus2103_aquarium.pdf. The song's message is delivered by one Colonel Vasin, who is mentioned in the section heading. —Trans.

126 Bykov, *ZhD*, 45.

The sadomasochistic nature of the Varangians' military (and other) operations is reinforced by the Varangian ideology, the pagan/Slavic/Nazi beliefs (that, in particular, justify the routine shooting of their own soldiers to galvanize the survivors) and crudely interpreted samurai practices (along the lines of the "path of the samurai is death"): "only a dead soldier ... was the absolute embodiment of the Norman spirit, having lost his individuality, which is superfluous in war. ... The sole drive of the small, unlovely military monad ... should be toward death, and as speedily as possible."[127]

Yet the author's invective is directed not just at the army but at everything. So, for instance, in the circles of power, "insignificance was a guarantee of might and an inability to make sense of reality was the highest virtue,"[128] Russia's intelligentsia has suffered "lumpenization," the simple people are "scum," and the Varangians and Varangian history possess all the most negative qualities ascribed to Russians in partisan commentary.[129]

> No one wanted to work. The few who had to were held up as idiots and made the object of sympathy at best and of animosity at worst. ... Nobody in Russia felt secure in the land, an apartment, a woman. Anything could be taken away at any moment. ... The task of any Russian power structure—irrespective of where it came from, what it was like, and how long it could continue—was first and foremost the annihilation of its own people. ... In Russia, that hatred for life, for the continuance of life, and for the timid, slavish hope of eking out that dismal servitude as long as possible was primarily revealed in the quirks of man's three chief mentors and comforters: priests, doctors, and teachers. ... Everyone in Russia was busy validating himself and not doing a whole lot else. ... The Russian terror grew eccentrically from below, and it didn't take much. All the authorities had to do was take out or make off with a few dozen for the ordinary people to start exterminating hundreds of their own ... yet there could not, by definition, be one nation in Russia. ... The public was not entitled to principles. And to make sure that it would not succeed in developing any and rebelling, once every decade it had to be filled with a new faith. ... The public no longer had faith in any law, divine or human.[130]

---

127 Ibid., 34.
128 Ibid., 438.
129 Ibid., 66.
130 Ibid., 178–82.

The previously encountered theme of emptiness, virtuality, and the sadomasochistic repression of all national symbols and institutions reaches its apogee here. Yet the isolationism and catastrophilia (the consequence of all the above-listed woes) turn out to be equally illusory. Even the catastrophilia, which would have been natural in this situation, is not a sensation common to all in a Russia that has neither "principles" nor "laws."

Bykov's rendition of internal and external geopolitical conflicts is equally schematic, presented as the realization of society's banal fears. "The Caucasus was smoldering," but even the "completely conflicting reports" can be confirmed only from Western radio stations. "Domestic production has entirely shut down," and the factories have moved to China.[131] A horrifying bureaucracy flourishes, and censorship runs rampant (the radio is muzzled and only six newspapers are being published), which is evidently symbolic of the legacy of Soviet times, while the present day of new-Russian capitalism, with its rebirth of all that is "immemorially Russian," is flagged by such phenomena as community liaison offices decorated in the florid *khokhloma* style.[132]

The book's easily guessed denouement, with its apocalyptic denial that Russia, living "with unique amiability outside of history,"[133] has any future at all, pronounces sentence on the country: "Moscow had seceded from the country and now lived its own life. The war had run dry all on its own. The earth had done what it did best, slowly overrunning, waterlogging, hiding the traces of a civilization that had exhausted itself."[134] At the end, the main characters leave for the village of Zhadrunovo (the novel's symbol of Russia immemorial) "where the unknown awaited them," in a finale reminiscent of the reply of Sorokin's prophetess that "nothing will happen."

* * *

The image of our country formed from the books of our selected authors is perhaps best described by Gloucester in *King Lear*: "We have seen the best of our time: machinations, hollowness, treachery, and all ruinous disorders follow

---

131 Bykov's main characters assume that the "folks upstairs" believe in "druidic horoscopes with quotations from Confucius" (Ibid., 225). (I remind the reader of the pseudo-Chinese horoscopes in Dorenko's book.)
132 Ibid., 296.
133 Ibid., 416.
134 Ibid., 652.

us disquietly to our graves."[135] This "picture of the world" ties directly into the fact that the works we have examined here primarily showcase a historical pessimism, an eschatological alarmism, and a "dearth of collective symbols that is acutely experienced by many groups. The 'old' symbolic configurations familiar to them are losing their social authority and are increasingly often flagged as negative, whereas the 'new' are alien, in terms of both life experience and ideological coloration, and any that might somehow combine and harmonize 'old' and 'new' are absent" (Boris Dubin).[136] In the dystopian worlds created here the old symbols, in the form of the "immemorially Russian" from Soviet times (and even the Middle Ages), subsist on a par with contemporary or futurological tokens, forming an ultimately discrete reality. That reality may not be characterized as merely simulative (virtual) or even implosive ("implosion" being the term that Baudrillard used to imply a "hypertrophy of the virtual" into which "reality effects disappear").[137] This is, rather, a third order of reality, essentially the same as in Ol'ga Slavnikova's *Immortal* [Bessmertnyi], a novella in which the stratum of real current events (post-Soviet life) and the stratum of the virtual (a world in which the Soviet Union did not disintegrate but continued to exist, fabricated to calm a sick pensioner) come together to form the eclectic world in which the characters exist. The sources of this aesthetic are to be sought not only in the hostile frustration of certain of our contemporaries but also in a reaction to the policy of Russia's ideological leaders, who have informed contemporary society with modern, Soviet, and archaic (premodern) values simultaneously.[138]

That being so, topicality (imagine it in quotes) attaches not only to the Soviet past but also to conflicts dating back almost a century. The revolutionary confrontation of "Reds" and "Whites" from the days of October and the Civil War persists and is experienced anew. But choosing the simulative restoration of the past over the formulation of a truly *new* future is an extremely dangerous tendency:

The mass reversion to an artificial past does not pass without consequence. What matters here is not the actual reinforcement of traditionalism but that

135 *King Lear*, Act I, Scene 2.
136 Dubin, *Slovo—pis'mo—literatura*, 157.
137 See Zh. Bodriiiar, *Paroli. Ot fragmenta k fragmentu*, trans. N. Suslov (Ekaterinburg: U-Faktoriia, 2006), 32. [The quoted terms are taken from Jean Baudrillard, *Passwords*, trans. Chris Turner (New York: Verso, 2003), 40, 42. —Trans.]
138 Several well-known films—not only Wolfgang Becker's *Good Bye, Lenin*, which is often discussed in connection with *Immortal*, but also Emir Kusturitsa's *Underground*—are structured on an embodiment of the idea of hybridizing historical reality with the illusion that is created to replace it.

traditionalism is a variant of social primitivization, which degrades the
structures of identity and appreciably affects the most diverse spheres. ...
It is not intellectual effort that has set the traits of the age but successive
periods of crisis and transitory mobilizations, accompanied by phases of
social asthenia, apathy, or indifference. They have followed one another
through recent years, leaving behind them a space bereft even of the
hallmarks of idealism (not a dreamy reverie but the potential and will to
self-perfection).[139]

The age has taken on the traits of a "petrified modernity" (an expression
borrowed from Karl Jaspers).

Much like the construction of a new building from rotten planks, the shaping of a new society from old patterns, using ideological elements from ages so
crisis-ridden they might have been handpicked for the purpose (in the books
examined here, the annexation of outlying principalities, the oprichnina, Soviet
times), is fraught not only with depression but also with armed conflicts, both
uprisings and wars, which we find in almost all our authors. Here, too, we can
discern an "inverse parallel" with previous ages, which explains, incidentally,
the isolationist tendencies of the social organism described here: whereas the
manifestation of a constant state of military mobilization in Soviet society was
a defense against the "enemy without," now the battle is against the "enemy
within."[140] The concomitant of the most profound social problems is that the
outside world (other countries and their experience) is simply unnecessary—
as unnecessary as Russia is to it.[141]

---

139 Gudkov, *Negativnaia identichnost'*, 166.

140 "That domestic conflicts can be neutralized by foreign military successes rests on a
socio-psychological mechanism that governments have repeatedly exploited." See Iu.
Khabermas, *Vovlechenie drugogo: ocherki politicheskoi teorii*, trans. Iu.M. Medvedev (St.
Petersburg: Nauka, 2001), 213. [This quotation is from Jürgen Habermas, *The Inclusion of
the Other: Studies in Political Theory* (Cambridge: MIT Press, 1998), 116. The page reference for the other citation from this edition is given below in square brackets. —Trans.]

141 Il'ia Kukulin provides examples of this introversion: "Volokhov, the hero of Bykov's
novel *ZhD*, finds himself in Israel, which is described under the transparent pseudonym
of the khanate of Khazar, but encounters there only Russophone émigrés still dwelling on
arguments begun in Russia. In Slavnikova's novel *2017*, an elderly secondary heroine
ends up by accident (after winning the lottery) in Spain, where shortly thereafter
a hurricane sweeps her off the beach (which is the last presentation of Spain or any
other foreign country in the novel)." Kukulin relates this "spatial and temporal hermeticity"
to Saltykov-Shchedrin's *History of a Town* [*Istoriia odnogo goroda*]. See I. Kukulin,
"Zamykanie gorizonta: ozhidanie sotsial'nykh katastrof v literature sovremennoi Rossii"

Yet our country's image is carried beyond isolationism: the new novels present Russia as fictive, nonexistent. As is evidenced by numerous direct and indirect statements, most of the authors examined here predict the imminent collapse—if not tomorrow, then any day now—not only of society and the state but also of certain fundamental categories of worldview. In Slavnikova's novel, for example, there is the disappearance of history, revived only in the form of civil disturbances. Moreover, in the world described in the "new dystopias" neither a political opposition nor mass media nor any type of civil association nor even a well-considered union of oppositionist forces is even feasible. Furthermore, the authors are convinced that authentic social activism either does not exist or can occur only as an impromptu outflow of emotion and is productive only in extreme situations (the obtrusive image of a "National Bolshevik revolt"). All the works we have analyzed here contain not so much as a hint of any positive program for building the future and even deny that such a program could be formulated under current circumstances. If one is to believe the messages delivered in the newest dystopias, essentially no social actor in the country (from pensioners to oligarchs) is satisfied with the current state of affairs. But they are all "completely disoriented" and "in a vacuum" (Smolenskii/Krasnianskii) and alienated from any involvement in history, regardless of their chosen political path. Ivanov and Smolenskii/Krasnianskii make diametrically opposite assertions—Ivanov that a simple person will only suffer from his involvement in politics and Smolenskii/Krasnianskii that "people of sound mind" should be involved in politics but only when "standing alongside the president." These two frames of reference, however, are equally pessimistic in their implications: both paths conspicuously highlight the space wherein the political in contemporary Russia disappears.

Unification with the Other is unrealizable, because it is impossible to determine the source of the cataclysms (everything blows up on its own) or at least identify the guilty person, phenomenon, or institution. Although the "conceptual field of sociality is, as things currently stand here, stipulated from the outset by antagonism or hatred toward ghostly but concretely irritating figures that materialize when the situation is right,"[142] the Caucasians and even

---

[Closing horizons: Anticipation of social catastrophe in contemporary Russian literature] in *Sbornik dokladov po itogam konferentsii "Puti Rossii" Mezhdunarodnoi shkoly sovremennykh nauk 2007 g.* [Proceeds from the conference "Russia's paths" at the International School of Modern Sciecnes, 2007] (in press).

142 Gudkov, *Negativnaia identichnost'*, 282.

the Russian state cannot successfully be made into the Other. The Other is, rather, described in the category of rumor and hence realized as a spectral figure consisting of those rumors. The cause of the crisis is thus designated as the crisis itself, which leads only to the heightening of crisis-centric eschato- logical sentiments, which are all the more harmful in that the source of the fear remains undefined while the fear implants itself firmly into the life of society. "Collective fears in Russia are … not timely reactions to what is happening but a mechanism whereby the surroundings are reaccentuated and the pres- ent delimited and redesignated. … In those terms, specific fears (as a part of culture, as a unique 'culture') may be viewed as a symptom of the continuous conservative stonewalling of institutional changes in Russia."[143]

The end result is that the conflict in society, lacking articulate political watch- words, is aimed not at a specific regime or specific individuals but masochistically at the society as a whole, becoming thereby traumatic but altogether amorphous. It is clear from the novels analyzed here that the manner in which our society sought to erase its psychological traumas in the 1990s has gone unexamined and is incomplete. Consequently, it remains to this day open-ended and, judging by Slavnikova's prediction, not even armed conflict will bring it to an end. Hence, too, the ludic, theatrical, meretricious nature of the revolution her novel describes ("as if nothing was happening. No default, no crisis, no presidential address").[144] Masochism is theatrical per se, and Slavnikova's novel is not the only place where it belongs.[145] Sorokin's novel, too—with its gang rapes, orgies, and murders, pub- licly perpetrated and, as always with Sorokin, garishly ritualized—is rooted in the same (sado)masochistic theatricality. Hence the conclusion that the revolution is not only "in masquerade" and derivative but nonexistent, since "what we call revolution is the active transfiguration of the political present into the guise of the

---

143 Ibid., 82.
144 Slavnikova, 2017, 456.
145 "Masochism always has a theatrical quality." See Zh. Delez [Gilles Deleuze], "Predstavlenie Sakher-Mazokha," trans. A.V. Garadzhi, in L. von Zakher-Mazokh [Leopold von Sach- er-Masoch], Zh. Delez, and Z. Freid [Sigmund Freud], *Venera v mekhakh. Predstavlenie Zakher-Mazokha. Raboty o mazokhizme* (Moscow: Kul'tura, 1992), 233. [The English quotation here is from Jean McNeil's translation of Deleuze's *Sacher Masoch: An Interpreta- tion* (London: Faber and Faber, 1971), p. 49. —Trans.] The sadomasochistic relationship between state and individual presents most conspicuously in the dystopian paradigm, even one patterned as "nonclassically" as in the model analyzed here: "This cross-movement [where the sadism of the state meets the masochism of the individual —A.C.] is nowhere more evident than on the social level of antiutopian reality" (B. Lanin, "Anatomiia litera- turnoi antiutopii," *Obshchestvennye nauki* no. 5 [1993], 162).

political future. That transformation presumes the *negation* of the present—that is, is not a simple *development* of what is already contained (embryonically) in that entity."[146] So the revolution in Slavnikova's novel is not just a development, an extrapolation of current conflicts, but a fully realized "transfiguration of the present" in the *guise of the past*.[147]

History—which the individual is barred from having any hand in shaping—has ended, time has disappeared, and the state is doomed to become "nothing" (Sorokin) or to die (Slavnikova and Bykov). But the power of the defunct, as Alexandre Kojève has proven in his study of the nature of power, is far stronger than the power of the living. "The reason for this lies in the fact that no response can possibly be made to the *defunct*."[148]

A state that is weak and sick in itself and from which society is isolated, precluded from any active involvement, gradually perishes. The authors examined here portray that destruction of the state with energy and gusto, making no attempt to propose any ideological program to replace it. Being set on fairly evident foundations (shame, a sense of guilt), the negation of the history of the prior (Soviet) decades, which typified the literature of the 1990s and the early 2000s, has been replaced in the literature of the last two years by a negation not only of all history but also of the present, and that literally *in real time*. This state of affairs could be considered a positive if the negation of old values were backed by a tendency to follow it up with the formulation of new social reference points. But the present situation unfortunately does not allow for such optimism. "In accordance with this transformation, prior values do not merely succumb to devaluation but, above all, the *need* for values in their former shape and in their previous place ... is uprooted."[149] This may happen because the political actors of recent years are banally incapable of reaching agreement among themselves, and if on rare occasions they do manifest an aspiration for political dialogue, they go into it with *no*

---

146 A. Kozhev, "Poniatie Vlasti" [Alexandre Kojève, "La notion d'autorité"], trans. A.M. Rutkevich (Moscow: Praksis, 2006), 155 [retranslated from the Russian—Trans.].

147 "An antiutopia is [always] about others, about those yet to come. But *2017* is about us" (O. Slavnikova, "'Spisok finalistov napominaet olimpiiskuiu sborniu' [Interv'iu]," *Knizhnoe obozrenie* nos. 27–28 (2006): 6) [available at http://1001.vdv.ru/arc/knigoboz/issue74/. —Trans.]

148 Kozhev, "Poniatie Vlasti," 26.

149 Khaidegger, "Evropeiskii nigilizm," 83 [6]. Heidegger's exegesis of Nietzsche's concept of pessimism may also serve as a description of the authors being compared here: "pessimism as weakness and decline sees only the dark side of everything, is ready with a reason for each new failure, and fancies itself the attitude that knows in advance how it will all turn out" (Ibid., 138 [54]).

common foundations on which to begin a properly grounded discussion and not the slightest wish to abandon their political camp's frames of reference. "Whereas parties who negotiate a compromise might accept the result for different reasons, participants in argumentation must reach a rationally motivated agreement, if at all, for the same reasons. Such practices of justification depend on a *jointly and publicly reached* consensus."[150] Unfortunately, the situation described by Habermas is in our day the stuff of utopia.

While the new dystopias may portray a repressive, stable society (*Day of the Oprichnik*) or one that is disintegrating and no longer has anything to hold it together (*ZhD*), both societies are ahistorical, both have "fallen away" from history. The negation of history is per se characteristic of a utopia (in that the embodiment of the social ideal is tantamount to the end of history, its redundancy going forward); by contrast, the assumption made relative to an antiutopia is that it does propose, albeit apophatically, a theory of the future. The lack of purposefulness and the negation of time are accompanied by an extreme historical pessimism that finds parallels in the literature of the 1980s (Aleksandr Kabakov's "Defector" [Nevozvrashchanets], Vladimir Voinovich's *Moscow 2042* [Moscow 2042], etc.).[151] The most likely explanation for this is that, just as the end of the totalitarian system was most certainly attended not only by a joyful feeling of liberation but also by a plunge into social depression, the sense that a new-model authoritarian or repressive society is in the making is even more persistently accompanied by acedia, perplexity, and resignation.

The impossibility of offering a plan of one's own for the future is, unfortunately, typical of the present situation in this country, which is characterized by the general fragmentation of intellectual and social groups: the "intellectual community is in no condition to make any new proposals that society would find attractive or persuasive. The 'intelligentsia' ... is increasingly working with ready-made and undervalued models and resources."[152] But until society pulls together, the "antiutopia factory" will evidently continue with its documentation of destructive mental tendencies.

---

150 Khabermas, *Vovlechenie drugogo*, 173–74 [86, emphasis in original].

151 The halting of time is generally characteristic of antiutopian literature, as in Zamiatin's *We*, Platonov's *Chevengur*, and Nabokov's *Priglashenie na kazn'* [Invitation to a Beheading], the stigmatizing of the parent/child relationship in Aldous Huxley's *Brave New World*, and so on.

152 Gudkov, *Negativnaia identichnost'*, 683.

Index

Note: Page numbers followed by 'n' denotes Notes

2001: A Space Odyssey, 284

Biocosmist manifesto, 110n96
biocosmists, 110–111
biogenetic law, 43
Bite of an Angel (2000), 347
Blade Runner, 282
Blazing Abysses, 132–135, 137, 138
Blok, Alexander, 8
blood transfusion, 47–48
Bobrov, N., 205
Bobrov, S., 11
Bogdanov, Alexander, x, 9, 30–50, 117, 118n2
Bogdanovich, Peter, xvi
Bogdanovism, 50
"Bogdanov's Inner Message," 33
Bolsheviks, Bolshevism, 31, 50, 80, 115,
    127, 189
Bolshevik utopia, x
Bonfiglio, T. P., 192n33
Bor'ba mirov, 95n48
Bor'ba za zhiznesposobnost', 49
Borenstein, Eliot, xvi
Boris Godunov, 1
bourgeois specialist, 170
Brake, Mark L., 120
Brave New World (1932), 35
Britikov, A. N., xiin11
Brooks, Jeffrey, 95, 95n47, 97n54
Brown-Sequard, Charles Eduoard, 196n43
Bryusov, Valery, 8, 70, 70n40
Bucke, Richard Maurice, 211
Buck-Morss, Susan, 292
Bukharin, Nikolai, 129
Bulgakov, Mikhail, 11, 140, 140n82, 178–200,
    199n51
Bulgarin, Thaddeus, 2
bureaucracy, 244–245, 256
Burke, Kenneth, 148
Burroughs, Edgar Rice, 16, 36, 40
Bykov, Dmitrii, 329, 329n2, 361

C
camera equipment, 221–222
Cameron, James, 287
Capek, Karl, 35
capitalism, 5, 37
Carpenter, William, 66n33
catastrophe novel, 11
Catherine, Empress, 2
Chaadaev, P., 360n116
Chaianov, Aleksandr, 348
Chantsev, Aleksandr, xvii
Chapayev and Void (*Chapaev i Pustota,* 1996),
    293, 302

Chariots of the Gods, 224
Chebrikov, Viktor, 288
Chelomei, Vladimir, 105
Chernetsky, Vitaly, 293, 293n13
Chernov, V., 94n41
Chernyshevsky, Nikolay, 5–7
Chikolev, V., 9, 65n30
Chizhevskii, A. L., 111n102
Christianity, 1, 13, 86, 89, 182
Christie, I., 167n2
The City of Truth (1923), 11
civilization, 33, 36–39, 42, 60, 182, 193, 212,
    243, 267, 271, 291, 297, 302, 306, 315,
    321, 364
civil society, 7
Civil War, 75, 170, 172
Clair, Jean, 87n22
Clark, Katerina, 53n7, 237
class, 1, 3, 4, 22, 34–36, 61, 64, 105, 130, 133,
    170, 186, 188, 189, 191, 194, 216, 237,
    238, 246, 280, 318
class conflict, 36
Cockrell, Roger, 118n4
Coldtown (1917), 9
Cold War, ix, xii, 79, 215
collapse of country, 358–361
The Coming Russia, 119
The Coming World, 10, 125, 126, 128
Common Task, 73
communism, 37, 51, 83, 131, 167, 171, 180,
    291, 292, 305
Comte, Auguste, 46
Conquest of Space (1954), 220
conservation of life, 351–358
Cooke, Leighton Brett, 155, 158
Coopersmith, Jonathan, 52, 52n5
Coppola, Francis Ford, 287
Cornell University, 178
Cor Serpentis, 23
cosmic egg, 77–78
Cosmic Flight (1936), 209
Cosmic Journey, 214, 217
Cosmic Landscape (1923), 106
cosmic societies, 90–95
Cosmic Symphony (1925), 109
Cosmic Voyage, xvi
cosmism, 82, 85–90, 105, 116
cosmonaut, xiii, xvi, 19, 79, 80, 105, 116, 214,
    221–228
cosmopolitans, 81, 98–101
cosmos, x, xi
    imagining, 79–116
Crime and Punishment, 8

Izvestiia, 91, 110, 111

J

Jahannum, 343
Jameson, F., x, xn3, 249n34, 290n1
"Jim Dollar," 10
The Journal of Latest Discoveries and Inventions, 62
Journal of Manufacturing and Trade, 58
A Journey from Petersburg to Moscow, 2, 56
The Journey of My Brother Alexei to the Land of Peasant Utopia, 124
Journey to the Center of the Earth, 122
Jünger, Friedrich Georg, 339

K

Kaempffert, Waldemar, 213
Kafkaesque Forest Study and Exploitation Authority, 258
Kammerer, Paul, 183n13
Karazin, Nikolai, 67
Katayev, Valentin, 10, 11
Kats, R.C., 119n7
Kaverin, Venyamin, 11
Kazus, Igor, 106
Kelvin, Kris, 282
Kern, Garry, 136n64
Khan-Magomedov, S. O., 108n93
Khlebnikov, Velimir, 71, 72n44, 75n51
Khochu vse znat', 95, 95n48
Khrushchev, Nikita, ix
kinship, forces of, 306–327
Kirpichnikov, Mikhail, 139
Klibanov, A., 69n36
Kliuchareva, Natal'ia, 345, 357
Klushantsev, Pavel Vladimirovich, xvi, 214–230
Klustis, Gustav, 75
Knowledge Is Power (Znanie—Sila), ix, 16, 204
Knyazhinsky, Alexander, 286
Kollontai, Aleksandra, 172n6
Kol'tsov, Nikolai Konstantinovich, 182
Komarov, N., 9
Komsomol, 204
Komsomolskaya Pravda, 285, 287
Köngäs, Elli, 250n36
Koryukov, Mikhail, 217, 228
Kosack, Wolfgang, 135n61
Kostin, Vladimir, 108n91
Kozhev, A., 369n146
Kramarov, Grigorii, 93, 105
Krasnaia nov', 95n48
Krasnianskii, Eduard, 358

Krivomazov, Omon, 299, 300
Kropotkin, Peter, 40, 40n31, 110
Kruchenykh, Alexei, 72
Krutikov, Georgii, 108
Krylov, Ivan, 296
Kubrick, Stanley, xi, 284
Kukulin, Il'ia, 366n141
Kuleshov, Leo, 216
Kuprin, Alexander, 9

L

Lacan, Jacques, 316n24, 317
Lamarckianism, 192
Land of Gonguri (1922), 10
Land of the Happy (1931), 10
Langemak, G. E., 207
Lang, Fritz, 176
Lapirov-Skoblo, M. Ia., 91n33, 92, 113
Larri, Ya., 10
Lasswitz, Kurt, 36
The Last Fairy Tale, 277–279
The Last Man, 4
Lavrenev, Boris, 10
Lavrent'yev, Anatolii, 218
Lefebvre, Henri, 297
Legend of the Sultan Mahomet, 2
Lem, Stanislaw, 260, 262, 281, 282
Leninism-Marxism, 131
Lenin, V. I., 44n41, 51n1, 84n10, 180
Lennauchfilm Studio, 218
Lents, E. Kh., 58, 58n15
Leonov, Leonid, 19
L'évolution créatrice (1907), 46
Lieut. Gulliver Jones (1905), 36
"Life on the Planet Mars," 41
"Lightning Sisters," 72, 73, 75
linguistic consciousness, 158
Linnik, Iurii, 109n95
Lipovetsky, Mark, xvii, xviin18
Lissitzky, Lazar (El), 108, 202
literary genre, 117–146
literary postmodernism, 290–327
    Soviet matrix, 298–301
    space and time, 293–298
Literature and Revolution, 84, 114, 118, 180
literature, literary, xii, 1–3, 8, 10, 12, 20, 23, 40, 92, 96, 101, 102–103, 117–146, 290–305, 328–370
Liushin, Vladimir, 108
"Living Communication," 97
Lombroso, Cesare, 193
Lomonosov, M., 55, 55n9, 56n10

CPSIA information can be obtained
at www.ICGtesting.com
Printed in the USA
BVHW03s1101180418
513722BV00008B/160/P